DHANAPĀLA AND HIS TIMES

A Socio-cultural Study Based upon his Works

GANGA PRASAD YADAVA

CONCEPT PUBLISHING COMPANY
NEW DELHI

The Indian Council of Historical Research, New Delhi gave the financial support towards the publication of this work. The Council, however, is not responsible for the views expressed therein.

First Published 1982

Ganga Prasad **Yadava** (*b*. 1939-)

Published by

Naurang Rai
Concept Publishing Company
H-13, Bali Nagar
NEW DELHI-110 015 (India)

Printed by

Cameo Printers
at Mohan Printing Corporation,
Padam Nagar
DELHI-110 007

To

My Revered Gurus

the late Pandit L.N. Mishra

and

R.C. Jain

Who have made me what I am

FOREWORD

The early medieval history of North India bristles with some significant ups and downs, both in the political and cultural fields. After the Classical Age of the Gupta emperors, several dynasties in North and Central India continued the administrative system and the socio-cultural norms stabilized during the Gupta period. Among these dynasties, mention may be made of the Vardhana, the Gurjara-Pratihāra, the Pāla, the Chandella, the Kalachuri and the Parmāra dynasties.

The all-India political outlook of the Mauryas and the Guptas, however, was lacking during the early medieval times (*c.* A.D. 550-1200) due to the disintegrating factors which had begun to crop up after the death of Harṣavardhana. During the 10th-11th centuries A.D., these factors became more striking and led to the political downfall of the country.

In the cultural field, the *Varṇāśrama* system of the society, the *Smārta-Paurāṇika* religion and the use of Sanskrit as the chief language of communication and literary compositions continued in the period. The same can be said about architecture, sculpture, painting and other fine arts.

The major religion of the people during the early medieval period was Hinduism based on the main *Smritis* ranging from the *Manu Smriti* to the *Devala Smriti*. The Paurāṇika lore of the later Vedic pantheons was followed by the respective adherents of the Vaiṣṇava, Śaiva, Śākta, Saura and other cults. In a way, the Hinduism of this period can be called a broad-based one, having absorbed and accommodated the tenets and injunctions of Buddhism, Jainism and several other faiths. This tendency of assimilation had started in the Śuṅga-Sātavāhana period culminating in an admirable cultural function during the Gupta Age.

The broad-based Hindu religion of the post-Gupta period has rightly been designated as 'New Brāhmaṇism' due to obvious reasons. The centre of religion had then almost totally shifted from the *Yajñas* (sacrifices) to temples. The

Devāyatanas (temples) became not only the centres of ritualism but also educational and social centres.

Out of the two chief protestant religions—Buddhism and Jainism—the former was restricted to parts of Eastern India and a few other patches here and there, such as the region of south-Kosala and parts of Orissa. Mahāyāna and Vajrayāna, the two chief Buddhist cults of the period, found much in common with the New Brāhmaṇism. The Tāntricism, a salient trait of Vajrayāna, had become part and parcel of the then Hindu pantheon. The code of conduct, for a large number of Buddhist householders, was almost similar to the one enjoined in the Vedic-Smārta religions. Gautama Buddha had now been accommodated among the chief ten Avatāras of Viṣṇu-Nārāyaṇa.

During the period Jainism had spread in much wider regions than was the case with Buddhism. The centres like Mathura in the North, Devagarh and Chanderī in Central India and a good number of centres in the Maharashtra and Karnataka regions contributed largely to the propagation of Jainism. Architecture and art flourished at various Jaina centres of the country side by side with the art of the Brahmaṇical faiths.

The Buddhists and Jainas did not raise any protests, worth mention, against the Hindu social order. On the other hand, they found in the then existing set-up a congenial atmosphere for the development of their own social, economic and religious interests. The old Vedic sacrifices were not in vogue now. Majority of the Hindu kings and merchants made no distinction between a Hindu, Jaina or Buddhist in so far as their common interests and an over-all national spirit among them was alone considered.

In Central India, the Parmāra rulers, notably Muñja and Bhoja, played a commendable role towards the advancement of various branches of learning. They gave patronage to a large number of scholars who wrote on literary and scientific subjects. The creations in literature and other fine arts of the period of these two rulers and their successors eloquently prove the existence of a bracing atmosphere in which great writers and artists produced their monumental works.

Among the great writers of the 10th-11th centuries A.D. can be mentioned the name of Sanskrit writer Dhanapāla. He is the celebrated writer of *Tilaka-mañjarī* and a few other works. For the cultural study of the period, these works contain a variegated wealth of information.

Dr Ganga Prasad Yadava has done an appreciable service to the cause of Indology by producing his present study on the works of Dhanapāla. He has critically analysed, in detail, the cultural data found in the works of the versatile writer. The evidence found in the works of Dhanapāla has aptly been corroborated by other contemporary source-material. I hope this new publication will be a welcome addition to the studies on ancient Indian culture.

K.D. BAJPAI

Tagore Professor & Head of the Department of
Ancient Indian History, Culture & Archaeology,
SAUGAR UNIVERSITY (RETD.).
SAGAR

Ex-Chairman, NUMISMATIC SOCIETY OF INDIA,

Chairman, EPIGRAPHICAL SOCIETY OF INDIA,

President, INDIAN ARCHAEOLOGICAL SOCIETY,

Visiting Professor, PUNJAB UNIVERSITY, CHANDIGARH.

10th April, 1982.

PREFACE

The present work entitled, "Dhanapāla and his Times: A Socio-cultural Study Based upon his Works" aims at reconstructing, with the help of my source materials, a fairly realistic picture of the social and cultural life of the times of Dhanapāla, a Śvetāmbara Jaina poet and litterateur who graced the court of the imperial Parmāras of Malwa in the glorious reigns of King Muñja and King Bhoja Paramāra, the great patrons of art and culture and wielders of the pen and the sword with equal felicity : becoming by virtue of it two of the most dazzling figures of Medieval India in the 10th and 11th centuries.

A word about the nature and contents of the source material will not be out of place here. While Dhanapāla's works written in Saṁskṛta, Prākṛta and Apabhraṁśa have naturally been my primary sources, I have freely used relevant evidence that came my way from such secondary sources as contemporary (and, at times, even later) literature, epigraphs, reference works and the like, for purposes of comparison, corroboration, explication and elucidation. I have also quoted, where necessary, from the works of modern historians on Ancient and Medieval India to corroborate my findings or to respectfully differ from them on (what, to me, were) valid grounds. All the works in Saṁskṛta, Prākṛta and Apabhraṁśa, cited and used as primary sources, are available (and not readily, at that) in the language of original composition and neither English nor Hindi translations are available, much to the dismay of the interested research worker who must fall back on his own resources to cope with the situation.

It will be seen from (even a cursory glance at) the ensuing pages that, of all the works of Dhanapāla, I have been leaning most heavily on the poet's magnum opus, *Tilaka-mañjarī*, which is cast as a prose-romance and, next to it, on *Pāiyalcchī-nāmamālā*, a work in Prākṛta lexicography. Between them, these two works (especially the former) yielded me the richest harvest of my basic data. Other works of Dhanapāla are of devotional character and I have used them, for what they are worth, in dealing with the religious conditions of the period.

The prose-romance structure of *Tilaka-mañjarī* may, at first glance, tempt an unwary reader to dismiss it as a beautiful work of poetic invention and, in the process, completely overlook and miss the sociological and historical aspect of the work. In fact, *Tilaka-mañjarī* belongs to the great tradition of the Jaina Prabandhas and Caritas which, to quote professor Bühler, were written "to edify the Jain community, to convince them of the glory and power of the Jain religion, or, in cases where the subject is a purely secular one, to provide them with an agreeable entertainment".[1] Dhanapāla has himself stated in the opening verses of *Tilaka-mañjarī* that he has written the romance to gratify the curiosity of King Bhoja in respect of Jina Dharma. Obviously, Dhanapāla who was a convert to the orthodox faith of Lord Mahāvīra (and as comes natural to a convert imbued with religious fervour and ardour to try to win over others to his new faith) must have gone all out for the prize-catch of a sovereign of King Bhoja's stature and eminence. That his efforts were crowned with success is testified by Merutuṅga in *Prabandhacintāmaṇi*, but in the absence of any reference to this effect in the works of Dhanapāla or in contemporary inscriptions etc., it would, at best, remain a conjecture. Merutuṅga's account of Bhoja's conversion compares favourably with his account of the conversion of another renowned Hindu king, Vikramāditya, and belongs, properly speaking, to the category of folklore rather than history. The knowledgeable scholar, C.H. Tawney, writes: "In accordance with their custom of annexing all the heroes of Indian tradition, the Jainas maintain that Vikramāditya was converted to the Jain faith by Siddhasena".[2]

It is interesting to note, in passing, that even where the conversion of a Hindu King to the faith of Lord Mahāvīra is a fact of history beyond any shadow of doubt as in the case of King Kumārapāla of Gujarat, the converted King "managed to combine with it a lurking regard for Śiva, the family-god of the Calukyas of Gujarat. This halting between two or more opinions in religion has been characteristic of many Indian sovreigns".[3] Probably for this very reason the Jaina poets who flourished in their courts are seen, at times, to strike ambivalent attitudes in religious matters and oft pay homage, if only out of consideration for the sentiments of their kings, to Hindu gods and goddesses. Thus it is that the sage Hemacandra was not ashamed to bow himself in the house of Somanātha in the company of his sovereign, and this explains, too, why Dhanapāla invokes the goddess Sarasvatī at the commencement of *Tilaka-mañjarī* along with several other gods and goddesses of the Hindu pantheon.

With regard to the historicity of my principal primary source namely, the narrative work, *Tilaka-mañjarī*, it will not be too presumptuous to suggest that all the works of great art are, by implication, more dependable documents of social and cultural history (than social histories as such) of the age in which they are produced, for the simple reason that a great artist is, first and foremost, a product of his age in whom the age finds the most conscious and the most articulate mouthpiece of its social and cultural ethos. Shakespeare's works are justly held to belong to all ages but we need not forget that, apart from and in spite of their universality, they also belong to an age—to Elizabeth's England, to be precise—faithfully mirroring, as they do, the milieu and the manners of the Elizabethan society. Granted that Shakespeare's *Hamlet* concerns itself with the human imponderables, yet it remains, for all that, a typical Elizabethan tragedy. Similarly, Chaucer's crowning achievement, *The Canterbury Tales*, may be read as an apotheosis of the universal human pilgrimage, yet through the jolly assemblage of his characters Chaucer has also presented "a cross-section of the 14th century English society".[4] The same is true of Kālidāsa's *Abhijñāna Śākuntala*, Bāṇa's *Kādambarī*, Dante's *Divinia Comedia* and Goethe's *Faust*.

Dhanapāla may not, as reputations go at present, be counted among the frontline Immortals but none can deny that he has tasted nectar. We shall not be surprised if, one of these days, a gifted scholar should come forward and demonstrate that Dhanapāla's *Tilaka-mañjarī* has an allegorical framework comparable with that of Spenser's *Faerie Queene*, or pay some such salute to the genius of Dhanapāla. The authenticity of

Dhanapāla's works as social documents stand self-vindicated yet, not resting content with that, I have sought further confirmation by examining (to the best of my capacities) the data yielded by his works in the light of evidence provided by secondary sources (contemporary, later or modern). I was happily egged on in my work by Professor Bühler's conviction, stated by Tawney in these words: "He (Bühler) warns us that they (the Jaina Prabandhas and Caritas) are to be used with the greatest caution. But, at the same time, he reminds us that their testimony is often confirmed by inscriptions and other evidence of a trustworthy kind".[5]

Though I do not follow the faith of Lord Mahāvīra, yet preparation of the present thesis has been, I must confess, a labour of love to me. It was both a privilege and a source of pure pleasure for me to browse through the works of erudite scholars and historians bearing upon my thesis and I have acknowledged my indebtedness to them in footnotes in the main body of the thesis. I am deeply indebted to late Dr. Buddha Prakash who suggested me this topic for research and rendered me all possible help. I am personally obliged to Dr V. C. Pandey, Head of the Department of Ancient History, Culture and Archaeology, Punjab University, Chandigarh, who was kind enough to give me valuable guidance on certain chapters of my work. I gratefully record the debt I would never be able to repay to my most revered teacher, the late Pandit Lakshmi Nath Mishra, Principal, D.S.N. College, Unnao, whose unbounded love, affection and erudition have always been a source of inspiration and instruction to me in my life, to whom this work is dedicated. I have also been very fortunate to have received from my eminent supervisor, Dr Roop Chand Jain, then Principal, J.V. Jain College, Saharanpur, ungrudging attention, infinite patience and thorough understanding all the time.

I feel very thankful to Dr B.N. Puri, late Prof. R.K. Dikshit, Pandit Ayodhya Nath Sharma, Dr B.N.S Yadava and Dr Raj Kumar from whom I received unfailing inspiration and valuable suggestions in the preparation and completion of this work.

I was fortunate enough to receive unbounded favour from the great savant Prof. K.D. Bajpai, formerly Head of the Department of Ancient Indian History, Culture and Archaeology, Saugar University, M.P., whose occasional help gave him insight into the subject. The debt of gratitude, I owe him immensely increased on account of his crowning this humble work with his learned Foreword.

I shall be failing in my bounden duty if I do not express my deep gratitude to 108 His Holiness Muni Sri Vidyanandji for having enlightened me in respect of certain crucial, if less known, aspects of Jaina religion and metaphysics.

I must also record my sincere thanks to Sri Bhura Lal, Librarian, Sarasvitī Pustaka Bhandāra, Hāthī Khānā, Ahmedabad, Gujarat, for making available to me related, and sometimes rare, literature on the topic from time to time.

Finally, I have to thank my wife, Suman, who cheerfully put up with all domestic worries and enabled me to devote my time to the present study.

In conclusion, I crave the readers' indulgence for any lapses and errors, typographical or other, that may still be found in the book, in spite of my best efforts to weed them out.

REFERENCES

1. Bühler, *Uber das Leben des Jaina Monches Hemacandra*, p. 6, quoted by C.H. Tawney (tr.), *Prabandhacintāmaṇi* (Calcutta, The Asiatic Society of Bengal, 1901), vi, p.
2. C.H. Tawney, op. cit., vii, p.
3. Tawney, xiv, p.
4. Grierson and Smith, *A Critical History of English Poetry* (London), p. 33.
5. Tawney, vi, p.

CONTENTS

TRANSLITERATION TABLE

अ	a	ठ्	ṭh
आ	ā	ड्	ḍ
इ	i	ढ्	ḍh
ई	ī	ण्	ṇ
उ	u	त्	t
ऊ	ū	थ्	th
ऋ	ṛ	द्	d
लृ	ḷ	ध्	dh
ए	e	न्	n
ऐ	ai	प्	p
ओ	o	फ्	ph
औ	au	ब्	b
anusvāra	ṁ	भ्	bh
visarga	ḥ	म्	m
क्	k	य्	y
ख्	kh	र्	r
ग्	g	ल्	l
घ्	gh	व्	v
ङ्	ṅ	श्	ś
च्	c	ष्	ṣ
छ	ch	स्	s
ज्	j	ह्	h
झ्	jh	क्ष्	kṣ
ञ	ñ	त्र्	tr
ट्	ṭ	ज्ञ्	jñ

ABBREVIATIONS

ABORI	:	Annals of Bhandārkar Oriental Research Institute
ARE	:	Annual Report of South Indian Epigraphy
ARIE	:	Annual Report of Indian Epigraphy
ASI	:	Archaeological Survey of India, Annual Reports
ASR : *ASIR* : *ASIAR* :	}	Archaeological Survey of India, Annual Report
ASWI	:	Archaeological Survey of Western India, Annual Reports
BKI	:	Bombay-Karnātaka Inscription
BG	:	Bombay Gazetteer
EI	:	Epigraphia Indica
IA	:	Indian Antiquary
IHQ	:	Indian Historical Quarterly, Calcutta
JAOS	:	Journal of the American Oriental Society
JASB	:	Journal of the Asiatic Society of Bengal, Calcutta
JBBRAS	:	Journal of the Bombay Branch of the Royal Asiatic Society, Bombay
JRAS	:	Journal of the Royal Asiatic Society of Great Britain and Ireland, London
PAIOC	:	Proccedings of the All India Oriental Conference
PIHC	:	Proceedings of the Indian History Congress
PRAS, WC	:	Progress Report of the Archaeological Survey of India, Western Circle

1

Dhanapāla—Man and Works

DATE

Introduction

Dhanapāla was a renowned Jaina thinker, intellectual, scholar and poet. A steady stream of Jaina ācāryas and poets has profoundly enriched almost every aspect of Indian culture—religious, social and intellectual. Their ideas have penetrated to the roots of religion, philosophy, literature and art of this ancient land. Indian thinkers of all classes and complexions owe a great deal, on the conscious or unconscious level, to the Jaina scholars who have left a lasting imprint on the currents and cross-currents of Indian thought by means of their works written in different languages and dialects of their times. Dhanapāla, a versatile genius, following in the footsteps of his illustrious literary predecessors, made a significant contribution to the political, social, economic and religious life of his time by virtue of the works of great intrinsic value he wrote in Saṁskṛta, Prākṛta and Apabhraṁśa. His masterpiece *Tilaka-mañjarī*, to mention but one for the present, besides revealing Dhanapāla's multifaceted genius, throws a flood of light on the history of the Paramāra dynasty.
Date:— Four Dhanapālas are known in the history of Jaina Saṁskṛta, Prākṛta and Apabhraṁśa literature. One with whom this study is concerned is Dhanapāla of Paramāra period who wrote *Tilaka-mañjarī* in Saṁskṛta, the other three being Dhanapāla (Dhakkara), writer of *Bhavisayatta-kahā* (Bhavisyadatta-kathā) in Apabhraṁśa who flourished in the X century, Dhanapāla (pallīvāla), author of *Tilaka-mañjarī-*

kathāsāra written in Saṁskṛta in XII century A.D. and Dhanapāla, the author of *Bāhu-balicarita* in Apabhraṁśa who lived in XV century A.D.[1]

Scholars do not differ much with regard to the date, time and ancestory of the poet Dhanapāla. Nathu Ram Premi is of the opinion that Dhanapāla, the creator of *Tilaka-mañjarī*, was the contemporary of Sīyaka II, Vākpati Muñja, Sindhurāja and Rājā Bhoja of Paramāra dynasty and was the court poet of the kings Vākpati Muñja and Bhoja.[2] His parents belonged to Sāṅkāśya village, now part of Farrukkābād district in Uttar Pradesh, who had later migrated to Malwa. Dhanapāla was not favourably disposed towards Jainism in the beginning but later under the influence of his younger brother, Śobhana, he was converted to Jainism and became a follower of Śvetāmbara sect. *Tilaka-mañjarī* informs us that he was a prominent figure in the court of king Muñja who decorated him with the title of Sarasvatī.[3]

Dhanapāla spent several years in the court of king Bhoja and was held in high esteem by the king. He became instrumental in making Bhoja realize the futility of Brāhmaṇical sacrifices and finally converted him to Jainism.[4] Dhanapāla composed his prose romance, *Tilaka-mañjarī*, for the gratification of king Bhoja's curiosity about Jinadharma.[5] This is also corroborated and confirmed by the author of *Prabhāvakacarita* who states that Dhanapāla composed *Tilaka-mañjarī* consisting of 12,000 verses in order to satisfy the curiosity of king Bhoja.[6]

Dr. S.N. Das Gupta opines that Dhanapāla wrote *Tilaka-mañjarī* in the reign of Muñja, Vākpati of Dhārā in about A.D. 970.[7] Another scholar, Dr. Lallan Ji Gopal is also of the same opinion.[8]

But we find it difficult to agree with the views of these scholars since neither of them has provided incontestable evidence in support of their opinion. On the other hand, the internal evidence and the clues provided by Dhanapāla's own observations in *Tilaka-mañjarī* appear more authentic and reliable.

Additional evidence gleaned from other important sources such as *Prabhāvakacarita* of Prabhācandrācārya and *Prabandha-*

cintāmaṇi of Merutuṅga points to the same conclusions, that is, Dhanapāla lived in the times of Rājā Bhoja Paramāra. It has been recorded in *Prabhāvakacarita* that once a poet named Dharma came to the court of king Bhoja and proudly claimed that none could trounce him in a debating contest. He appeared so brilliant and formidable a challenger that really none of Bhoja's courtiers dared to pick up the gauntlet.[9] At that time Dhanapāla was at Sācore (in present-day Rājasthāna). Smarting with the pain of insult at the hands of king Bhoja who had in a fit of anger thrown the manuscript of his *Tilaka-mañjarī* into fire, Dhanapāla had left Malwa with a vow never to set eyes on Bhoja again for the rest of his life.[10]

At this critical moment when the prestige of his court and kingdom was at stake, Bhoja sent his emissaries to Dhanapāla with the request, "You are the eldest son of Muñja and I am his youngest one. Can you disobey me? Mahārāja (Muñja) had conferred on you the title of 'kūrcālasarasvatī' by taking you in his lap. By ill-chance you left the kingdom, the elders and us all. Avanti is yours. It should be your concern whether it gets the glory of victory or indignity of defeat".[11] Dhanapāla could retain himself no longer. He returned to Avanti and defeated the challenger.[12]

The above description establishes the fact that Dhanapāla was connected with Vākpati Muñja and Bhoja. Dr. K.M. Munshi connects Dhanapāla with three Paramāra rulers -- Sīyaka II, Vākpati Muñja and Sindhurāja. He considers Dhanapāla as the court poet of Muñja and Sindhurāja.[13]

Of Dhanapāla, G.V. Devasthali, writes: "He was a contemporary of Halāyudha, Padmagupta, Dhanañjaya and enjoyed the patronage of kings Sīyaka and Vākpati of Dhārā".[14] The same opinion has also been shared by Dr. H.C. Ray who places Dhanapāla in the last quarter of the X and first quarter of the XI century.[15] Dr. Gulab Chandra Choudhary also places Dhanapāla in the courts of Vākpati Muñja and Bhoja.[16] Dr. D.C. Ganguly connects Dhanapāla with king Bhoja only and confidently affirms that "Dhanapāla flourished at the end of the tenth and the beginning of the eleventh centuries".[17]

P.T.S Ayyangar declares Dhanapāla as the protégé of Vākpati Muñja and Bhoja II.[18]

European scholars also connect Dhanapāla with Paramāra dynasty. A.B. Keith is of the opinion that Dhanapāla was patronized by Sīyaka and Vākpati of Dhārā.[19] On the other hand, J.N. Farquhar's statment connects Dhanapāla with Muñja and Bhoja. According to him, "Two brothers belonging to the latter half of the tenth century, Śobhana and Dhanapāla, the later a protégé of both Muñja and Bhoja, kings of Malwa, distinguished themselves greatly as writers of sacred odes in Sanskrit".[20]

However, a more authentic proof of Dhanapāla's date and time is found in the concluding verses of Dhanapāla's *Pāiyalacchīnāmamālā* wherein the poet states that he has composed the work for his sister, Sundarī, "when one thousand years of Vikrama era and twenty nine besides had passed away and at the time when Mānyakheṭa (the capital of the Rāṣṭrakūṭas of Deccan) was plundered and sacked in an attack by the lord of Malwa".[21] This account is corroborated by the *Udaipur Praśasti* wherefrom we learn that the king of Malwa was no other than Sīyaka II who took away the wealth of king Khoṭṭiga of Mānyakheṭa (Śloka 12). The imperial treasury of the Rāṣṭrakūṭas was completely looted and the victor carried away even the office copies of the copper plate charters lodged in the record office.[22]

From the above account it is evident that Dhanapāla composed *Pāiyalacchī* in V.E. 1029 (A.D. 972) and can, therefore, be safely placed in the later part of the X century.[23] The above account makes Dhanapāla a contemporary of Sīyaka II.

Dhanapāla has also given his version of Mahmud Ghazanavī's invasion on Somanātha (V.E. 1081 A.D. 1024 *c.*) in his work *Satyapurīya-Śrī-Mahāvīra-Utsāha*. According to *Utsāha*, Mahmud looted Śrīmalladeśa (the territory of Śrīmala or Bhīnmal) and after sacking Anhilvārā, Candrāvatī, Sortaha and Dilwara destroyed the temple of Someśvara ('the giver of the pleasure to the hearts of people'). But he could not destory the idol of Mahāvīra of Satyapura (present-day Sāncore in Rajasthāna), "for can even a large number of stars dim the light of the Sun or snakes swallow Garuḍa"?[24]

The Vividha-Tīrtha-kalpa gives practically an identical version. According to it, when the lord of Gajjanī (Ghaznī) reached Satyapura on his way back after plundering Gurjara (Gujarat), he saw the lovely temple of Jina and tried to demolish the idol installed there. But neither elephants nor bullocks succeeded in pulling off the brass idol of Mahāvīra. The ropes snapped as elephants tried to pull down the idol. Elephants and horses fell. The blows aimed at the body of Mahāvīra struck the strikers themselves; though they left marks on the idol, they could not break it.[25]

The account of *Satyapurīya-Śrī-Mahāvīra-Utsāha* mentioned above has led us to believe that Dhanapāla was alive when Mahmud of Ghazīn's invasion of India took place in A.D. 1024 and that he may have written *Utsāha* in that year or sometime later. In case Dhanapāla was around 20 when he composed *Pāiyalacchī* in A.D. 972, he might have been nearly 72 when he wrote *Utsāha.* In all likelihood the poet remained alive for about twenty years or more after the composition of *Utsāha.* In that case he might have left this world at the age of 82 or 90.[26]

Dr. K. M Munshi's observation in the matter informed as it is by historic authenticity and reliability may be noted: "Dhanapāla, the poet of Dhārā, wrote his *Pāiyalacchī* just after the sack of Mānyakhcṭa by Sīyaka II in A.D. 972. He must then have been in middle life, but even if he had only been twenty-five or thirty at that time, he would have been seventy-five or eighty in A.D. 1024. But the poet must have written this song still later.......".[27]

In his monograph, *Yaśastilaka and Indian Culture*, K.K. Handiqui states that Somadeva, the author of *Yaśastilaka* (A.D. 959), was followed by a number of prominent poets who flourished in the last quarter of the X century and the first quarter of the XI century, Dhanapāla being one of them.[28] From the above account it becomes established that Dhanapāla was a contemporary of Somadeva, the court poet of Kṛṣṇa III. As we know, Kṛṣṇa III remained in power from A.D. 939 to A.D. 969[29] and Sīyaka II of Paramāra dynasty sacked Mānyakheṭa in V.E. 1029 (A.D. 972), the year in which Dhanapāla composed *Pāiyalacchī.* At that time khoṭṭigadeva, the immediate successor of Kṛṣṇa III, was killed in war. It may be deduced from K.K. Handiqui's thesis that Dhanapāla lived in the latter half of the X century A.D.

From the views expressed by the scholars of both Indian and foreign extraction and from an intimate study of Dhanapāla's own works and those of his contemporaries, it becomes sufficiently evident that Dhanapāla had witnessed the reigns of four Paramāra kings viz., Harṣa *alias* Sīyaka II (A.D. 945-972),[30] Vākpati II (A.D. 974 to 994),[31] Sindhurāja (A.D. 997-1010),[32] and Bhojadeva (A.D. 1011-1055).[33]

Being on terra firma we can confidently say that Dhanapāla belonged to the Paramāra period and flourished from the latter half of the X century to the first quarter of XI century A.D.

LIFE

Although no autobiography (ātmacarita) as such is known to have been written by Dhanapāla, yet we can build up a fairly authentic account of his life by piecing together evidences provided by such sources as his own works, works of his contemporary poets and scholars and the researches of the later-day scholars working on him. The prominent sources which may be cited in this context are Merutuṅga's *Prabandhacintāmaṇi*, Prabhācandrācārya's *Prabhāvakacarita*, Dhanapāla's *Tilaka-mañjarī* and *Pāiyalacchīnāmamālā*, Someśvara's *Kīrtikaumudī*, Nathu Ram Premi's *Jaina Sāhitya Aur Itihāsa* and that invaluable publication—*Jaina Sāhitya Saṁśodhaka*.

Parentage

Dhanapāla reveals his parentage in the opening pages of his *Tilaka-mañjarī*. A scion of a vipra (Brāhmaṇa) family, he was the son of Sarvadeva and the grandson of Devarṣi. His ancestors belonged to Kaśaypa gotra (clan) and hailed from the town of Śaṅkāśya in Madhayadeśa.[34] Nathu Ram Premi identifies this town as the present-day Śaṅkiśā in Farrukkābād district of Uttar Pradesh.[35] Dhanapāla's parents are known to have migrated to Dhārā and settled there.[36]

Dhanapāla had a younger brother named Śobhana and a sister named Sundarī. He was married to Dhanaśrī.[37] He had a daughter, Bālā Paṇḍitā.[38]

Conversion

What turned the entire course of Dhanapāla's life and gave a new bearing to his art was his conversion from orthodox Brāhmaṇism to Jainism wrought by a stirring instance of exemplary non-violence practised by his younger brother Śobhana.[39] The story needs telling at length. We read in *Prabhāvakacarita* that a Jaina Ācārya, Mahendra Sūri of Candragaccha, happened to be passing through Dhārā in the course of his itinerations. Sarvadeva who was deeply impressed by the piety and erudition of the Jaina preacher waited upon him along with his two sons. The Ācārya moved by the humility and devotion of Sarvadeva asked him the purpose of his visit. Sarvadeva who had learnt of the holy man's powers of getting at the secrets of hidden things wanted to know the whereabouts of the treasure of his ancestors. The Ācārya agreed to unearth the treasure provided he would be given half the portion of his own choice.[40]

Being gifted with extra-sensory powers, Ācārya Mahendra Sūri fulfilled his promise by restoring to Sarvadeva the ancestral wealth to the tune of forty lakh gold coins from under the earth.[41]

Sarvadeva delightfully laid one-half of the recovered treasure at the feet of the hermit as agreed between them but the Ācārya declined to accept the gold coins. What he had meant to have, he said, as his share was one of the two sons of Sarvadeva which constituted, more than his ancestral gold, the real family wealth of the vipra. Sarvadeva was rudely taken aback by the unexpected development. His head swam and he was at his wit's end, but being bound by the solemn agreement, he was left with no choice but to accept the Saint's demand. Reaching home he flung himself on his bed and lay brooding on what appeared to be a bolt from the blue. Dhanapāla, returning from his court, saw his sire sunk in sorrow and was alarmed. He solicited his father to tell him the cause of his sudden sorrow. Sarvadeva who was loath to tell his son how dearly he was obliged to pay for the ancestral gold he had acquired could not but reveal the whole truth in reply to his son's queries.[42]

Dhanapāla reacted very violently to the Jaina Ācārya's demand which he felt was tantamount to a high handed act of double coercion. For it involved the conversion of one of Sarvadeva's sons to Jaina faith and his renunciation of the world to become a follower of Mahendra Sūri. Dhanapāla was so much enraged and infuriated that he described the whole transaction as a dirty trick played on his unsuspecting and unsophisticated sire by a sophist. When Sarvadeva sorrowfully reminded his son that he was obliged to send him to Jaina Ācārya, Dhanapāla bluntly told him that he was not going to do anything of the kind. It would be a sheer sin on his part to step into the Jaina temple.[43] For a vipra's son would fain be mauled and trampled by an elephant than go to a Jaina temple.[44] Dhanapāla categorically declared that he had no wish to become guilty of pushing his ancestors into hell.[45] He gave vent to his spleen by describing Jaina saints as mean Śūdras.[46]

Dhanapāla's ranting and railing against Mahendra Sūri dismayed his father and tears rose to his eyes. As he sat alone, Dhanapāla's younger brother, Śobhana, came there. Sarvadeva acquainted him with all that had transpired. Śobhana who was devoted to his father begged him not to feel distressed at all and prayed that he be sent to the Jaina saint to honour his father's words. Let alone going to a Jaina temple, he would not wince even if his father were to throw him into a well or hand him over to an assassin for murder. Śobhana's words charged with the fire of filial devotion resolved the crisis and ended Sarvadeva's mental torment. Sarvadeva took Śobhana to Mahendra Sūri who made Śobhana his desciple.[47]

At the court of king Bhoja where he reigned supreme among the paṇḍitas,[48] Dhanapāla narrated the story of his brother's conversion to Jainism. King Bhoja's sire was roused and at Dhanapāla's instance he decreed that Jaina saints were forbidden from entering his country for a period of 12 years.

Meanwhile, Ācārya Mahendra Sūri initiated Śobhana into the intricacies and subtleties of Jaina philosophy and raised him to the eminence of 'Vācanācārya'. Śobhana now sought and got the Ācārya's permission to visit his native town and wandering from habitation to habitation finally entered Dhārā along with other hermits.[49]

As Śobhana was entering the city, paṇḍita Dhanapāla, who was accompanying the king on his royal circuit, not recognising Śobhana, said to him ironically, "All hail ass-toothed mendicant".[50] The hermit Śobhana answered, "Good luck befall you, my friend with a mouth like 'kapivṛṣaṇa".[51] Dhanapāla felt astonished at Śobhana's dexterity in speech. Dhanapāla again said to Śobhana, "Whose guests art thou"? It immediately elicited the reply from the hermit, "We are your guests, sir". Greatly impressed, Dhanapāla sent Śobhana along with his attendant novice to his own place and on returning from court he invited the hermits to dinner.[52]

But they refused. Dhanapāla earnestly enquired what objection could be taken to his food. Thereupon, they replied, "A hermit should eat food collected as bees collect honey, even if the donors were families of Mleccha....... He should not eat a regular meal even if offered by one equal to Bṛhaspati".[53] They explained that "as meals exclusively prepared for them were forbidden by their religious precepts, they collect food from different families".[54] Dhanapāla was struck by their admirable practice.

When Dhanapāla was going to bathe, two hermits (Śobhana and another) arrived on their begging round. Dhanapāla's wife who had not cooked meals by then brought some kept milk for them. They wanted to know whether it had been kept for several days. At this Dhanapāla jocularly quipped if they suspected there were maggots in it. Dhanapāla's wife told the hermits that the milk had been kept for two days whereupon they said, "undoubtedly, there are maggots in it". Hearing these words, Dhanapāla got up from his bathing stool and peering at the milk bowl saw that on a piece of red-coloured cotton which the hermits had placed in the vicinity of the sour milk tiny creatures coming out of the milk bowl were climbing making it white as clot of milk.[55]

From the spectacle which he saw, it dawned upon Dhanapāla that the pervading spirit of Jaina religion was compassion towards all living creatures. He embraced his younger brother, Śobhana, with love and, affected to the core of his soul by Śobhana's exemplary conduct, adopted Jainism.[56]

Career as Court Poet

A revolutionary change occurred in Dhanapāla's attitude and he began to have a great regard for the sanctity of life, both human and animal. Once when king Bhoja went out for hunting in the company of Dhanapāla he questioned the poet:

"Dhanapāla, what, pray, is the cause that these deer leap up towards the sky, while the boars furrow the ground"? The quick-witted Dhanapāla answered:

"King, terrified by your weapons, they seek to take refuge with their kind", The deer with the deer in the deer—marked noon, the boars with the primeval boar".[57]

When the king pierced a deer with an arrow he looked at the face of Dhanapāla, expecting an appropriate śloka of praise from him for his skill as a hunter. But the śloka that issued from the poet's lips was to the following effect:

"Your valour in hunting deserves but a place in the region of hell;
It's evil as policy, he who takes refuge is always held guiltless;
That the weak one is slain by the mighty is always a matter of sorrow;
Oh' Woe worth the day when this happens;
it shows that the world is then kingless."[58]

Getting something different from that he had expected, the king indignantly asked the poet to explain what he meant. The poet readily answered:

"Even foes who take grass in their mouths are reprieved from sentence of death. Can you slay these most innocent beasts who have always green grass in their mouths?"[59]

Then a great pity rose in the heart of the king and he

resolved to break his bow and renounce the sinful habit of hunting for the term of his natural life.[60]

Dhanapāla who was endowed with a highly versatile and accomplished wit was verily the brightest luminary in the galaxy of poets surrounding king Bhoja and often delighted the king with his literary flashes. Once a merchant came to the court of king Bhoja and presented him some laudatory stanzas impressed on a tablet of wax. The king asked him wherefrom he had brought the tablet. The merchant replied, "My ship suddenly stopped in the mid ocean and when the sailors began to sound the sea, they saw submerged in it a temple of Śiva, and though the waves were surging round it, they saw that, inside, it was free from water, and perceiving that there were letters on a certain wall, they applied a tablet of wax to it, in order to find out what they were and here is the tablet with the letters that came off on it".

When the king heard that, he applied a tablet of clay to the wax tablet, and had the letters that then appeared on it, read by paṇḍitas.[61]

While the complete stanzas were read in the royal presence by some paṇḍitas, they came upon the following incomplete verse:

"Alas! indeed the results of deeds formerly done
Are terrible in the case of living creatures".

When more than a hundred scholars failed to complete the verse, Dhanapāla was asked by the king to accomplish the challenging task. He improvised the following lines to complete the fragmentary stanza:

"Alas! Alas! those very heads, which gleamed on the head of Śiva.
Are now rolled about by the feet of kites".[62]

The king remarked with admiration that the second half produced by Dhanapāla appeared to harmonize with the first. Dhanapāla boldly asserted: "If this is not found both in words and sense on the wall that contains this panegyric and Rāmeśvara I will henceforth renounce the profession of poet until the end of my life". Hearing this, the king ordered soldiers to sail for Rāmeśvara forthwith. Putting out to sea they reached the temple in six months, applied a tablet of wax to the inscription and brought it to the king. When the king saw that the second half of the stanza brought by them tallied syllable by syallable and letter by letter with what Dhanapāla had extemporized, he gave the paṇḍita the reward that he deserved for his adroitness.[63]

Dhanapāla at times displayed rare audacity by openly criticising king Bhoja's Brāhmaṇical beliefs and practices, while yet present in the court, he could turn a compliment as neatly as any other courtier:

"The Creator wished, O Lord of Dhārā to count the earthly kings,
Then made a streak in the sky with a piece of chalk to note you down,
The streak became this stream, for none can equal you,
He let the chalk drop down, and it became Himālayas."[64]

When the other paṇḍitas criticised the stanza as dripping with exaggeration, Dhanapāla retorted:

"Vālmīki makes the sea to be bridged with the rocks that were brought by the monkeys and Vyāsa by the arrows of Arjuna, and yet they are not charged with exaggeration."[65]

Conversion of Bhoja

Dhanapāla was also instrumental in making king Bhoja to give up the Vedic practice of sacrificing animals for the propitiation of gods. Once the king, while in the company of Dhanapāla, heard the plaintive bleating of a goat which was fastened to a yūpa (sacrificial post) in the Yajñaśālā ('shed for sacrifice'). He asked the poet Dhanapāla, "what does the animal say"? Dhanapāla replied, "It is entreating not to be slain". It says', "I am not desirous of enjoying the fruits of heaven, I never asked you for them, I am always satisfied with eating grass, this conduct does not become you, holy man. If the living creatures sacrificed by you assuredly go to heaven, why do you not offer sacrifice of your mother and father, your sons and brothers and likewise".[66]

Dhanapāla added by way of hitting the hail on the head, "If one goes to Heaven by erecting sacrificial post, slaying beasts and shedding blood, by doing what does one go to hell?

Truth is my sacrificial post, penance indeed is my fire, deeds are my fuel. The sacrifice of one who offers harmlessness as a burnt-offering wins the approval of the good".[67]

Although ironically stated, Dhanapāla's argument was so convincing that the king heard his vigrous condemnation of his religious beliefs without anger.

Dhanapāla even went so far as to ridicule the gods whom Bhoja worshipped without ruffling his temper. He once visited a temple in the company of his master, and there noticed the statues of Kāmadeva (the God of Love) and of his wife Rati. The poet, then, laughed. When the king asked him the cause of his laughter, the paṇḍita said:—

"Through the three Worlds is Śiva famed for self-restraint but yet,
For fear of parting makes Umā a part of his own self,
So we are conquered by this God, are we?
Saying this, and patting with his hand.
The hand of his beloved, triumphs laughingly the god of love".[68]

On another occasion Dhanapāla ridiculed the worship of the cow, as was practised by Bhoja and the majority of his subjects. Dhanapāla ironically stressed on the worship of the buffalo:

"She (Cow) feeds on filth. She does not show the discernment in her love, she weds her own son, she smites all creatures with her hoofs and horns, what good in her does make you worship her? It is because she gives you milk? So does the buffalo. There is not seen in the cow even the slightest superiority to the other."[69]

By these and other observations he made in the king's presence and by bringing home to him that those who preached the gospel of doing harm to living beings were in effect Rākṣasas in the form of Brāhmaṇas, he made king Bhoja well disposed towards the Jaina religion.[70]

Once when Bhoja was walking in the temple of 'Sarasvatī kaṇṭhābharaṇa', he said to Dhanapāla, who was always praising the founder of Jainism (Lord Mahāvīra), "Admitting that there once was an All-knowing one", "is there now any superiority of knowledge in his sect"? Dhanapāla answered, "The book called *Arhaccūdāmaṇi* written by the Arhat, contains true information about all objects in the three worlds of the past, present and future". When Dhanapāla said this, the king was in the maṇḍapa (ante-chamber) of the temple which had three doors. In his eagerness to cast a slur on the Jaina treatises, Bhoja said, "By what door are we going out"? Then Dhanapāla, proving the truth of the version, "The really auspicious thirteenth is intellect only'', wrote the answer to the king's question on a leaf of birch-bark, and placed it in an earthen jar, and gave the jar to the betel-box bearer. Then he said to the king, "Set on your foot, your Highness". Thinking that Dhanapāla must have fixed on one of the three doors, the king had the lotus slab of the ante-chamber removed by masons and went out by that aperture. Then he broke the jar and lo! the precise mode of his exit from the temple was written on the birch leaf. This incident made a deep impression on Bhoja's mind and he praised the law of the Jina.[71] By these and other telling strokes Dhanapāla led Bhoja ultimately to renounce the religion of his ancestors and embrace Jainism.

Rupture with Bhoja

At one stage Dhanapāla's happy relations with king Bhoja were ruptured. The king who had been listening with rapt attention to Dhanapāla's recitation of the original draft of his magnum opus, *Tilaka-mañjarī*, was so much taken in by the beauty of the work that he wanted to be made the hero of it. As Dhanapāla refused to oblige the king, Bhoja got into a rage and threw the manuscript of *Tilaka-mañjarī* into the fire. Smarting with humiliation meted out to him by the insolent sovereign, Dhanapāla left Dhārā in disgust and settled at Sācore (the present day Sanchor in Rājasthāna). There in the big temple of Lord Mahāvīra, the poet immersed himself in the worship of the Lord Mahāvīra and composed the book *Satyapurīya-Śrī-Mahāvīra-Utsāha* in praise of Lord Mahāvīra.[72] As stated earlier (p. 3), king Bhoja later recanted, made suitable amends to Dhanapāla and brought him with due honour to

Avantipura where Dhanapāla fought a poetical contest trouncing the challenger-Dharma.

Devotion to Religion

Dhanapāla used his wealth for the uplift of the seven orders of Jaina monks e.g., 'Śrāvakā', 'Srāvikā, 'Sādhu', 'Sādhvī, Jinacaity, Jinabimba and Śāstra.[73]

He got erected a big Jaina temple, installed therein the statue of Ṛṣabhadeva and composed *Ṛṣabhapañcāśikā* in praise of Ṛṣabhadeva.[74]

Though he himself was a staunch and devout Jaina, Dhanapāla's attitude towards other religions was refreshingly compassionate and tolerant. There are numerous references scattered in the pages of *Tilaka-mañjarī* and *Pāiyalacchī*, which provide convincing proof of his generous and universal outlook.

Learning and Education

Dhanapāla was a polyglot genius. His mastery over the principal literary languages of the time e.g., Saṁskṛta, Prākṛta and Apabhraṁśa stands revealed in his works in these languages. He had drunk deep and long at the fount of knowledge so that his erudition took in its stride all the principal branches of learning e.g., the Veda, Vedāṅga, Smṛti, Itihāsa and Purāṇas.[75]

Travels

Dhanapāla was a widely travelled man. In the course of many pilgrimages he himself (after his conversion) to far-flung Jaina Shrines throughout the length and breadth of India, he was able to visit Koraṇṭaka, Śrīmāladeśa, Dhārā, Āhāḍa (Āghāṭa), Narāṇā, Aṇahilavāḍu-Pāṭaṇa, Vijayakoṭṭa and Pālītāṇa.[76]

Summing up

Destiny had assigned three roles to Dhanapāla—those of the

man, the poet and the convert and it may be conceded without any reservation that he filled each of them with equal competence and becoming grace. His well-spent life was informed by a deep-seated love of humanity, a heart-felt devotion to religion and a total commitment to the art of poetry.

There can be no better tribute than one paid to him by one of his own contemporaries, Someśvara, who asserts that there was no living being who was not overpowered by the sweet words and generous heart of Dhanapāla.[77]

WORKS

There is near consensus among the scholars and researchers with regard to the works written by Dhanapāla. Shāntyāchārya[78] and H.R.D. Kapaḍiya[79] have attributed the following works to Dhanapāla:

1. *Pāiyalacchīnāmamālā* (Prākṛta lexicon).
2. *Tilaka-mañjarī* (Saṁskṛta romance).
3. *Śrāvaṇa vidhi Prākaraṇa* (Prākṛta).
4. *Śrīvīrastuti* (Prākṛta hymn).
5. *Śobhana Stutivṛtti* (Saṁskṛta Commentary).
6. *Ṛṣabhapañcāśikā* (Prākṛta hymn).
7. *Satyapurīya-Śrī-Mahāvīra-Utsāha* (Apabhraṁśa hymn).
8. *Vīra Stuti* (Hymn in Saṁskṛta and Prākṛta).
9. *Nāmamālā* (Prākṛta lexicon).

Pāiyalacchīnāmamālā (Prākṛta lexicon)

Pāiyalacchī occupies a prominent place in the field of Prākṛta lexicography. Dhanapāla's *Pāiyalacchīnāmamālā* and *Deśīnāmamālā* of Hemacandra were discovered first by Dr. Bühler in the last quarter of the 18th century.

Pāiyalacchī was composed in V.S. 1029 (A.D. 972 *c.*) when Mānyakheṭa, the capital of the Rāṣṭrakūṭas of Deccan was sacked and looted by Sīyaka II of Paramāra dynasty of Malwa.[80]

Dhanapāla composed the book for the edification of his younger sister, Sundarī, while residing at Dhārā, the capital of of Paramāras.[81]

Dhanapāla calls the *Pāiyalacchī* a 'deśī' or 'deśi' 'Śāstra',[81] yet includes in it more 'tatsama' and 'tadbhava' words than those belonging strictly to deśī etymology. It may be presumed that as Prākṛta was the language of popular literatures, while Saṁskṛta that of literati, Dhanapāla has chosen to call it 'deśī', e.g., a work in popular tradition.

Bühler has remarked in the 'Introduction' of his edition to *Pāiyalacchīnāmamālā* that the deśī words "are all or nearly all derived from Sanskrit words...... They are formed according to the more occult phonetic and grammatical laws differing from the obvious ones, which the grammarians have embodied in their vyākaraṇas".[83] Thus for instance the words *Kallā*,[84] *Cūo*,[85] *duggulla*,[86] *herambo*[87] are very closely related to Saṁskṛta *Kalya*, *Cūcuka* (*cūta*), *dukūla* and *heramba* respectively.

There are 279 verses in the koṣa and synonyms of 998 deśī words[88] are given.

In the maṅgalācaraṇa of *Pāiyalacchī*, Ṛṣabhadeva, Brahmā[89] and other Brāhmaṇical deities like Pārvatī, Durgā, Kālī, Kalyāṇī and Caṇḍī are invoked.[90] At the end of the third part, the name of Tīrthaṅkara Mahāvīra[91] is mentioned.

The last three verses are of topical interest wherein the poet dilates on the purpose of composing the lexicon. In the last śloka the poet states, "I have arranged here these words rich in flavour which are commonly used by the bards in their poetic compositions. May they gladden the hearts of clever men".[92]

Pāiyalacchī is a work of considerable importance from the historical point of view. It throws some very significant light on the relations between Paramāras and the Rāṣṭrakūṭas of Deccan. The sack of Mānyakheṭa, the capital of Rāṣṭrakūṭas, which is mentioned in *Pāiyalacchī* helps the students of ancient Indian history in fixing the periods of various kings of Paramāra and Rāṣṭrakūṭa dynasties. It also provides valuable information with regard to the religious, social and economic conditions of Dhanapāla's time.

Tilaka-mañjarī

It is a prose-romance in Saṁskṛta modelled admittedly on the famous classical Saṁskṛta novel, Bāṇa's *Kādambarī*. The work gives, like its model, a continuous narrative without any division into chapters with the significant difference that whereas *Kādambarī* is essentially in prose, Dhanapāla has used verses as well. Nevertheless the verses are not so numerous as could entitle *Tilaka-mañjarī* to be classified as a Campū kāvya.[93]

Dr. S.N. Das Gupta has opined that Dhanapāla wrote *Tilaka-mañjarī* under the patronage of Muñja of Dhārā at about A.D. 970.[94] But from the internal evidence provided by *Tilaka-mañjarī*, it is revealed that the book was written by Dhanapāla to satisfy the curiosity of king Bhoja about Jina-dharma.[95]

There is a story associated with the work, a story that has many parallels in Saṁskṛta literature as in the case of the *Uttararāmacarita* and the *Āścaryacūḍāmaṇi*, where the author burnt the manscript and then someone else had to reproduce the whole work from memory. The work (*Tilaka-mañjarī*) was written out for the king and it used to be given to him part by part. Before the work was finished, the author lost the favour of the king and the king ordered that the entire manuscript be burnt. But the author had a daughter who had been committing every line of it to memory and so she was able to rewrite the whole work from memory. The work bears her name, which is the name of the heroine.[96]

The legend about the origin and composition of *Tilaka-mañjarī* has also been narrated by Merutuṅga in *Prabandhacintāmaṇi*. Dhanapāla, according to Merutuṅga, remained absent for a considerable time from the royal Court of Rājā Bhoja. When after his arrival Bhoja enquired the cause of his absence the poet, Dhanapāla replied that he had been busy in composing '*Tilaka-mañjarī*'. The king, being very eager, went through the book and was very much impressed by its merits. King Bhoja then asked Dhanapāla to make certain changes in the book. He said to Dhanapāla, "Make me the hero of this tale and put Avanti in the place of Vinītā and let the shrine of Mahākāla take the place of the holy Śakrāvatāra and then I will give you whatever you like to ask". The self-respecting Paṇḍita thereupon exclaimed: "There is a vast difference between the two sets of things, as there is between a fire fly and the Sun, between a grain of mustard seed and the golden mountain, between glass and gold, between a dhatūrā plant and the wishing tree of Paradise".[97]

Dhanapāla continued, "Double-mouthed speeches, covetous minded javelin-like creature, what are we to say to you? Weighing gold with guñjā-seeds, you have not gone to the subterranean world".

When the Paṇḍita reproached him in these words, king Bhoja, being indignant threw the MS into the blazing fire.

Humiliated, depressed and enraged as he felt, Dhanapāla stood up and vowed, "I will never come again".

At home the Paṇḍita who was utterly dispirited and crest-fallen flung himself down on an old couch in the back part of his palace and lay sulking there. His daughter, (Bāla Paṇḍita) roused him from his stupor with loving attention and made him bathe and eat and then recollecting the first half of *Tilaka-mañjarī* which she had gone through, she wrote it out and the second half she composed anew in order to complete the book.[98]

It goes in *Prabhāvakacarita* that originally *Tilaka-mañjarī* had twelve thousand ślokas of which a thousand ślokas were reproduced by the poet's daughter from memory and remaining three thousands were added by her as new ones.[99]

Tilaka-mañjarī, named after its heroine, like *Kādambarī*, is an elaborate tale of love and union of Tilaka-mañjarī and Samaraketu. Like Kādambarī, Tilaka-mañjarī, too, is 'Mugdhā' and 'Pragalbhā' and in the beginning is bent upon not to marry. In the same manner the hero, both in Bāṇa and Dhanapāla, is 'Dhīrodātta'.

In the introductory verses Dhanapāla gives the genealogy of the Paramāra kings of Dhārā and among the poets mentions Vālmīki, Vyāsa, Jīvadeva, Kālidāsa, Bāṇa, Māgha, Bhāravi, Bhavabhūti, Vākpatirājā, Bhadrakīrti, Bappabhaṭṭa, Rāja-śekhara, Mahendra Sūri, Rudra and Kardamarāja.[100]

Tilaka-mañjarī is one of the important works in Saṁskṛta prose-romance and sheds valuable light on the contemporary social, religious, economic and political conditions of the time. It contains vivid descriptions regarding habitation of cow-herds and the stir caused in a village by an army on march. It graphically describes a naval expedition to Dvīpāntara and gives interesting information about Indian shipping and trade in South East Asia. Its manifold descriptions taken from the mythology and from Nature and also from different classes of lore like, religion and philosophy and sciences, from the customs and manners and practices of the people provide valuable and reliable data for the study of the socio-economic life of those times.

Śrāvaṇavidhi Prakaraṇa

The work remains untraceable despite my best efforts.

Vīrastuti or Mahāvīrastuti

It is a poem of 30 verses in Prākṛta composed in praise of Lord Mahāvīra. All the verses have been cast in the mould of 'double entendres' and the poem bears an unmistakable stamp of Dhanapāla's poetic ingenuity and virtuosity. It is recorded in *Prabhāvakacarita* that on leaving Dhārā, after being insulted by Rājā Bhoja on the issue of the composition of *Tilaka-mañjarī*, Dhanapāla settled at Sācore and there meditating in the temple of Lord Mahāvīra composed *Mahāvīra-stuti.*[101] The work sheds interesting light on the life and personality of Lord Mahāvīra. It begins with the verse:

> *Nimmalanahe vi aṇahe jiṇāṇa calaṇuppale paṇamiūṇaṁ/*
> *vīramaviruddhavayaṇaṁ thuṇāmi sa viruddha vayaṇa mahaṁ//*[102]

in which the poet dedicates himself to the worship of Vardhamāna Mahāvīra.

In the succeeding verses Dhanapāla dilates on the well-known Jaina tenets and concepts of 'Triratna' (śloka 4), Triveda (śloka 19), 'Syād-vāda' (śloka 9), Kāṣāya (śloka 2), Guṇasthāna (śloka 7) and the like.

Śobhanastutivṛtti

Śobhana, the younger brother of Dhanapāla, wrote a hymn,

variously known as *Caturviṁśati-Jinastuti* or *Śobhanastuti* in honour of the different Tīrthaṅkaras. *Śobhanastutivṛtti* is a commentary written by Dhanapāla on the work of his younger brother.[103]

Ṛṣabhapañcāśikā

Ṛṣabhapañcāśikā is a Prākṛta poem of 50 stanzas, a hymn in honour of the first Tīrthaṅkara, Lord Ṛṣabhanātha.

Dhanapāla credits Ṛṣabha with having taught art, craft, mathematics and scripts to his subjects. He is said to have taught 72 male arts and 64 female arts. He taught 100 crafts including those of warfare, agriculture and trade.[104]

Ṛṣabha's grandson Namivinamī (son of Bharata) is said to have risen to the eminence of Vidyādhara (heavenly god) by virtue of his devotion to Ṛṣabha. Dhanapāla thus lays great stress on Ṛṣabha's worship. For the worship of the gurus always bears fruit.[105]

Among other things discussed in the body of the poem, Dhanapāla has referred to Nayavāda,[106] the kālas, e.g., 'Avasarpiṇī' and 'Utsarpiṇī'.[107]

Dhanapāla also speaks of the seven hells, namely, 'Ratnaprabhā', 'Sarkarāprabhā', 'Valukāprabhā', 'Paṅkaprabhā', 'Dhūmaprabhā', 'Tamaḥprabhā' and 'Mahātmaḥ' situated in 'adholoka'. Man and fish are assigned to the seventh hell. Dhanapāla also mentions the theory of transmigration and rebirth and dwells on the numerous births before the soul gets nirvāṇa.[108]

Eulogising the importance of Namaskāra formula (Vacanāmantra) which runs thus :

Ṇamo arahaṁtāṇaṁ, ṇamo siddhaṇaṁ, ṇamo āiriyāṇaṁ, ṇamo uvajjhāyāṇaṁ, ṇamo loye sabba sāhuṇaṁ.

Dhanapāla confidently asserts that the soul possessed by mithyātva (perverted attitude) becomes conscious and changed into Samyaktva (right attitude) by hearing the words of Salutation mantra.[109] Such is the miraculous power of this mantra.

In the conclusion the poet invokes the great Tīrthaṅkara, "Thus praised with devotion by me, a man of small understanding only, whose karma is consumed like fuel in the fire of meditation, mayest thou (O Ṛṣabha) reward me by pure knowledge which is a boat to cross the ocean of existence".[110] Commenting upon the style of the book, Winternitz says, "It is written in a very artificial style but not without poetical beauty".[111]

Satyapurīya-Śrī-Mahāvīra-Utsāha[112]

It is a poem of 37 verses in Apabhraṁśa in praise of Lord Mahāvīra's image at Sācore (Satyapura). It was composed in V.S. 1081 (A.D. 1024) when Mahmūd of Ghaznī invaded India. It sheds light on Mahmūd's route which he took during his vandalic outrage on Somanātha. Muni Jina Vijai is of the opinion that the poet Dhanapāla of this poem is identical with the author of *Tilaka-mañjarī* of the same name.[113]

Vīrastuti[114]

It is a poem of 11 verses in which the first line of every śloka is in Saṁskṛta and the second in Prākṛta. Fashioned after *Mahāvīrastuti*, it begins with the following verse :

> *Sarabhasanṛtyatsurayuvati kucataṭatruṭita hāratārakitam/*
> *jayaṁ siddhattha narindamaṅdiraṁ jassa jammammi//*
> (*Śloka* 1, p. 269)

According to Śvetāmbara tradition, Lord Mahāvīra was married to Yaśodā and a daughter named Priyadarśanā was born to them. Dhanapāla, obviously working within the same tradition, mentions in *Vīrastuti* that bound by the unbounded love and affection of his parents lord Mahāvīra, though keen on renouncing the world, stayed for a time with his family for the sake of their pleasure filling the house with his divine radiance :

Mātāpitroḥ premānubandbamadhikaṁ vibudhyayaḥ sthitavān/
divvālaṁkāra phuraṁta viggaho cattasaṅgo vi//
(*Śloka 5*)

In another verse Dhanapāla praises Lord Mahāvīra for having protected a cāmara-mṛga (gazelle) which came to his feet terrified with the burning vajra (missile) thrown on him by the god Indra :

Pṛakupita surādhipa vikṣiptā dīpta dambholibheda sambhrāntaḥ/
camaro calaṇuppala mūlamāgao rakkhio jeṇe//
(*Śloka 8*)

Nāmamālā

It is another Prākṛta lexicon attributed to Dhanapāla. Dr. Bühler confirms that the author of *Pāiyalacchī* wrote another Prākṛta Kośa (Nāmamālā) and that Hemacandra's quotations are drawn from it.[115] Śrī Vikramavijayamuni has shared the same opinion. He writes that Dhanapāla wrote another saṁskṛta Kośa consisting of 1800 verses in Saṁskṛta :

Temaṇe 1800 śloka pramāṇa Saṁskṛta bhāshāno kośa banā vyāno ullekha maleche.[116]

These opinions have, however, been contradicted by prof. P.V. Ramānuja Swāmī who writes : "I venture to suggest that Dhanapāla quoted by Hemacandra is quite different from the author of *Paīyalacchī.* If they were identical, it would be impossible to conceive how one person could teach one and the same word in two different works. Again, I do not see any reason why he should compose two Kośas of the same kind instead of one a comprehensive one".[117]

REFERENCES

1. Nathu Ram Premi, *Jaina Sāhitya aur Itihāsa* (Bombay: Hindi Grantha Ratnākara, 1956), pp. 408-411. While Premi has listed

three Dhanapālas, Parmānanda Śāstrī has mentioned the fourth one also, the author of *Bāhubalicarita*. ("Dhanapāla nāma ke cāra Vidvān Kavi," *Anekānta-kiraṇa*, VII-VIII, p. 82).

2. Op. cit., p. 409.
3. Dhanapāla, *Tilaka-mañjarī*, ed. Bhavadattaśastrī (Bombay: Nirṇaya Sāgara Press, 1938), p. 7, śloka 53.
(All refs. in this dissertation are to this ed. unless otherwise indicated).
4. *Tilaka-mañjarī*, ed. Shantyacharya, (Bombay: Nirṇaya Sāgara Press, 2008 (V.E.), Pt. I, p. XVII (Introd.).
5. *Tilaka-mañjarī*, p. 7:

Niḥśeṣavāṅganayavido'pijināgamoktaḥ
śrotum kathāḥ samupajāta kutūhalasya/
Tasyāvadātacaritsya vinodaheto
Rājñaḥ sphuṭādbhutarasā racitā katheyam//

(*Śloka* 50)

6. Prabhācandrācārya, *Prabhāvakacarita*, ed. Jinavijayamuni, "Siṅghī Jaina Granthamālā" (Calcutta, 1940), p. 145:

Ekadā nṛpatiḥ smārttakathāvistaranistuṣaḥ/
Vayasyamavadajjaiṇakathāṁ śrāvaya kāmapi//
Dvādaśātha sahastrāṇi granthamānena tāṁtataḥ/
Paripūryatato Vidyatsamūhairavadhāritām//
Yathārthāṁ kācadoṣasyoddhārāt Tilaka-mañjarīm/
Rasenakavitārūpacakṣunairmarlyadāyinim//

(*Ślokas* 194—196).

7. S.N. Das Gupta & S.K. De, *History of Sanskrit Literature* (Calcutta: Cal. Univ., 1947), pp. 430-431.
8. Lallan Ji Gopal, *Economic Life of Northern India* (Delhi: Moti Lal Banarsi Das, 1965), p. xx.
9. *Prabhāvakacarita*, p. 148, ślokas 263—265.
10. Ibid., p. 146, ślokas 213—215.
11. *Prabhāvakacarita*, p. 148:

Śrī-Muñjasya mahībhartuḥ pratipanna sutobhavān/
jyeṣṭho' haṁ tu Kaniṣṭho' smi tat kiṁ gaṇyaṁ laghorvacaḥ/
Purā jyāyānmahārājastvāmutsaṅgopaveśitam/
Prāheti viradaṁ te'stu śrī kūrcāla saravati//
Tyaktā vayaṁ tvayā vṛddhā rājyamāptā sca bhāgyataḥ/
jaye parājaye vāpyavantideśaḥ sthalaṁ tava//

(*Ślokas* 270—272)

Bhoja was not the real son of Muñja, but he loved him as his own son. The term '*Pratipanna sutaḥ*' indicates that king Muñja loved Dhanapāla too as his own son.

12. Merutuṅga, *Prabandhacintāmaṇi*. "Siṅghī Jaina Granthamālā" (Sāntiniketana, Bengal, 1933), p. 41.
13. K.M. Munshi, *Glory That was Gūrjara Deśa* (Lucknow, 1954), p. 197.

14. *History and Culture of Indian People*, Vol. IV (Bombay, 1955). p. 186.
15. H.C. Ray, *Dynastic History of Northern India*, Vol. II (Calcutta, 1931), p. 856.
16. Gulab Chandra Choudhary, *Political History of Northern India from Jaina Sources* (Amritsar: Sohan Lal Jain dharma Pracharak Samiti, 1962), pp. 94,105.
17. D.C. Ganguly, *History of Paramāra Dynasty* (Dacca, 1933), p. 282.
18. T.S. Ayyangar, *Bhoja-Rājā* (Madras, 1931), p. 25.
19. A.B. Keith, *A History of Sanskrit Literature* (Oxford, 1928), p. 332.
20. J.N. Farquhar, *An Outline of Religious Literature of India* (Delhi, 1969), p. 279.
21. Dhanapāla, *Pāiyalacchīnāmamālā*, ed. Bacharadasa Jivaraya Doshi (Bombay, 1960), p. 38:

    Vikkama kālassa gaye auṇattīsuttare sahassammi|
    Mālva narinda dhāḍīe lūḍie manna kheḍammi||
    Dhārānayarīe pariṭṭhieṇa magge ṭhiāe aṇavajje|
    Kajje kaṇiṭṭha bahiṇīe 'sundarī' nāma dhijjāe||
    Kaiṇo andhajaṇa kivā kusalatti payāṇa mantimāvaṇṇā|
    Nāmammi jassa kamaso teṇesā viraiyā deśī||

    (*Ślokas* 276—278)
22. *E.I.*, I, p. 234.
23. See also Becharadasa Jivaraja Doshi, Introd. to *Pāiyalacchī*, p. 15.
24. Dhanapāla, *Satyapurīya-Srī-Mahāvīra-Utsāha* in "Jaina Sāhitya Samśodhaka", II, No. 3. (Ahmedabad), p. 1:

    '*Bhañje viṇusirimālādesu anu aṇihilavāṅgaū*
    Bhāgu na siri............turuṣka......'
25. Jinaprabha Sūri, *Vividha-Tīrtha-kalpa*, "Siṅghī Jaina Granthamālā X" (1934), p. 29:

    Tao annayā anno gajjanavaī gujjaraṁ bhañjitā tao vaṁtato|
    Patto saccaure dasaseya ikkāsīe vikkama varise miccharājo||
26. See Becharadasa Jivaraja Doshi, Introd. to *Pāiyalacchī*, p. 31.
27. K.M. Munshi, op. cit.. p. 197.
28. K.K. Handiqui, *Yaśastilaka and Indian Culture* (Sholapur, 1949), pp. 9-10.
29. Op. cit., p. 6.
30. Pratipal Bhatia, *The Paramāras* (Delhi, 1967), p. 37.
31. Op. cit., p. 46.
32. Op. cit., p. 58.
33. Op. cit., p. 74.
34. *Tilaka-mañjarī*, p. 7:

    Āsīddvijanmākhila madhyadeśe prakāśaśāṅkāśajaniveśa janma(?)/
    Alabdha devarṣiriti prasiddhiṁ yo dānavarṣitva Vibhūsito'pi||

Śāstreṣvadhītī kuśalaḥ kalāsu bandhe ca bodhe ca girām prakṛṣṭaḥ|
Tasyātmajanmā samabhūnmahātma devaḥ svayambhūriva sarva-devaḥ||
Tajjanmā janakoṅghripañkja rajaḥ sevāpta vidyālayo||
Vipraḥ śrī Dhanapāla ityaviśadāmetāmabadhanātkathām|
Akṣunno'pi viviktasūktiracane yaḥ sarvavidyābdhinā
Śrī Muñjena Sarasvatīti sadasi kṣoṇībhṛtā vyāhṛtaḥ||

35. Nathu Ram Premi, op. cit', p. 409.
36. *Pāiyalacchīnāmamālā*, ed. Becharadasa Jivaraja Doshi, Introd. (Hindi), p. 16.
37. *Tilaka-mañjarī*, ed. Shantyacharya, Pt. I, Introd. (Sanskrit), p. 16.
38. *Prabandhacintāmaṇi*, p. 41: *Bālapaṇḍitayā tatsutāyā...*
39. *Pāiyalacchīnāmamālā*, ed. Becharadasa Jivaraja Doshi, Introd. (Hindi), p. 24.
40. *Prabhāvakacarita*, p. 138. *Prabandhacintāmaṇi*, p. 36.
41. *Prabhāvakacarita*, loc. cit.
42. *Prabhāvakacarita*, p. 138.
43. *Prabhāvakacarita*, p. 139. *Prabandhacintāmaṇi*, p. 36.
44. *Tilaka-mañjarī*, ed. Shantyacharya, Pt. I, Introd., p. 16:
Hastinā tāḍyamāno' pi na gacccheta Jaina mandiram.
45. *Prabhāvakacarita*, p. 139, śloka 46:
Ekastvamṛṇato mocyaḥ pātyāḥ sarve'pi pūrvajaḥ|
Imaṃ kuvyavahāraṃ nādhāsye sajjananinditam||
46. Ibid., p. 139, śloka 45.
47. Ibid., pp. 139-140, ślokas 49—67.
48. *Prabandhacintāmaṇi*, p. 36: *Dhanapālena Śrī Bhoja prasāda samprāpta samasta paṇḍita praṣṭha pratiṣṭhena.*
49. Ibid., p. 36. *Prabhāvakacarita*, p. 140.
50. Loc. cit.: *Gardabhadanta bhadanta ! namaste.*
Tr. C.H. Tawney (Calcutta, Asiatic Society of Bengal), p. 53.
51. Loc. cit., *Kapivṛṣaṇāasya! sukhante.*
52. Loc. cit., see Tawney, p. 53.
53. *Prabandhacintāmaṇi*, p. 36: *Bhajenmādhukarīṁ vṛttiṁ munir malecchakulādapi|*
Ekānnaṁ naiva bhuñjīta bṛhaspatisamādapi||
See Tawney, p. 53.
54. Ibid., p. 36:
Svasamaya parasamayābhyāṁ niṣiddhaṁ kalpitmāhāraṁ pariharantaḥ śuddhāsana bhojinovayamiti.
See Tawney, p. 53.
55. Ibid., pp. 36-37. It is a tenet of Jaina religion that maggots are produced in sour milk if it is kept for three days:
Muggamāsāipamuhaṁ vidila Kaccami gorase paḍai|
Ta tasajīvuppatī bhaṇanti dahie tidiṇuvarim||
56. *Prabandhacintāmaṇi*, p. 37.

57. Ibid., p. 37:

Bhojarājaḥ prāha-kiṁkāraṇaṁ nu Kavirāja mṛgāyadete vyomotpatanti vilikhanti bhuvaṁ varāhāḥ?
Dhanapālaḥ prāh-deva tvadastracakitāḥ śrayituṁsvajātineke mṛgāṅkamṛgamādi varāhmanye||
(*f.n.*)

See, Tawney, p. 55.

58. *Prabhāvakacarita*, p. 143:

Rasātalaṁ yātu yadatra pauruṣaṁ kva nītireṣā'śaraṇo hyadoṣavān|
nihanyate yada balina'pi nirbalo hahā mahā Kaṣṭamarājakaṁ jagat||
(*Śloka* 50)

59. *Prabandhacintāmaṇi*, p. 37:

Vairiṇāpi hi mucyante prāṇānte tṛṇabhakṣaṇāt|
tṛṇāhārāḥ sadaivai te hanyante paśavaḥ katham||
(*Śloka 91*)

60. *Prabandhacintāmaṇi*, p. 37:

Ityadbhutasañjāta kṛpeṇa nṛpeṇa dhanurbāṇabhaṇga-bhaṇgī kṛtyājīvitānta saṁnyastamṛgayāvyasanena......|

61. Ibid., pp. 40-41, see Tawney, p. 59.

62. *Prabandhacintāmaṇi*, p. 40:

Ayi khalu viṣamaḥ purā kṛtānāṁ bhavti hi jantuṣu karmaṇāṁ vipākaḥ|
Hara śirasi śirāṅsi yāni rejurhari hari tāni luṭhaṅti gṛdhra pādaiḥ||
(*Śloka* 101)

See Tawney, p. 60:

"According to Tawney, the above mentioned two lines are found in *Bhoja Prabandha* (p. 246, Bombay Edition, 1895) but the second line begins Śiva Śiva, tāni, This suggests the reading 'Hara, Hara, tāni', "Alas"! means literally "O Viṣṇu',. In *Bhoja Prabandha* the inscription is found by fisherman on a stone in the Narmadā'."

63. *Prabandhacintāmaṇi*, p. 41. See Tawney, p. 60.

64. Ibid., p. 41:

Dharādhīśa dharāmahīśa gaṇane kautūhalīyānayaṁ vedhāstvadgaṇanaṁ cakāra khaṭikākhaṇḍena rekhāṁ devi|
sīveyaṁ tridaśapagā samabhavatvatulya bhūmīdha vāmā vatta tyajatismaso'yamavanīpīthe tuṣārācalaḥ||
(*Śloka* 69)

See Tawney, pp. 61-62.

65. *Prabandhacintāmaṇi*, p. 42:

Śailairbandhayatisma vānarahṛtairvālmīkirambhonidhiṁ
Vyāsaḥ pārthaśaraistathapina tayoratyukti rudbhāvyāte|

Vastu prastutameva kiṁcanavayaṁ brūmstāthāpuccakair-
loko'yaṁ-hasati prasārita mukhāstubhyaṁ p atiṣṭhe namaḥ//

(*Śloka* 70)

See Tawney, pp. 61-62.

66. Ibid., p. 38:
Nāhaṁ svargaphalopabhogatṛṣito nābhyarthitastvaṁ mayā
saṁtuṣṭastṛṇabhakṣaṇena satataṁ sādho na yuktaṁ tavā/
Svargaṁ yānti yadi tvayā vinihatā yajñe dhruvaṁ prāṇino-
yajñaṁ kiṁ na karoṣi mātṛpitṛbhiḥ putraistathā bāndhavaiḥ//

(*Śloka* 92)

67. *Prabandhacintāmaṇi*, p. 38:
Yūpaṁ kṛtva pāśūn hatyā kṛtvā rudhira kardamam/
yadyevaṁ gamyate svarge narake kena gamyate//
Satyaṁ yūpaṁ tapo hyagniḥ karmāṇi samidho mama/
ahiṁsāmāhutiṁ dadyādeśa yajñaḥ sanātanaḥ//

(*Ślokas* 93-94)

68. Ibid., p. 40:
Sa ēṣa bhuvanatraya prathitasaṁyamaḥ Śaṁkarovibharti
vapuṣā'dhunā viraḥ kataraḥ kāminīm/
anena kila nirjitā vayamiti priyāyāḥ karaṁ kareṇa
paritāḍayan jayati jātahāsaḥ smaraḥ//

(*Śloka* 96)

69. *Prabandhacintāmaṇi*, p. 38:
Amedhyamaśnāti vivekaśūnyā
svanandanaṁ kāmayate'abhiṣaktā/
khurāgraśṛṅgairvinihanti jantūn
gaurvandyate kena guṇena rājan//
Payaḥ pradāna sāmarthyādvandyā cenmahiṣi na kim/
Viśeṣo dṛśyate nāsyāṁ mahiṣīto manāgapi//

(*Ślokas* 57-58)

70. Ibid., p. 38:
Ityādi-śukasaṁvābdoditāni vacāṁsi narendrasya purataḥ
paṭhan hiṁsāśāstro padesino hiṁsraprakṛtīn brahmarūpeṇa
rākṣāsāṁstāñjñāpayan nṛpamahardharmābhimukhaṁ cakāra.

71. *Prabandhaciintāmaṇi*, p. 39. See also Tawney, pp. 56-57.

72. *Pāiyalacchī*, ed. Becharadasa Jivaraja Doshi, Introd., p. 29.

73. Ibid., Introd., p. 30.

74. Ibid., p. 30.

75. *Tilaka-mañjarī*, ed. Shantyacharya, Pt. I, Introd., p. 16.
Akhila veda vedāṅga-smṛtītihāsa-purāṇeśu prakāṇḍapāṇḍityam

76. *Pāiyalacchī*, ed. B.J. Doshi, Introd., pp. 30-31.

77. *Kīrtikaumudī*, ed. Puṇya Vijaya Sūri (Bombay, Bharatiya Vidya-Bhavana, 1961) I, p. 3:
Vacanaṁ Dhanapālasya candanaṁ malayasya ca/
sarasaṁ hṛdivinyasya ko'bhūnnāṃ na nirvṛtaḥ//

(*Śloka* 16)

78. *Tilaka-mañjarī*, ed. Shantyacharya, Gujarati Edition (Ahmedabad, V.S. 2008), Pt. I, Introd,, p. 26.
79. *Ṛṣabhapañcāśikā-vīrastuti dvayarūpa Kṛti kalāpaḥ*, ed, Hira Lala Rasika Dasa Kapadiya. Gujarati Ed. (Bombay, 1933), Introd., p. 16.
80. *Pāiyalacchīnāmamālā*, p. 38:

    Vikkama kālassa gaye a-uṇattīsuttare sahassammi|
    mālava nariṅda dhāḍīe lūḍie mannakheḍammi||
    (*Śloka* 276)

81. Ibid., p. 38:

    Dhārānayarīe pariṭṭhieṇa magge thiāe aṇavajje|
    kajje kaṇiṭṭha bahiṇie 'Sundarī' nāma dhijjāe||
    (*Śloka* 277)

82. Ibid., p. 38:

    Ka-iṇo aṅdha jaṇa kivā Kusalatti payāṇa maṁtimā vaṇṇā|
    nāmammi jassa kamaso teṇesā vira-iyadesī||
    (*Śloka* 278)

83. *Pāiyalacchīnāmamālā*, ed. G. Bhüler (Bhavanagar, V.S., 1973), p. 14.
84. *Pāiyalacchīnāmamālā*, ed. Becharadasa Jivaraja Doshi, p. 28, śloka 211.
85. Ibid., p. 18, śloka 145.
86. Ibid., p. 36, śloka 266.
87. Ibid., p. 11, śloka 96.
88. According to Keith, "Some of the words are referable in Sanskrit, but most are not and their provenance is still extremely uncertain". (A.B. Keith, *A History of Sanskrit Literature*, London: Oxford Univ. Press, 1928), p. 415.
89. *Pāiyalacchīnāmamālā*, p. 1. *Nābhi saṁbhavaṁ* indicates Ṛṣabha and *Purisuttamanābhi saṁbhavaṁ* denotes Brahmā.
90. loc. cit.
91. Ibid., p. 11:

    Titthā hivaī jiṇo arahā.

92. Ibid., p. 38:

    Kavvesuje rasaḍḍhā saddā bahuso kaṭhi bajjhanti|
    te ittha ma-e ra-iā ramaṇtu hiae sahiayāṇaṁ||
    (*Śloka* 279)

93. C. Kunhan Raja, *Survey of Sanskrit Literature* (Bombay, 1962), p. 216. 'The admixture of prose and metrical passages in more or less equal proportions in Sanskrit is known as Campū. In *Tilaka-mañjarī* the prose is the normal vehicle and the employment of verse is not so free and frequent as in a Campū'............However, Becharadasa (Op. cit.), calls it a Campū-kāvya· (*Pāiyalacchī* "Introduction", p. 37).
94. S.N. Das Gupta and S.K. De, op. cit., p. 431.
95. *Tilaka-mañjarī*, p. 7, śloka 50.
96. Kunhan Raja, *Survey of Sanskrit Literature*, p. 334.

97. *Prabandhacintāmaṇi*, p. 41. See Tawney, pp. 60-61.
98. *Prabandhacintāmaṇī*, p. 41, See Tawney, pp. 60-61.
99. *Prabhāvakacarita*, p. 146, ślokas 221-22.
100. *Tilaka-mañjarī*, pp. 3-4, ślokas 20—36.
101. *Prabhāvakacarita*, p. 146:

Paścimāṁ diśāmāśritya parispaṅdaṁ' vinā' calat|
prāpa satyapuraṁnāṁa puraṁ paurajanottaraṃ||
Tatra śrimanmahāvīra-caitye nitye pade iva|
dṛṣṭe sa paramānandamāsasāda vidāṁvaraḥ||
Namaskṛtya stutiṁ tatra virodhābhāsa saṁskṛtām|
cakāra prākṛtāṁ deva (?) *nimmaletyādisā' stica||*

(*Ślokas* 224—226)

102. *Ṛṣabhapañcāśikā-vīrastuti dvayarūpa kṛti kalāpaḥ*, p. 200.
103. Nathu Ram Premi, op. cit, p. 410.
104. *Ṛsabhapañcāśikā-vīrastutidvayarūpa kṛti kalāpaḥ*, p. 42:

Dāviavijjāsippovajjariāsesaloavavahāro|
jāo si jāṇa sāmia, payāo tāokayatthāo||

(*Śloka* 10)

105. Ibid., p.51:

Muṇiṇo vi tuhallīṇā, namivinamī khearāhivā jāyā|
guruāṇa calaṇasevā, na niṣphalā hoi kaiā vi||

(*Śloka* 14)

106. *Ṛṣabhapañcāsikā-vīrastutidvayarūpa kṛti kalāpaḥ*, p. 117:

Vāīhiṁ pariggahiā, Karaṁti vimuhaṁ Khaṇeṇa paḍivakkhaṁ|
tujjhanayā nāha! mahāgaya vva annunnasaṁlagnā|

(*Śloka* 40)

107. Ibid., p. 43:

Araeṇaṁ taieṇaṁ, imāi ussappinīi tuha jamme|
phuriaṁ kaṇagamaeṇaṁ, va Kālacakkikkapāsaṁmi||

(*Śloka* 7)

108. Ibid., p. 137:

Vucchaṁ apaṭṭhiāgaya-macchabhavaṁto muhuttavasieṇa|
chāvaṭṭhī ayarāiṁ, niraṁtaraṁ appaiṭṭhāṇe||

(*Śloka* 43)

109. Ibid., p. 112:

Micchattavisapasuttā saceyaṇā jiṇā! na huṁti kiṁ jīvā?
Kaṇṇammikamai ja-i ki-ttiaṁpi tuha vayaṇamantassa||

(*Śloka* 38)

110. *Ṛṣabhapañcāsikā-vīrastuti dvayarūpa kṛti kalāpaḥ*, p. 162:

Ia jhāṇaggipaliviakammiṁdhaṇa! bāla budhiṇā vimae|
bhattīi thuo bhavabhayasamudda bohittha! bohiphalo||

(*Śloka* 50)

111. Winternitz, *Jainas in the History of Indian Literature* (Ahmedabad, 1946), p. 19.
112. Published in *Jaina Sāhitya Saṁśodhaka*, Pt. II (Gujarati).
113. Quoted by Gulab Chandra Choudhary, op. cit., p. 238.

114. "The Śvetāmbaras hold that though Mahāvīra was keen on renouncing the world earlier, he promised his mother that during his parent's life time he would not become an ascetic. The promise was in response to the persuasions of his mother. Even after his parent's death, Mahāvīra took his elder brother's permission and then only renounced the world". (Gopalan, *Outlines of Jainism*, Delhi, 1973, p. 25).
115. Hema Chandra, *Deśīnāmamālā*, ed. R. Pischel with Introduction, Critical Notes and Glossary by P.V. Ramanujaswami M.A. (Poona, 1938), p. 13.
116. Quoted by Becharadasa Jivaraja Doshi in the Introduction to *Pāiyalacchī*, p. 37.
117. P.V. Ramanujswami, op. cit., p. 13.

2

Political Conditions

THE PARAMĀRAS

In the pages of *Tilaka-mañjarī* Dhanapāla has incidently (or, may be, by deliberate design) thrown light upon (not more than) two (historically most crucial) points concerning his Paramāra patrons, viz.: (*i*) their legendary origin, and (*ii*) their celebrated genealogy upto his time, which need to be examined at some length, especially in the context of some recent researches on the Paramāra dynasty.

As regards the first, Dhanapāla states in *Tilaka-mañjarī* that the Paramāras originated from the fire-pit of Vaśiṣṭha at Ābū. "The Gurjaras of the Mountain Ābū (Arbuda) still sings the glory of the king Paramāra, who sprang from the fire-pit of sage Vaśiṣṭha who was defeated by Viśvāmitra".[1]

The mythical origin of the Paramāras is given credence to by *Udaipur Praśasti*, wherein it is stated :

There is in the west a son of the Himālayas, that lofty mountain, called Arbuda (Ābū), that gives the desired reward to those possessing (true knowledge) and (is) the place where the conjugal union of the 'Siddhas' is perfect. There Viśvāmitra forcibly took from Vaśiṣṭha (his cow). Through his (Vaśiṣṭha's) power a hero arose from the fire-pit, who worked the destruction of the enemy's army. When he had slain the enemies, he brought back the cow, then the sage spoke, you will be a lord (of kings) called Paramāra.[2]

The same account is lent support by various inscriptions such as, Nāgpur stone inscription,[3] 'Vasañtagarh inscription',[4] Arthuna inscription of Cāmuṇḍarāja,[5] Jaina inscription of the temple of Neminātha,[6] Doṇagaragrāma inscription.[7] Paṭṇārāyan inscription[8] and the Jainād inscription.[9]

The fire-pit origin of the Paramāras is also subscribed to in *Navasāhasāṅkacarita* of Padmagupta, the court poet of Vākpati Muñja and Sindhurāja. The poet says:

"There (on mount Arbuda) the wise house-priest (Vaśiṣṭha) of the Ikṣvākus made a sage's grove, rich in wild rice, fruits, roots, fire-wood and Kuśa-grass.

His wish-granting cow was once stolen and carried away by the son of Gādhi (Viśvāmitra) as was that of Jamadagni by Arjuna, Kṛtavīrya's off-spring.

Arundhatī, upon whose bosom the silk garment was bathed with streams of tears, became a log, on account of her husband's wrath.

Thereupon the first of the judges of the Ātharvaṇa songs (Vaśiṣṭha) with holy sayings threw an offering into the fire, which kindling up with broad flames seemed to bear an ascetic's hair braid.

Quickly a man sprang out of the fire with bow and crown and golden armour.

By him the cow of the wise man, led away by Viśvāmitra was brought back, as Sun brings back the light of day, which has been led away by thick darkness.

Then the grove-maidens took the cheek, wet with tears of joy, from the supporting hand which is worshipped by the devout.

He received from the sage the fitting name of Paramāra-killer of the enemy—and a ruler's power over the globe, before whom all the parasols of all other kings were shut."[10]

The *Dvyāśrayamahākāvya* also states that the Paramāras were created by Vaśiṣṭha to teach Viśvāmitra a lesson when the two sages quarrelled over the cow Nandin.[11]

According to *Pṛthvīrāja Rāso*, an important bardic tale, Viśvāmitra, Agastya, Vaśiṣṭha and other sages began a great sacrifice on Mount Ābū. Daityas (miscreant demons) rendered it impure. With a view to saving his companions from the nuisance, Vaśiṣṭha created from the sacrificial pit three warriors in succession, the Pratihāra, the Solankī and the Paramāra. None of them, however, succeeded in completely rooting out the danger posed by the demons.[12]

Abul Fazl, the renowed author of *Āin-i-Akbarī*, also subscribes to the mythical tradition of the 'Agni-kula' origin of the Paramāras. But he records the tradition of the fire origin in a different version: the hero is born in a temple of fire to protect fire worship against the intrigues of the Buddhists. To quote from *Āin-i-Akbarī* "Two thousand, three hundred and fifty five years, five months and 27 days before the 40th year of the Divine era (i.e. 761 B.C.) an ascetic named Mahābāha kindled the first flame in a fire temple and devoting himself to the worship of God resolutely set himself to the consuming of his rebellious passions. Seekers after eternal welfare gathered round him, zealous in a life of mortification. About this time Buddhists began to take alarm and appealed to the temporal sovereign asserting that in this fire temple many living things were consumed in flaming fire and that it was advisable that the Brāhmaṇical rites should be set aside and that he should secure the preservation of life. It is said that their prayer was heard and prohibition against the said people was enforced. These men of mortified appetites resolved on redress sought by prayer' a deliverer who should overthrow Buddhism and restore their own faith. The Supreme Justice brought forth from this fire temple now long grown cold, a human form resplendent with divine majesty and bearing in its hand a flashing sword. In a short space he enthroned himself on the summit of power and renewed the Brāhmaṇical observance. He assumed the name of Dhanjī and coming from the Deccan, established his seat of government in Malwa and attained to an advanced age.

When Pūtarāja, the fifth in descent from him died without issue, the nobles elected Āditya Ponwar as his successor and this was the origin of his sovereignty of this house".[13]

Some European and Indian scholars have interpreted this 'Agnikula' myth to mean that the Paramāras belonged to the Hūṇa Gurjara stocks and after the performance of some ceremony they became fit to be admitted into Hindu caste system. Commenting upon the Agnikula origin of the Paramāras, Dr. R.S. Tripathi observes :

> The probable significance of this mythical derivation from fire (Agnikula) appears to be that like the Pratihāras and

other clans, the Paramāras were also of foreign extraction and they became fit to be admitted into Hindu caste system after the performance of some fire ceremony.[14]

Historians like Watson, A.M.T. Jackson, Campbell, Forbes, Kielhorn, D.R. Bhandarkar and H.C. Ray hold that Paramāras were an off-shoot of the Gurjaras, a tribe which is believed to have entered India with the Hūṇas in the V and VI centuries after the downfall of the imperial Guptas.[15] Another argument regarding Paramāras having been foreign settlers runs thus, "According to legend, the Chāpas belonged to the Paramāra race, the Paramāras were allied to the Pratihāras, the Cāhamānas and the Cālukyas and were, therefore, Gurjaras, and as the Gurjaras were foreigners, the Paramāras were foreigners also".[16]

Although the Agnikula story was not accepted per se by the European writers, they gradually used it as corroborative evidence in favour of the theory of the fire origin of the Rājpūts. V. Smith quotes Crook's remark with apparent approval that the story "represents a rite of purgation by fire, the scene of which was southern Rajasthan whereby the impurity of the foreigners was removed and they became fit to enter into Hindu caste system".[17]

The story of the foreign origin of the Rajputs formulated on the premise that they were of Gurjara stock is not convincing. For 'Gurjara' is the nomenclature denotive not only of a particular people but also of a specified tract of land and its inhabitants irrespective of the distinctions of caste or clan.[18] In the opinion of Dr. Dasharatha Sharma "the Pratihāras were called Gurjaras because they belonged to a geographical tract called Gurjara".[19] Smith's view that "Bhoja, his predecessors, and successors, belonged to the Pratihāra clan of Gurjara tribe,"[20] thus becomes suspect, so do the theories of the foreign origin of the Paramāras and the Rājpūts built up by the European historians.

In Dr. D.C. Ganguly's opinion Paramāras were neither Gurjaras nor born of the fire-pit, but were the descendants of the imperial Rāṣṭrakūṭas of Mānyakheṭa.[21] In support of his view Dr. Ganguly cites the evidence provided by the Harsolā copper-plate grant of Harṣa Śīyaka II. The Harsolā inscription[22] (A.D. 948) states that the Paramāra ruler Vappairāja (Vākpati I) was descended from the family (kula) of the Rāṣṭrakūṭa ruler Akālavarṣa (Kṛṣṇa III). Dr. Ganguly identifies Akālavarṣa with Kṛṣṇa III, king of Mānyakheṭa (A.D. 940-951), contemporary of Paramāra Sīyaka II (A.D. 949-969) and Vappai with Vākpatirājā I, the father of Vairisiṁha II of Paramāra dynsty.[23] In Dr. Ganguly's view the connection between the Rāṣṭrakūṭas and Paramāras is further substantiated from the fact that Vākpati Muñja had assumed distinctive Rāṣṭrakūṭa titles like 'Amoghavarṣa', 'Śrīvallabha' and 'Pṛthvīvallabha'.[24] Dr. Ganguly further argues that the original home of the Paramāras must have been in the Deccan which formed the home dominion of the Imperial Rāṣṭrakūṭas.[25]

Dr. Dasharatha Sharma questions the theory of Kinship of the Paramāras with Rāṣṭrakūṭas and observes: "*Navasāhasāṅkacarita* was written under the direction of Sindhurāja, a son of that very ruler who issued the Harsolā plates. Therefore, what was known as the true origin of the family to Sīyaka could not have so readily been forgotten by his son and the son's protégé, Padmagupta. Nor would they have dared describe Sindhurāja as an Agnikula, if on fact he had been a Rāṣṭrakūṭa of the Deccan".[26]

To my mind Dr. Ganguly's thesis is neither erected on perfectly logical postulates nor supported by incontestable concerete evidence. A question may be posed here to further scrutize the veracity of Dr. Ganguly's thesis: Did the Paramāras have any blood relation with Rāṣṭrakūṭas of Mānyakheṭa? And if they had, do we find corroborative evidence in contemporary literature or inscriptions? Since no literary or inscriptional evidence to this effect is available, it is hardly possible to accept the theory propounded by Dr. Ganguly. Dr. Pratipal Bhatia rejects Dr. Ganguly's thesis out of hand with the remark: "In fact, those who ascribe a Rāstrakūṭa origin to the Paramāras direct or indirect should read the account left by Padmagupta, the court poet of Vākpati Muñja".[27]

In the opinion of Dr. Pratipal Bhatia Paramāras were originally Vaśiṣṭha Brāhmaṇas, who became Kṣatriyas by adopting the profession of warriors.[28] In support of her contention, she quotes Halāyudha, the court poet of Muñja who writes in *Piṅgalasūtravṛtti*:

Brhmakṣtra·kulīnaḥ samasta sāmaṅta cakranuta caraṇaḥ|
Sakala-sukṛtaika-puñjaḥ śrīmānmuñjaściraṁ jayati||[29]

"The poet has used the word 'Brahmakṣtra' for his patron in his *Piṅgalasūtravṛtti*. The expression means that Muñja belonged to a family which had the attributes of the Brāhmaṇa, as well as the Kṣatriyas. Paramāras like the Śuṅgas, the Sātavāhanas, the Kadambas, the Cāhamānas and Guhilas were descended from an ancestor who, though originally a Brāhmaṇa had, on account of adopting the profession of arms came to be regarded as Kṣtariya".[30]

Of all the theories about the origin of the Paramāras the theory of the 'Agnikula' origin as alluded to in *Tilaka-mañjarī* and supported by various historical accounts and inscriptions possesses credibility under its symbolical interpretation than all the other theories on the subject.

Although Paramāra families ruled, as per archaeological records, over various regions of western India, but the poet, Dhanapāla, speaks in *Tilaka-mañjarī*, of only the Paramāras of Dhārā or Malwa. He traces the genealogy of the Paramāras only from Vairisiṁha II onwards. Eulogizing the personal traits and prowess of Vairisiṁha the poet says: "He was a paraśu to cut the creeper in the form of drawing lines upon the cheek of the wives of the enemies and was like a wall of the shore of four seas to break the teeth of strong military elephants".[31] The poet adds that Vairisiṁha was succeeded by his son, Sīyaka who was the proven protégé of Śrī (Goddess Lakṣmī).[32] Harṣa was his other name. His real name was Sīyaka. Sīyaka is said to have conquered and looted Mānyakheṭa, the capital of the Rāṣṭrakūṭas in A.D. 1029.[33] Sīyaka begot two sons, Vākpatirājā *alias* Muñja and Sindhurāja.[34] Muñja was the elder son.

Speaking of Vākpati, the poet says that he was the first among the heroes and through the prowess of his bow, he had measured all the four parts of the world.[35] Muñja conferred on Dhanapāla the title of Sarasvatī.[36] About Sindhurāja Dhanapāla states that he was a man of great fame, a leader among heroes and a lion for the line of rutting elephants of Indra.[37] Sindhurāja had a son named Bhoja whose feet were marked with auspicious signs and being considered absolutely fit for the highest seat of the country he was anointed and put on the throne by king Vākpati *alias* Muñja.[38] Merutuṅga in his *Prabandhacintāmaṇi* states that after the death of Muñja, Bhoja was placed on the throne: "Then the ministers in the country of Malwa hearing that event, placed Bhoja—the son of Muñja's brother, on the throne".[39] But Padmagupta writes in his *Navasāhasāṅkacarita* that 'Muñja placed the world in Sindhurāja's arm which was marked by scars of bow-string'.[40] This fact is also confirmed by the Udaipur Praśasti.[41] But there is overwhelming evidence forthcoming from other ancient and modern sources to confirm the fact that Bhojarāja became the successor of Muñja Paramāra.

The pedigree of the Paramāras deriveable from the account given by Dhanapāla in *Tilaka-mañjarī* is depicted below in the genealogical tree beginning with Vairisiṁha:

Vairisiṁha
↓
Sīyaka (Harṣa)
↑
Vākpatirāja (Muñja) — Sindhurāja
↓
Bhoja

From other Paramāra records we can derive a longer genealogy of the Imperial Paramāras of Malwa as depicted in the following genealogical tree:

(Upendra) Kṛṣṇarāja

↑

Vairisiṁha — Dambara Siṁha

↓

Sīyaka I

↓

Vākpati I or Vappaiyarāja

↓

Vairisiṁha II or Vajaratsvāmin

↓

Sīyaka II *alias* Harṣa

↕

Vākpati II (Muñja) — Sindhurāja

↓

Bhojarāja

Dhanapāla seems to have deliberately omitted the genealogy of four Paramāra kings from Upendra to Vākpati I. It may be due to the fact that these early Paramāras held their authority in subordination to the Rāṣṭrakūṭas of Deccan and were not independent rulers. It was Vairisiṁha II and his successors who established and maintained their independent sovereignty by the power of their sword. This has been corroborated by Udaipur Praśasti which records :

"By that king (Vairisiṁha II) the famous Dhārā was indicated, when he slew the crowd of his enemies with the edge of his sword".[42]

Regarding Sīyaka II D.C. Ganguly observes: "He was the real founder of Paramāra kingdom and the first Imperial ruler of his family".[43] It, therefore, goes without saying that Vairisiṁha II and Sīyaka II had established independent authority over their dominions. As Dhanapāla was the court poet, he might have thought it more dignified to trace the genealogy of the Paramāra kings from their first truly independent sovereign viz. Vairisiṁha.

OTHER CONTEMPORARY DYNASTIES

Dhanapāla has not for obvious reasons attempted in his writings a systematic chronicling of the deeds and careers of the Paramāra kings though he has alluded to particular events or episodes related to his literary or religious purposes. For gaining a proper perspective of the political conditions of Dhanapāla's times which were marked by an internecine warfare among the rulers of Indian kingdoms and principalities for political supremacy, we will do well to briefly recapitulate here the careers of other contemporary dynasties.

After the death of Harṣa in A.D. 647 the empire that he had established crumbled to pieces. A period of political chaos and anarchy followed. In A.D. 712 the country was invaded by Muhammad Bin Qasim who conquered Sindh. "In the north, the Arab Invasion had greater effect, some of the older dynasties disappeared and political power passed into the hands of the leaders who either rallied the forces of resistance against foreign invaders or gave peace to the territories by ending matsya nyāya—a condition in which might was right".[44]

In the first half of the VIII century A.D. there emerged on the political scene of India three Imperial dynasties—the Pālas, the Pratihāras and the Rāṣṭrakūṭas. In the later part of the VIII and beginning of the IX century there was a long protracted war for supremacy among Pālas, Pratihāras and Rāṣṭrakūṭas of Mānyakheṭa. This tripartite struggle forms the most interesting episode of the early medieval history of our country. In the middle of the X century A.D., the Pratihāra empire collapsed and was divided amongst a number of independent ruling dynasties; the Paramāras of Malwa, the Candellas of Bundelkhand, the Kalacuris in Jabalpur, the Cālukyas of Gujarat, the Cāhamānas of Mārwār and Guhilas of Mewar. In the later part of the XI century A.D., Kanauj was conquered by the Gāhaḍavālas and in the early years of the XII century A.D., the Senas wrested the sovereignty of Bengal from the Pālas. Thus the Paramāras, Cālukyas, Cāhamānas, Guhilas, Kalacuris, Candellas, Gāhaḍavālas and the Senas were the last great Hindu ruling dynasties of Northern India. They held sway over it with unquestioned supremacy, till they were overthrown by the Muslims.[45]

Besides the above-mentioned big dynasties there were some

other dynasties as well which were contemporaries of Paramāras.

The Hindu Śāhī Kingdom

On the North Western Frontier the Śāhī kings of Ḳabul held sway. This Śāhī kingdom extended from the river Chenāb to the Hindukush monutains. The Śāhī royal house had resisted, single-handed, the Arab encroachment successfully for 200 years. It was, however, compelled to abandon a part of Afghanistan, including Kabul and to shift its capital to Udbhāndapura or Waihind. The Śāhī king, about the end of the X century, was the famous Jaipāla who was a brave soldier and an able ruler. Jaipāla was defeated at the hands of Mahmud of Ghaznī on 27th November, A.D. 1001 near Peshāwar. Jaipāla could not bear the shock of humiliation, he had experienced at the hands of a cruel foreigner, and burnt himself to death.[46] He was succeeded by his son, Ānandapāla, in A.D. 1002. Anandapāla fought valiantly with the Turkish invader but could not stem the flood of invasion. Ānandapāla's son, Trilocanapāla, was also defeated by Mahmud. Trilocanapāla's descendent, Bhimapāla, also died in A.D. 1026. With his death the Hindu 'Śāhī' kingdom came to an end.[47]

Utpala Dynasty

The next notable kingdom was that of Kashmir. Avantivarman founded the Utapala dynasty in A.D. 855. Avantivarman was a benevolent king. He increased the prosperity of the land. After his death, his son, Śankara Varman, (A.D. 883—A.D. 902), followed an aggressive policy. He extended the boundaries of Kashmir in several directions, seized certain territories from the Pratihāra king, Mehendra Pāla I. He died in A.D. 902 fighting with the people of Urasad, the modern Hazāra district. The Utpala dynasty came to an end in A.D. 939. Śūravarman II was the last king of the dynasty.[48]

The Line of Parva Gupta

(*i*) After Śūravarman II, the Brāhmaṇas elected Yaśaskara

as king. During his benevolent reign of nine years (93—948) peace and prosperity returned to the country. His son and successor, Saṁgrāma, was killed in A.D. 949 by his Minister, Parvagupta, who usurped the throne himself. Parvagupta's son and successor was Kṣemagupta (950-958). During his time his queen, Diddā was the virtual ruler. This powerful lady ultimately seized the throne and crowned herself as Queen. She ruled over Kashmir till A.D. 1003. After her death the throne passed over to Saṁgrāmarāja who became the founder of Lohara dynasty.[49]

(*ii*) Lohara dynasty came to power in Kashmir in the early years of XI century. Sāṁgrāmarāja sent his minister Tunga to help the Śāhī Trilocanapāla against Mahmud of Ghaznī. Mahmud left no stone unturned to conquer Lohara but failed to achieve his end.[50] This dynasty remained in power till A.D. 1172. Vantideva was the last ruler of this dynasty.

Pratihāras

The imperial city of Kanauj passed into the hands of Pratihāra dynasty in the second quarter of VIII century A.D. A notable ruler of the Pratihāra dynasty, was Mihira-Bhoja (A.D 836-885). The Imperial Pratihāras suffered a severe blow on account of the Rāṣṭrakūṭa and Pāla invasions. Their former feudatories, the Candellas of Bundelkhand. the Cālukyas of Gujarat and Paramāras of Malwa became independent. During the reign of Rājyapāla (A.D. 1018) Mahmud of Ghaznī invaded India. when Mahmud attacked his kingdom, he fled away. This act of Rājyapāla enraged the Candella chief, Gaṇḍa, and he sent a force under the command of Vidyādharadeva who killed Rājyapāla and placed his son Trilocanapāla on the throne. The last ruler of his family was Yaśapāla who is referred to in an inscription of the year A.D. 1036.[52] According to Dr. A.L. Srivastava, "the Pratihāras continued to exercise sway over Kanauj and Madhya Deśa and to fight, sometimes successfully and at other time unsuccessfully, with their neighbours in the north and the south".[53]

Pālas of Bengāl

Devapāla of Pāla dynasty died about A.D. 850. His successors were weak and the kingdom of Bengāl rapidly declined under them. The later Pāla kings came into conflict with the Pratihāras of Kanauj and brought sufferings to their people. Mahīpāla I (988-1038) who was the contemporary of Rājā Bhoja Paramāra succeeded in partly restoring the fortunes of his family. He gave a new lease of life to his kingdom. But a part of Bengal had already fallen into the hands of the powerful vassals who only vaguely recognised the over-lordship of the Pāla kings.[54]

Cālukyas of Aṇahilavāḍa

This dynasty was founded in the X century A.D. by Mūlarāja (*c.* A.D. 941-995) and grew in power in the reigns of Bhīma I (A.D. 1021-1063), Karṇa (A.D. 1063-1093), Jaya Siṁha Siddharāja (A.D. 1093-1143) and Kumārapāla (A.D. 1143-1172). This kingdom comprised of Saurāṣtra, Gujarat, Malwa, Nādol, and Ābū (after the downfall of Paramāras) and Konkaṇa. The Paramāra king Muñja over-ran the kingdom of Mūlarāja. Mūlarāja fled to Mārwār.

Mahmud of Ghaznī invaded India during the reign of Bhīma I (*c* A.D. 1021-1063). Bhīma instead of offering resistance sought safety in flight. Mahmud plundered Somanātha and slaughtered the Hindu infidels (Kāfirs). When the Sultan returned to Ghaznī, Bhīma recovered his capital and revived the Cālukya power. He constituted a coalition with Lakṣmī Karṇa Kalacuri and completely devastated Malwa. Bhoja Paramāra died in the course of the struggle, fighting with the combined forces of his adversaries. During the reign of Karṇa (A.D. 1063-1093), the son and successor of Bhīma I, the power of the Paramāras once more waxed. For Udayāditya Paramāra is credited with a victory over Karṇa. Jaya Siṁha Siddharāja carried on a protracted war with the Paramāra potentates, Narvarman and Yaśovarman. Eventually, Dhārā fell and the victor assumed the title of 'Avantinātha' in commemoration of the subjugation of Malwa.[55]

The Cauhāns

The Cāhamānas, later known as the Cauhān Rajpūts, are known to have been ruling in different parts of Gujarat and Rājpūtāna as early as the VII and VIII centuries A.D. The most important Cauhān branch ruled over Sapādalakṣa country with its capital at Śākambharī, now known as Sambhara in Jaipur. The Cāhamāna rulers of this kingdom acknowledged the suzerainty of Pratihāras. The Cāhamānas were loyal to the Pratihāras till the beginning of the X century. But after the disastrous defeat of Mahīpāla Pratihāra (A.D. 912-940) at the hands of Rāṣṭrakūṭa king, Indra III, they gradually asserted their independence. Vākpatirāja I, who ruled in the first quarter of the X century A.D. is said to the harassed Tantrapāla who was coming with a message of his over-lord. If this over-lord was Mahīpāla I Pratihāra, we must presume that Vākpatirāja had already begun to defy the authority of his suzerain. His son and successor, Siṁharāja (A.D. 956-972), declared independence and assumed the title of 'Mahārājādhirājā'.[56] His son and successor, Vigraharāja II, over-ran the Cālukya kingdom and Lāta and carried his victorious arms upto the bank of Narmadā. "In the closing years of the X century, the kingdom of the Cāhamānas of Śākambharī extended at least upto Sīkāra on the north, the town of Jaipur in the east, Puṣkara near Ajmer in the south and Parbatsar, in Jodhpur, in the west''.[57] The most powerful and gallant ruler of this dynasty was Prthvīrāja III who was defeated at the battle of Tarain by Mohammad Gaurie.

The Cāhamānas of Nādol

Lakṣmaṇa, the youngest son of the Cāhamāna Vākpatirāja I (X century) of Śākambharī founded a kingdom at Naddūla, modern Nādol in Jodhpur, which flourished for several centuries. Lakṣmaṇa was succeeded by his son, Sobhita, who annexed Mt. Ābū. His son and successor was Balirāja who had to surrender Mt. Ābū and the adjoining territory to the Paramāra Muñja, who appointed the princes of his family to rule over Mt. Ābū, Jalor and Bhīnamala which were situated to the southern border of the Cāhamāna kingdom of Nādol.

Two other branches of Cāhamāna family ruled in Dholpur and Pratāpgarh as feudatories of the Imperial Pratihāras.

Guhilas of Mewar

The Guhila-putras or Guhilotas of Medāpaṭa (Mewar) later known as Śisodiyā Rājpūts, occupy a unique place in the medieval history of India. Śrī Bappā is said to be the founder of this dynasty. All the chronicles place him in the first half of the VIII century A.D. He is said to have faced the onslaughts of the Arab invaders and distinguished himself by brave resistance against them.

There was another branch of Guhilas which was ruling in Jaipur. Both the branches acknowledged the suzerainty of Pratihāras.

In the second quarter of the X century A.D. the Guhila ruler Bhartṛpaṭṭa (A.D. 943) threw off the yoke of the Pratihāras. His son and successor, Allaṭa, whose known dates are A.D. 951 and 953 killed in battle Devapāla, probably the Pratihāra king.

The Guhila kingdom flourished till the reign of Śakti Kumāra the great grandson of Allaṭa when the Paramāra king, Muñja, attacked the kingdom and destroyed Āghāta the capital city and the priod of Medāpaṭa.[58] Śakti Kumāra was badly defeated in the war. He took shelter under the Rāṣṭrakūṭa Dhawala of Hasti Kuṇḍi.[59]

Tomaras

The kingdom of Cāhamānas of Śākambharī was bordered on the northeast by that of the Tomaras. They ruled the modern Harayāṇā country from their capital Dhillika, modern Delhi. In the X century the Tomaras came into conflict with the Cāhamānas of Śākambharī. The Tomaras continued to rule over the region round Delhi until they were overthrown by the Cāhamāna king, Vigraharāja III Viśāladeva, in the

XII century. Mahīpāla Tomara, a powerful ruler, succeeded in wresting the forts of Hānsi, Thāneśwara and Nagar Koṭa from the Ghazanavids in A.D. 1043. He also attempted to capture Lahore from the Ghaznavids but could not succeed. Tomaras were rivals and enemies of Cāhamānas and when they found Cāhamānas' pressure unbearable they entered some sort of understanding with Ghazanavids. The results of this policy proved disastrous.[60]

Candellas

The Candellas rose into prominence in the IX century A.D. and established their kingdom at Jejākbhukti in the Bundelkhand region. The capital of this kingdom was Kharjuravāhaka, represented by the modern village of Khajurāho in Chhatarpur (M.P.)[61] The Candellas were feudatories of the Pratihāras and their chief, Harṣadeva (*c.* A.D. 900-925), assisted Mahipāla in regaining his kingdom. Yaśovarman, son of Harṣadeva, was "a scorching fire to the Gurjaras in that he easily conquered the fort of Kalinger".[62] He threw off the allegiance and became independent. He made extensive conquests in North India and consolidated his power. Candella power rapidly advanced during the reign of Dhaṅga (A.D. 954-1002). Vidyādhara Candella (*c.* A.D. 1017-1029), who was the contemporary of Rājā Bhoja Paramāra, "was the most powerful ruler of his time and his reign marked the zenith of Candella supremacy".[63] D.C. Ganguly thinks that Bhoja Paramāra attacked the Candella kingdom when Vidyādhara was on the throne, but with no favourable result.[64] He is said to have fought against Mahmud Ghaznī. His grandson, Paramārdin (A.D. 1165-1202), had to suffer at the hands of Pṛthvirāja III, Cāhamāna of Śākambharī who raided his territory sometime in A.D. 1182.[65]

The Kacchapaghātas

The Kacchapaghātas were among those aspirants who became independent after the disintegration of the Gurjara Pratihāra power. They established a powerful kingdom to the east of the Cāhamānas in the later part of the X century A.D. Three branches of the Kacchapaghātas family are known. They ruled in Gwalior, Dubkund and Narwar.[66]

Kacchapaghātas of Gwalior

The earliest known chief of the Gwalior branch is Lakṣamaṇa. Gwalior was under the sway of Candella king, Dhaṅga, a feudatory of the Pratihāra Vināyakapāla of Kanauj in the third quarter of the X century A.D. In or before A.D. 977, Mahārājādhirājā Vajaradāmana, son of Lakṣamaṇa, established his supremacy over Gwalior by defeating the king of Gādhinagar (Kanauj) who may be identified with the Pratihāra Vijayapāla. Vajaradāmana was followed by Mangalarāja and Kīrtirāja. Kīrtirāja is said to have defeated a Malwa king who may be identified with Bhoja Paramāra.[67]

The Kacchapaghātas of Dubkund

A branch of the Kacchapaghātas' family ruled in Dubkund. The history of the Dubkund branch of the dynasty is known from a Jaina inscription. From the genealogy of Kacchapaghātas given in the Jaina inscription we learn of the following kings—Yuvarāja, his son Arjuna, his son Abhimanyu, his son Vijayapāla and his son Vikrama Siṁha.[68] Arjuna assisted the Candella Vidyādhara in defeating and killing Rājyapāla Pratihāra.[69] Bhoja Paramāra entered into an alliance with Abhimanyu on the eve of the northern expedition.[70] Abhimanyu was succeeded by his son, Vijayapāla, and Vijayapāla by his son Vikrama Siṁha. The known date of his reign is A.D. 1088.[71]

Kacchapaghātas af Narwar

Three generations of the kings of this family are known. They are Gangāsiṁha, his successor Śarada Siṁha, and Śarada Siṁha's successor Vīra Siṁha, who issued an inscription from Nalapura durga (fort) in A.D. 1120.[72]

Kalacuris

Kalacuris for Cedis claimed their descent from the Haihayas, famous warriors of Vedic period. The Kalacuris rose into prominence under Kokalla I who founded a kingdom at Tripuri Dahala, i.e., Jabalpore region. He flourished about the last decade of the IX and early part of the X century A.D. He married a Candella princess named Naṭṭadevī and gave the hand of his daughter to Rāṣṭrakūṭa Kṛṣṇa II (A.D. 875-911).[73] Yuvarāja II (A.D. 975-1000) a contemporary of Vākpati Muñja Paramāra was defeated by him (Muñja).[74]

Gāṅgeya Deva (A.D. 1019-1041) a powerful ruler of the dynasty was the contemporary of king Bhoja Paramāra (A.D. 1010-1055). He extended his sway to Prayag. Karṇa or Lakṣmī Karṇa, son and successor of Gāṅgeya Deva, was the most powerful personality among the Kalcuri rulers. Karṇa defeated Bhoja Paramāra of Dhārā with the help of Bhīma I, Cālukya of Gujarat (A.D. 1022-1064). Karṇa also defeated his Candella contemporary identified with Vijayapāla. But towards the close of his career, he met a series of disasters. Cālukya Someśvara I Ahavamalla (*c.* A.D. 1042-1068) and Kīrtivarman Candella defeated him. With Gāya Karṇa (A.D. 1128-1164) the Tripurī Kalcuris finally sank into insignificance.[75]

Gāhaḍavālas

Candradeva founded the Gāhaḍavāla dynasty at Kanauj between A.D. 1080-1085. Candradeva was followed by Govindacandra, Vijayacandra, Jayacandra and Hariścandra. The most important event of Jayacandra's reign was the invasion of Sihābuddīn Ghori. In 1194 Sihābuddīn marched towards Kanauj and met Jayacandra on the plain between Candāvara and Etawah. Jayacandra was defeated and slain by Ghori.[76]

Senas

The Senas who belonged to Kṣatriya clan of Karnataka came in power after the disintegration of the Pālas of Bengal.

In the opinion of Dr. R.S. Tripathi they were of southern origin. The founder of this dynasty was Sāmantasena who founded his empire in Rādhā (West Bengal). Vijayasena (A.D. 1095-1158), Vallālasena (A.D. 1158-1178) and Lakṣmaṇasena (A.D. 1178-1205) were the popular and powerful rulers of this dynasty. Vijayasena conquered Bengal after defeating the Pāla king, Madanapāla. Lakṣmaṇasena fought with Gāhaḍavālas and conquered Benaras and Allahabad. After the death of Lakṣmaṇasena the Senas exercised their authority in Eastern Bengal for almost half a century. After that it came into the possession of Muslims.[77]

Rāṣṭrakūṭa Empire

Dantidurga (A.D. 752-758) was the founder of this dynasty. He was the feudatory of Cālukyas of Veṅgī. The capital of Rāṣṭrakūṭas was Mānyakheṭa. The king Khoṭṭiga of this dynasty was defeated by Paramāra king, Sīyaka II, in A.D. 972. The Rāṣṭrakūṭa capital was plundered and sacked.[78] Khoṭṭiga's nephew, Karka, was a weak personality. Cālukya Tailapa II defeated him in A.D. 973 and after Karka the Rāṣṭrakūṭa empire remained no more.[79]

Cālukyas of Kalayāṇi

Tailapa was the founder of this dynasty. He, after overthrowing the last Rāṣṭrakūṭa king, Karka II, in A.D. 973-74, re-established the sovereignty of the Cālukyas in the Deccan.[80] Tailapa led six invasions against Malwa, but he was repulsed on all occassions by Muñja Paramāra. At last Muñja took the offensive in order to put a stop to further aggression of the Cālukyas. Muñja crossed the Godāwarī and led a compaign against Tailapa. Tailapa defeated him, took him priscner and beheaded him. Tailapa's successor, Śatyāśraya (A.D. 997-1042), was defeated by Bhoja Paramāra. Someśvara I Ahvamalla (A.D. 1042-1068) invaded Malwa and ravaged Manḍu and Dhārā. Bhoja Paramāra fled towards Ujjain. Somésvara IV (A.D. 1181-1189) was the last Cālukya ruler.[81]

Foreign Kingdom

In the X century there were two foreign kingdoms on our soil, namely, Multan and Mansura or Sindha. There were also Arab colonies in Southern India, particularly in Malābār.

Other Dynasties

There were also other dynasties in Eastern Deccan as the Kākatīyas, Eastern Cālukyas, the Eastern Ganges, the Colas, Pallavas and Yādavas of Devagiri. They played important roles in Rajpūt period.

The Rajpūts in the X and XI centuries fought among themselves for political supremacy. There was no political unity and no proper organisation. It has been rightly said, "Indeed the most striking thing in Indian History during this period is the constant warfare going on between Indian rulers at the very moment when the Muslim armies were carrying fire and sword into the heart of India, even one Indian ruler attacking another who was actually engaged in fighting with the Muslims or was in a position to do so, if left unhampered by his Indian enemy...........it becomes painfully evident that the people lacked a true conception of Indian or Hindu nationality".[82]

REFERENCES

1. *Tilaka-mañjarī*, p. 5 :
   Vāśisṭhaiḥ smakṛtasmayo varaśatairastyagnikuṇḍodbhavo |
   Bhūpālaḥ Paramāra ityabhidhayā khyāto mahīmaṇḍale ||
   Adyāpyudgataharṣagadgadagiro gāyanti yasyārbude |
   Viśvāmitrajayojjhitasya bhujayorvisphūrjitaṁ Gurjarāḥ ||
   (*Śloka* 39)
2. *E.I.*, I, p. 236.
3. Ibid., II, pp. 182-83.
4. Ibid., IX, pp. 12-13.
5. Ibid., XIV, pp. 297-98.
6. Ibid., VIII, pp. 208-209.
7. Ibid., XXVI, p. 183.

8. *I.A.*, XLV, pp. 77-79.
9. *E.I.*, XXII, pp. 59-60.
10. Padmagupta, *Nava-Sāhasāṅkacarita*, ed. V.S. Islam Purkar (Bombay, 1895), XI., ślokas 64—76.
11. Hemacandra, *Dvyāsrayamahākāvya*, ed., A.V. Kathavate (Bombay, 1915), XVI, śloka 34.
12. Canda Bardāī, *Pṛthvīrājarāso*, ed. M.V. Paṇḍit and Samsundardas (Benaras, 1913), pp. 45-51,
13. *Āin-i-Akabarī*, tr. Blochmann and Jarret, Vol. II (Calcutta, 1948), p. 215.
14. R.S. Tripathi, *History of Ancient India* (Delhi, 1942-60), p. 378.
15. *J.R.A.S.*, (1907), p. 988: Smith, *Early History of India*, 4th Ed. (Oxford, 1962), p. 427.
16. Hoernle, *J.R.A.S.* (1905), p. 31.
17. V. Smith, op. cit., p. 428.
18. *Tilaka-mañjarī*, p. 5, śloka 39.
19. Dasharatha Sharma, *Lectures on Rajput History and Culture* (Delhi, 1970), p. 2.
20. V. Smith, op. cit., p. 427.
21. D.C. Ganguly, op.cit., p. 9.
22. *E.I.*, XIX, pp. 241-42.
23. D.C. Ganguly, op. cit., pp. 8-10.
24. Op. cit., p. 9 :

    Amoghavarṣa-devaparābhidhāna-śrīmad Vākpatideva—Pṛthvīvallabha śrīvallabha-narendra devaḥ kuśalo . . . .
25. Op. cit., Abul Fazl subscribes to this tradition (*Āīn-i-Akbari*), Vol. II, tr. Blochmann and Jarret, p. 214 ff).
26. Quoted by Pratipal Bhatia, *Paramāras* (Delhi, 1970), p. 18.
27. Pratipal Bhatia, op. cit,, p. 19.
38. Op. cit.
29. Halāyudha, *Mṛtasañjīvanī* (Kāvyamālā Series, No. 91), p. 34.
30. Pratipal Bhatia, op. cit , p. 19.
31. *Tilaka-mañjarī*, p. 5 :

    Tasminnabhūdripukalatrakapolapatra-
    vallīvitānaparaśuḥ Paramāravaṁśe |
    Śrī Vairisiṁha iti durdharasainyadanti-
    dantāgrabhinnacaturarṇāvakūlabhittiḥ ||

    (*Śloka* 40)
32. Ibid. :

    Tatrābhudvasatiḥśriyāmaparayā Śrī Harṣa ityākhyayā
    vikhyātścaturamburāśirasaanādāmnaḥ praśāstā bhuvaḥ |
    bhūpaḥ kharvitavairigarva garimā Śrī Siyākaḥ sāyakāḥ
    pañceṣoriva yasya pauruṣaguṇāḥ keṣāṁ na lagnā hṛdi ||

    (*Śloka* 41)

    It is beyond dispute that Sīyaka and Harṣa were the names of one and the same king as mentioned in *Tilaka-mañjarī*.

33. *Paīyalacchīnāmamālā*, p. 38, ślokas 276-277.
34. *Tilaka-mañjarī*, p. 5 :

    Tasyodagrayasāḥ samastasubhaṭagrāmāgragāmī sutaḥ
    siṁhodurdharaśakrasindhuratateḥ Śrī Sindhurājo'bhavat /
    ekādhijyacaturjitābdhivalayāvacchinnabhūryasya sa
    Śrīmad Vākpatirājadeva nṛpatirvīrāgraṇīragrajaḥ //
    (*Śloka* 42)

    In the *Nāgpur praśasti* Vākpati is described as Muñja and in the rest of the inscriptions he is mentioned as Vākpati. (*E.I.*, Vol. II, p. 184, śloka 23). That Vākpati and Muñja were of one and the same king is borne out by the following verse of *Tilaka-mañjarī*:

    Ākīrṇāṅghritalaḥ sarojakalaśacchatrādibhirlāñcchanai-
    stasyājāyata māṁsalāyatabhujaḥ Śrī Bhoja iīyātmajaḥ /
    prṭtyāyogya iti pratāpavasatiḥ khyātena Muñjākhyayā
    yaḥ sve Vākpatirājabhūmipatinā rājye'bhisiktaḥ svayam //
    (*Śloka* 43)

35. *Tilaka-mañjarī*, śloka 42.
36. Ibid., p. 7 :

    Śrī Muñjena Sarasvatīti sadasi kṣoṇibhṛtā vyāhṛtaḥ. . . .

37. Ibid., śloka 42.
38. Ibid., śloka 43.
39. *Prabandhcintāmaṇī*, p. 25 :

    Atha mālava maṇḍale tadvṛtāṅtavedibhiḥ sacivaistad bhrātṛvyo Bhojanāmā rājye'bhiṣicyat.

40. *Navasāhasāṅkacarita*, XI, śloka 98.
41. *E.I*, XIX, p. 61.
42. *E.I.*, Vol. I, p. 235.
43. D.C. Ganguly, op. cit., p. 44.
44. Pratipal Bhatia, op. cit., pp. 21-22.
45. D.C. Ganguly, op. cit. (Introd.), pp. ii-iii.
46. A L. Srivastava, *The Sultnate of Delhi* (Agra, 1966), p. 53.
47. Op. cit., p. 55.
48. R.S. Tripathi, *History of Ancient India* (Delhi : Motilal Banarsi Dass, 1960), pp. 347-348.
49. A.L. Srivastava, op. cit., p. 44.
50. *History and Culture of Indian People*, Vol. V, p. 97.
51. *History and Culure and Indian People*, Vol. IV, pp. 36-37.
52. R.S. Tirpathi, op. cit., p. 326.
53. A.L. Srivastava, op. cit., p. 45.
54. *History and Culture of Indian People*, Vol. IV, pp. 51-55.
55. R S. Tripathi, op. cit., pp. 385-90.
56. R.C. Majumdar, *Ancient India* (Delhi, 1960), pp. 297-98.
57, *History and Culture of the Indian People*, Vol. IV, p 107.
58. R.C. Majumdar, op. cit., pp. 297-99. *I.A.* XXII, pp. 80-81.
59. D.C. Ganguly, op. cit., p. 51.
60. *History and Culture of the Indian People*, Vol. IV, pp. 110-11.

61. R.C. Majumdar, op. cit., p. 290.
62. *E.I.* I, p. 132, śloka 23, p. 133, śloka 31.
63. N.S. Bose, *History of the Candellas* (Calcutta, 1956), p. 51.
64. D.C. Ganguly, op. cit., p. 104.
65. N.S. Bose, op. cit., p. 94.
66. *History and Culture of the Indian People*, Vol. V, p. 56.
67. *I.A.*, XIV, p. 9, ślokas 9-10.
68. *E.I.*, II, pp. 233-37.
69. *E.I.*, II, pp. 237-38.
70. D.C. Ganguly, op. cit., p. 105.
71. *History and Culture of the Indian People*, Vol. V, p. 57.
72. Op. cit.
73. R.S. Tripathi, op. cit., pp. 369-70.
74. D.C. Ganguly, op. cit., p. 49.
75. R.S. Tripathi, op. cit,, pp. 370-73.
76. R.S. Tripathi, op. cit., pp. 327-30.
77. R.C. Majumdar, op. cit., p. 320.
78. *E.I.*, XIII, p. 180, *Pāiyalacchīnāmamālā*, p. 38, ślokas 276-77.
79. A.S. Altekar, *The Rāṣṭrakūtas and Their Times* (Poona, 1934), p. 131.
80 *History and Culture of Indian People*, Vol. V, p. 161.
81. Op. cit., pp. 161-183.
82. R.C. Majumdar, op. cit., p. 314.

3

System of Administration

THE KING

In the pages of Dhanapāla's *Tilaka-mañjarī*, we can have a fair glimpse of the administrative set-up of Paramāra age. For convenience, we may study it under such broad heads as Rājpūt polity; theory of kingship; the rights and duties of the king in administering the kingdom; the mantrimaṇḍala, its composition and functions; various categories of State Officers and their respective functions; provincial administration; feudal system; army administration and the like. *Mānasollāsa* of Someśvara and *Kṛtyakalpataru* of Lakṣmīdhara, the court poet of Govinda Canda Gāhaḍavāla, '*Sṛngāramañjarī kathā* '*Yuktikalpataru*' and '*Samarāṅgaṇa Sūtradhāra* of king Bhoja, Somadeva's '*Nītivākyāmṛtam*' and *Yaśastilaka*, Alberunī's *India* also provide supplementary information in regard to the administration of Dhanapāla's age.

Kingship :— Kingship or monarchical form of government existed during the medieval period of Indian history. Dr. V. B. Mishra is of the opinion that "The monarchs exercised despotic powers and except their immediate advisers, the people in general had no right to participate in their deliberations".[1] *Tilaka-mañjarī* bears eloquent testimony to the fact that their suzerainty was acknowledged by a number of feudatories who very often assisted them in their campaigns and rendered them personal attendance when required. They also brought presents with them for the king who was the head of the State.[2]

Kingship hereditary

The institution of kingship was hereditary. The heir apparent was selected during the lifetime of the ruling king. The Arab traveller, Sulaiman, also records that the princes in India appointed their own successors.[3] We learn from *Tilaka-mañjarī* that Muñja proclaimed Bhoja to be his successor in his lifetime.[4] King Meghavāhana also thinks to coronate his son, Harivāhana, as Yuvarāja.[5] Such examples are numerous in history. Dr. Altekar gives certain other examples of Madana Pāla and Govinda Candra of Gāhaḍavāla dynasty who were selected as crown princes by their fathers and also cites similar cases of Tribhuvana-pāla and Rājya-pāla of the Pāla dynasty.[6]

The age at which the Kumāra (prince) was made a Yuvarāja (crown prince) was probably at or about sixteen.[7] The king Meghavāhana is described to have been coronated in his boyhood.[8]

Generally, the eldest son was made the heir apparent. A younger brother or a nephew was at times selected as crown prince under special circumstances. In the selection of Kumāras, as heir apparents, the merits of the candidate were taken into consideration, for we are told in *Nītivākyāmṛtam* that no prince should be coronated as heir apparent or successor, howsoever he may be well born, unless he is otherwise qualified for the post.[9] The selection of Bhoja by Vākpati as his heir apparent, while he was a minor[10] (leaving aside the candidature of his younger brother Sindhurāja and even two sons)[11] testifies that Bhoja was selected for his extraordinary merit.[12] The Cālukya Durabharāja installed his nephew Bhīma I as his successor, who in turn installed his son, Karṇa, instead of his eldest son, Kṣemarāja. Likewise Kumārapāla won the throne by virtue of his proven ability.[13]

Titles

The royal titles viz., 'lokapāla',[14], 'kṣitipāla',[15], 'Kṣitipāti,'[16] 'kṣoṇīpāla,'[17] 'prajāpati,'[18] 'bhūmipāla,'[19] 'narendra,'[20] 'Budhajanaikavallabha'[21] are indicative of the king's eminence as a Father-figure and his role as protector of the country and the people. King Vākpati II assumed the titles 'Śrīvallabha', Pṛthvīvallabha' and 'Amoghavarṣa'[22]

Imperialism

During Dhanapāla's time the king was a sovereign monarch and therefore the state of imperialism seems to have existed. King Meghavāhana in *Tilaka-mañjarī* has been styled 'Sārvabhaumarājā'[23] which points to his imperial status. Hindu imperialism is denoted by the grandiloquent epithets attributed to Meghavāhana 'samastaika-visṭapādhipatayā'[24] or 'aruṇasāratherekarathākāntacaturabdhisīmā'.[25] Dr. Beni Prasad says that, "It was not long before public opinion and political philosophy held up to admiration the ideal of the big kingdom, the kingdom extending upto the sea, the universal dominion. Constant efforts were made to realise the ideal in some practical form or other in reality or name".[26] *Tilaka-mañjarī* bears testimony to this ideal. The rulers of the Rājpūt dynasties sought to acquire samarājya by extending their kingdoms. In *Tilaka-mañjarī* Meghavāhana is described to have conquered the whole land up to the sea.[27]

King Meghavāhana is called a 'Cakravartin' king in *Tilaka-mañjarī*.[28] About a Cakravartin king, J.B. Gokhale comments: "The Cakravartin in the Arthaśāstra has been depicted as the universal conqueror, one whose sway extends over the known earth. The idea of conquest has been intimately associated with the Cakravartin. Perhaps a case can be made for a different interpretation of the universal ruler. This view may be more appropriate to the Buddhist tradition than the Hindu, although evidence for this view can be inferred from the *Arthaśāstra* also. This interpretation portrays the Cakravartin as a universal ruler but not by virtue of conquest alone. His power radiates across the continents and men everywhere respond to his appeal. He is bathed with an almost supernatural effulgence, yet he represents the best that is in man. He stands between man and God extracting awe from the man and respect from the other".[29] King Maghavāhana is Cakravartin, not being so much a universal conqueror as by virtue of his attainments both temporal and spiritual.

Divinity of Kingship

Tilaka-mañjarī upholds the divine character of Hindu

monarchy. King Meghavāhana is himself equated to 'Prajāpati'.[30] He is also compared to sea,[31] moon,[32] sun,[33] pṛthvī[34] and other divine personalities like, 'Acyuta',[35] 'Sarasvatī'.[36] He is referred to as the God incarnate.[37] Upendra arose as an incarnation of Viṣṇu to give protection to the country and its culture. Upendra and Kṛṣṇa are identical.[38] In the Paramāra copper plates we find "the flying figure of Garuḍa holding a snake in his left hand".[39] It is the representation of Garuḍa śakti for the liberation of motherland from the clutches of snakes (kāli-bhujaṅga). The king Meghavāhana in *Tilaka-mañjarī* is described as the supreme deity with a divine spark.[40] The king is regarded as the supreme deity because he protects the mortals and also the gods, the gods being unable to protect themselves.[41]

The kings, Candra and Govinda Candra of Gahaḍavāla dynasty, were regarded as the incarnations of Brahmā and Hari respectively.[42] *Viṣṇu-purāṇa* says that a number of divinities reside in the person of the king.[43] Dr. A.S. Altekar opines on the divine function of the kings thus, "The majority view thus points only to the functional resemblance between the king on the one side and the various divinities on the other. It does not say that the king is himself a god but observes that his functions are similar to those of some gods. Most Hindu writers have thus advocated the divinity not of the person of the king, but of his office, because of the resemblance between his functions and those of some deities".[44] The king Meghavāhana resembles the god 'Fire'[45] because he burns the wicked by his power, the god 'Sun'[46] because he sees everything through his spies, the god 'Acyuta'[47] because he will relieve the earth of the calamities. Like Acyuta (Viṣṇu) who is having 'śaṅkha' and 'cakra' with him as symbols of well-being and destruction of the wicked, king Meghavāhana provides good to the virtuous people, protects 'dharma' but destroys the evil mongers.

King's Character and Qualities

In *Tilaka-mañjarī* king Meghavāhana is described to be a man of pure character,[48] gifted with countless merits and virtues.[49] He is calm and tranquil like saints,[50] religious minded[51] and of self-sacrificing nature.[52] He is described to be brave and valiant possessing the dash and drive of a lion.[53] He is cool-headed and has got patience of mind.[54] Like an ocean, he is both deep and grave and terrible.[55] According to Somadeva, "a good king is expected to be a man of religious temperament, with good family traditions, endowed with pure character, dignity and valour".[56] All these qualities of character are attributed to the kings of Rājpūt period.

The ancient Indian thinkers have emphasized on the character formation in kings. King Meghavāhana is immune from the evils called 'Vyasanas'.[57] He attaches no value to sexual pleasures and regards them as trifles.[58] He is far removed from the evils which arise from excessive pride in wealth.[59] Somadeva rightly advises the king to remain aloof from 'Vyasanas'.[60]

Like Kauṭilya, Śukra, Bṛhaspati and other thinkers, Dhanapāla asserts that 'ṣaḍvarga-ari' i.e., six-fold enemy must be suppressed and subdued in order to attain self-control.[61] Śukra describes these six vices as passion, anger, stupidity, greed, pride and arrogance which should not be indulged by kings.[62]

Dhanapāla attaches even greater attributes to his ideal of a king. The ideal king, Meghavāhana, is firm and stable like earth.[63] He is equal to the Sun in radiance[64] and to Sarasvatī in eloquence.[65] He is sweet as Nectar[66] and shines in fame like the full-beamed Moon.[67] He is benevolent and has earned the love of the people with his charity.[68] He is of keen intelligence[69] and is well-versed in all the works on ethics.[70] In the manner of holy men, he has propensity for good actions.[71] Although erudite in all the branches of knowledge, yet he views things with equanimity.[72] His pleasure lies in solving the intricate problems.[73]

Like other ancient Indian thinkers, Dhanapāla lays down certain specifications for the king. King Meghavāhana in *Tilaka-mañjarī* is said to have mastered four branches of learning,[74] which according to Somadeva deal with Ānvīkṣikī (knowledge of self), Trayī (knowledge of sacred Vedas, Śikṣā, Kalpa, Vyākaraṇa, Nirukta, Chanda, Jyotiṣa and Itihāsa,

Purāṇa, Mīmaṁsā, Nyāya and Dharma Śāstra), Vārtā (the science of agriculture, cattle breeding and commerce), Daṇḍa-nīti (the principles of politics).[75]

'Guṇas' or expedients dictated by policy occupied a very high place in the medieval Hindu thought. King Meghavāhana in *Tilaka-mañjarī* is described to be proficient in the use of the six principal policies,[76] which according to Manusmṛti,[77] were as follows: (1) sandhi (peace or alliance), (2) vigraha (war), (3) yāna (march or expedition), (4) sthāna or āsana (halt), (5) saṁśraya (shelter), and (6) dvaidha or 'dvaidhibhāva' (duplicity).

King Meghavāhana is said to be wielding 'daṇḍanīti' in order to ensure law and order in his country.[78] According to Śukra, 'Daṇḍa' means the king and his policy which he applies to regulate, govern and guide his subjects is called 'Daṇḍanīti'.[79] Somadeva also lays stress on the need for the kings to follow the policy.[80]

Equally great emphasis was laid on the all-round training of the princes. A case in point is that of Cakrasena in *Tilaka-mañjarī* who is said to have mastered, in his boyhood the skill of using all kinds of weapons, learnt all the treatises on kingly craft and secured proficiency in all the languages used in the sciences.[81] Tāraka is said to have got training in shipping.[82] The *Prabandhacintāmaṇi* says that Bhoja had studied all the treatises on kingly craft, learnt the use of thirty-six weapons and acquired seventy-two accomplishments.[83] King Meghavāhana is said to have gained specialisation in all the philosophies.[84]

The kings of Dhanapāl's time were benevolent rulers, not autocrats. The king was expected to rule the kingdom according to the laws enjoined by the holy books.[85] The kings were fully conscious of their responsibilities and duties to the State and their subjects. The realisation of 'trivarga' was an ideal which the kings held before themselves. The king was advised to follow 'Dharma', 'Artha' and 'Kāma' within proper limits and not to pursue the one at the cost of another.[86] King Meghavāhana in *Tilaka-mañjarī* acts in such a manner which neither spoils his dharma nor dissipates his wealth (artha). He acts so wisely that goddess 'Lakṣmī' never disfavours him, his fame knows no decline, his glory never fades, his virtues do not wear off, his friends are never unhappy and his enemies are not in a position to challenge him.[87] Such is Meghavāhana, the ideal king, who respects and honours men of learning and knowledge[88] and maintains the integrity and glory of his family.[89] He displays modesty in his demeanour.[90]

To maintain law and order in the kingdom and to protect the property and lives of the people from internal and external disturbances and to safeguard their welfare and happiness were among the primary duties of the king. King Meghavāhana in *Tilaka-mañjarī* stands the test of an ideal king prescribed by Someśvara who observes that "the king with his honesty, fortitude, youth, alacrity, ability etc., should prove his worth and incur the implicit confidence of his subjects. He should be compassionate and just and should work for the welfare of his subjects".[91] We find king Meghavāhana ever ready to protect the poor.[92] With his manifold virtues and accomplishments, he has been able to please all the people living on earth[93] and maintain law and order in the kingdom. The country is free from the enemies. There is no danger on the highways.[94] The Paramāra State was a welfare State. The descriptions in *Tilaka-mañjarī* are sufficiently convincing that the rulers of the time took keen interest in public welfare. The king always assisted his subjects.[95] providing succur not only to men but also to animals.[96] The main duty of the king, according to *Tilaka-mañjarī*, was to protect his subjects.[97]

We learn in '*Pṛthvīrājavijaya*' that people's happiness (prajāsukha),[98] protection and prosperity (prajākṣema)[99] were the most important concerns of a king who was the support[100] and sustenance of the country ('vasudhāmababhāra').[101] King Meghavāhana in *Tilaka-mañjarī* is described as being capable of carrying the burden of the whole earth.[102]

The responsibility of the rulers of ancient India in maintaining social order (varṇāśrama) stressed in several other works of Hindu polity[103] is also emphasised in *Tilaka-mañiarī.* King Meghavāhana is described to have fixed in due order the laws pertaining to the four classes in society.[104] As a just king he maintained the system of 'Varṇas', and saw to it that each 'Varṇa' performed its proper function. In his reign the 'aśrama' system functioned so well that it earned for him the encomium, the protector of the four stages of life.[105]

To the multiple qualities of an ideal king, Dhanapāla makes the addition that he is one who keeps all the 'Sāmantas' and the 'mantrimaṇḍala' under his sway, wins friends, appoints trusted and tried men in his forts[106] and uproots 'adharma' (Evil) from his kingdom.[107]

Supporting learned Brāhmaṇas holding assemblies of poets and scholars, making gifts of lands to religious and educational institutions and promoting advancement of learning in every sphere have always been the cherished concerns of ancient Hindu kings. King Meghavāhana in *Tilaka-mañjarī* is described taking keen interest in the education of Brāhmaṇas by providing ample facilities for their studies.[108] He also presides over the religious functions arranged by Devas, Brāhmaṇas, Kṣatriyas, Vaiśyas and ascetics.[109] He attends 'goṣṭhis' (meetings) where stories based on Rāmāyaṇa, Mahābhārata, Purāṇas and other Mahākāvyas (epics) are narrated.[110] Vākpati Muñja and Bhoja also patronised poets and other learned men. For their patronage of art and literature, Paramāra rulers can be placed among the front rank of Indian monarchs.

The kings of Rājpūt period took keen interest in works of public utility. In *Tilaka-mañjarī*, we hear king Meghavāhana ordering the artisans to repair and restore the dilapidated temples atonce, asking the officers to fill up the charity homes with fresh provisions of bedding, medicines and other amenities for travellers and the sick and ailing, and ordering the forester (udyānapāla) to protect the trees planted on the sides of tanks and rivers.[111]

Śukranītisāra lays down that the king should personally inspect villages, towns and districts every year.[112] Manu states that royal officers have a natural tendency towards corruption and oppression; the king should, therefore, pay frequent visits to the towns to find out whether people are pleased or displeased with them.[113] This advice was regularly followed by the Paramāra kings. In order to keep his subjects satisfied and in good humour, king Meghavāhana in *Tilaka-mañjarī* is described visiting the people of the capital in the spring season and on special occasions.[114]

Knowing fully well that his ministers were conscientious in performing their duties, that the administration was quite efficient, that the intelligence men (spies) were obedient and faithful and that the people were devoted to him, the king still spared time from his own sensual pleasures and went round the empire all alone in disguise in the night (like Cupid) to know first hand the people's well-being.[115] The king stopped at meetings of prominent persons to listen to rumours. At some places he visited make-shift structures built of grass and straw stalks and talked to the travellers, who coming from all sides, made halts there. In order to know the inner feelings of his subjects, the king in disguise discussed administrative affairs with the people. He would criticise himself (the king), ministers and other officers about lapses and shortcomings in their work and conduct. But the people who had no cause for complaint would not listen to any criticism directed at the king and his officials and expressed their disapproval of the unfounded criticism by angrily rebuking the disguised king. The words of rebuke made the king very happy.[116]

The Sovereign being the centre of the State in ancient India, much of the success in administration depended on his personal involvement and attention to State affairs. He had to attend to details, to infuse life into the governmental machinery and check corruption among the offices placed in authority in distant areas. With this end in view, Meghavāhana in *Tilaka-mañjarī* appears to have essayed the difficult task of keeping the offices of his dominion under his personal surveillance. The king freely went to the midst of the populace to make the imperial decrees more effective. The same procedure of inspecting the empire was adopted by Harṣavardhna. We are told by Yuvan chawng that "the king made visits of inspection through out his dominions, not residi ng long at any place of sojourn and he did not go abroad during the three months of rainy seasons".[117]

Following the traditions of the kings of Maurya and Gupta dynasty, king Meghavāhana installed pillars on all the borders of his State. The victories and achievements of the king were engraved on these pillars.[118]

Tilaka-mañjarī throws light on the daily routine of the king.

The king remained busy from morning till evening in various activities—religious, administrative and the like. The first quarter of the day was devoted to the performance of religious rites for his personal purification. He worshipped gods and heard discourses ('upadeśa') from religious teachers. Thereafter the king held his private Court attended by his prime minister and secretaries, prominent Brāhmaṇas, feudatories, kinsmen, friends and invited citizens. The king discussed with them important and secret business of the State. He also conferred with foreign ambassadors on matters of mutual interest. He made donations to dependents and admirers. On special occasions he visited the temples of the city and inspected the public works department. He returned at mid-day to his palace and after giving food and alms to mendicants took his meals surrounded by friends and companions. Then he repaired for a while to his picture galleries for enjoyment and relaxation. He enjoyed musical concerts and poetry recitations. In the afternoon he held his general court (āsthānamaṇḍapa) where he transacted the routine business of the State. He also received foreign kings and gave audience (darśana) to the general public who came to see him. Sometimes he attended wrestling matches, elephants' fights and such other pastimes. Having spent the busy day the king finally returned to bed.[119]

The coronation of a king was always a special event in ancient India. Before a new king was installed on the throne certain rituals and celebrations took place. Abhiṣeka or anointing was the first among them. The 'Mūrdhābhiṣiktas' only were regarded as the real kings of our period.[120] The king alongwith the citizens performed the coronation ceremony[121] to the accompaniment of great fanfare and festivity. The city resounded with the noise of a variety of bands[122] and singing parties.[123] Pitchers made of gold were filled with water brought from all the holy places.[124] Water mixed with camphor, sandal and the essence of many kinds of flowers was poured on the head of the king by other kings, feudatories, ministers, merchants, princes and other respectable citizens.[125]

The above description leads us to the conclusion that the kings in Dhanapāla's time were benevolent. They took keen interest in the welfare of the public, attended personally the minutiac of government, kept a keen watch over the work and conduct of his officers and were able to give a clear and efficient administration.

CENTRAL ADMINISTRATION

The king was the head of the State in the Rājpūt polity. He was assisted in his administration by a council of ministers. We find frequent mention of prime ministers and ministers of the king in *Tilaka-mañjarī* which points to the existence of a council of ministers. The author of *Tilaka-mañjarī* has used for the council the term 'mantrimaṇḍala'.[126] Almost all well-known authorities on law have recognized the importance of 'mantrimaṇḍala'. Somadeva, for instance, says that without the council, the king becomes an autocrat, he plans for ruin due to his hasty actions.[127] Dealing with the strength of the council, Somadeva puts the number of ministers at three, five or seven.[128] According to Śukra, the ministry with the strength of ten, was to consist of Sumantra (Minister of Finance), 'Paṇḍita' (Minister of Law), Mantrin Pradhāna (President of the Council), Saciva (Minister of War), Amātya (Minister of Revenue and Agriculture), Prāḍvivāka (Minister of Justice and Chief Justice), Pratinidhi (Representative), Purohita (Minister of Religion), Dūta (Minister of Diplomacy).[129]

Though Dhanapāla has not specifically given the strength of 'Mantrimaṇḍala' in *Tilaka-mañjarī*, the offices of 'Purohita'[130] 'Pradhānamantrin',[131] 'Saciva',[132] 'Amātya',[133] 'Mantrin,[134] Dharmastheyas',[135] 'Ratnakoṣādhayakṣa',[136] and Dūta[137] are mentioned. It may be presumed that these were the members of 'Mantrimaṇḍala' or 'Mantripariṣad' which existed during Dhanapāla's time. 'Pradhānamantrin', 'Dharmastheyas' and 'Ratnakoṣādhayakṣa' of *Tilaka-mañjarī* may be regarded as synonyms respectively of 'Pradhāna', 'Paṇḍita' and 'Sumantra' of *Śukra-nīti-sāra*.

In *Tilaka-mañjarī*, 'Amātyas' are mentioned as finance ministers proficient in economic matters.[138] K.P. Jayaswal, on the basis of *Sukra-nīti-sāra*, calls the revenue minister as 'Amātya'[139] and Dr. Altekar is of the opinion that his (Amātya's) duty was "to have a correct inventory of villages, towns and forests in the country and of the income expected from each.

His office had also an accurate account of the land under cultivation and the land lying fallow as also of the expected produce from the different mines".[140] In *Tilaka-mañjarī* Saciva and Mantrin are referred to as councillor[141] and minister proper,[142] respectively. But according to *Śukra-nīti-sāra* the Mantrin was the Home Minister and Saciva the Minister of War.[143] Dr. Kāṇe's view that the words 'Mantrin', 'Saciva', and 'Amātya' are usually interchangeable,[144] seems to be correct.

The 'Purohita' or the royal chaplain was an important member of the ministry. Learned Brāhmaṇas, well-versed in 'Dharmaśastras' and other sacred literature, were given this title and were patronised by the king. The 'Purohita' assisted the king in the maintenance of 'dharma'. The 'Purohita' officiated at the religious ceremonies of the palace and inevitably exercised influence on the administrative affairs relating to religion. The 'Purohita' was expected to ward off natural and supernatural calamities threatening the kingdom.[145] Dr. K.P. Jayaswal is of the view that 'Senāpati' was the military member in the council.[146] But Somadeva opposes the inclusion of Senāpati or military officers in the council saying that 'Military authorities should not be authorities in political councils', for the obvious reason that 'war mongering leaders have a natural hankering after war'.[147]

The ministers of the king are described in *Tilaka-mañjarī* to have studied all the 'Dharmaśāstras'. They follow the principles as laid down by their fore-fathers and are fully aware of the interest of the king and work according to his will. They endeavour to remove the difficulties of the subjects.[148] According to Somadeva, the ministers should be faithful and courageous.[149] They must be endowed with theoretical and practical knowledge, for of what use are those who do not know the interest of the king and cannot remove his difficulties.[150] Dilating upon the qualities of the minister, Dr. B.G. Gokhale writes, "The most valuable qualities of a minister were loyalty, ability, knowledge, wisdom, boldness, eloquence, dignity, influence, prestige and character".[151]

The Central Secretariat which was responsible for running

the entire machinery of the State was established at the capital city, the place of the royal residence (rājadhānī) and was called Srīkaraṇa.[152] The king's seat in the Secretariat was called Kāryāsana.[153]

According to Dr. Dasharatha Shamra, "the royal court had two sections, the Mahāsthāna and the Abhyantara-sthāna or the inner court. Attendance in the latter was restricted to a select number of the people enjoying the ruler's fullest confidence, e.g., the rājñī, the Yuvarāja, the ministers and the senāpati. The Mahāsthāna, on the other hand, was attended by the representatives of all the classes who had any stake in the State".[154] In *Tilaka-mañjarī*, the word Sabhā[155] is for 'Mahāsthāna' and 'Mantrimaṇḍala' for 'Abhayantara-sthāna'. The 'Sabhāsadaḥ'[156] who participated in the meeting of the 'Sabhā' consisted, inter-alia, of 'Mantrins',[157] 'Sainya-nāyakas',[158] 'Mahāpratihāras',[159] Purohitas,[160] 'Dharmastheyas',[161] 'Saints, Śrotriyāḥ, 'Pradhānamantriṇaḥ', Amātyavṛdhāḥ, Mahā-sāmantāḥ, king's relatives and friends, prominent persons of the city,[162] learned Brāhmaṇas,[163] vandiputras[164] (bards), physicians[165] etc.

Somadeva remarks that single handed, one can do nothing, therefore, to maintain administrative efficiency, a number of State officers are required.[166]

According to Dr. R.S. Tripathi, "Since administration means many functions and not one, which are moreover not restricted to a single place, success in government must largely depend upon the efficient organisation of the Bureaucracy".[167] We may, therefore, list below some of the State functionaries, civil and military, mentioned in *Tilaka-mañjarī* who assisted the king to carry on the day-to-day administration.

(1) *Pradhāna mantrin*[168] (Prime Minister) : The position of Prime Minister during Dhanapāla's time was very important. He controlled all the officials and was himself subordinate to the king. The king always consulted him on all important occasions,[169] but was free to follow or ignore his advice.[170] Sometimes he set aside his counsels and proceeded according to his own discretion. We know from *Prabandhacintāmaṇi* that Vākpati Muñja, inspite of being dissuaded by his Chief Minister,

Rudrāditya, crossed the river, Godāvarī.[171]

Pradhāna Mantrin was also called 'Mahāmantrin'[172] and 'pradhānāmātya'[173] and was authorised to transact the royal seal and signet.[174]

In *Tilaka-mañjarī*, the terms 'Pradhanamaṅtrinaḥ,[175] and 'Pradhāna Sacivāḥ'[176] denote a variety of ministers. Some of them were in charge of the Secretariat and some were councillors of the king.

Under the Prime Minister there were heads of several departments. In *Tilaka-mañjarī*, they are called 'Amātyavarga' and 'Amātyavṛddhas'.[177] They are described to be proficient in all matters relating to morality and ethics.[178] Somadeva says that income, expenditure, royal safety and maintenance of order are the chief concerns of these ministers.[179]

(2) *Buddhi-Saciva* :[180] In *Tilaka-mañjarī*, one of the ministers was designated as the Buddhi-Saciva. His duty, as his designation implies, must have been to give advice when solicited by the king. It appears that the Paramāra kings adopted the old method of appointing two categories of officers (ministers) viz., the Buddhi-Saciva or 'Matī-Saciva' or 'dhīsaciva' i.e., minister whose duty was to give counsel to the king on State matters and 'Karma-Saciva' whose duty was to assist the king in the execution of State policy. Under the Śakas of Western India there were two types of Sacivas—'Mati-Sacivas' or Councillors proper and Karma-Sacivas or administrative heads.[181] Pradhāna Buddhi-Saciva is also referred to in *Tilaka-mañjarī*.[182]

(3) *Nārma-Saciva* : Narma-Saciva was probably meant to entertain the king.[183]

(4) *Yuvarāja*[184] or Crown Prince : The eldest son of a king who was generally regarded as heir-apparent was called Yuvarāja, while other princes were known by terms as Rājāputras.[185] 'Yuvarāja' held an honourable position in the realm. He was associated with the government. Sometimes the Yuvarāja was in charge of the provincial administration. In *Tilaka-mañjarī*, prince Harivāhana, the heir-apparent, was given the charge of the administration of 'Sakala Uttarāpatha' alongwith its chief towns and villages.[186]

Like the chief queen, the 'Yuvarāja' was invested with

certain royal prerogatives, such as granting villages and land. Princes Harivāhana and Samaraketū are mentioned in *Tilaka-mañjarī* to distribute towns and villages of their 'Bhuktis' among the Rājaputras, who were responsible for administration there.[187]

(5) *Mahāmātras* :[188] In *Tilaka-mañjarī*, the term 'Mahāmātra' is used in the sense of minister. According to Dr. A.S. Altekar, they were high judical and executive officers.[189] Dr. K.P. Jayaswal calls them high ministers.[190] The conquered province of Kaliṅga was governed in the time of Aśoka Maurya only by a council of mahāmātras.[191]

(6) *Pratihāra*[192] (Chamberlain) : The office of the chamberlain has always been a prominent one in the states of ancient India. Visitors and ambassadors were ushered into the royal presence by the officer known as Pratihāra. This officer is also mentioned in the records of the Pratihāra kings.[193]

(7) *Mahāpratihāra*[194] (i.e. Chief Warder or Usherer) : *Tilaka-mañjarī* gives a very graphic account of the duties and functions of the Mahāpratihāra. He is mentioned as "imposing the vow of silence on the loquacious, making all officials do their prescribed duties, turning out people who had no right to be there, asking those who stood to sit down, showing respect with folded hands to those who deserved it, threatening the impudent ones and bearing himself with pride. He taught novices the right way to salute".[195]

Pratihāra,[196] dvārapāla[197] and dauvārika[198] mentioned in *Tilaka-mañjarī* are synonyms denoting the same officer i.e., the door-keeper.

(8) *Dūta* :[199] The foreign affairs of the State were under an officer who was called 'Dūta'. These officers constituted a diplomatic corps responsible for maintaining proper relations with foreign powers. In *Tilaka-mañjarī*, Pradhānadūta is sent to the neighbouring countries to know their war policy whenever the country came under the shadow of an attack.[200] Thus according to the narration of *Tilaka-mañjarī*, it may be deduced that dūtas were foreign ministers.

(9) *Adhyakṣas*[201] (Superintendents) : Dhanapāla makes a mention of the 'adhayakṣas' in *Tilaka-mañjarī*, which shows

that the subordinate officers were placed under their departmental superintendence. This term is also found in Bāṇa's *Harṣacarita*[202] and the records of the Pālas of Bengal.[203]

(10) *Sainyādhipati* :[204] He was the commander of the royal troops. He is also called 'Senāpati',[205] 'Sainyapati'[206] and 'Senādhipati'.[207]

(11) *Balādhikṛta* : In *Tilaka-mañjarī*, Balādhikṛta is mentioned as a military officer. He was a trusted man. We read in *Tilaka-mañjarī* that money was put in bronze vessels and conveyed to the house of the 'Balādhikṛta' to be kept as a nyāsa (pledge) with his ladies.[208] Dr. Dasharatha Sharma is of the opinion that Balādhikṛta was generally a military officer put in charge of a town.[209] Dr. B.N. Puri says, "We, therefore, propose that 'Balādhikṛta' was an officer attached to the secretariat for handling the military department. Such an appointment was made by the king".[210]

(12) *Daṇḍanāyaka* :[211] Daṇḍanāyaka was primarily a military officer. Sometimes he could be put in charge of newly conquered territories and asked to discharge not only military but also civil functions. The *Tilaka-mañjarī* speaks of two 'Daṇḍanāyakas', one in charge of South[212] and the other of North.[213] Dr. B.N. Puri discusses the significance of the term Daṇḍanāyaka thus:

"The exact meaning and significance of this term is not yet determined. It has been translated as 'trying magistrate' (Prinsep), 'the great leader of the forces' (Fleet), 'Prefect of Police' (Auriel Stein), 'Commissioner of Police' (R.S. Pandit) and some times left untranslated (Nāgārjunakuṇḍ Inscriptions). It appears that he enjoyed a fairly high status.......... He was distinct from the Senāpati (*E.I.*, Vol. XV, p. 283), but was at the same time connected with the army (*E.I.*, Vol. VI, p. 92, *C.I.I.*, Vol III, p. 10). His assistance was sought even in civil administration (*I.A.*, Vol. V, p. 49). Such a title was hereditary (*E.I.*, Vol. VI, p. 92; C.II., Vol. III, p. 10) and kings sometimes gave their daughters in marriage to 'Mahādaṇḍanāyakas' (*E.I.*, Vol. XX, pp. 1ff.)". It appears that Daṇḍanayākas were feudatory chiefs.[214] Dr. Puri does not agree that the terms 'Daṇḍanāyaka', 'Balādhikṛta' and 'Senāpati' convey the same meaning, namely, the commander of the forces.[215]

(13) *Mahādaṇḍanāyaka*: In '*Tilaka-mañjarī*, Mahādaṇḍanāyaka is referred to as a feudal lord and also the commander of the forces. The king consulted the Mahādaṇḍanāyaka on important matters of the State.[216] About Mahādaṇḍanāyaka, Dr. Dasharatha Sharma says, "on military matters, the ruler must have conferred with his 'Mahādaṇḍanāyakas' ".[217] Dr. U.N. Ghoshal is of the opinion that he was the chief commander of the forces.[218]

(14) *Mahāsāmanta* :[219] He was the chief of the feudatories.

(15) *Dharmastheyas*: Judicial officers, who decided the questions of law and religion, were called 'Dharmastheyas'. In *Tilaka-mañjarī*, the term stands for a justice. His main function was to advise the king in judicial matters and to prevent injustice being done.[220] The officers of this cadre were know as 'Dharmamahāmātras' under the Mauryas, 'Śramaṇamahāmātras' under the Sātāvāhanas, 'Vinayasthitisthāpaka' under the Guptas[221] and 'Dharmāṅkuśas' under the Rāṣṭrakūṭas,[222] 'Viniyuktaka' under the Pālas and 'Dharmādhikaramika' under the Gāhaḍavālas.[223]

(16) *Nagarapāla* :[224] The officer in charge of the city administration was called Nagarapāla.

(17) *Mahānāgaraka* :[225] He may be superintendent of big cities. In Kauṭilya's Arthaśāstra, [226] he is called 'Nāgaraka'.

(18) *Antarveśika*[227] (superintendent of seraglio) : As kings often used to have several wives, the special officers were appointed to look after the needs of the harem, who were known as 'Antarveśika'. They were generally old in age (p. 153).

(19) *Pradhānāntarveśika* :[228] He was the head superintendent of seraglio.

(20) *Akṣapaṭalika* :[229] He was the keeper of the records, who kept a full account of the income of the State and also of its expenditure. The Akṣapaṭalika was generally a Kāyastha by caste.[230] He registered grants of 'jāgīras'. Sudṛṣṭi in Dhanapāla's *Tilaka-mañjari* shows to prince Harivāhana, the record of all the maṇḍalas with their cities granted to rājaputras. He did all the business of seal relating to the drawing up of documents (paṭṭaka).[231]

(21) *Udyānapāla* :[232] The officer in charge of the royal gardens was called Udyānapāla.

(22) *Śayyāpāla* :[233] The officer incharge of the royal

bed-chamber was know as Śayyāpāla.

(23) *Naimittika* :[234] He was the State Astrologer and was responsible for forecasting the effects of particular conjunctions of the stars, planets etc. It was probably after his reading of the omens and portents that undertakings were embarked upon.

(24) *Mauhūrtika* :[235] He was a State Astronomer.

(25A) *Bhiṣak*[236] (Physician) : He looked after the health of the king and of the members of the royal household and was perhaps the head of the public health department.

(25B) *Ratnakoṣādhyakṣa* :[237] The officer in charge of the royal treasury and jewels was called Ratnakoṣādhyakṣa.

(26) *Paurogava* :[238] The officer in charge of the royal kitchen was known as Paurogava.

(27) *Aṅgarakṣaka* :[239] The king had a bodyguard of his own, called 'Aṅgarakṣaka'.

(28) *Sevaka* :[240] This denotes a menial servant in State employ.

(29) *Lekhahāraka*[241] (Letter-carrier) : Lekha-hāraka's duty was to carry the king's lekha (i.e. letters). This term is also found in Bāṇa's *Harṣacarita*.[242]

(30) *Vetra-dhārī* :[243] He was the holder of the royal sceptre.

(31) *Chatracāmaragrāhāḥ* :[244] These were the holders of royal umbrella and fly whiskers.

(32) *Kañcukin* :[245] He had a free access to the king as well as the inmates of the harem. He gave reports of the happening in the harem to the king. He was usually of ripe age and enjoyed great confidence of the king.

(33) *Bandiputra* :[246] He was the royal bard.

(34) *Karisādhanādhyakṣa* :[247] The officer in charge of the royal elephants was known as 'Karisādhanādhyakṣa'. In the Gāhaḍavāla records, he is known as Karyā-adhikārapuruṣāḥ.[248]

(35) *Nausādhanādhyakṣa* :[249] He was the superintendent of the navy. He is known as 'Naukādhyakṣa'[250] under the Pratihāras and Nāvādhyakṣa in the records of the Pālas[251] and under the Mauryan administration.[252]

(36) *Guḍhapuruṣas* :[253] They were probably officers of the secret service.

(37) *Pradhānapuruṣas* :[251] They were probably in great confidence of the king.

(38) *Sthāpatya* :[255] These were the officers who were posted outside the harem as guards.

(39) *Tāmbūladāyaka*:[256] He was the king's betel carrier. Other prominent officers of the time not mentioned in *Tilaka-mañjarī* included the following:

(40) *Sandhivigrahika*: [57] The officer in charge of the affairs of peace and war was known as 'Sandhivigrahika'.

(41) *Daṇḍāpāśika* : [58] The towns had their police officers called Daṇḍāpāśikas, whose duties consisted of acting as watch and ward as well as of investigating crimes, arresting the criminals and producing them before the court.

MILITARY ORGANISATION

The Four-fold Army : The four-fold army constituting elephants (hasti), cavalry (aśva), chariots (rathas) and infantry (padāti) employed in warfare during Rājpūt period is appropriately mentioned in *Tilaka-mañjarī*.[259] Paramāra army, according to D.C. Ganguly, consisted mainly of infantry, cavalry and elephants.[260] Chariots, though not a very important military force, were still in use as they are referred to in *Yuktikalpataru*.[261] Ships (naukās) made of strong timber were used for carrying cargo as well as for conquering islands.[262] Dhanapāla gives a vivid description of the naval expedition of Rājaputra Samaraketū who proceeds to punish tribulent feudatories of Dvīpāntara.[263] Samaraketū is said to have entered the cabin erected in the forepart of the vessel.[264]

At the time of a naval expedition all the essential articles prescribed by the experts for keeping physical sustenance were taken. Among them the fuel (indhana),[265] oil (taila), medicine (auṣadha) and blankets (Kambala) were of primary importance.[266] All the water jars were filled with sweet water.[267] Arms of various kinds were also taken.[268] The people of that age seem to be god-fearing. From *Tilaka-mañjarī* we learn that before proceeding on a voyage God Ratanākara (sea-God) was worshipped, in the course of which groups of ladies in beautiful dresses sang songs in praise of His serenity, grandeur, honour and other qualities.[269] Before the ship set to sail maid servants applied the auspicious paint of gruel with their five fingers.[270]

During Rājpūt period it was a tradition to divide the army into different *vyūhas* where all the forces could be effectively pressed into service. In *Tilaka-mañjarī*, we hear of 'Cakravyūha' contrived by Vajrāyudha, the commander of the forces.[271]

Various kinds of weapons were used in ancient times for offensive and defensive purposes. Dhanuṣ[272] (bow), gadā[273] (mace or heavy club), aśi[274] (sword), Kunta[275] (lance), cakra[276] (discus), nārācā[277] (iron, tipped arrow) prāsa[278] (battle axe) are particularly mentioned.

Dhanapāla names some musical instruments which too were used during the war. It was to the rhythm of the beat of the drum that forces marched to war. They advanced towards the battlefield to the accompaniment of martial music, the thrilling notes reminding them of their past glory and the achievements of their ancestors. These musical instruments consisted of tūrya,[279] dundubhi,[280] ghantā,[281] śaṅkha,[282] paṭaha,[283] bherī[284] and jhallerī.[285]

The army commander or general was known (as stated earlier) variously as 'Senāpati',[286] 'Daṇḍanāyaka',[287] 'Mahādaṇḍanāyaka',[288] 'Balādhikṛta',[289] 'Daṇḍādhipati',[290] 'Mahādaṇḍādhipati',[291] 'Kārisādhanādhyakṣa',[292] and 'Nausadhanādhyakṣa'.[293].

We are told by Dhanapāla that whenever an attack was inminent upon the empire, all possible steps were taken for defence and safety. Woods in the neighbourhood of all villages were burnt.[294] All the tanks outside the city were dried up.[295] Fuel, corn and husk were collected in considerable quantities.[296] The vāpīs cleared of mud were filled with fresh water.[297] The ailing and emaciated soldiers were removed from the army.[298] The strangers were prohibited from entering the city.[299] The 'gulmaka' (the army division) commanded by army officers trusted by the king was posted at every pratolī (subsidiary city gate).[300] Stones were piled by the city-wall.[301] The deadly weapons (yantras) were collected at the top of the city-wall.[302] A roving ambassador was despatched to the neighbouring kings to ascertain their attitude, *vis-a-vis*, the impending war.[303] The troops of the feudal lords (Sāmantas) were requisitioned.[304]

Dhanapāla mentions that canon-like machines vomitted fire and/or hot oil to disperse the infantry of the enemy.[305] Stones were hurled upon those who tried to force entry into the city after breaking the planks of the pratolī.[306]

LAW AND JUSTICE

The king was the chief administrator of law and justice. He administered justice according to the law sanctioned by the 'Dharmaśāstras',[307] e.g., the Vedas, Saṁhitās, the 'Brāhmaṇas', the 'Upanisads' and 'Smṛits' etc.[308] These sacred books were interpreted by religious teachers ('gurus') of the king and practically these laws were enumerated by them.[309] The Brāhmaṇa, according to K.P. Jayaswal, was absolutely necessary for dharma administration.[310] We are told by Alberunī that "they (Hindus) believe that their religious law and its single precepts derive their origin from Riṣis, their sages, the pillars of their religion and not from the prophet i.e., Narāyana".[311] So it is evident that Brāhmaṇas or Purohitas had a great hand in the formulation of laws. The office of the Purohita is mentioned in *Tilaka-mañjarī.*[312] The king is described in *Tilaka-mañjarī* abiding by the moral code (dharma).[313] He did not act against the law.[314]

Not only the king but ministers as well worked according to the laws as codified in 'Dharmaśāstras'.[315] They followed the 'Vyavahāra' of their ancestors.[316]

The behaviour of the officials towards the subjects was not harsh.[317] No one could harm and hurt the people.[318]

The king was just,[319] calm and quite,[320] impartial,[321] pious,[322] and religious.[323] It was his duty to protect his subjects[324] and the 'āśramas'[325] to set in order varṇas and āśramas.[326] The king was determined to uproot evils (unrighteousness).[327]

It was within the moral laws to pay due respect to saints, Brāhmaṇas and old men.[328]

Next to the court of the king, there were lower courts to dispense justice. *Tilaka-mañjarī* refers to two officers of justice named 'Mahādaṇḍanāyaka'[329] and 'Dharmastheya'.[330] The former was probably the Sessions Judge (Chief Criminal Judge), while the latter appears to have been the Chief Justice.

Somadeva, contemporary of Dhanapāla, mentions that the cases decided in the village tribunals or city tribunals could be put before the king for appeal.[331] It shows that some other types of courts in the form of 'Grāma Pancāyata' or Tehsīla might have existed during Dhanapāla's time. But it goes without doubt that the king was the highest court of appeal. He heard the cases sitting in his court (Sabhā) which included, according to *Tilaka-mañjarī*, 'Rājaputras', 'Mantrins', Sainyanāyakas, Mahāpratihāras, Pradhāna-mantrin, learned Brāhmaṇas, Mahāsāmantas and the like.[332] In *Tilaka-mañjarī*, a court of law is named Sabhā[333] and the presiding Judge of the court is known as Sabhāpati[334] as referred to in *Nītivākyāmṛta*. Assisting judges or juries are known as 'Sabhāsadas'.[335]

The king's verdict was the final word of justice.

PROVINCIAL ADMINISTRATION

For administrative convenience, the Paramāra kingdom was divided into a number of provinces. According to Dhanapāla's *Tilaka-mañjarī*, these administrative units were generally called 'Bhuktis'[336] and 'Maṇḍalas'.[337] But Dr. D.C. Ganguly[338] and Dr. Pratipal Bhatia[339] mention the division of the empire into 'Maṇḍalas' only. From *Tilaka-mañjarī*, it is evident that 'Maṇḍala' was the next lower unit after 'Bhukti' and that the two were not synonymous terms. Dr. B.N. Puri firmly believes 'Bhukti' to be the highest administrative unit in the administrative system.[340] Dr. R.S. Sharma is of the opinion that 'Bhukti' was a large administrative unit, for the enjoyment of the governor under the emperor's direct and close control.[341] From *Tilaka-mañjarī* we learn that the whole of 'Uttarāpatha' alongwith its chief towns and villages were granted to prince Harivāhana as 'Kumārabhukti'. In that unit Kaśmīr Maṇḍala and some other cities and villages were included.[342]

Aṅga was similarly granted to Harivāhana's companion Samaraketū as his assignment[343] and the lands to the west of Aṅga were made over to army commander (Senānī) Kamalagupta.[344]

This division of the empire into 'Bhuktis' as provincial units also existed under the reigns of Guptas,[345] Vardhanas,[346] Pratihāras,[347] Pālas[348] and Candellas.[349]

Maṇḍala was therefore the next higher unit after 'Bhukti'. In the inscriptions 'Maṇḍala'[350] has always been taken in the sense of a district lower than 'Bhukti', but higher than 'Viṣaya' in the administrative set up. *Tilaka-mañjarī* mentions Kashmir,[351] Kāñci[352] and Kāmarūpa[353] as 'Maṇḍalas'. In *Rajātaraṅgiṇī*, Kashmir is mentioned as a 'Maṇḍala'.[354]

The following maṇḍalas have been mentioned in the Paramāra inscriptions:—

Pūrṇapathaka-maṇḍala,[355] Ārddhāsta-maṇḍala,[356] Vyāpura-maṇḍala,[357] Hūṇa-maṇḍala,[358] Upendra-maṇḍala,[359] Sthalī-maṇḍala,[360] Vindhya-maṇḍala,[361] Mahādvādaśaka-maṇḍala,[362] 'Sangamakheṭaka-maṇḍala',[363] 'Avanti-maṇḍala',[364] 'Nīlagiri-maṇḍala',[365] 'Sihara-maṇḍala',[366] 'Uparahādā-maṇḍala',[367] 'Maru-maṇḍala',[368] 'Arbuda-maṇḍala',[369] 'Chachchuroṇī-maṇḍala',[370] 'Kheṭaka-maṇḍala'.[371]

The provincial governor or the officer-in-charge of the 'Bhuktis' was generally the Yuvarāja or a Kumāra who was member of the royal household. Kumāra Harivāhana, officer in charge of the Uttarāpatha, is the crown-prince. We are told in *Purātana Prabandha-Saṅgraha* that Prithvīrāja III appointed his so-called brother Yaśorāja in Kumārabhukti at Aśinagara.[372]

The provincial governors wielded wide powers. They maintained huge regular armies at provincial headquarters and were responsible for the maintenance of internal peace, law and order and the protection of their territories from external invasions. They ensured the collection of the taxes and kept accounts of receipts and expenditure.[373]

The governors had their own ministers. The governors of the provinces had to see if their ministers functioned well under their administration.[374] This shows that they had a sort of cabinet to consult now and then. Dr. A.S. Altakar is, however, doubtful about the cabinet functioning at the provincial headquarters.[375]

It was a feudal society during Dhanapāla's time. There

were feudal chiefs who administered the territory of the Paramāra kingdom.[376] They were known as 'Sāmantas'[377] and were also designated by various other titles like 'Mahāsāmanta',[378] 'Nṛpa'[379] and 'Rājaputra',[380] 'Daṇḍādhipati'[381] or 'Mahādaṇḍādhipati'.[382] *Tilaka-mañjarī* states that the Paramāra court was full of these 'Sāmantas'.[383] The Sāmantas were under the control of the emperor and owed allegiance to him.[384] They had to pay their personal homage to the emperor.[385] In *Tilaka mañjarī*, the dispossessed kings accept the vassalage of their sovereign lord and bring presents to him.[386] In *Nagpur Praśasti*, the Paramāra kings are described as the ones whose feet were reddened with the lustre of the jewels in the crowns of the kings who bowed at their feet.[387]

The samantas maintained small armies and occasionally offered their services to their sovereign in the time of war. Sometimes they themselves joined military duty and led their armies in battle. There are numerous references in *Tilaka-mañjarī* to show that the 'sāmantas' invariably accompanied the lord in military expenditions.[388]

Feudatories that rebelled were attacked and defeated.[389] The Paramāra chief Vikramasiṁha of Ābū was dethroned and replaced with his nephew by Kumārapāla Cālukya who suspected treachery on the part of Vikramasiṁha.[390]

The feudal lords owed suzerainty over their respective territories. The measure of internal autonomy enjoyed by the feudatory lords varied according to the circumstances. Big feudatory chiefs enjoyed a fairly large amount of internal autonomy. They could create their own sub-feudatories. They could divide their lands among their dependants. In *Tilaka-mañjarī* the princes Harivāhana and Samaraketū do not themselves administer their charges. They become free from anxiety after distributing the property (consisting of towns and villages) of their 'Bhuktis' among the 'Rājaputras' who served them. The distribution of territory was made to the recipients according to their merit.[391]

Smaller feudatory chiefs enjoyed far less freedom. They were required to take permission of the king for the alienation of land or land revenues which was usually countersigned by the overlord.[392]

Thus according to *Tilaka-mañjarī*, 'Bhukti' was the biggest division. Next to it was the 'Maṇḍala'. Maṇḍala was again sub-divided into the cities and villages. There is no reference to the term 'Viṣaya' (district) in *Tilaka-mañjarī* which occurs in Paramāra inscriptions.[393]

The village was the lowest territorial unit in the administration. The village administration was placed under the supervision of the village headman known as Grāmaṇī[394] in *Tilaka-mañjarī*. The village granted to the Brāhmaṇas was known as 'agrahāra' village.[395]

REFERENCES

1. V.B. Mishra, *The Gurjara Pratihāras and Their Times* (Delhi: S Chand and Company, 1966), p. 56.
2. *Tilaka-mañjarī*, p. 184:
   Upaninyuśca nijanija deśājātāni jataprītayaḥ pradhānānī tasmai prābhṛtāni.
3. Elliot and John Dowson, *History of India As Told by Its Own Historians*, Vol. I, p. 20.
4. *Tilaka-mañjarī*, p. 6:
   Ākīrṇāṅghritalaḥ saroja kalaśacchatrādibhirlāñcchanai-
   stasyājāyata māṁsalāyatabhujaḥ Śrī Bhoja ityātmajaḥ |
   Krītyā yogya iti pratāpavasatiḥ khyātena Muñjakhyayā
   Yaḥ sve Vākpatirāja bhūmipatinā rājye'bhiṣiktaḥ svayam||
   (*Śloka 43*)
5. Ibid., p. 80:
   kartukārmaśca yaurājyabhiṣekaṁ tasya.......
6. A.S. Altekar, *State and Government in Ancient India* (Delhi: Motilal Banarsi Das, 1972), p. 365.
7. *Tilaka-mañjarī*, p. 80.
8. Ibid., p. 16:
   Sarājā bāla evādhigata rājyābhiṣekaḥ sakala-bhuvanābhibhāvinā.........
9. Somadeva, *Nītivākyāmṛta*, "Māṇikchand Granthamālā Series" No. 22, (Bombay, 1922), p. 56.
10. Pratipal Bhatia, op. cit., p. 207.
11. D.C. Ganguly, *History of Paramāra Dynasty* (Dacca, 1933), p. 64.
12. *Tilaka-mañjarī*, p. 6.

13. Gulab Chandra Choudhary, *Political History of Northern India from Jaina Sources* (Amritsar, 1963), p. 337.
14. *Tilaka-mañjarī*, p. 39.
15. Ibid., p. 78.
16. Ibid., p. 101.
17. Ibid., p. 72.
18. Ibid., p. 13.
19. Ibid., p. 70.
20. Ibid., p. 65.
21. Ibid., p. 190.
22. *I.A.*, XIV, p. 160.
23. *Tilaka-mañjarī*, p. 14:
    Sārvabhaumo rājā Meghavānhano nāma......
24. *Tilaka-mañjarī*, p. 12.
25. Ibid.
26. Beni Prasad, '*State in Ancient India*' (Allahabad, 1928), p. 4.
27. *Tilaka-mañjarī*, p. 16:
    Sakala bhuvanābhibhāvinā bhujabalena nirjitya saptāmburāśiraśanākalāpāṁ kāśyapīm......
28. *Tilaka-mañjarī*, p, 39:
    Cakravartilakṣaṇaiḥ sakhalu bhavānmadhyamalokapālo rājā Meghavāhanaḥ......
29. J.B. Gokhale, "Hindu and Buddhist Political Tradttions, A Comparison", *A Journal of Indian History*, Vol. XLIX (April, August and December, 1971), University of Kerala, Trivandrum), p. 203.
30. *Tilaka-mañjarī*, p. 12:
    ...yathārthaḥ prajāpatiḥ.........
31. Ibid., pp. 13-14:
    ...sarvasāgarairivotpāditagāmbhīryaḥ......
32. Ibid., p. 14:
    ...Sarvacandrodayairiva racitakīrtiḥ......
33. Ibid., p. 14:
    ...Tigmāṁśumaya iva tejasi......
34. Ibid., p. 14:
    ...Pṛthvīmaya iva sthairye,......
35. Ibid., p. 13:
    ...acyuta iva śaṁkhacakrābhyām......
36. Ibid., p. 14:
    ...Sarasvatīmaya iva vacasi...
37. *Tilaka-mañjarī*,, p. 12.
38. H.C. Ray, *Dynastic History of Northern India*, Vol. II (Calcutta, 1931), p. 844.
39. Ibid., pp 861—863.
40. *Tilaka-mañjarī*, p. 13.
41. Vādibha-Siṁha, *Kṣātra-Cūḍāmaṇi*, ed. Kuppu Swami Shastri (Tanjore, n.d.):

Rājānaḥ prāṇināṁ prāṇāsṭeṣu satsvevajīvanāt/
tattatra sadasatkṛtyaṁ hi loka eva kṛtaṁ bhavet//
Evaṁ rājadruhāṁ hanta sarvadṛohitva saṁbhave/
rājadhrugeva kiṁ tasmāt pañcapātakabhājanam//
rakṣantyevātra rājāno devān deha bhṛto'pi ca/
devāstu nātmano'pyevaṁ rājāhi paraṁ devatā//

(Canto I, *Ślokas* 46—48)

42. *I A.*, XVIII, p. 15, *E.I*, IX, p. 319.
43. *Viṣṇū-purāṇa*, (Gorakhpur: Gita Press, samvat 2018):
Brahmājanārdano Rudra Indro Vāyuryamo Raviḥ/
hutabhugvaruṇo dhātā pūṣā bhūmirniśākaraḥ //
ete cānye ca ye devāḥ śāpānugrhakāriṇaḥ/
nṛpasyaite śarīrasthāḥ sarvadevamayo nṛpaḥ//

(*Ślokas* 13—14)

44. A.S. Altekar, op. cit., p. 92.
45. *Tilaka-mañjarī*, p. 92:
Sarvajvalanairiva janitāpratāpaḥ......
46. Ibid,. p. 14.
47. Ibid., p. 13:
...Acyuta iva śaṁkha cakrābhyām...
48. *Tilaka-mañjarī*, p. 13.
49. Ibid., p. 13
50. Ibid., p. 14.
51. Ibid., p. 39.
52. Ibid., p. 39.
54. Ibid., p. 14.
54. Ibid., p. 13.
55. Ibid., p. 13:
...Ambhasāṁpatirivāmṛtavāḍavābhyāmabhirāmabhīṣaṇo yaśaḥ pratābhyām......
56. Somadeva, *Nītivākyāmṛta*, p. 180:
Dhārmikaḥ kulācārabhijana viśuddhaḥ pratāpavānnyānu gatavṛttiścasvāmī.........
57. *Tilaka-mañjarī*, p. 14:
...Vyasana cakra pīḍābhiranākṛṣṭaḥ......
58. Ibid., p. 21:
...Mūle'ti madhureṣvapi viṣayopabhoga sukheṣukāśastambeṣviva tṛṇabuddhiṁ......
59. Ibid., p. 14:
...Lakṣmī mada vikārairakhalī kṛtaḥ......
60. *Nītivākyāmṛta*, pp. 177, 179:
Vyasana samuddeśaḥ ekenāpi vyasanenopahataśca caturaṅgavānapi rājā vinaśyati kiṁ punrnāṣṭa daśabhiḥ...
61. *Tilaka-mañjarī*, p. 167:
Śatru ṣaḍvarga nigrahaparaḥ......

62. Śukrcārya, *Śukranīti*, ed. G.Oppert, (Madras, 1882), tr. B.K. Sarkar, 2nd ed. (Allahabad, 1923), , 142:
Kāmaḥkrodhastathā moho lobho māno madastathā|
Ṣaḍvargamutsṛjadenamasmistyakte sukhī nṛpaḥ||
63. *Tilaka-mañjarī*, p. 14:
...Pṛthvīmaya iva sthairye...
64. Ibid., p. 14:
Tigmāṁśumaya iva tejasi......
65. Ibid., p. 14:
Sarasvatīmaya iva vacasi......
66. Ibid. p. 14:
Sudhāmaya iva mādhurye......
67. Ibid., p. 14:
sarvacandrodayairiva racita kīrtiḥ......
68. Ibid., p. 14:
Dānavyasanī janānāmarthitayāprīyata......
69. Ibid., p. 14:
Kuśāgrīya buddhiḥ......
70. Ibid., p. 16:
Viditaniḥśeṣa nītiśāstra saṁhateḥ......
71. Ibid., p. 14:
śritaviśuddhasādhu samācāro'pi sarvakālomuvryā bhujaṅgatayā bhrājitaḥ......
72. Ibid., p. 13:
sarvalokānāṁviśeṣajño'pi samadarśanaḥ...
73. Ibid., p. 14:
kāryāṇāṁvaiṣamyeṇa jaharṣa......
74. *Tilaka-mañjarī*, p. 13:
Catasṛṣvapi vidyāsu labdhprakarṣaḥ......
75. *Nītivākyāmṛta*, p. 60:
Ānvīkṣikī, trayī vārtā, daṇḍanītiriti ca taśro rājavidyāḥ...
76. *Tilaka-mañjarī*, p. 13:
ṣāḍguṇya prayoga caturaḥ......
77. *Manusmṛti*, (Bombay, 1923), VII, p. 160:
Saṁdhiṁ ca vigrahaṁ caiva yanamāsanameva ca|
dvaidhībhāvaṁ saṁśrayaṁ ca ṣaḍguṇāṁścintayetsadā||
78. *Tilaka-mañjarī*, p. 13:
sannihita daṇḍanītiḥ......
79. *Śukranīti*, p. 22, ślokas 313-14.
80. *Nītivākyāmṛta*, p. 10:
yathādoṣadṇḍaṁ praṇayan daṇḍanītiḥ......
81. *Tilaka-mañjarī*, p. 168:
śaiśvābhyastaniravadyaśāstrāśastravidyasya......
82. Ibid., p. 129:
śikṣitānena sakalāpi naupracāravidyā......

83. *Prabandhacintāmaṇi*, p. 22:
So'bhyastasamastaśāstraḥ ṣaḍtriṁśaddaṇḍāyudhānyadhītyadvāsaptatikalākūpārapāraṅgamaḥ samasta lakṣaṇa lakṣito vavṛdhe.
84. *Tilaka-mañjarī*, p. 13:
Sarvadarśanānāṁ viśeṣajño'pi......
85. *Tilaka-mañjarī*, p. 13:
Gurūṇāṁ vitīrṇājñā śāsano...
...Satprāsaṁ śāsitasyeva gurukṛtena śrutidharmeṇa...... p. 21.
86. *Tilaka-mañjarī*, p. 28:
Anayāsmākamavikalā trivargasampattiḥ......
Cf. *Nītivākyāmṛta*, p. 33:
śāmaṁvātrivargaṁ sevet...
87. *Tilaka-mañjarī*, p. 19:
Yathā na dharmaḥ sīdati yathā nārathaḥ kṣayaṁ vrajati yathā na rājalakṣmīrumanāyate yathā na kīrtirmandāyate yathā na pratāpo nirvāti yathā na guṇāḥ śyāmāyante yathā na śrutamupahasyate yathā na parijano virajyate yathā na mitravargo mlāyati yathā na śatravastaralāyante tathā sarvamanvatiṣṭhat.
88. Ibid., p. 19:
Ārādhakaṁ vidagdhānām...
89. *Tilaka-mañjarī*, p. 19:
Tadaparamapyavikalatayā vivekasya sthiratayā kulābhimānasya......
90. Ibid. :
svabhyastatayā vinayasya bhūyiṣṭhatayā ca satvavṛtteḥ...
91. Someśvara, *Mānasollāsa*, ed., G,K. Shrigondekar (Baroda, 1930), p. 29.
92. *Tilaka-mañjarī*, p. 14:
Satatamavanecarataḥ......
93. Ibid., p. 21:
Tasya ca rājñaḥ sakala bhuvanābhinanditodayā...
94. Ibid., p. 16:
Sukhapracārārthamiva niṣkaṇṭakāḥ kakubhaḥ...
95. *Tilaka-mañjarī*, p. 19:
Prajāsupakṣpātasya paravaśā vṛttirāsīt...
96. Ibid., p.21:
Apatyaparivāra nirvṛtebhyo na varaṁ paurebhyohpaśubhyo'pi-spṛhayāṁcakāra...
97. Ibid., p. 299:
Prajārakṣaṇamātrakarttvyānāṁ narapatinām...
98. Candra Bardai, *Pṛthvīrājarāso*, ed. Kaviraj Mohan Singh Mehta (Udaipur, V.S. 2012), III, p. 21.
99. Ibid., VIII, p. 65.
100. Ibid., IX, p. 66.
101. Ibid., IX, p. 67.

102. *Tilaka-mañjarī*, p. 13:
sakalabhūbhāradhāraṇakṣamaḥ...
103. Cf. *Manuṣmṛti*, IV, p. 126.
104. *Tilaka-mañjarī*, p. 12:
yathāvidhivyavasthāpitavarṇāśramadharmo...
105. *Tilaka-mañjarī*, p. 13:
Trātacaturāśramaḥ...
106. Ibid., p. 16:
Vaśikṛtasamastasāmantamāyattamaṁtrimaṇḍalamupagṛhītamitravargamāptapuruṣādhiṣṭhita durgam...
107. Ibid., p. 14:
Sakalādharma nirmūlābhilāṣī...
108. Ibid., p. 15:
Dvijātikriyāṇāṁ śākhoddharaṇam...
109. Ibid., p. 19:
Dharmapakṣapātitayā ca devadvijāti tapasvijanakāryeṣu mahatsu kāryāsanaṁ bheje...
110. Ibid., pp. 10, 75, 107, 163, 172.
111. Ibid., p. 66:
kvacidāsanna sevaka niveditadānavicchedaāsu dānaśālāsudīnānātha pathika sārthasya saviśeṣmannapānaśayanauṣadhādidānamdhikṛtaiḥ pravartayataḥ, kvacitsvakhāniteṣu saraḥ sutaṭaropitānāṁ vayasvacchā diviṭapināṁ pālanārthmudyānapālānudyamayataḥ, mārgaghaṭitaṁ ca sūktavādinaṁ daridrayācakasārthamarthasaṁbhāreṇa bhūriṇā kṛtārthīkurvātaḥ, tīvratigmāṁśukaranīpātopatāpitaḥ svaduḥkhamā cikhyāsuriva prtyāsasāda madhyānhsamayaḥ|
112. *Śukranīti-sāra*, I, pp. 751-752.
113. *Manusmṛti*, VII, p. 123.
114. *Tilaka-mañjarī*, p. 19:
Pauralokaparitoṣahetosca vasantādiṣu saviśeṣa pravṛttotsavāṁ nirgatya nagrīmapaśyat|
115. *Tilaka-mañjarī*, p. 19.
116. Ibid. :
kiṁvadantīśuśruśayā ca tatra sthāne saṁniviṣṭā viśiṣṭajanagoṣṭhīrjagāhe|
Pratiśryakuṭīṣu ca digantarāgatapathikasatatasaṁbādhāsvaḍhaukata|
Rājavyāpārakathāprakrama ca paurāṇāmāśayapa īkṣārthamavanīpateramātyasya tadadhikṛtānāṁ ca yathāsambhavaṁ parikalpya doṣānudakīrtayat|
Taiśca praśānta nikhilopadravatayā sarvadā sukhitaiḥ svāmisacivādhyakṣa mithyā parivādaśravaṇabaddhama rṣairapratybhijñānsya doṣeṇa puruṣākṣaramadhikṣipyamāṇaḥ parāṁ mudamuvāha||

117. Samuel Beal, *Life of Yuan Chwang* (London, 1911), I, p. 215.
118. *Tilaka-mañjarī*, p. 16:
...Samāropitasvanāmavarṇāh śreṇīkānāropyadiśāmaṣṭānāmapi paryanteṣu jayastambhān...
119. *Tilaka-mañjarī*, pp. 62-71.
120. *Tilaka-mañjarī*, p. 27:
Mūrdhābhiṣiktakṣatriyāmnāye mānanīyā...
121. Ibid., p. 424:
...Nagarapaurainnṛpabhiṣekamāṅgalikasampādanāya...
122. Ibid., p, 269:
Vyadhiyanta vaiṇikairitastataḥ prahatatantrīparīkṣita-kaladhvanibhirniścalāḥ kalā vallakīṣu vitīrṇa vividhamārjanāni sadṃāni /
123. Ibid.:
...Agre gāyanīgaṇamupāviśnvāṁśikāḥ prakṣālanpavitrapāṇibhiḥ...
124. Ibid.:
Upānīyanta pānīyena sākalatīrthāhṛtena pūritāḥśātakumbhakumbhāḥ...
125. *Ādi-purāṇa*, XVI, pp. 223-230.
126. *Tilaka-mañjarī*, p. 16.
127. Somadeva, *Nītivākyāmṛta*, MDJG Series, No. 22 (Bombay, 1922), p. 149:
Svatantraḥ sahaśākārityāt vināśayati...
128. Ibid.. p. 128.
Treyaḥ pañca saptavā mantrigaṇāstaiḥ kāryāḥ...
129. *Śukranītisāra*, ed. Jivananda, Vidyasagara Bhattacharya (Calcutta, 1890), II, 71-72:
Aṣṭaprakṛtibhiryukto nṛpaḥ keścitsmṛtaḥ sādā/
sumantraḥ paṇḍito mantrī pradhānaḥ sacivastathā/
Amātyaḥ prāḍvivākaśca tathā pratinidhiḥ smṛtaḥ//

II. 84-87:
Sarvadarśī pradhānastu senāvit sacivastathā
māṅtrī tu nītikuśalaḥ paṇḍito dharmatattvacit
lokaśāstra nayajñastu prāḍvivākaḥ smṛtaḥ sadā//
Deśa kāla pravijñātā hyamātya iti kathyate/
āya vyaya pravijñatā sumaṅtraḥ sa ca kīrtitaḥ
ingitākāraceṣṭajñaḥ smṛtimandeśakālavit//
Ṣāḍguṇyamantravidvāgmī vītabhīrdūta iṣyate
ahitañccāpi yatkāryaṁ sadyaḥ kartuṁ yadocitaṃ
akartuṁ yaddhitamapi rājñaḥ pratinidhiḥ sadā//
Bodhayetkārayetkuryyanna kuryyānna prabodhayet
satyaṁ vā yadi vāsatyaṁ kāryajātañca yatkila
sarveṣāṁ rājakṛtyeṣu pradhānastadivacintayet//
130. *Tilaka-mañjarī*, p. 63.
131. Ibid., p. 62.
132. Ibid., p. 20.
133. Ibid., p. 85.

134. Ibid., p. 15.
135. Ibid., p. 15.
136. Ibid., p. 81.
137. Ibid., p. 17.
138. Ibid., p. 82.
139. K.P. Jayaswal, *Hindu Polity* (Bangalore, 1943), p. 293.
140. A.S. Altekar, *State and Government in Ancient India* (Delhi, 1972), p. 173.
141. *Tilaka-mañjarī*, p. 20.
142, Ibid., p. 182.
143. *Śukranītisāra*, p. 173, śloka 84.
144. Kāṇe, *History of Dharmaśāstras*, Vol. II (Poona, 1930), p. 104. B.G. Gokhale is also of the opinion that, "three terms are used to designate a minister; Saciva, mantrin and amātya" and are synonymous (*Ancient India*, Bombay: Asia Publishing House, p. 108).
145. *Tilaka-mañjarī*, p. 15:
    Dhārmikataiva duritāni praticakāra (na) prapañcaḥ purodhasaḥ...
146. K.P. Jayaswal, op. cit., p. 297.
147. *Nītivākyāmṛta*, p. 136:
    Śasyādhikāriṇo na māntrādhikāriṇaḥ syuḥ/
    Śastropajīvināṁ kalahamantreṇa bhaktamapi bhuktaṁ na jīyati/
148. *Tilaka-mañjarī*, p. 20:
    Sacivaloko'pi śrutatvadharmaśāstrāṇāmapekṣhtitvā datīta puruṣa vyavahārāṇāmakarkaśatvādāśayasya parijñātatvāñca prabhucitta vṛtteḥ pariharanprajā khedamakhilaṅyapi rajakāryāṇi cakre //
149. *Nītivakyamṛta*, p. 109, Sūtra 10,
150. Ibid., p. 110, Sūtra, 12.
151. B.G. Gokhale, *Ancient India* (Bombay : Asia Publishing House, 1962), p. 108.
152. Purana Chandra Nahara, *Jain Lekhā Saṅgraha* (Calcutta, 1918, 1929) Vol. I, p. 233.
153. *Tilaka mañjarī*, p. 19:
    sabhamaṇḍapamadhyasta......karyasanaṁ bheje......
154. Dashratha Sharma, *Lectures on Rajput History and Culture* (Delhi, 1970), p. 110.
155. 'Sabhā', according to C.N. Puri, consisted of both official and non-official elements *The History of the Gurjara Pratihāras* (Bombay, 1957), p. 114.
156. *Tilaka-mañjarī*, p. 111.
157. Ibid., p. 15.
158. Ibid., p. 14.
159. Ibid., p. 70.
160. Ibid., p. 63.
161. Ibid., p. 15.

162. *Tilaka-mañjarī*, p. 62 :
...Maharṣayaḥ śrotriyaḥ pradhānamantriṇo'matya vṛddhā mūrdha-bhiṣiktanṛpatyo mahāsāmanta jnatayaḥ suhṛdaḥ samagra nagaralokāgresarāsca paurāḥ samājagmuḥ /
163. bid., p. 62.
164. bid., p. 15.
165. bid., p. 78.
166. Somadeva, *Nītivakyamṛta*, p. 130:
Ekohipuruṣo keṣu nāma kāryeṣvātmānaṁ vibhajate/
167. R.S. Tripathi, *History of Kanauj* (Delhi, 1964), p. 136.
168. *Tilaka-mañjarī*, pp. 62, 181.
169. *Tilaka-mañjarī*, p. 181.
170. Ibid., p. 181.
171. *Prabandhacintāmaṇi*, p. 22:
Rudrādityanāmnā mahāmātyena niṣiddhyamāno'pitaṁ pratipratiṣṭhāsuḥ...
172. *Tilaka-mañjarī*, p. 402.
173. Ibid., p. 114.
174. *I.A.*, XIL, p. 202.
175. *Tilaka-mañjarī*, p. 62.
176. Ibid., p. 99:
Rājyacintakāḥ p adhānasacivāḥ...
177. *Tilaka-mañjarī*, pp. 17, 62.
178. Ibid., pp. 16-17:
...Viditaniḥśeṣanitiśastrasaṁhateramātyavargasyāyattamakarot.
179. Somadeva, *Nītivākyāmṛta*' p. 156:
Āyavyoyo svāmirakṣā mantrapoṣaṇāṁ cāmātyānāmadhikāraḥ...
180. *Tilaka-mañjarī*, p. 33:
Buddhisacivānāṁ ca yathā vṛttaṁ sarvameva munivṛttāntamākhyat,......
181. B.G. Gokhale, op. cit., p. 108.
182. *Tilaka-mañjarī*, p. 401.
183. *Tilaka-mañjarī*, p. 15:
...Rūpameva manasvinīḥ prasādamanayadvinodo narmasacivāḥ...
184. Ibid., p. 182.
185. Ibid., p. 161.
186. Ibid., p. 103.
187. Ibid., p. 103.
188. Ibid., p. 184.
189. A.S. Altekar, *State and Government in Ancient India*, p. 315.
190. K.P. Jayaswal, *Hindu Polity*, p. 295.
191. Ibid.
192. *Tilaka-mañjarī*, p. 107.
193. *E.I.*, XVIII, pp. 107-110.
194. *Tilaka-mañjarī*, p. 70.

195. Ibid., p. 70. English translation by Dr. Dasharatha Sharma in his book *Lectures on Rajput History and Culture*, p. 111.
196. *Tilaka-mañjarī*. p. 107.
197. Ibid., p. 68.
198. Ibid., p. 91.
199. Ibid., p. 17.
200. Ibid., p. 82.
201. Ibid., p. 64.
902. R.S. Tripathi, op. cit., p. 143.
203. *The Age of Imperial Kanauj*, p. 243.
204. *Tilaka-mañjarī*, p. 81.
205. Ibid., p. 82.
206. Ibid., p. 82.
207. Ibid., p. 81.
208. Ibid., p. 120:
...Kāṁsyapātrikāsūtrakaṁ valayaprāyaṁ balādhikṛtadhāmanya-bālājananyāsī Kurvardbhiranekavṛttāntair grāmeyakaira-valokyamāṇabalasaṁhatiḥ...
209. Dasharatha Sharma, op, cit., p. 113.
210. B.N. Puri, op. cit., p. 111.
211. *Tilaka-mañjarī*, p. 182.
212. Ibid., p. 80:
...Dakṣiṇāpathādāgato dakṣiṇa daṇḍādhipatervajrā yudhasya...
213. Ibid., p. 182:
...Uttaradiganta daṇḍanāyakena......
214. B.N. Puri, op. cit., p. 111.
215. *Idem.*
216. *Tilaka-mañjarī*, p. 71.
217. Dasharatha Sharma, op. cit., p. 112.
218. *Ths Age of Imperial Kanauj*, p. 242.
219. *Tilaka-mañjarī*,, p. 62.
220; Ibid., p. 15.
221. A.S. Altekar, op. cit., p. 205.
222. *The Age of Imperial Kanauj*, p. 242.
223. *History of Kanauj*, p. 344.
224. *Tilaka-mañjarī*, p. 322.
225. Ibid., p. 110.
226. Quoted by A.L. Basham, op. cit., p. 103.
227. *Tilaka-mañjarī*, p, 330;
Vṛddhāntarveśikasamūhena...... (p. 153)
228. Ibid., p. 72.
229. Ibid., p. 103.
230. Ibid., p. 246:
Akṣapaṭalamāsthāya kāyasthena......
231. Ibid., p, 103:
Sudṛṣṭināmākṣapaṭalikaḥ praviśya paṭṭakāropita-

niravaśeṣaviśeṣamabhyarṇavartibhiranekaiḥ kāśmīrādi maṇḍalapratiboddhaiḥ...

232. Ibid,, p, 178.
233. Ibid., p. 73; p. 375.
234, Ibid.. p. 403.
235. Ibid., p. 131.
236. Ibid., p, 78:

...sarvāyurveda pāragairbhiṣagbhiḥ......

237. Ibid., p. 81.
238. Ibid., p. 69.
239. Ibid., p. 142.
240. Ibid., p. 66.
241. Ibid., p. 195.
242. Ed. Jivananda Vidyasagara (Calcutta, 1892), p. 60.
243. *Tilaka-mañjarī*, p. 414.
244. Ibid., p. 15.
245. Ibid., p. 76.
246. Ibid., p. 108.
247. Ibid., p. 184.
248. *E I.*, IV, p. 250.
249. *Tilaka-mañjarī*, p. 126.
250. *E.I,*, IV, p. 250.
251. *The Age of Imperial Kanauj*, p. 242.
252. R.K. Mookerji, *Chandragupta Maurya and His Times* (Madras, 1943), p. 179.
253. *Tilaka-mañjarī*, p. 15.
254. Ibid., p. 39.
255. Ibid., p. 15:

...Saubhāgyamevāntaḥ puramarakṣatisthitiḥ stāpatyāḥ......

256. Ibid., p. 105.
257. Dasharatha Sharma, op. cit., p. 111.
258. Bhoja, *Śṛṅgāramañjarī-kathā*, ed. Dr. (Miss) K. Munshi (Bombay, 1958), p. 87.
259. *Tilaka-mañjarī*, p. 26:

Hastyaśvarathapadāti prāyo...

260. D. C. Ganguly, op. cit., p. 245.
261. Bhoja, *Yuktikalpataru.* ed., Ishvar Chandra Shastri (Calcutta, 1917), p. 7, śloka 45.
262. *Tilaka-mañjarī*, p. 140:

...Dṛḍhanipātaniṣṭhurakāṣṭhakīlaniyamitanaukeṣu......

263. Ibid., p. 131:

Kumārasyāpi śakravijayāya sajjīkṛtā vijayayātrabhidhānā nauḥ...

264. Ibid., p. 131:

Saparigrahe ca purobhāgavartinaṁ mattavāraṇakam-adhyamadhyāsya baddhāsane mayi kṛtottarīyasaṁ-caraṇāscaraṇābhyāmeva satvaramupasṛtya sarve rājaputraḥ saparijanāḥ svāni svāni yānapātrāṇyaviruruhuḥ, pratasthire ca parivārya mām/

265. *Tilaka-mañjarī*, p. 131:

...samāropitamapramāṇamindhanam......

266. Ibid., p. 131:

...Taila kambaloṣadhaprāyaḥ......

267. Ibid., p. 131:

...Āpūritāni svādhunā salilena kṛtsnānyudaka pātrāṇi...

268. Ibid., p. 131:

...Gṛhīta nānāvidhāstraḥ......

269. Ibid., p. 123:

...Udāraveṣayoṣidvṛndagīyamānagāmbhīryamahima maryādādijalanidiguṇāmācamanapūta purohitagṛhītakanakārgha pātra nikṣiptadadhidūrvākṣatāṁ svayamavekṣitairbhakṣyabalibhirvilepaṇaiḥ puṣpadāmbhiraṁśukairatnālaṁkāraiṣca bahuvikalpairupetakalpitāmanalapyā bhaktayā bhagavato ratnākarasya pūjāṁ prātiṣṭhapam/

270. Ibid., p. 132:

...Sthagita niḥśeṣa saṁdhirandhryā dāsapuraṁdhridattapiṣṭapañcāṅgulayā......

271. Ibid , p. 89.
272. Ibid , p. 114.
273. Ibid., p. 87; p. 114.
274. Ibid., p. 114.
275. Ibid., p. 114.
276. Ibid., p. 114.
277. Ibid., p. 87.
278. Ibid., p. 114.
279. Ibid., p. 83:

...Nirdaya prahatatūryarava paryāsitakātarakaraśastrāṇi...

280. Ibid., p. 370.
281. Ibid., p. 87.
282. Ibid., p. 132:

...Dadhānadhvajinyā'mukhe mukharaḥ prayaṇa maṅgalaśaṅkhaḥ...

283. Ibid., p. 132.
284. Ibid., p. 87:

...Samarabherīṇāṁ bhāṅkāreṇa...

285. Ibid., p. 132.
286. Ibid., p. 82.
287. Ibid., p. 82.
288. Ibid., p. 71.
289. Ibid., p. 120.
290. Ibid., p. 80.
291. Ibid., p. 81.
292. Ibidr, p. 184.

293. Ibid., p. 126.
294. Ibid., p. 82:
...Auvahaṁ ca dahyamānāsannagrāmakakṣām......
295. Ibid., p. 82:
...Upahata bahirjalśāyām...
296. Ibid., p. 82:
...Antaḥ praveśitaprabhūta dhānyāmupasāṁgṛhītapracurayavasaindhanām......
297. Ibid., p. 82:
...Udaktajīrṇavāpīkūpapaṅkām......
298. Ibid., p. 82;
...Niṣkāsitniḥśeṣāsāralokaṁ viṣamitaprākāramūlasamabhūtalāmavatāra mārgadurgāmīkṣatakhātavalayāṁ......
299. Ibid., p. 82:
...Nivāritāvijñātajananirgama praveśām......
300. Ibid., p. 82:
...Apramattāptapuruṣagulmakapratipannasakalapratolirakṣām...
301. Ibid., p. 82:
...Pāṇikśepaṇīyapāṣāṇakūṭasthapuṭitaprākārāsannasthalām...
302. Ibid., p. 82:
Prākāraśikharotsaṅgasūtritavicitrayantra......
303. Ibid., p, 82:
...Aparityaktasamarābhilāṣaśca sahāyakadheyasa vidhavartināmavanipālānāmanuśaṁdhānāya pradhānadūtamaharhaḥ prāhiṇota...
304. Ibid., p. 83:
Sāmantaśca sajjīkṛtasamadasāmajaghaṭā vighaṭanāya durgasya tena kṛtavisargaḥ krameṇanirjagmuḥ...
305. Ibid., p. 83:
...yantravikṣiptāganitaptātailacchaṭavighaṭāmānavikaṭapadātigumphāni......
306. Ibid., p. 83:
...kuthāratāḍita pratolīkapāṭaniḥ svanānusāranipatatprabalapāṣāṇavarṣaṇi......
307. Ibid., p. 15:
yasmiśca rajnyanuvartitaśāstramārge praśasati......
308. K.P. Jayaswal, op. cit., p. 323.
309. *Tilaka-mañjarī*, p. 14:
Guruvitīrṇa śāsana...
310. K.P. Jayaswal, op. cit., p. 324.
311. Sachau, op. cit., p. 106.
312. *Tilaka-mañjarī*, p. 63.
313. Ibid., p. 19:
...Dharmapakṣapātitayā...
314. Ibid., p. 19:
Na dharmaḥ sīdati...

315. *Tilaka-mañjarī*, p. 20:
Sacivaloko'pi śrutatvāddharmaśāstrāṇāmapekṣitatvāt ..
3 6. Ibid., p. 20:
...Atītapuruṣavyavahārāṇāmakarkaśatvādāśayaya pariṇātatvāñca...
317. Ibid., p. 20.
318. Ibid. p. 15:
...Na nidhuvana Krīḍasu tarjana tāḍanāni...
na timīnāṁ galagrahaḥ...
319. Ibid., p. 13:
...Samyagjñātaheyopādeyavibhāgaḥ......
320. Ibid., p. 14:
...sarvamunibhiriva nirmito paśmaḥ......
321. Ibid., p. 13:
...samadarśanaḥ......
322. Ibid., p. 13:
...svaritena caritena pavitrita tribhuvanāvaniḥ......
323. Ibid., p. 19:
...Vinayasa bhūyisṭhatayā c satyavṛtteḥ...
324. Ibid., p. 19:
...Prajānurāgo'pi......
325. Ibid., p. 13:
...Trāta caturāśramaḥ...
326. Ibid., p. 12.
327. Ibid., p. 14:
...sakalādharmanirmūlanābhilāṣī......
328. Ibid., p. 19.
329. Ibid., p. 71.
330. Ibid., p. 15.
331. Somadeva, *Nītivākyāmṛta*, p. 302.
332. *Tilaka-mañjarī*, p. 62.
333. Ibid., p. 102.
334. *Nītivākyāmṛta*, pp. 296-297.
335. *Tilaka-mañajrī*. p. 111.
336. Ibid., p. 182:
...yuvarāja Samaraketoḥ bhuktiriti/
337. Ibid., p. 103:
...Kaśmīrādi maṇḍala...
338. D.C. Ganguly, op. cit., p. 235.
339. P. Bhatia, op. cit., p. 215.
340. B.N. Puri, *The History of the Gurjara-Pratihāras* (Bombay, 1957), p. 108.
341. Ram Sharan Sharma, *Aspects of the Political Ideas and Institutions in Ancient India* (Delhi, 1959), p. 208.
342. *Tilaka-mañjarī*, p. 103:
...Anekaiḥ kaśmīrādimaṇḍala pratibaddhaiḥ pradhānanagara grāmairupetaṁ kumārabhuktāva khilamuttarāpathamarthayāṁbabhūva/

The Damodarpur Copper Plate Inscriptions mention 'Punḍravardhana Bhukti' or province adminstered by the Uparika Cirātedatta who was selected by the Gupta monarch Kumāragupta (*E.I.*, Vol. XV, pp. 130ff.).

343. *Tilaka-mañjarī*, p. 103:
Samaraketoścasarvadāyasahitānaṅgādijanapadānprāyacchat/

344. Ibid., p. 182.

345. *E.I.*, Vol. V, p. 130, & Vol. XX, p. 61.

346. R.S. Tripathi, *History of Kanauj* (Delhi: Motilal Banarsi Das, 1964), p. 344.

347. B.N. Puri, op. cit., p. 108. *E.I.*, Vol. XV, p. 130 & Vol. XX, p. 61.

348. *The Age of the Imperial Kanauj* (Bombay: Bharatiya Vidya Bhavan, 1955), p. 242.

349. *I.A.*, Vol., XV, pp. 304-310.

350. According to Hirananda Sastri, "the term 'maṇḍala' connotes a larger area than a 'viṣaya' which in majority of cases seems to include a 'maṇḍala' (*E.I.*, Vol. XVII, p. 316).

351. *Tilaka-mañjarī*, p. 103.

352. Ibid., p. 82.

353. Ibid., p. 349.

354. Kalhaṇa, *Rājtaraṅgiṇī*, ed. and translated by Pandeya Rāmatej Sastrī, (Kashi, 1960), p. 27.

355. *E.I.*, III, p. 48.

356. *E.I.*, XXXIII, p. 197.

357. *E.I.*, II, p. 188.

348. *E.I.*, XIII, p. 108.

359. *E.I.*, XX, p. 106.

360. *E.I.*, XI, p. 182; *I.A.*, XLI, p. 201.

361. *I.A.*, XVI, p. 254.

362. *I.A.*, XIX, p. 352, *E.I.*, XXIV, p. 232.

363. *P.A. I.O.C.* (1919), p. 319, D.C. Ganguly, op. cit., p. 236.

364. *E.I.*, XXIII, p. 112.

365. *J.A.S.*, VII, (1838), p. 737.

366. *I.H.Q.*, 1961, p. 163, 1.2.

367. *I.A.*, XX, p. 84; *A.S.I.*, X, p. 31.

368. *I.A.*, LXI, p. 136.

369. *E.I.*, IX, p. 13.

370. *E.I.*, XXIII, p. 135.

371. *E.I.*, XIX, p. 242.

372. Jina-vijaya-muni, *Pnrātana-Prabandha-Saṅgraha*, Sindhi Jaina Granthamala No. 11 (Calcutta, 1936), p. 86.

373. A.S. Altekar, *State and Government in Ancient India* (Delhi, 1936), p. 213.

374. *Tilaka-mañjarī*, p. 82:
...śaratasamaye senāpatirarthaśāstra parāmarśapūta-matibhiramātyaiḥ...

375. A.S. Altekar, op. cit., p. 214.
376. *Tilaka-mañjarī*, p. 182.
377. Ibid., p. 16.
378. Ibid., p. 62.
379. Ibid., p. 426:
...*Samaraketu-kamalaguptādinā parivāra nṛpasamājena*......
380. Ibid., p 427:
...*Kamalaguptādhibhiḥ pradhāna rājaputraiḥ*...
381. Ibid., p. 80.
382. Ibid., p. 81.
383. Ibid., p. 62.
384. Ibid., p. 16:
...*Vaśīkṛtasamastasāmantam*......
385. Ibid., pp. 63, 81.
386. Ibid,, p. 81.
387. *E.I.*, II, p, 185, V. 29.
388. *Tilaka-mañjarī*, p. 83:
Sāmantāśca sajjikṛtasamadasāmajaghaṭāvighaṭanāya durgasyatena kṛtavisargāḥ krameṇa nirjagmuḥ|
389. Ibid , p. 63.
390. G.C. Choudhary, op. cit., p. 196.
391. *Tilaka-mañjarī*., p. 103.
392. *E.I.*, XXXII, pp. 155-156.
393. D.C. Ganguly, op. cit., p 235.
394. *Tilaka-mañjarī*. pp. 87, 398.
395. Ibid., p. 182.

4

Social and Economic Conditions

VARṆA, CASTE, AND FAMILY LIFE

It is universally recognized that literature reflects the spirit of the age, that the artist is the product of the age and that the works of art portray a fairly faithful picture of the life and manners of the age. Being a poet and a gifted one, at that—Dhanapāla was naturally an acute observer of the life around him. His works, informed as these are through and through with the zeitgeist, may be taken as reliable guide manuals by the student of ancient Indian history.

Hindu society, as is well-know, had adopted the Varṇa system as far back as the Vedic period. It divided society into four great classes, viz., the priest (Brāhmaṇa), warrior (Kṣatriya), peasant (Vaiśya) and Serf (Śūdra) which have survived to the present day. We read in *Tiloka-mañjarī*[1] that among the four varṇas a sharp distinction was drawn between the members of the three higher classes and the Śūdras who occupied the lowest rung of the social cadre. The first three varṇas were known as 'dvija'[2] or twice born (because of their natural birth and again at their initiation when they were invested with the sacred thread).[3] Dr. Basham is of the opinion that, "In later texts the term 'twice born' was often reserved for Brāhmaṇas, but strictly it applies to Kṣatriyas and Vaiśyas also, if they have been initiated".[4] John Garrett explains the term 'dvijā' thus : "Twice born, a Brāhmaṇa whose investiture with the sacred thread constitutes religiously and metaphorically his second birth, in this sense it may be applied to Kṣatriya and Vaiśya".[5] In *Tilaka-mañjarī*, the term 'dvija' is generally used in the context of 'Brāhmaṇas Further the word 'yācaka dvija'[6] (mendicant) occurring in the work makes it evident that it was applied only to Brāhmaṇas, as a Kṣatriya could not beg. It is interesting to note that at one place Dhanapāla describes the 'dvija' a very cruel person.[7] It appears that Dhanapāla must have in mind those Brāhmaṇas who were working as purohitas of the Bhīlas.

Dhanapāla enumerates the duties and functions of a Brāhmaṇa : studying,[8] teaching,[9] sacrificing[10] and receiving gifts and land grants (agrahāras).[11] As regards the position of the Brāhmaṇas in society, the statement in *Tilaka-mañjarī*, that the blessings of 'devās' and Brāhamaṇas bear fruit,[12] points to the fact that the Brāhmaṇas were still the most esteemed class in society and were revered by the people at large.[13] The purohitas enjoyed an exalted status which is borne out by the selection of certain categories of royal officers such as Dharmastheyas[18] and 'Mauhūrtikas'[15] from the Brāhmaṇa class. Alberunī confirms that the Brāhmaṇas were honoured by the Indians as forming the most noble and illustrious caste.[16] The Brāhmaṇas who recited Vedas were know as 'śrotriyas'.[17]

Regarding the duty and position of the Kṣatriya class, Dhanapāla provides us the required clue while cataloguing the duties of king Meghavāhana in *Tilaka-mañjarī* who is a Kṣatriya.[13] The king is expected to maintain the varṇas and āśramas[19] in their proper order, to uproot evil,[20] to favour, protect and please the people[21] and to give donations.[22] He offers oblations to the fire[23] and acts according to the rules laid down by Dharmaśāstras.[24]

Protection of the people from internal and external aggressions was the primary duty of the 'Kṣatriyas'. According to Alberunī they could learn the Vedas but they were not permitted to teach them.[25] In *Tilaka-mañjarī* we read that prince Harivāhana has learnt and mastered the fourteen vidyās (four Vedas, six Vedāṅgas, Purāṇa, Nyāya, Mīmāṁsā and Dharmaśāstras).[26]

Of the Vaiśyas (the third Varṇa), we learn from Dhanapāla that they were timid by nature.[27] Being cowardly, they were averse to fighting; their duty was trade and business.[28] They sat in their shops selling provisions.[29] According to *Smṛtis* the occupation of the Vaiśyas included agriculture, cattle breeding,[30] trade and money-lending.[31] '*Tilaka-mañjarī*'[32] and *Pāiyalac-*

chīnāmamālā,[33] speak of Vaiśyas as 'Vaṇikas', probably for the reason that by then they had become a mercantile community who dealt in buying and selling. According to Alberunī Vaiśyas and Śūdras were not allowed to hear 'Vedas', much less to pronounce and recite it. If such a thing was proved against one of them, Brāhmaṇas dragged him before the magistrate and he was punished by having his tongue cut off.[34]

However, Bhaṭṭa Lakṣmīdhara, who knew Hindu society better than Alberunī, vouchsafes the study and recitation of the Vedas open for Vaiśyas[35] too. *Tilaka-mañjarī* corroborates this account. Tāraka, a merchant in *Tilaka-mañjarī*, listens to Śāstras which include Vedas as well.[36] The authenticity of Alberunī's evidence becomes somewhat dubious.

Śūdras were the lowest among the four varṇas. Their duties, though not referred to in *Tilaka-mañjarī*, as such, have been specified in other accounts. The duties of 'Śūdras', writes B.G. Gokhale, were to serve the 'twice born' and to practise all branches of occupational arts.[37] Alberunī gives the following account of their life. "The Śūdra is like a servant to the Brāhmaṇa, taking care of his affairs and serving him. Though being poor in the extreme, if he still desired not to be with a Yajñopavīta, he girded himself up only with one linen. Every action which is considered as the privilege of a Brāhmaṇa such as saying prayers, the recitation of the Veda, offering sacrifices to the fire is forbidden to him".[38]

From Dhanapāla's works we learn that Śūdras were divided into various sub-castes based on different vocations and occupations, viz., the artisan (śilpī),[39] farmer (halika),[40] carpenter (baḍhaī or 'vardhakī'),[41] potter (Kumbhāra),[42] fisher ('dhīvara'),[43] barber ('caṇḍila'),[44] 'cāṇḍāla',[45] garland-maker ('puṣpalāvī'),[46] hunter (vāha),[47] cowherd (gvālā),[48] washerman (śodhaka),[49] weaver ('tantuvāya'),[50] dyer (chimpā),[51] actor (Kuśīlava),[52] female dancer (nartakī),[53] sailor or boatsman (nāvika),[54] charioteer (sārathi),[55] gardener (udyānapāla)[56] courtesan (veśya,[57] gaṇikā),[58] dealers in betel leaves,[59] wrestler (malla),[60] niṣāda,[61] and Kirāta[62] etc.

In this context it may be interesting to note that Dhanapāla in *Pāiyalacchīnāmamālā* mentions the term 'Prākṛta' equating it with 'adhama', 'itara' and 'nīca',[63] Halāyudha takes

Prākṛta in the sense of a manual labourer of sorts. Under this head he places the washerman, the distiller of liquids, the fisherman, the butcher, the meat-seller, the shoe-maker, the fowler and the cāṇḍāla.[64] Dr. B.N. Sharma in his monograph, *Social Life In Northern India,* quotes *Skanda Purāṇa* in which as many as eighteen sub-castes, of 'Prākṛtas' have been listed viz. 'Śilpī', 'Nartaka', 'Kāsthakāra', 'Prajāpati', 'Vardhika', 'Citraka', 'Sūtraka', 'Rajaka', 'Gacchaka', 'Tantukāra', 'Cakrika', 'Carmakāra', 'Sunika', 'Dhvanika', 'Kaulhika', 'Matsyaghātaka', 'Aunāmika' and 'Cāṇḍāla'.[65]

In addition to the Śūdras, the system of slavery appears to have been prevalent in Dhanapāla's days as there occur several references to slaves[66] in *Tilaka-mañjarī.* Both male[67] and female slaves[68] (dāsas and dāsīs) served as domestic servants residing in the houses of their masters and performing all types of house-hold and menial duties entrusted to them.

FAMILY LIFE

Family has always been the base of the Hindu society. In Dhanapāla's times joint families were the order of the day. The discipline and administration of the house were looked after by the head of the family who was known as 'kulapati'.[69] The headship formally vested in the father who was the head of the house and administrator of joint property.[70] The son was also the natural protector of the family after the passing away of the father. However, young he might be, it was his moral duty to look after the family. Within the family, the atmosphere was one of filial love and discipline. We read in *Tilaka-mañjarī* that Tāraka and Priyadarśanā, crazy in love with each other, await their parent's permission before marriage,[71] as it was expected of them not to offend the head of the family.[72] Women in *Tilaka-mañjarī* are described to be obeying the instructions of the head of the family. They serve the guests according to the instructions of the head of the family.[73] It does not mean that women were regarded inferior to men. They were very much respected in the family. It was the duty (dharma) of the householder to look after the welfare of the ladies.[74]

It appears that no distinction was made between the male and female child during Dhanapāla's time. The birth ceremony of the female child was also celebrated with the same eclat and enthusiasm as that of the male child.[75]

The family was bound together by 'Śrāddha'[76] (the rite of commemorating the ancestors at which balls of rice called piṇḍa were offered). Sons, grandsons and great-grandsons of the deceased joined in Śrāddha and three generations of the dead were believed to participate in the benefits of the ceremony.[77] In *Tilaka-mañjarī*, King Meghavāhana also observes Śrāddha ceremony in order to please his forefather.[78] At the ceremony of some one's birth and marriage or of some festival, the relatives and friends were also invited. When prince Harivāhana is born his father invites his friends, relatives, kinsmen and throws a sumptuous feast to them.[79]

In the words of Brijendra Nath Sharma: "The position of father in the family was one of great authority. He could give out of love every thing to his children and even accede to their unreasonable demands. He could disinherit his son and expel a daughter from his house if he found that they had committed some offence which he regarded as heinous or socially unpardonable. The mother did not have the father's authority, but she had generally all the love and affection that children could give. She had also plenty of influence on the formation of boy's character. In the Rajpūt society, a mother preferred death of her son to his fleeing from the battlefield and the same high estimate came in due course to be entertained by her daughters and daughters-in-law".[80]

SOCIAL LIFE

Besides being a work of art of great beauty in its own right, the prose romance, *Tilaka-mañjarī*, is also a social document of great value—a veritable mine, that is, of sociological data. It provides the discerning reader vital information on the pattern of the contemporary social life reflected in the prevailing customs and manners, modes of dress and personal adornment, foods and drinks, pleasures and pastimes, festivals and seasonal rejoicings, and the like.

Saṁskāras

In Dhanapāla's days great emphasis was laid upon the observance of the sixteen 'saṁsakāras'.[81] A saṁskāra was a "religious ceremony of refinement in various stages of life that polished and made a disciplined child of a man unaffected by good or bad".[82] The performance of saṁskāras was regarded as a social obligation. In *Tilaka-mañjarī*, Dhanapāla takes up for special enumeration the important saṁskāras such as 'Puṁsavana', 'Jātakarma', 'Nāmakaraṇa', 'Annaprāśana', 'Upanayana'[83] and 'Vivāha'.[84]

Vedavyāsa, one of the earliest thinkers of ancient India, lays down the sixteen saṁskāras as 'Garbhādhāna', 'Puṁsavana', 'Sīmanta', 'Jātakarma', 'Nāmakaraṇa', 'Niṣkramaṇa', 'Annaprāśana', 'Vapanakriyā' (Muṇḍana or Cūḍākarma), 'Karṇavedha', 'Vratādeśa or Upanayana', 'Vedārambha', 'Keśānta', 'Snānam', (Samāvarttana), 'Vivāha' and 'Tretāgni-Saṅgraha'.[85]

Garbhādhāna

This saṁskara was observed for inducing conception and preserving it in the gestation period.[86]

Puṁsavana

It was meant to secure the birth of a male child.[87] Usually, this saṁskāra was performed in the third month of pregnancy i.e., before the formation of embryo. King Meghavāhana in *Tilaka-mañjarī* performs all the rites related to Puṁsavana saṁskāra in order to be blessed with a son. He worships his family deity, adores saints and ācāryas, worships jewels, makes oblations to Dikpālas (Indra etc.), helps the poor and destitutes by way of charity, pleases Brāhmaṇas by paying due respect to them, donates cows to the 'śrotriyas', observes śrāddha on pañcamī, and performs yajña with the help of purohita. He proceeds on with these ceremonies for a number of days. The Brāhmaṇas recite mantras for blessing the king with a son.[88] All the women of his harem observe fasts of various kinds.[89]

Sīmanta

It literally means the partaking of the hair. This saṁskāra was observed in the sixth or eighth month of the gestation period.[90]

Jātakarma

It denotes the ceremony held at the birth of the child.[91] Dhanapāla has given a vivid description of 'Jātakarma' saṁskāra in *Tilaka-mañjarī.* Soon after Harivāhana's birth, volleys of conchshells (Śaṅkha), 'jhallarīs', drums (mṛdaṅga), kettle drums (dundubhī) are sounded in every house. The teachers (ācāryas) and students disengaging themselves from their studies move towards the royal palace reciting verses from holy works. The students who are dull in studies walk in the front carrying jars full of water. Women from the city and the king's own harem begin to dance.[92] The warriors (vīrapuruśāḥ) carrying swords stand on guard on all sides of the nursing home (prasūtigṛha). The top plank of the gateway of the 'prasūtigṛha' is decorated with strings of fresh leaves of the trees. A pair of the auspicious jars ('maṅgala-kalaśa') filled with water is placed on the porch. The 'guggulu' incense is burnt to clear the air of the nursing home. Elderly ladies of the family after having washed their feet enter the nursing home ('prasūtigṛha) and pray for the new born's long life. They bless the new born by scattering flowers and rice (akṣata). Songs expressive of joy and blessing are sung. The courtyard of the palace is decorated with the paste of sandal ('hari candana'). The main (toraṇa) gate of the palace is decked for the occasion. The auspicious 'svastika' emblem is made everywhere with powdered gems.[93] On the sixth day, Goddess 'Ṣaṣṭhī Devī' (Skandamātā) is worshipped,[94] and a night-long vigil is observed.[95] The line of protection from evil influence (rakṣāmantrabhūtirekhā) is drawn near the bed of the mother with the recitation of mantras. The holy water is sprinkled and the auspicious lamps are lit. The elderly ladies sitting beside the bed of the mother recite 'mantras'.[96]

Nāmakaraṇa

According to *Tilaka-mañjarī,* the 'Nāmakaraṇa' saṁskāra was observed on the tenth day after the birth of the child.[97] But according to *Vyāsa Smṛti*, it fell on the eleventh day after the birth.[98] That very day all the temples of the city were visited for worship. The friends, relatives and gurus were paid due respects. Loads of gold and thousands of cows were gifted to Brāhmaṇas.[99]

Niṣkramaṇa

It was the ceremony of taking the infant out to see the sun. It took place in the fourth month of infancy.[100]

Annaprāśana

This saṁskāra, observed in the sixth month, marked the formal weaning of the sucking infant and his first feeding with solid (cereal) food.[101]

Cūḍākarma

This saṁskāra was celebrated generally in the third year after birth.[10] It was held to give tonsure to the child.

Karṇavedha

It was the ceremony of piercing the lobes of the child's ears.

Upanayana

It means initiation. Through this ceremony, the child entered upon the new life of 'Brahmacarya'. Dhanapāla gives a vivid description of this saṁskāra. According to him, the child was initiated to the austere life of a student on an auspicious day[103] at the age of six.[104]

On this day he wore Uttarīya of Kṣauma-cloth after taking bath. His body was besmeared with the fragrant sandal paste. Tilaka (auspicious mark) was applied on his forehead. He wore 'gaṇḍamālā' and worshipped Goddess 'Sarasvatī'.[105]

'Vedārambha', 'Keśānta' and 'Samāvartana'

These ceremonies were performed during the student life of a boy.

Vivāha

The Vivāha saṁskāra marked the end of the period of Brahmacarya and commencement of full manhood with entry into 'Gṛhastha Āśrama', which entailed the leading of married life and shouldering the responsibilities of a householder. From *Tilaka-mañjarī's* account it becomes evident that Vivāha saṁskāra was observed with great rejoicings. The marriage ceremony was not only the carrying out of a major saṁskāra but was also a festive occasion. Dhanapāla gives graphic descriptions of the preparations made before Tilaka-mañjarī's (the heroine's) wedding. The marriage ceremony is fixed for an auspicious hour determined by astrologers who are proficient in astronomy (grahagaṇita).[106] Friends and relatives are cordially invited to grace the occasion. A great maṇḍapa is erected. Delicious meals are served to the guests. The 'gurus' and Brāhmaṇas are paid the reverence due to them. Beggers are given alms.[107]

Tretāgni-Saṁgraha or Antyeṣṭi

With this saṁskāra ended one's bodily career on earth.

The existence of the four-fold āśrama system also becomes evident from the above account. King Meghavāhana in *Tilaka-mañjarī* is described as a protector and care-taker of the four varṇas as well as the four āśramas.[108] The āśrama system was a natural concomitant to the varṇa system. The four āśramas were : Brahmacarya (student life), Gṛhastha (married and domestic life), Vāṇaprastha (life in a hermitage) and Sannyāsa (life of renunciation and detachment).

Food and Drinks

The eating and drinking habits of the people of Northern India in Dhanapāla's days were the same as in earlier centuries.

"Śāli"[109] (rice) was a common cereal. It had various varieties, one of which known as 'kalama'[110] was particularly relished. Various preparations were made of it which are still liked. Rice, cooked in milk known as 'khīra', was very popular.[111] Another preparation was made by cooking rice in curds and was known as 'karamba'.[112] N.G. Mazumdar is of the opinion that rice cooked in curds and ghee was also offered to the Hindu gods.[113]

Another important cereal was barley (yava).[114] Dhanapāla speaks of the common corn[115] (Sādhāraṇa anna) known as 'yava' which was the staple food of the peasants and poorer sections of the society.[116]

Though wheat has not been particularly mentioned by Dhanapāla in his works, it was also a popular corn. Wheat is frequently referred to in contemporary literature.[117]

In his monograph, *Food and Drinks in Ancient India*, Dr. Om Prakash has quoted an ancient writer, Kṣīrasvāmin, who mentions the existence of the following food-grains in ancient India :

"Vrīhi, yava, masūra, godhūma, mudga, maṣa, tila, caṇaka, aṇu, priyaṅgu, kodrava, makuṣṭha, śāli, āḍhakī, kalāya, kulattha and ṣaṇa."[118]

Dhanapāla speaks of milk[119] in terms of an important food item of daily use. Curds (dahī), butter (sappī) and 'ghee' were prepared from milk.[120] A preparation made from it and mixed with spices was known as rasālā or 'mañjikā'.[121] In *Mānasollāsa*, we are also told that churned curds mixed with sugar and fumigated with camphor were also used as an invigorating drink.[122] In the opinion of Dr. Om Prakash, "Rasālā continued to be the most popular preparation of curds".[123]

Among the vegetables of the day, *Pāiyalacchīnāmamālā* mentions bottle gourd[124] (tumbaka) and beam[125] (samī). In *Mānasollāsa* cucumber, radish, brinjal and onions are mentioned.[126]

The notable fruits mentioned in Dhanapāla's works are cocoanut (nālikela) whose milk was also liked as a beverage,[127] plantain (kadalī), jackfruit (panasa), dates (piṇḍa khajūra),[128] orange (nāraṅga),[129] wood apple (bilva)[130] mango (āmra),[131] jujube (badarī),[132] tamarind (āmlikā)[133] etc. According to Dr. Om Prakash the common fruits in use during the period,

A.D. 750,—A.D. 1200, referred to in such works as *Pauma-cariu*, *karpūra-mañjarī*, *Bhavisayattakahā* were : orange, grape, dates, cocoanut, pomegranate, karamarda, mango, lakuca, banana, bread fruit and kapittha.[134]

Dhanapāla's society consisted of both the vegetarian and non-vegetarian people. Cooked meat[135] is referred to at various places. Various kinds of fish, big[136] as well as small,[137] were also used. Probably many an Āryan clan and other predominant races had been meat and fish eaters. At least meat eating was not anathema to them.

Alberunī states that animals and birds killed for obtaining meat included sheep, goat, gazelle, hare, rhinoceros, buffalo, fish, water and land fowl, sparrow, ringdoe, francolin doe, peacock etc. which were neither loathsome to men nor noxious.[138] From the food habits of Tāntrikas and Kāpālikas referred to in *Tilaka-mañjarī*, it is obvious that meat-eating was common in certain sections of contemporary society.[139]

Drinking of spirituous liquor was apparently quite common in Dhanapāla's time. Some of the popular liquors in use included Kâpiśāyana,[140] madirā, madhuvāra, sīdhu, Saraka or Śarkarā, madhu, Apakvarasa (avakkarasa) Kādambarī, prasannā, Hālā, Vāruṇī, Vinṭasurā, and piṭṭhakhauriā.[141] Vāgbhaṭṭa has listed eight kinds of liquors namely, surā, vaibhitakī, mārdvika, Kharjūra, Śarkarā, gauḍa, Śīdhu and madhvāsava.[142] In the opinion of B.N. Sharma 'surā' was the common name for all intoxicating liquors.[143] Rājaśekhara mentions that women liked to drink vāruṇī wine.[144] Special cups wrought with pearls were used for taking wine.[145] From *Tilaka-mañjarī* we learn that madirā (wine) was not taken by dvijas.[146] Dhanapāla has given an interesting description of a 'madhupānotsva' (drinking-festival). For such a party or function the members of the royal family resorted to pleasure gardens, in the company of their women folk (Vanitāsakhaiḥ).[147] The royal women also enjoyed drinking.[148] The Pānotosava appears to have been a common indulgence among the aristocracy in the XI century.[149] We are also told in *Mānasollāsa* that the members of the royal party on the occasion of a 'Pānotsava' sang, danced, laughed, muttered indistinct words abandoning themselves to the mood of the occasion. Under intoxication they sometimes rebuked one another and slept on bare ground.[150]

There are repeated references in *Tilaka-mañjarī* to the use of betel leaves[151] which were greatly relished by the gentry.[152] *Tilaka-mañjarī* speaks of the bearers carrying betels.[153] Betel leaves were offered to the guests on ceremonial occasions such as a birth-day party, a marriage party, and the like.[154] Betels were generally taken after meals.[155] Śriharṣa also refers to the custom of chewing betels[156] after a meal. Chewing of betels scented with camphor was popular among men as well as women.[157]

The pre-eminence enjoyed by the betel is borne out by the fact that the betel leaf was one of the essential articles used in offerings to the deities.[158]

In the pages of *Tilaka-mañjarī* Dhanapāla has drawn a very vivid and graphic picture of a dinner party held at the king's palace. The head of the kitchen ('paurogava') is well provided with stores of all kinds of provisions in the royal kitchen. The courtyard is sanctified with the coating of Cowdung for the Brāhmaṇas to sit there. Thousands of utensils of different shapes and sizes made of gold have been laid for dinner. The invitees numbering thousands gather in the courtyard for dinner. The had of the kitchen had standing instructions to take special care of the people of common stock among the invitees. With welcoming eyes, he observes their arrival, their partaking of food and departure.[159] When the cooking is over and the food is ready to be served, the 'Vaidya' who has occupied his seat near the king inspects the preparations thoroughly, In order to satisfy himself that the food is edible and free from poisonous elements he gives portions of it to birds such as the parrot, merle, cakora (red legged partridge), heron, cuckoo, etc. On clearance from him the food is then served by courtesans wearing glittering ornaments studded with pearls and attractive costumes.[160]

While serving, the courtesans cut jokes with the members of the royal families and their friends.[161] The modern cabaret dinners may bring to our mind these dinner parties of ancient India.

After the dinner is over, the guests clean their hands and

mouths, inhale sweet scent of camphor and musk mixed together and partake of betels.[162]

These dinners were so elaborate and sumptous that our forefathers in ancient India were without doubt far advanced in the culinary sciences and their cuisine can only make us envy them.

Cosmetics

In Dhanapāla's period people were obviously very fond of living fashionably. They used a variety of means to adorn themselves. *Tilaka-mañjarī* and *Pāiyalacchīnāmamālā* shed valuable light on the ornaments, hair styles, cosmetics and beauty aids popular in those days. King Meghavāhana in *Tilaka-mañjarī* uses a cosmetic (ointment) prepared with such ingredients as musk, camphor and sandal.[163] Camphor powder was used as face powder.[164] The 'abhisārikās' applied musk-based cosmetics upon their bodies including their private parts.[165]

The practice of applying collyrium to the eyes was quite common.[166]

Coiffure

The women of those days appear to be very particular about their coiffure. Dhanapāla has mentioned a number of hair-do's such as veṇī[167] (braided hair falling down on the back like a tail), kabarī, kuntalahāra, (braid), dhammilla (cluster of hair), keśahastaka (braid), mukuta (top lock); cūlā (top lock), śikhā (top lock), śikhaṇḍa (top lock), siṁhaliyā (top lock), chiḍā and caṭakas (top lock).[168] Great varieties in hair styles can be witnessed from the sculptures of khajurāho.

Costumes

Men and women of the day were fond of dressing well. Women wore uttarīya[169] (a piece of cloth like 'dupaṭṭā' or an 'oḍhanī' which covered the upper part of the body), kañcuka[170] (or bodice which was specially designed to cover the breasts) and nivasana[171] (an upper garment or petticoat worn round the waist). The nīvī,[172] a kind of cloth belt tc fasten the petticoat, is also mentioned. The abhisārikās often wore blue silk sarees in the night.[173]

From *Tilaka-mañjarī* we learn that in winter women put on Netra 'Kurpāsaka.[174] Alberunī mentions a female dress, namely, 'Kurtaka', a short shirt, with sleeves extending from the shoulders to the middle of the body and having slashes on both the right and left sides.[175] 'Kūrpāsaka' was like the 'Kurtaka' mentioned by Alberunī.

The veil is also referred to by Dhanapāla in *Pāiyalacchī-nāmamālā.*[176] Dr. B.N. Sharma is of the opinion that " 'Uttarīya or an aṁśuka used with a long Kañcuka was used to cover the head and might have served also as a veil".[177]

The two garments—the 'adhovastra' (Kaṭibhava)[178] and 'uttarīya'[179] (upper dress) were sufficient to cover the whole body of a man. Both the garments did not need any tailoring. The former was put on the lower part of the bady and the latter on the upper one. The 'uttarīya' appears to have been used both by men and women as mentioned in *Tilaka-mañjarī.*[180] Rājaśekhara is also of the same opinion.[181]

Men's head dress was called uṣṇīṣa (turban).[182] In *Tilaka-mañjarī* prince Samaraketū sits on horse back wearing a silk turban with his tunic firmly drawn.[183]

The cut and sewn garments of men were 'Kuñcuka' and vārabāṇa.[184] Kañcuka was a long robe of full sleeves coming upto the knees.[185] In *Pāiyalacchīnāmamālā* 'vārabāṇa' is referred to in terms of 'kañcuka'.[186] Prof. B.N. Sharma says, "Vārabāṇa, as it appears from the name, was a dress peculiar to soldiers. It is suggested by scholars that the design originally belonged to Irān and was later on adopted by the Indians. It was a full-sleeved coat coming upto the knees and thus less longer than a kañcuka.... The Persian name baravan, the Aramaic name varapanak, the Syriac name gurmanaka and the Arabic name zumanaqah are probably derived from one and the same original Iranian name".[187]

In *Tilaka-mañjarī*, we find references to different varieties of cloth such as 'dukūla',[188] 'aṁśuka',[189] citrapaṭṭa',[190] cīnāṁśuka,[191] paṭṭāṁśuka[192] and 'kṣauma'.[193] King Meghavāhana wears a 'dukūla vastra' while observing celibacy,[194] while *Tilaka-mañjarī* describes it as a variety of cloth.[195] Dr. Moti Chandra is of the opinion that dukūla was made from the bark of trees. The bark was beaten in a mortar to separate the fibres after being soaked in water. The fibres were turned into twines to be spun later on.[196] Dr. V.S. Agrawal on the other hand thinks that it was known as dukūla because it was available in the form of long pieces with two borders.[197] In *Pāiyalacchī-nāmamālā* aṁśuka is used as synonymous with cloth.[198] In *Amarakośa* as well, it is treated as synonymous with 'vastra' (cloth).[199] Dr. Agrawal holds that aṁśuka was a silk cloths.[200] In all probability, aṁśuka was a special kind of cloth, cotton as well as silken. About 'Cīnāṁśuka' and 'paṭṭāṁśuka' B.N. Sharma confidently asserts that these were silken cloth.[201] 'Citrapaṭṭa', in the opinion of Dr. V.S. Agrawal, might have been a variety of damask.[202] In *Tilaka-mañjarī* it is utilized for drawing paintings.

On the basis of Kṣīrsvāmin's commentary it becomes certain that Kṣauma was a variety of cloth prepared from Kṣauma or linseed flax.[203]

Ornaments

In Dhanapāla's time both sexes appear to have been fond of wearing various kinds of ornaments wrought in gold and studded with jewels and pearls. Some of the ornaments mentioned by Dhanapāla are hāra[204] (necklace), nūpura[205] (anklet), keyūra (bracelet), mekhalā[206] (girdle), cūḍā[207] (arm ring), kuṇḍala[208] (ear-ring), avacūla (a pendant ornament) also known as pralamba.[209] Dhanapāla names some varieties of hāra as, "muktāvalī,[210] (pearl string), 'muktāhāra,[211] 'nābhīcakracumbano hāra'[212] (the string falling down to the navel), ekāvalī[213] (single string), Krauñcamālā.[214]

Of Nūpura, he lists the important varieties as haṅsaka, mañjīra,[215] Śabdāla (noisy anklet), Siñjīra (noisy anklet), kaṇira,[216] keyūra was also known as 'angada'.[217] Notable varieties of 'Mekhatā' were 'kacchā', 'Kañcī' and 'rasanā'.[218] Cūḍā had its different varieties, namely, valayavāhu,[219] 'kanaka-kankana',[220] 'kalācikā'[221] 'kalāiā (forearm) and paṭṭā.[222]

Kuṇḍala's many varieties included Karṇāvataṁsa,[223] tala-patra,[224] uttaṁsa, avataṁsa, karṇāvalī, karṇapūra,[225] dantapātra and karṇapāśa.[226]

Superstitions & Occultism

The people during Dhanapāla's time were superstitious as is evident from *Tilaka-mañjarī.* The itching of the right eye was regarded auspicious.[227] A jackal crossing one's path from the right to left was considered a good omen. The blowing of air in the direction one was to go was also regarded to be auspicious. The working of the left nostril during the night was also thought to be a good omen.[228]

From the supernatural as well as medical (āyurvedika) point of view the burning of 'guggulu' incense was considered good. It was believed that its smoke killed germs. In *Tilaka-mañjarī* guggulu incense was burnt in the 'prasūtigṛha', so that the newly born child of queen Madirāvatī may not be adversely affected by the ill omened looks of the wicked women.[229]

Another occult practice prevailing in Dhanapāla's days was the wearing of amulets to get a desired results or to guard against evil. King Meghavāhana, in *Tilaka-mañjarī* ties an amulet to the arm of queen Madirāvatī with the chanting of mantras, so that she may beget a male issue.[230] The worship of ornaments and jewels was also considered propitious.[231]

The dreams occurring to the parents particularly to the mother before the birth of a child were variously interpreted as good or bad by the medieval astrologers. In Jaina literature a mother usually beholds certain dreams before conceiving a child. We learn from *Tilaka-mañjarī* that at the time of conceiving Harivāhana his mother saw the Airāvata elephant (Surendra-Vahāna) in her dream just before the break of dawn when tūrya (a musical instrument) was played upon to herald the day.[232]

At the time of the conception of Lord Mahāvīra, the last 'Tirthaṅkara' of Jains, his mother dreamt fourteen dreams in which she saw an elephant, a bull, a lion, the besprinkling of goddess Śrī, a garland, the moon, the sun, a banner, a jar, a lotus-pool, the sea, the celestial-palace, a heap of jewels and fire respectively.[233] Queen Māyā, the mother of Gautama Buddha, dreamt that a star in the form of a white elephant was entering into her womb.[234]

On account of the prevailing occult practices it is not surprising that Naimittika,[235] (fortune tellers) and Mauhūrtikas[236] (astrologers) and Śakuna-pāṭhaka,[237] (omen readers) commanded equal respect from the king and the pauper. Whenever any important enterprise was to be undertaken, astrologers were invariably consulted about the most auspicious time likely to yield successful results.[238] In *Tilaka-mañjarī*, astrologers are appointed to honoured positions in the royal court.[239]

General standard of the people

In the pages of *Tilaka-mañjarī* Dhanapāla projects an image of a cultured society where the common man is neither poor,[240] illiterate,[241] wicked,[242] or irreligious.[243] Most of them are satisfied[244], happy,[245] philanthropic[246] and used to virtuous life.[247] In spite of the fact that they are well read in 'policy', they are not deceitful.[248] They read 'Purāṇas', 'Dharmaśāstras', works of history,[249] poetry (kāvyas), drama (nāṭaka), prabandhas (epics),[250] tales and fables.[251] They are proficient in dramaturgy.[252] Habitually calm and peaceful, they never get angry.[253] They have learnt many languages.[254] Their conversation shines with flashes of wit.[255] In spite of the fact that they are quite adept in the erotic art,[256] they do not indulge in prostitution.[257] They are always inclined to adopt the virtues of others.[258] They are endowed with goodness, sincerity and purity.[259]

Although they are humorous, yet they do not make fun of others.[260] Though they are spirited and powerful, yet they are calm.[261] They are generous,[262] sweet-speaking.[263] Their good actions have ushered in 'Kalāyuga'.[264] In this congenial atmosphere Brāhmaṇas are happy.[265]

Means of Recreation

From a number of accounts recorded in *Tilaka-mañjarī*, we get a glimpse of the pleasures and pastimes which were in vogue in the X and XI centuries. Story-telling was the commonest source of amusement.[266] Story-telling sessions were held after meals.[267] The stories were generally based on Purāṇa and Itihāsa.[268] The people also took pleasure in listening to good poetry.[269] 'Kāvya-goṣṭhīs' were held for that purpose.[270] The learned held literary goṣṭhīs where the discussion centred round important questions of religion, ethics, philosophy and logic.[271] 'Subhāṣita-goṣṭhīs' are frequently mentioned in *Tilaka-mañjarī*.[272] In this type of goṣṭhī (gathering), self-composed witty sayings were recited.[273]

Jesters with their multi-coloured masks and motley dresses were a source of much amusement particularly to the ladies.[274] Performance of strange feats with artificial horses and elephants was another source of popular entertainment.[275]

People used to enjoy themselves through various types of games and pastimes. Gambling was a very popular pastime in ancient India.[276] Members of royal families played at stakes with pearls and jewels.[277]

An outdoor sport which was very popular among the Kṣatriya rulers was hunting. Royal princes were very fond of hunting.[278]

There were some indoor pastimes. One of these was playing with pet birds.[279] Another such pastime was painting pictures. Men and women often painted pictures of persons whom they loved and painting was considered as an essential part of the training of an accomplished girl.[280] It was usual for aristocrats to have in their mansions a room set apart for painting which was called citra-śālā.[281]

From *Tilaka-mañjarī* we learn that members of the royal family often amused themselves by arranging visits to pleasure gardens in the centre of which there was generally an artificial lake.[282] In shady bowers, artificial ponds, lakes and rivers the members of the royal family played games of all kinds.[283] They played water sports with the ladies of the harem in artificial ponds adjacent to the palace. Water-sports are frequently referred to in *Tilaka-mañjarī*. While playing water-sports, sometimes the rings of the ladies of the harem were thrown into the pleasure-pond. The members of the royal party then tried to salvage the rings from water. We are told by Dhanapāla that even, the hip-cloth worn by the ladies was removed from their hips.[284] Sometimes the rich enjoyed shower baths in special bath rooms (dhārāgṛha) in the summer season.[285] Ladies plucked flowers from the gardens and derived pleasure by arranging them in different forms.[286]

In the spring season when the cool and fragrant breeze of the south blew and the atmosphere was full of the pollen of flowers, the king often derived pleasure by arranging a visit to some nearby forest.[287] Groups of ladies enjoyed playing with bouncing balls.[288]

On the full-moon day of the spring season the members of the family derived pleasure from swaying on the swings slung across trees in the open.[289]

Festivals

Spring season was the occasion for the celebration of vasantotsava,[290] which according to Alberunī fell on the full-moon day of the month of 'Caitra'. He describes it as the festival for women when they put on their best dresses and ornaments and demanded presents from their husbands. The king was expected to participate in the festival.[291]

'Anaṅgotsava' (festival of the god of love) was another source of pleasure for the people.[292] According to *Sṛṅgāra-mañjarī-kathā* quoted by B.P. Majumdar in his *Social and Economic History of Northern India*, it fell on the 14th day of the bright half of Caitra and was celebrated with dancing, songs and merry-making.[293]

Dīpotsava[294] or Dīvālī was an important festival which was celebrated on the darkest night (amāvāsyā) in the month of Kārttika (October-November). According to *Yukti-kalpataru* all the houses in the city were white-washed and decorated with white flags and rows of lights on the terraces.[295]

Another popular festival, kaumudī-mahotsava,[296] mentioned in *Tilaka-mañjarī* fell on the full-moon day in the month of Kārttika. On this occasion houses and shops were decorated with flowers and flags. Both men and women put on their best clothes on this festive occasion and enjoyed themselves with singing and dancing.[297]

Lord Mahāvīra's birth ceremony (Jinajanma-mahotsava)[298] and death ceremony (niravāṇadivasa)[299] were also celebrated with great reverence.

Festivities were also arranged on some other occasions such as the birth of a son, on the sixth day after the birth of the child and on naming the child on the tenth day.[300] Another occasion of festive gathering was provided by the thirteenth day of the bright fortnight in 'Caitra' when the king derived pleasure from sprinkling coloured water on other people in the afternoon after lunch.[301]

The populace also enjoyed vocal and instrumental music.[302] Music conferences were organised.[303] Dancing was also a means of recreation.[304] Dramatic performances were also a source of popular amusement. Almost every house had a dramatic hall during those days.[305]

POSITION OF WOMEN

Women have contributed to the march of civilization everywhere in human society by filling every role assigned to them by nature —of sister, wife, mother and mistress of the house. Woman is the axis of the wheel of family. 'There is no family life without the mistress of the house', say our writers. Dhanapāla's *Tilaka-mañjarī* provides ample material for assessing the position of women in his times.

Dhanapāla, while drawing a vivid picture of the beauty of Ayodhayā[306] in *Tilaka-mañjarī*, mentions the manifold qualities of the head and heart possessed by the women of his age. They are described to be always busy in household affairs,[307] obeying their husbands and gurus.[308] They are hospitable and serve the guests in accordance with the instructions of the head of the family.[309] Their hospitality is not affected even when they are in sorrow.[310] They are modest,[311] tender,[312] peaceful[313] and indifferent to carnal pleasures.[314] They scrupulously follow the canons of their respective families.[315] They do not give up modesty, even if they are harmed.[316]

Even when they are angry, their faces do not betray any sign of it.[317] They speak sweet words, even when they are in conflict with others.[318] Dhanapāla chooses to call them noble ladies born of noble families.[319] The author of *Kuṭṭanīmata* says that a wife coming of a noble family is to a wiseman, the means of reaping good fruits of life here and hereafter.[320] The women in *Tilaka-mañjarī* are described to be the embodiment of 'Sakala-puruṣārtha' ('dharma', 'artha', 'kāma' and 'mokṣa').[321]

It is interesting to note that if Dhanapāla draws, on the one hand, a flattering picture of women of high morality, he does not hesitate to balance it by depicting ladies who are coquettish, fickle, unchaste and unfaithful. Dhanapāla blames it all on bad company saying that they are not wicked by nature.[322] They think of others, not of their husbands in their dreams.[323] While assuming chastity, they are not found constant and their fidelity is belied.[324] They are not tired of self-decorations and adornments.[325] Daṇḍi's *Dasakumāracarita* gives instances of conjugal infidelity yet lays stress on the wife's chastity and obedience to her husband as the ideal of Hindu woman.[326]

By and large, women of the day were religious-minded. In *Tilaka-mañjarī*, old women are described wearing white dress and carrying pots of copper on their way to the temples.[327] Dhanapāla describes women plucking flowers for the worship of 'devas' (deities).[328] The wives of Brāhmaṇas are represented as taking keen interest in the religious activities of their husbands.[329]

The cultivation of fine arts like music, dancing and painting as desirable accomplishments for girls of goods families was recognized in ancient India. Among the arts which ladies in cultured families were expected to cultivate, the *Kāmasūtra* assigns the most important place to dancing and music.[330] In *Tilaka-mañjarī*, we meet Malaya Sundarī who is not only a well-read girl but also an expert dancer.[331] The heroine, Tilaka-mañjarī, is an accomplished girl in practically every art that a princess or a girl of an aristocratic family was expected to cultivate.[332] Gandharvadattā, a girl of ten years, is described to be proficient in the art of dancing ('lāsyavidyā').[333] Not only the ladies of royal blood but the women of common stock were also adept in fine arts. Citralekhā, the nurse, in *Tilaka-mañjarī* is said to be well-versed in the art of painting,[334]

Tilaka-mañjarī describes women to be well-versed in all the branches of knowledge, proficient in languages spoken in all the States and well read in 'Paurāṇic' stories.[335] They write letters to their spouses.[336] The heroines in *Viddhaśālabhañjikā*[337] and *Karpūra-mañjarī*[338] are represented as composing poems and writing letters to their husbands.

Girls in ruling and Kṣatriya families used to receive a fairly good amount of military and administrative training. The girls of royal blood in *Tilaka-mañjarī* are described learning 'dhanurveda'[339] (knowledge in the use of bow). We hear of thousands of women in *Tilaka-mañjarī* working as body-guards.[340] From classical sources we learn that Candragupta Maurya had a guard of women.[341] In *Karpūra-mañjarī*, we find the queen's attendants bearing swords, shields, bows, arrows, lances and staffs.[342]

Women discharging a number of responsible duties are mentioned in *Tilaka-mañjarī*. Some women worked as gate-keepers,[343] messengers,[344] treasury-incharge,[345] post-carriers,[346] śayanapālī[347] (incharge of bed chamber) and spies.[348] But according to Dr. Altekar, these careers were probably not open to women from higher classes.[349]

As a general rule men were monogamous, and polygamy was an indulgence that the rich and ruling sections of the society could alone afford. The kings and princes considered it a royal prerogative to have a crowded harem. King Meghavāhana in *Tilaka-mañjarī* is said to have many wives.[350] Alberunī's observations in the matter are quite interesting. He says, "Some Hindus think that the number of the wives depends upon the caste; that accordingly, a Brāhmaṇa may take four, a Ksatriya three, a Vaiśya two wives and a Śūdra one".[351]

Love marriages were not unknow during this period. We hear of Gāndharva[352] and Svayaṁvara[353] marriages in *Tilaka-mañjarī*. But by and large, society recognised the father's right to find a suitable match for his daughter, to give her away in marriage to a bridegroom. A very fine intance of this convention is provided in *Tilaka-mañjarī* by the couple, Tāraka and Priyadarśanā, who are crazily in love with each other yet await their parent's sanction before marrying.[354]

Similarly the marriage of Tilaka-mañjari with Harivāhana was arranged by the parents of both the parties. Their marriage took place on the auspicious day[355] fixed for the ceremony and the bridegroom and his party were received at the bride's house with great honour and were entertained with food, drink etc.[356] Thus the forms of marriage mentioned in *Tilaka-mañjarī* may be classified into three types: Gāndharva, Svayaṁvara and arranged marriages.

Early marriages appear to have been in vogue during Dhanapāla's time. *Tilaka-mañjarī*'s account with regard to this is interesting, where we read that marriages were sometimes arranged even before birth.[357] Alberunī informs us that the Hindus married at a very young age.[358] A Brāhmaṇa was not allowed to marry a woman above twelve years of age.[359] The prevalance of early marriage is also attested by *Nītivākyāmṛta* of Somadeva which says that a girl of twelve and a youth of sixteen are fit for matrimonial alliance.[360] In aristocratic families the marriage of girls took place on their reaching the age of sixteen or so. In *Tilaka-mañjarī* we find Priyadarśanā,[361] Malaya Sundarī[362] and heroine, Tilaka-mañjarī[363] fully grown up before they are married.

Sometimes the parents of the girl preferred to keep their son-in-law in their own house, instead of sending their daughter to her mother-in-law's house. (This practice called 'ghara jamāī' in the vernacular continues to the present day). In *Tilaka-mañjarī*, Tāraka, the son-in-law of Jalaketu began to live in his father-in-law's house after marriage. Jalaketu who was well-to-do, gave all his property including his boats to his son-in-law and made him head of the mariners in his employ.[364]

Satī-system also seems to have been prevalent at this time. *Tilaka-mañjarī* mentions slave girls preparing to burn themselves on the funeral pyre on hearing the death of their husbands.[365] Alberunī's statement also confirms this practice. According to him, "If a wife loses her husband by death, she cannot marry another man. She has only to choose between two things—either to remain a widow as long she lives or to burn herself and the latter eventually is considered the preferable, because as a widow she is ill-treated as long as she lives".[366] Among the instances of women who committed 'satī' during this period are a Queen of king Yaśaskara of Kashmir and a Queen of his successor, Kṣemagupta.[367]

Courtesans enjoyed an important position in ancient India.

They were the cynosure of Indian cities and courts. Amaracanda in his *Kāvyakalpalatāvṛtti* insists that the description of a city should among other things touch upon a 'Veśyā' most probably because the institution was one of its common features.[368] Dhanapāla dutifully includes them in the description of the city of Ayodhyā.[369] B.N. Sharma is of the opinion that, "if one king could grace his court and capital with a team of courtesans, the other too felt induced to imitate him whatever his own views might have been about the matter".[370] "The kings", observes Alberunī, "make them an attraction of their cities, a beat of pleasure".[371]

The courtesans in ancient days were not degraded women but were talented women of physical, intellectual and artistic charm whose company was much sought after by respectable citizens. Dhanapāla speaks very highly of courtesans in *Tilakamañjarī*. They are said to be very beautiful and have the likeness of the maidens of 'Alakāpurī'.[372] The beauty of their feet excels that of lotuses.[373] Some of them surpass even the goddess Pārvatī in beauty.[374]

These courtesans worship the moon-goddess daily for preserving their beauty.[375] The god Kāmadeva himself is allured by the bewitching beauty of their faces and desires them.[376] Even kings are easily infatuated by their beauty and would fain sacrifice every thing for them.[377] These courtesans are not unduly conceited of their looks, though they are adept in the erotic art.[378] They are not over-conscious of their dresses and do not care for make up.[379] They are not proud of their youth[380] and do not hanker after luxurious living.[381] The ornaments they wear are no less than a burden to them.[382] In spite of the fact that they know nine ways of Rati, they do not indulge in love making with men of low dignity.[383] They are not after lucre only,[384] but are attracted by men's virtues in the manner of goddess Lakṣmī who was attracted by the virtues of Viṣṇu.[385]

The courtesans also do benevolent and virtuous deeds.[386] They are proficient in observing social etiquettes.[387] They believe in the principle that the world is to be enjoyed.[388] They are unaware of the yoga-mārga.[389]

The courtesans are described to be adept in fine arts. From

Kalāvilāsa we learn that they were expected to be proficient in as many as sixty-four 'kalās' (arts).[390] In *Tilaka-mañjarī* they are described to be adept in the art of coition.[391] Another fine art in which the courtesans were well-versed was that of 'Vaiśika'.[392] Jagdish Chandra Jain is of the opinion that in order to learn this art people from distant places approached the courtesans.[393] The courtesans had expert knowledge of human psychology and were skilled in painting.[394] The *Bṛhatkalpa-bhāṣya* refers to a courtesan who had a nice picture gallery in which she had painted the characteristics of different castes and also the different phases of *ars amoris*, beautifully depicting the reconciliation of lovers. She took every visitor to her picture gallery and asked what pictures he liked most. From the answer of the man she understood his caste, his artistic taste, the weakness as well as the strength of his nature.[395]

We hear in *Tilaka-mañjarī* about Kṛṣṇābhisārikās who having put on black dress, long braided hair, and cosmetics of musk and nut solicit men in the night from far and near.[396] The apsrās arranged dance shows in the evening.[397] The prostitutes who entertained the people in various ways are referred to in *Tilaka-mañjarī* by the names of 'paṇyavanitās,[398] vāravanitās,[399] Veśyas,[400] and gaṇikās.[401] We find concrete instances of the better types of gaṇikās[402] as well as of the common variety.[403] A gaṇikā in ancient India was highly respected by the people in general. According to Vātsyāyana her mind was cultivated and trained by a thorough education and she was a woman of various artistic accomplishments.[404]

From the evidence provided by Dhanapāla we may conclude that the women of his age were mostly religious, hospitable, educated, adept in fine arts and efficient in managing the affairs of the family. The prostitutes were not fallen women but highly talented entertainers. Polygamy, early marriage and the custom of satī were in vogue. Members of the royal families indulged in prostitution and were polygamous.

EDUCATION

Education (Vidyā) rightfully occupied the pride of place in

social set up in ancient times. The renowned author of *Nītiśataka* says: "Vidyā is the highest ornament that a man possesses. It is a valuable hidden thing to be carefully guarded for it gains food, glory and blessing. It is the lord of the lords and is honoured among kings even more than wealth. A man devoid of education and wisdom is noting but a beast".[405]

Dhanapāla's *Tilaka-mañjarī* throws sufficient light on the educational system of his age, touching on such subjects as the "Gurukula system" the subjects of study for men and women including facilities available for training in fine arts. One of the Saṁskāras, 'Upanayana', which literally means leading a student to the teacher, was the first step towards the education of a child. In *Tilaka-mañjarī*, we read that the education of a boy began with this Saṁskāra[406] at the age of six.[407] Bāṇa also corroborates this. Like Harivāhana in *Tilaka-mañjarī* Candrāpīḍa, the hero of Bāṇa's Kādambarī, was sent to school when he was six.[408] Apparently the school-going age in those days was six.

But from other sources we learn that boys of the three higher varṇas (classes), viz., 'Brāhmaṇa', 'Kṣatriya' and Vaiśya, were initiated to education when they were eight, eleven and twelve years respectively.[409] The initiation of the child into three R's took place on an auspicious day in a festive atmosphere. We are told by Dhanapāla that the child after bath wore Uttarīya made of 'kṣauma' cloth, sandal wood paste was applied on his body, a garland of pearls was put around his neck and tilaka (auspicious paint of gruel) was applied on his forehead. Sarasvatī, the goddess of learning, was worshipped and gurus were venerated.[410] By the time a boy attained the age of sixteen he was expected to have become the master of all sciences and arts.[411] Thus according to *Tilaka-mañjarī*, within the course of ten years the boy theoretically knew all the subjects of study. During his student life, he worked deligently and regularly.[412]

Subjects of Study

According to *Tilaka-mañjarī* there were four faculties of education (vidyā),[413] namely, Ānvīkṣikī (philosophy), Trayī (the knowledge of four 'Vedas', 'Sikṣā', 'Kalpa', 'Vyākaraṇa',[414]

'Nirukti', 'Chhandas', 'Jyotiṣa',[415] 'Itihāsa', Purāṇas, Mīmāṁsā, 'Nyāya' and 'Dharmaśāstras', etc.), Vārtā (the science of agriculture, cattle breeding and commerce) and Daṇḍanīti[416] (politics). These four traditional faculties were further subdivided into fourteen vidyās[417] (disciplines).

The fourteen vidyās according to *Yājñavalkayasmṛti*[418] included the four Vedas, six Vedāṅgas (Chhandas—metre, 'Sikṣā'—phonetics, 'Nirukti'—exegesis, 'Kalpa'—ritual, 'Vyakaraṇa'—grammar and 'Jyotiṣa'—astronomy—astrology), 'Purāṇas', 'Nyāya', 'Mimāṁsā' and 'Dharmaśāstras'.

Fine arts like dancing, music and painting[419] are also mentioned by Dhanapāla as forming an essential part of the curriculum prescribed for the princes. According to Dhanapāla, Ethics,[420] Poetics,[421] Dramaturgy,[422] Mathematics,[423] Āyurveda,[424] Weaponry,[424] Archery[426] (Aśtravidyā), Shipping,[427] Omen-reading[428] and Spells and Magic[429] were some of the more popular subjects of study.

References in *Tilaka-mañjarī* reveal that the sciences of Linguistics,[430] Eroticism[431] and Lexicography[432] were regarded as important subjects of study.

Dhanapāla's account is corroborated by Haribhādra Sūri who lists eighty-five branches of learning in *Samarādityakathā*.[433]

Another work, *Milinda-pañho*,[434] mentions the following nineteen arts and sciences as subjects (śilipa) of study:—(1) Suti (holy tradition), (2) Sammuti (secular law), (3) Saṅkhyā (4) Yogā, (5) nīti (nyāya), (6) Visesikā, (7) Gaṇikā (arithmetic), (8) Gandhabbā (music), (9) Tikiccā (medicine), (10) Catubbedā, (11) Purāṇa, (12) Itihāsa, (13) Jotisā, (14) Māyā (magic), (15) 'Hetu' (Causation), (16) Mantanā (polity), (17) Yudha (art of war), (18) Chhandas (poetry), and (19) Muddā (Conveyancing).

Women's Education

Women of Dhanapāla's age were comparatively very well-read. They learnt fine arts like music, dancing[435] and painting.[436] Girls of royal families received military training and learnt archery ('dhanurvedaṁ').[437] Quite a number of women were very learned indeed and knew probably all the languages spoken in India in those days.[438] Courtesans who pursued the oldest profession on earth knew all that was there to know about the art of coition[439] and Vaiśika.[440]

In *Tilaka-mañjarī*, Dhanapāla has casually referred to eighteen scripts.[441] The names of these eighteen scripts are found in *Pannavaṇasūtra* thus:[442] (1) Bambhī, (2) Javanāli, (3) Dośapuriā, (4) Kharoṭṭhī, (5) Pukkharasāriyā, (6) Bhogavaiyā (7) Pahārāiyā, (8) Upaanta rikkhiyā, (9) Akkharapitthiyā, (10) Tevaṇaiyā, (11) Gi (ṇi) rāhaiyā, (12) Aṅkalivi, (13) Ganita-ilvi, (14) Gaṅdhavvalivi, (15) Ādaṅsalivi, (16) Māhesarī, (17) Dāmitnī, (18) Polindī. Harivāhana is described to have learnt a number of scripts.[443]

Literary Seminars (Goṣṭhīs)

Dhanapāla mentions literary Seminars and poetical symposiums where experts and scholars in such subjects as poetry, music and other fine arts met and discussed the topics of their interest in a lively manner. Sometimes kings and courtiers also participated in these literary gatherings and exercised their brains in interpreting verses and solving questions of intricate nature.[444] Bāṇa also makes a mention of such Goṣṭhīs.[445] The Goṣṭhīs mentioned in *Tilaka-mañjarī* must have done a lot to further the cause of education.

Centres of Education

Dhanapāla informs us that education was imparted in the gurukulas,[446] vidyāmaṭhas,[447] endowed with landed property[448] and agrahāra villages.[449] The institution of schools attached to temples and 'maṭhas' may have been an imitation of the Buddhist schools attached to the Buddhist Vihāras. Kalhaṇa has recorded that king Yaśaskara of Kashmir built a maṭha for the students of Āryadeśa who went there in quest of learning,[450] From *Tilaka-mañjarī* we learn that a 'Gurukula' situated in the heart of the capital was built by king Meghavāhana.[451] There were a number of eminent teachers employed in the school who were given assistance of all kinds by the king. The teachers. born of high families, were men of character and righteous inclination.[452]

Aims of Education

The aims of the Gurukula System, according to *Tilaka-mañjarī*, were to impart sound education in all the branches of sciences and arts[453] and to inculcate the virtues of truth and righteousness.[454] The student reading in a Gurukula also learnt manners, etiquettes and cultivated modesty and humility.[455] The Gurukula education was meant for allround development of a man's personality:[456] "It was so designed as to broaden the student's outlook on life, give him enlightenment, sharpen his intellect and establish his character through the development of his personality".[457] Besides mental development, the student developed a strong and healthy body in the gurukula.[458]

Dhanapāla has given a general account of education in *Tilaka-mañjarī* and has not specifically mentioned the courses prescribed for study for Brāhmaṇas, Kṣatriyas, Vaiśyas and Śūdras separately. For the most part, the picture of education which he has drawn is in relation to the princes and princesses of the ruling and royal Kṣatriya families. From the account given by Dhanapāla we learn that the princes were taught the four traditional subjects (ānvīkṣīki, trayī, vārtā and Daṇḍanīti),[459] though special stress in their case was laid on the science of politics (daṇḍanīti).[460] The princes were to be proficient in the use of different weapons of war. Harivāhana mastered all śastras and kalās[461] and also learnt the fine arts.[462]

So far as the education of Brāhmaṇas is concerned, it is exemplified in Dhanapāla's own case. He was able to attain proficiency in Saṁskṛta, Prākṛta and Apabhraṁsa and to compose a number of works in these languages. He was well-versed in Vedas, Vedāṅgas, Smṛitis, Itihāsa, Purāṇas and Dhārmaśāstras.[463] (A fuller account of Dhanapāla's life and works appears in Chapter 1).

Although a clear account of the education given to a Vaiśya has not been given by Dhanapāla, we may well presume that such learning as helped in making money through trade, agriculture and cattle breeding was considered desirable for a Vaiśya. In *Bhavisayattakahā* written by Dhanapāla, Dhakkara, the son of Jaina merchant, is said to have learnt Jaina scriptures, grammar, lexicography, astronomy and many practical arts like wrestling, archery, the science of horses and elephants and other similar arts.[464] In *Tilaka-mañjarī*, Tāraka, who is Vaiśya by caste, is said to have heard Dharmaśāstras and learnt arts and sciences deligently.[465] He has also learnt the art of shipping.[466]

About the education of Śūdras, we may deduce a lot from the example of Citralekhā, the nurse in *Tilaka-mañjarī*, who is said to be proficient in the art of painting. It is evident that even the lower classes had some acquaintance with fine arts, besides being proficient in machanical, technical and manual works traditionally done by them.

INDUSTRY AND TRADE

Industry

Tilaka-mañjarī and *Pāiyalacchīnāmamālā* bear testimony to the existence of many cottage industries in the X and XI centuries in North India. *Yuktikalpataru* of Bhoja also provides a detailed account of the principal industries existing during the period. However, there is no evidence to show that any large-scale industry existed in this period. Some cities, towns and regions became famous for particular industries. The artisans of the day were credited with exquisite workmanship bequeathed from father to son for generations.

Textile Industry

We know from the description of *Tilaka-mañjarī* and *Pāiyalacchīnāmamālā* that men and women used various kinds of clothes. Some of the principal types of cloth manufactured in textile industries were white-dukula,[467] 'aṁśuka'[468] (silk-cloth), 'raktāṁśuka'[469] (red-silk), 'harita-paṭṭāṁśuka'[470] (green-silk), 'kṣauma'[471] (linen cloth, prepared from linseed flax), 'citrapaṭṭa'[472] (canvas used for paintings), 'navaraṅga'[473] (garment of nine colours or red cloth) and 'Vitāna' (tent cloth).[474]

Among the garments worn by men & women 'uttarīya'[475] (upper garment), 'katibhava'[476] (lower garment), 'avaguṅṭhana'[477] (veil), 'kurpāsaka'[478] (cotton garment), 'kañcuka'[479] (bodice), 'uṣinīṣa'[480] (head dress) and 'kambala'[481] (woollen blanket) are particularly mentioned. Dr. B.P. Majumdar quotes *Yaijayantī* of Yādavaprakāśa to the effect that north Indians used mosquito-nets in the XI century.[482]

The main centres of textile industry, according to B.P. Majumdar, were Bengal, Kāmarūpa, Magadha, Madurā, Aparānta. Kaliṅga, Kāśī, Vatsa and Mahiṣa.[483]

It is of interest to note that *Pāiyalacchīnāmamālā* refers to the existence of 'kuvinda'[484] (weaver), 'Chimpā'[485] (dyer) and 'rajaka'[486] (washerman).

Iron and Metal Industries

Of the metal industries, the iron industry seems to have been the most important one, because various types of weapons of war, like swords, spears, machines, agricultural implements, weights and measures were made of iron.

In *Tilaka-mañjarī*, we read that the shops had locks which were made of iron.[487] Tavā[488] (pan) of iron for caking bread and iron spoon[489] are also referred to in *Pāiyalacchīnāmamālā*.

The setting up of famous Iron pillar at Dhārā, the capital of Paramāras, has been the greatest achievement of the Paramāra dynasty in the field of metallurgy.[490] It has been estimated to have originally reached a height of 50′ and is considered to be the highest pillar of its kind in the world.

Other important metal industries were of brass, silver[491] and gold,[492] as the household utensils in *Tilaka-mañjarī* are described to be made of these metals. Vimānas[493] and jars[494] were made of gold. Idols of deities were often made of gold. In *Tilaka-mañjarī* we find the idol of Mahāvīra made of gold.[495] A great variety of ornaments were made of gold and studded with precious stones.[496]

Mirrors

According to *Tilaka-mañjarī*, mirrors manufactured from gems were called 'ratnadarpaṇa,[497] or 'maṇidarpaṇa'.[498] We are told in *Yuktikalpataru* that mirrors were manufactured from gold (suvarṇa), silver (rajata), lead (trapu) and iron (loha).[499] It is the opinion of Dr. B.P. Majumdar that mirrors which figure in Pāla art, Khajurāho and Bhuvaneśvara were made of brass or gem.[500] *Pāiyalacchīnāmamālā* mentions mirrors made of glass also.[501]

Wood Industry

Wood has always been put to a great and varied use through the centuries. In *Tilaka-mañjarī*, we read of boats manufactured from hard wood.[502]

In *Yuktikalpataru* there is a detailed description of various kinds of boats used in ancient times. Different kinds of timber used for making these vessels has also been mentioned.[503] Chariots,[504] Carts,[505] pīṭhas[506] (seat or couch) and bed-steads[507] were also made of wood. The 'pīṭhas' studded with gold[508] and precious stones[509] are mentioned in *Tilaka-mañjarī*. Carpenters[510] skilled in the manufacture of wooden furniture are mentioned in *Pāiyalacchīnāmamālā*. A statue of goddess 'Lakṣmī' in *Tilaka-mañjarī* is described to be made of wood.[511] A fine statue of winged Garuḍa made of wood has been found during the excavations of Raghurāmapura. The statue is preserved now in Dacca museum.[512] Another example of excellent wood work is a pillar from the sun temple of Katārmal of the X century A.D. which has been brought from the Himalayan area of Uttar Pradesh.[513]

Sugar Industry

The cultivation of sugarcane[514] seems to have been popular during Dhanapāla's time. The existence of sugar industry can be verified from the fact that the accounts in the epigraphs mention gur or brown sugar being produced in such abundance that it was taxed by the kings.[515]

Umbrella-making

As referred to in *Pāiyalacchīnāmamālā*,[516] the making of umbrellas appears to have been a popular craft during those days. *Yuktikalpataru* supplies a detailed description about the making of umbrellas.[517] A copper plate grant of king Trilocanapāla Cālukya of Lāṭadeśa of the Śaka Era 972 (A.D. 1050) records the dedication of an umbrella to God Somanātha by Vatsarāja, father of Trilocanapāla.[518] In *Tilaka-mañjarī*, a painter has drawn a portrait of a girl who is shown beneath an umbrella held by her attendants.[519]

Ivory

The ivory industry appears to have been an important industry of the time. In *Tilaka-mañjarī*, we read that the balconies of the palace of king Meghavāhana were made of ivory.[520] The *Sṛṅgāramañjarī-kathā* of Bhoja[521] and *Mānasollāsa* of Someśvara[522] also corroborate this. We are told in *Mānasollāsa* that the king's seat, called 'sukhāsana', was covered with lion's skin and studded with gold. The ivory poles fixed under it enabled the four bearers to carry it aloft.[523] The legs of cots and bedsteads were also made of ivory.[524]

Jewels and Ornaments

The craft of the jeweller and ornament-maker appears to have been a very prominent one in ancient India. Different kinds of jewels like muktā,[525] maṇi[526] (pearl), ratna[527] (diamond), Cintāmaṇi,[528] Vaidūrya,[529] padmarāga[530] (ruby) are referred to in the works of Dhanapāla. The Tanjore temple inscriptions distinguish between numerous varieties of diamonds, rubies and pearls and enumerate the flaws to be found in these gems.[531] We read about 'Pradhanaratnakośa'.[532] (chief treasury of diamonds) and 'Pradhānaratnakośādhyakṣa'[533] (Treasury Officer, diamond treasury) in *Tilaka-mañjarī*. The people in general were fond of wearing ornaments. *Tilaka-mañjarī* and *Pāiyalacchīnāmamālā* describe various types of ornaments made of precious metals, like gold and silver and studded with various types of precious stones.[534]

Perfumaries

Men and women of Malwa made ample use of various kinds of perfumes.[535] This leads us to presume the existence of a highly developed perfumery industry.

The works of Dhanapāla refer to some other industries viz., making of watches[536] and musical instruments,[537] ropes[538] and armours,[539] pottery,[540] dyeing of clothes,[541] leather work,[542] small bells,[543] sword-hilts,[544] scabbards,[545] balls,[546] machinery for drawing water (water wheel),[547] metallic vessels,[548] cane work[549] etc.

It is evident that Northern India during Dhanapāla's time had made a significant advance in the field of cottage industries. The word 'śilpī' certainly refers to skilled workmen adept in different handicrafts. The artisans and craftsmen engaged in different industries generally carried on their work in their own cottages. As the joint family system was the order of the day, the industrial units in the X and XI centuries were owned and run by families rather than individuals. People belonging to the same vocational caste lived together in villages and towns and had separate localities assigned to them.

TRADE

India during Dhanapāla's time was a great trading centre engaged in inter-state and foreign trades. The merchants who took to inter-state trading generally travelled in groups and caravans for fear of robbers. Dhanapāla, describing the outskirts of a city in *Tilaka-mañjarī*, mentions the caravans of traders camping there.[550]

Trade was carried on both by land and sea. There are references to carriage streets in *Tilaka-mañjarī*.[551] Arrangements for the supply of drinking water to the way-farers were always made. *Tilaka-mañjarī* describes a water reservoir for the use of travellers on the outskirts of the city. Its banks were surrounded by circular white-washed cloister (varaṇḍikā). It was made of compact piles of bricks and had rows of stairs going down into the water.[552]

The conscientious kings maintained charitable houses where travellers coming from other parts were given food, hot water and oil to remove their fatigue and for the purpose of encouraging travelling and trading in the country. Adequate provisions were made for board and lodging in the night-halts built for the use of travellers.[553] In *Tilaka-mañjarī*, the king is found appointing officers and giving them the charge of providing food, drink, beds and medicine to the poor, the orphans, the travellers and the carvan men in the charitable houses which had reportedly been closed down.[554]

In *Tilaka-mañjarī* we read descriptions of traders, businessmen[555] (vaṇikas), trading centres and market places.[556] The capi tal cities as well as big towns had different markets specializing in different commodities. There occurs a reference to *haṭṭa*[557] in *Pāiyalacchīnāmamālā* meaning probably the market places in villages. According to *Tilaka-mañjarī*, shops in the main trading centre used to be built in lines.[558] Road-side trading was carried out through chariots.[559]

Though Dhanapāla has not specified the principal commodities in which the merchants traded, the epigraphic evidence indicates that internal trading was done mostly in wheat, barley, pulses, sugar, candied sugar, jaggery, clarified butter, oil, resins, spices like nutmeg and pepper, cocoanut, dates, sesame, musk, sandal, camphor, agar, hiṅgula, triphalā, mahuā. Bengal madder, mañjiṣṭhā, horses, cattle fodder, thread, textiles, gold, silver, ivory and the like.[560]

The rich merchants of the day did export and import trade with foreign countries such as Persia,[561] China,[562] Dvīpāntara[563] (South East Asia) and Siṁhaladvīpa[564] by the land and sea routes. The use of ships for trade is frequently mentioned in *Tilaka-mañjarī*[565] and other contemporary literature. Trade with Persia and China was carried on by the land route as well.

Dhanapāla has referred to Kāpiśāyana, the wine imported from Kapiśā valley (the military base of the Persians at Spet-verez)[566] in *Tilaka-mañjarī*. According to Dhanapāla, it was a favourite drink in royal circles and was reddish in colour like the eyes of a woman burning with hatred for her co-wife or the petals of the red lotus.[567] *Arthaśāstra* of Kauṭilya makes it crystal clear that 'Kāpiśāyana' was produced in the region around Kapiśī (Begram) from green grapes.[568] It is likely that this wine was imported into India from Persia during Dhanapāla's time. A few years ago, a Russian archaeological mission led by M.E. Masson discovered a large wine cellar in the remains of the Parthian capital at Nisa, eleven miles northwest of Ashkabad, the modern capital of Turkmenia. In that wine cellar nearly 200,000 litres of wine were once kept in clay pitchers.[569] This evidence suffices to believe that India had trade relations with Persia and wine from Kāpiśi came to India by the north-western route. Ibn Khordadbah has given a detailed account of a road to eastern countries from Karkuz in Persia to Nārmasīrā on the boundary between Persia and Sind and connected with Debal.[570] Al-Berunī has sketched the routes from the country of Nimroz or Sijistan and the route from Kabul to India, adding that there must be other possible routes.[571] According to Kālidasa, Raghu led his famous expedition against the Persians (Pārasīkas) along the land route.[572] A considerable number of horses imported into India came along the overland route. Yādavaprakāśa tells us that Bāhlīka (Balkha) was sending not only its horses[573] but also saffron and asafoetida to India.[574]

In the list of imports from China to India the pride of place goes to the Chinese silk which has been referred to in *Tilakamañjarī*.[575] In the mathematical text *Gaṇitasārasaṅgraha*[576] two problems are set involving numerous large places of Chinese silk. Dr. Lallanji Gopal is of the opinion that India also received gold and silver from China.[577] A Tamil inscription of the early years of the XI century indicates that South India was receiving Chinese gold by way of Indonesia.[578]

The overland route connecting India with China passed through Bihar to Tibet and from there to China: "It was the lucrative trade passing through Tibet and Assam to China that led Mongols and also Indian kings to make efforts to dominate these regions".[579]

Indian merchants went to Dvīpāntara (Suvarṇadvīpa or Indonesian islands of Jāvā, Sumātrā and Bāli) by sea route.[580] Camphor, areca-nuts, betel plants, sandal trees, lavaṅga, lavalī, cocoanut, plantain, panasa, piṇḍa-khajūra, rājatālī, tamāla and mandāra are described in *Tilaka-mañjarī* to be the prized products of Dvīpāntara.[581] We are also told that there were many mines of gems, gold and silver in the islands of South East Asia and that the area also abounded in pearls.[582] It may be presumed that Indian merchants used to buy camphor, sandal wood, silver, gold and gems from these islands. In *Samarāicchakahā*, we are told that merchants who went to the islands of South East Asia brought jewels from there.[583] They also brought with them blocks of gold marked with their names.[584]

As regards imports from Ceylon, probably the most important item according to the narration of *Tilaka-mañjarī*, was pearls. We are told that Meghavāhana's palace was filled with the hard stones of pearls brought from Ceylon.[585] Someśvara refers to the fine fabrics which were imported into India from Ceylon.[586]

India had trade relations with Arab countries too. Trade ties between India and Arabia were strengthened in the post-Harṣa period. The swords, iron-goods, ivory, pearls, jewels, teak-wood, cane, bamboo, camels, Sindhi fowl, velvet, cotton and silken textiles, camphor, sandal wood, mushk, ginger and a variety of spices and medicines were imported by the Arabs from India.[587] Abī Dulf Musir bin Mulhil, who visited India in A.D. 942-943, records that from Trāvancore was imported earthen-ware called Ghazayar which was known as China-ware in Arabia.[588] It has been recorded by Masudi and Bushārī that the shoes of Cambay were imported in abundance and were very much liked by the Arabs.[589] According to Masudi, peacocks were in great demand among the Arabs and a large number of them were exported to Iraq for breeding purposes.[590] "The love of Arabs for Indian commodities was so much that they used to name their favourite fair daughters as Hindā and Saifi-Hindī, after their dream land—India."[591]

AGRICULTURE

Agriculture has remained the mainstay of the Indian people since earliest times. In *Pāiyalacchīnāmamālā*, we hear of 'halika'[592] (husband man) who tilled the land with hala (plough).[593]

Crops

The principal crop throughout Northern India appears to have been that of paddy.[594] In *Pāiyalacchīnāmamālā*, women are referred to be watching the fields of rice.[595] A constant vigil kept by the night watchmen[596] makes it clear that theft of the standing crops must have been a real fear for the cultivators in those days. Among other grains barley[597] (yava) occupied a place next only to that of paddy. B.P. Majumadar quotes Hemacandra who has mentioned seventeen varieties of grains (cereals, pulses oil-seeds) grown in India in those days: 'Vrīhi',' yava', 'masūra', 'Godhūma', 'Mudga', 'Māśa', 'Tila', 'Caṇaka', 'Aṇava', 'Priyaṅgu', 'Kodrava', 'Mayushthaka', 'Śāli', 'Adhaki', 'Kulattha', 'Kalāya' and 'Saṇa'.[598]

Among the commercial crops sugarcane[599] and cotton[600] held the most important place. The fields of sugarcane are frequently referred to in Dhanapāla's *Pāiyalacchīnāmamālā*[601] and Bhoja's *Sṛṅgāra-mañjarī-kathā*.[602]

Among the coarse grains, the ordinary corn[603] which was the State food of the common man was produced in abundance. Other grains which can be placed in this category, 'kodrava' (Kodo-millet, a species of grain eaten by the poor), 'til' (sesame), 'mudga' (moong or kidney bean) and 'kaṇikā' (cumin seed) etc. are particularly mentioned.[604]

It is quite evident that Indian agriculture had become sufficiently advanced by then. *Tilaka-mañjarī* refers to agricultural products such as arcanuts, betel plants, sandal, lavaṅga, cocoanut, plantain, piṇḍa-khajūra, orange (nāranga), 'panasa' (jack tree) grown during Dhanapāla's time.[605] U.N. Ghoshal states that Gujarat was known for growing cocoanut, lemon, fruit, rice and honey.[606]

Means of Irrigation

Fields were irrigated both by natural reservoirs as well as artificial water-works. The ponds[607] (taḍa), lakes[608] (sarasī), rivers[609] (saritā), water-wheels[610] (rahaṭa) and wells (kūpa) were the means of irrigation during Dhanapāla's time.[611]

It was incumbent upon the king to provide necessary facilities for the supply of water for irrigation purposes by getting tanks, wells, canals etc. excavated. The Paramāra king Vākpati II got a tank called Muñjasāgara dug in Malwa. Bhoja Paramāra is also credited to have constructed a tank near Chittor called 'Bhoja sāgara'. Another big tank near Bhopala was also constructed for irrigation purposes by king Bhoja Paramāra.[612] The 'Sahasra linga' lake at Anhillapura was built by the Calukya ruler Siddharāja Jaya Siṁha of Gujarat. It was fed with the waters of Sarasvatī river by a net-work of canals.[613] The use of Persian wheels (arehata) and leather buckets for irrigation has also been mentioned in a record of A.D. 946.[614]

LAND SYSTEM

Ownership

Land in ancient India was regarded as a trust.[615] As Dr. Lallanji Gopal has observed: "For all practical purposes, the peasant was the owner of the land. The king, as the sovereign of everything in his State, had some claim over the land and received from the peasant a revenue as the wages for the protection he afforded to the people but all this did not amount to a proprietory right over the land".[616] There is strong evidence to suggest that while the peasant might have been the owner of land in theory but in practice the real control of the land was vested in the king and next to him in the feudal lords to whom donations of land were made by the king for various reasons. The feudal lords, in turn, freely exercised the privilege of donating lands in their control.

The Practice of Land Grants

King : It should become amply clear from the practice of land grants obtaining in medieval Hindu India under which lands (known as agrahāra)[617] were bequeathed to temples, monasteries and Brāhmaṇas, that the king had many claims over the village land. In the Paramāra records, whole villages are shown to have been donated to Brāhmaṇas, temples etc. alongwith rows of trees (sa-vṛkṣamālākula), houses, house-sites (gṛha-sthāna), granaries (khala), threshing floors (khalasthāna), pits (tala bhedyā), cow-sheds (go-vāṭikā), gardens, tanks, step-in wells (vāpī), wells etc.[618]

References to land grants made to the monasteries (maṭhas) are also found in *Tilaka-mañjarī*.[619] The Chinese traveller Hsuan Tsang informs us that the Nālandā Vihāra was maintained out of the revenues of about a hundred villages, granted to this institution.[620] Commenting upon the land-donations to temples and maṭhas, R.S. Sharma has very rightly observed, "As a result of the process of land grants these temples and monasteries developed as semi-independent areas enjoying immunities on religious grounds and gradually converted into medieval maṭhas rich enough to tempt Turkish invaders".[621] Large pasture lands were attached to every village. Kings sometimes donated pasture land or the right of grazing cattle free.[622]

The king did not restrict himself to making donations of land to Brāhmaṇas or maṭhas but settled lands to his feudal lords and other officers of State by way of rewarding them for their loyalty and distinguished services in times of war, as also occasionally on poets, scholars and artists for their services in the field of art and culture. This practice naturally resulted in increasing the power and pelf of the feudal chiefs as time went on. In *Tilaka-mañjarī*, we read that the area of Aṅga is granted to Samaraketū (a feudal lord and companion of Prince Harivāhana) and the lands to the west of Aṅga are made over to Senānī (War Lord) Kamalagupta. According to *Tilaka-mañjarī*, the distribution of land was duly recorded by the records officer (Akṣapaṭalika) on paṭṭaka.[623] The term 'deśapati' has been explained by Lakṣmīdhara to mean soldiers which suggests that the king donated lands to warriors for their service which carried with them some abiding claims of ownership.[624] In this connection Dr. Lallanji Gopal observes, "Such close political and administrative control over a limited area would often tend to help the emergence of rights of ownership".[625]

From the IX century onwards we get epigraphic references to confirm the practice of land grants made to officers and others and their subsequent increase from the XI century onwards.[626]

Feudal Lords: It will not be wrong to suggest that with the passage of time the concept of peasant ownership of land (which existed, at best, only in theory, and could never become a reality) receded into oblivion and the process of land grants came to be regarded by the ruling classes (the king and his feudatories) as a matter of right, and not merely a privilege enjoyed by a trustee. In *Tilaka-mañjarī*, we read that Prince Harivāhana and the feudal lord Samaraketū choose to become 'niścinta' (free from care) by dispensing with the responsibility of administration. All they have to do is simply to distribute the town and villages of their 'bhuktis' among the Rājaputras who served them. By way of satisfying their royal conscience they distribute estates on the principle of individual merit of the recipients.[627] Dr. Lallanji Gopal cites the case of king Avantivarman II, the feudatory ruler of Mahendrapāla, the Paramāra Emperor, who is said to have divided his kingdom among his relatives and officers in the form of estates and fields.[628] On the issue of the right of feudatory chiefs to donate lands Dr. Lallanji Gopal observes that theoretically the feudatory rulers were not entitled to make land grants,[629] but on the basis of epigraphic evidence,[630] he assumes that they could donate lands.[631]

From the above discussion it becomes clear that in Dhanapāla's time the real owners and administrators of land were not the ruled but the rulers, the traditional concepts of trusteeship and peasant ownership of land notwithstanding.

Assessment of the Land Revenue: The Naihati grant of Vallālasena mentions three types of land, namely Vāstu, Kṣetra and Khila. Vāstu land meant the land on which residential houses could be constructed.[632] Kṣetra was arable land and khila meant the fallow land. We read in Pratihāra records that village lands were measured by 'Parameśvarīyahastas' (royal yards) and 'nalukas' and were well-demacrated by boundaries.[633]

The amount of revenue seems to have been assessed according to the fertility of the soil, location of the land and also the use to which the land was to be put. Residential land owners had to pay a higher rate of revenue than arable land and for the land which was unfit for cultivation paid little or no rent.

Analysing the various rates of revenue income mentioned in the Naihati grant Dr. D.C. Sircar comes to the conclusion that a Droṇa of land consisting of house and garden had to pay $37\frac{2}{3}$ Purāṇa, but if it consisted only of plantation and no residential house the rent was $30\frac{2}{17}$ Purāṇas for a Droṇa. If the land happened to be covered with grass or jungle, the rent was 4 Purāṇas only per Droṇa; but if it was arable but not actually cultivated, the rent charged was a little higher, namely, $4\frac{11}{64}$ Purāṇas per Droṇa.[634] We do not have any information from the Paramāra sources regarding the rate of bhāga (land tax). Neither Lakṣmīdhara nor Someśvara lay down any specific rate at which land revenue was to be collected. *Mānasollāsa* simply says that 1/6, 1/8 or 1/12 of the share of the produce should be collected as bhāga.[635] It appears that land tax was mainly fixed according to the fertility of the land.

Officers connected with Land Administration: Besides Akṣapaṭalika, other officers connected with the land administration mentioned in the Paramāra land grants were 'Gokulika' and 'Paṭṭakīla'. 'Gokulika' seems to have been in charge of the gokulas or the pasture lands.[636] The 'Paṭṭakīla', was the most important officer in the village. His main duties may have been the assessment of the land and the fixation of the boundaries.[637] In Pratihāra records, Kṣetrapa or Supervisor of the cultivators[638] is mentioned.

CONTACTS WITH THE OUTSIDE WORLD

India's contacts with the outside world go back to the beginnings of its ancient civilization. In the making of what is distinguished as Asian Culture the contribution made by India is universally acknowledged. It has been noted, "Although original intercourse might have been inspired by commercial enterprise, it was soon overshadowed by missionary activity leading to a more or less complete cultural conquest over extensive regions. Besides, the Indians set up colonies and established political influence in many of these countries which brought into existence what may properly be called Greater India".[639]

From *Tilaka-mañjarī* we learn that India enjoyed extremely cordial relations with China,[640] Persia,[641] Ceylon[642] and Dvīpāntara[643] (countries of the South East Asia).

It is significant to note that Dhanapāla in *Tilaka-mañjarī* has eulogized international marriages which testifies to the cosmopolitan outlook of Indian culture. Malaya Sundarī, an Indian girl, is married to the Ceylonese prince Samaraketū[644] whereas Tāraka, a sailor from Suvarṇadvīpa (Indonesia) marries the daughter of an Indian sailor and after marriage settles down permanently[645] in the land of his father-in-law. These examples testify to the broad outlook of Dhanapāla who was steeped in the liberal spirit of Indian culture.

Likewise, the hero of another romance who is an Indian prince named Karkanda marries a Ceylonese princess during his visit to Ceylon (Siṁhala).[646]

The travels of the Indian and Chinese Buddhists in both directions gave a great fillip to a profitable cultural and economic intercourse between the two countries, bringing the two countries closer. According to Dr. Lallanji Gopal, "Relations between India and China were revived under the Sung dynasty to such an extent that Chinese chronicles themselves hold the number of Indian monks in the Chinese Court towards the close of the X and the beginning of the XI century as the highest in Chinese history".[647]

In A.D. 972 forty-four Indian Buddhist monks went to China.[648] The Pālas of Bengal took keen interest in propagating Buddhism outside India. An important institute, known as 'Yi-ching-yuan' (The Imperial Institute for Canonical Translations), came into existence as a result of the arrival of learned Indian monks at the Sung Court. Dharmabhadra, Dānapāla and Dharmadeva, prominent Buddhist scholars from India, who were put in charge of the Institute, translated most of the canons. Dharmabhadra was a native of Kashmir. He and his cousin Danapāla left India in A.D. 970 and arrived at the Sung Court in A.D. 980. Within a period of 20 years Dānapāla translated 18 works, whereas Dharmabhadra translated 72 works. Dharmabhadra died on September 4, A.D. 1000.[649]

In A.D. 973 Dharmadeva, alongwith a four member mission,

visited China. He was an expert linguist. He worked at the Institute till his death on January 15, A.D. 1018.

Another monk from Kashmir named Dharmapāla arrived at the Chinese Court in A.D. 1004. He was appointed co-translator in A.D. 1009. He worked at the Institute till his death in A.D. 1058. He translated 12 works into the Chinese language. The last translator connected with the Institute was Jih-Cheng (Sūryakīrtī).

A number of other Indian monks, including a prince of Western India, visited China between A.D. 970 and 1036. A large number of Saṁskṛta manuscripts from India were taken to China by these monks.[650]

A large number of Chinese pilgrims also came to India between A.D. 950 and 1033. In A.D. 964, 300 Chinese monks set out for India and this pilgrimage lasted for tweleve years. Two years later the Chinese Emperor issued an appeal to the Buddhist-monks and 157 of them came in pursuance of it to pay homage to the Buddhist holy places in India.

Political relations also existed between South India and China during the Sung period. A Cola king sent his embassy to the imperial court of China in A.D. 1015. The Indian ambassador carried with him presents from the king which included among other things, 21,000 ounces of pearls, 60 elephant's tusks and 60 catties of perfumes. In A.D. 1033 and 1077, the Cola king sent two more embassies to China.[651]

Numerous references in *Tilaka-mañjarī* to the use of Chinese Silk (Cināṁśuka) also testify to the existence of trade relations between India and China in those days.[652]

India's relations with South East Asia are also reflected in *Tilaka-mañjarī.* The sailors of India are described to have relations with the sailors of Suvarṇabhūmi (Jāvā, Sumātrā or Indonesia). Tāraka, the son of Vaiśravaṇa Vaiśya, resident of Maṇipura in Suvarṇadvīpa, sails to Dvīpāntra on trading voyages, alongwith other sailors. He (Tāraka) marries an Indian girl, the daughter of a master mariner, named Jalaketu. He settles in India after marriage and becomes, in due course, the head of the mariners.[653]

From the evidence gleaned from *Tilaka-mañjarī,* we become aware that Indian culture had spread to 'Suvarṇadvīpa'. The four Indian 'Varṇas' were in existence there also. The Vaiśya community's main profession was trade and commerce by sea. Moreover, we are told that like his Indian counterparts Vaiśravaṇa respected 'Devas', 'Brahmaṇas', 'Ācāryas' and 'Śramaṇas'.[654]

From the latter half of the VIII century we find influences from Northern India, especially from the Pāla dominions, becoming predominent in the culture of South East Asia. It is reflected not only in the use of pre-nāgarī script in a few Indonesian inscriptions,[655] but also in the Indo-Japanese bronzes[656] and probably architecture as well.[657] The growth of the Cola power towards the beginning of the XI century led to Southern India becoming the main Indian influence in Indonesian lands. However, there are indications which suggest that Eastern India continued to maintain direct contact with South East Asia[658]

The Southeast Asian countries are collectively known as Dvīpāntara and here the impact of the Indian religions and culture was the greatest. The countries included are Malaya, Indonesia, the erstwhile Indo-China, Siam, Cambodia[659] etc. "To these islands, culturally regarded as integral parts of Bhāratavarṣa, extended the specific Indian religious ceremony or institution known as Ijyā or sacrifice. As stated in the Vāmanapurāṇa, they were sanctified by the performance of pious deeds, like sacrifice (ijyā), by righteous war (yuddha), by trade (vāṇijya) and other deeds (karmabhiḥ)".[660]

The *Tilaka-mañjarī* describes a naval attack upon 'Dvīpāntara'. The descriptions given in this connection are so graphic and realistic as regards the culture and industrial products of the region that they imply a thorough and intimate knowledge of the areas. Dhanapāla mentions that the land was covered with dense forests of betel nuts. Every city had numerous palaces, which had many storeys. One could see in the islands here and there many mines of gems, gold and silver and also an abundance of pearls in the heaps of oysters piled in enormous quantities, even in the houses of the poor could be found innumerable gems fit for the ornaments of kings and glittering gold and silver pieces were neglected as if equal to dust.[661]

Referring to the culture of the land, Dhanapāla says that

works on poetry written on the leaves of palmyra trees in Saṁskṛta and local tongues in the Karṇātaka script existed there.[662] The people of Dvīpāntara were not sufficiently civilized.[663] They could not distinguish between good or bad actions.[664] Varṇāśrama order was not properly in vogue.[665] Men of high moral character were few and far between.[666] The dresses of their women were eye-catching though,[667] the language of the people was difficult to understand.[668] The built of their bodies was flawed[669] and some of them were deformed.[670]

In the tradition of the mythical Rāvaṇa they were in the habit of kidnapping the wives of others.[671] Like the fabled demons of Laṅkā, they were black.[672] They were by nature unfair and unjust.[673] They carried long daggers hanging from their waists.[674] They were believed to be under the protection of Niṣāda.[675]

From *Upamitibhavaprapañca-kathā* we learn that sight-seeing was one of the reasons for the people coming to the picturesque islands of Dvīpāntra. The visitors came to feast their eyes on the forests, monasteries, gardens and art of the islands.[676] It was the growing familiarity with the Indonesian lands that led Rājaśekhara to observe that in describing the things of Dvīpāntara, one should be faithful to its dress, customs and other details.[677] *Tilaka-mañjarī*'s description of Dvīpāntara justifies the above statement.

REFERENCES

1. *Tilaka-mañjarī*, p. 66.
2. Ibid., p. 64.
3. A.L. Basham, op. cit., p. 138. f.n.
4. Op. cit.
5. John Garret, *The Classical Dictionary of India* (Delhi Oriental Publishers, Reprint, 1971), I, p. 17.
6. *Tilaka-mañjarī*, p. 44.
   In *Pāiyalacchīnāmamālā*, Dhanapāla has regarded 'Dvija' as Brāhmaṇa, p. 12.

7. Ibid., p. 200:
...*Niṣādalokādadhikanirdayadvijātibhiḥ*...
8. Ibid., p. 68:
...*Adhyayanamukharonmukha dvijeṣu*...
9. Ibid., pp. 18, 79.
10. Ibid., pp. 63-64.
11. Ibid., p. 132.
12. Ibid., p. 64:
...*Devadvijaprasādādihāpi sarvaṁ śubhaṁ bhaviṣyati*...
13. *Tilaka-mañjarī*, p. 114:
...*Saṁpūjyavastrādyatisarjanena dvijātilokaṁ*......
14. Ibid., p. 15.
15. Ibid., p. 31.
16. Sachau, I, pp. 100-01.
17. *Tilaka-mañjarī*, p. 64.
18. Ibid., p. 27.
19. Ibid., p. 12.
20. Ibid., p. 14.
21. Ibid., p. 19.
22. Ibid., pp. 13, 64, 181-182.
23. Ibid., p. 63.
24. Ibid., p. 15.
25. Sachau, II, p. 136.
26. *Tilaka-mañjarī*, p. 79.
27. Ibid., p. 130:
Vaṇigjātisahabhuvābhīrutvena......
28. Ibid., pp. 67, 127, 130.
29. Ibid., p. 67.
30. *Manusmṛti* (Bombay, 1923), VIII, ślokas 88, 410.
31. Op. cit. IX, ślokas 326, 33.
32. *Tilaka-mañjarī*, p. 130.
33. *Pāiyalacchīnāmamālā*, p. 13.
34. Sachau, II, p. 136.
35. Lakṣmīdhara, *Kṛtya Kalpataru*, Edited with an Introduction by K.V. Rangaswami Aiyangar, Gaiekwad Oriental Series, (1944), Gṛhastha-kāṇḍa, II, p. 258.
36. *Tilaka-mañjarī*, p. 127.
37. B.G. Gokhale, op. cit., p. 120.
38. Sachau, II, p. 136.
39. *Pāiyalacchīnāmamālā*, p. 33, śloka 227; *Tilaka-mañjarī*, p. 220.
40. Ibid., p. 8, śloka 71.
41. Ibid., p. 12, śloka 103.
42. Ibid., p. 12, śloka 104.
43. Ibid., p. 13, śloka 105.
44. Ibid., p. 7, śloka 61.
45. Ibid., p. 13, śloka 105. *Tilaka-mañjarī*, p. 112.
46. Ibid., p. 13, śloka 106.

47. Ibid., p. 34, śloka 248.
48. Ibid., p. 12, śloka 104.
49. Ibid., p. 32, śloka 237.
50. Ibid., p. 32, śloka 238.
51. Ibid., p. 32, śloka 236.
52. *Tilaka-mañjarī*, p. 122.
53. Ibid., p. 18.
54. Ibid., p. 136.
55. Ibid., p. 92; *Pāiyalacchīnāmamālā*, p. 30, śloka 223.
56. Ibid., p. 66.
57. Ibid., p. 323.
58. Ibid., p. 18.
59. Ibid., p. 65.
60. Ibid., p. 141.
61. Ibid., p. 92.
62. Ibid., p. 76.
63. *Pāiyalacchīnāmamālā*, p. 12, śloka 103.
64. Halāyudha, *Abhidhānaratanamālā*, ed. Jay Shanker Joshi (Varāṇasi, śaka 1879) II, ślokas 593-598.
65. B.N. Sharma, op. cit., p. 56.
66. *Tilaka-mañjarī*, p. 285.
67. Ibid., p. 35.
68. *Pāiyalacchīnāmālā*, p. 12.
    Tilaka-mañjarī, p. 285.
69. Ibid., p. 202.
70. A.L. Basham, op. cit., p. 155.
71. *Tilaka-mañjarī*, p. 127.
72. Ibid., p. 336:
    ...*kathaṁ ca kulapatiṁ kupitamanuneṣyāṃi*......
73. Ibid., p. 331.
74. Ibid., p. 374:
    ...*Svadāra paripālana karma gṛhamedhināṁ dharmaḥ*......
75. Ibid., p. 263:
    ...*Putrajanmasadṛśamatiṁahāntamutsvamakārayat*...
76. Ibid., p. 64.
77. *The Wonder That Was India*, pp. 155-56.
78. *Tilaka-mañjarī*, p. 64.
79. Ibid., pp. 77-78.
80. *Social and Cultural History of Northern India* : c. A.D. 1900-1200 (New Delhi : Abhinav Publications, 1972), p. 77.
81. *Tilaka-mañjarī*, p. 78:
    ...*Nivartitānnaprāśanādisakalasaṁskārasya*...
82. C. Sivarama Murti, *Arts Asiatiques* (Paris, 1955), II, p. 4.
83. *Tilaka-mañjarī*, pp. 76—79.
84. Ibid., p. 425.
85. R.B. Pandey, *Hindu Saṁskāras* (Banaras, 1949), pp. 34-35.

86. *Laghu Āśvalāyana Smṛti*, ed. Vinaya Ganesh Apte (Poona, 1929), IV:17.
87. *Vyāsa Smṛti*, ed. Vinaya Ganesh Apte (Poona, 1929) I : 17.
88. *Tilaka-mañjarī*, pp. 63-64.
89. Ibid., p. 65 :
 ...putrakāmayantībhirantaḥpura kāminībhirvidhīyamāna vividha-vṛta viśeṣam...
90. *Laghu Āśvalāyana Smṛti*, IV : 2.
91. *Vyāsa Smṛti*, I : 18.
92. *Tilaka-mañjarī*, p. 76.
93. Ibid., pp. 76-77:
 ...Racayat sthāna sthāneṣu ratnacūrṇa svastikāna...
94. Ibid., p. 77:
 ...Āharata Bhagavatīṁ Ṣaṣṭhīdevīm...
95. Ibid., p. 78:
 ...Atikrānte ca ṣaṣṭhī jāgare...
 Sidharṣi Sūri describes that fearing lest Goddcss Sarasvatī should trouble the child, all the relatives and friends did not sleep in the night. (*Upamitibhavaprapañca-kathā*, ed. P. Peterson and H. Jacobi, Calcutta, 1899-1914), p. 731.
96. *Tilaka-mañjarī*, p. 78.
97. Ibid.
98. *Vyāsa Smṛti*, I : 18.
99. *Tilaka-mañjarī*, p. 78:
 ...samāgate ca daśame'nhi kārayitvā sarvanagara devatāyataneṣu pūjām, mānayitvā mitrajñativargam, abhyacryagurujanam, dattvā samāropiṭābharaṇāḥ savatsāḥ sahastrśogāḥ suvarṇa ca pracuram-ārambhaniḥspṛhebhyo viprebhyaḥ...
100. B.N. Sharma, *Social Life in Northern India* (Delhi, 1961), p. 429.
101. *Vyāsa Smṛti*, I : 18.
102. *Manu Smṛti* (Bombay, 1923), II : 35.
103. *Tilaka-mañjarī*, p. 79.
104. Ibid., p. 78.
105. Ibid., p. 79.
106. Ibid.. p. 423.
107. Ibid., p. 425.
108. Ibid., pp. 12-13.
109, *Pāiyalacchīnāmamālā*, p. 35, śloka 256.
110. Ibid.
111. Ibid., p. 32. śloka 240.
112. Ibid., p. 21, śloka 163.
113. N.G. Majumdar, *Inscriptions of Bengal*, III, pp. 86, 89-90:
114. *Pāiyalacchī* p. 34.
115. *Tilaka-mañjarīnāmamālā*, p. 417.
116. *E.I.*, pp. 47, 49-50, ff 10; *E.I.*, XI, p. 57.
118. Om Prakash, *Food and Drinks in Ancient India* (Delhi : Munshi Ram Manohar Lal, 1961), f.n. p. 203.

119. *Pāiyalacchīnāmamālā*, p. 15. śloka 123.
120. Ibid.
121. Ibib., p. 32, śloka 237.
122. Someśvara, *Mānsollāsa*, III : 1573:
Mathitamśarkarāyukta melācūrṇavimiśritam/
Karpūradhūpitamnamnābhañjiketyabhidhīyate//
123. Om Prakash, op. cit., p. 209.
124. *Pāiyalacchīnāmamālā*, p. 22, śloka 176.
125. Ibid., p. 17, śloka 137.
126. *Mānasollāsa*, III : 1553-64.
127. *Tilaka-mañjarī*, p. 250.
128. Ibid., p. 137:
...*Nirantarālaphalitanālikelakadalīpanasapiṇḍa kharjūra*...
129. Ibid., p. 260:
...*yatranāraṅga-panasa-kadalaka-prāyamaśanam*...
130. *Pāiyalacchīnāmamālā*, p. 18, śloka 148.
131. Ibid., p. 18, śloka 145.
132. Ibid., p. 34, śloka 254.
133. Ibid., p. 18, śloka 145.
134. *Food and Drinks in Ancient India*, p. 220.
135. *Pāiyalacchīnāmamālā*, p. 14, śloka 113:
Pisiam sullam mamsam...
136. Ibid., p. 5. śloka 40:
...*Sa-ulā saharā mīṇā timī jhasā aṇimisāmmacchā*...
137. Ibid., p. 16, śloka 128:
Kaḍuyālā kubarā ya lahumacchā.
138. *Alberuni's India*, tr. Sachau, Vol. II (Delhi, 1964). p. 151.
139. *Tilaka-mañjarī*, pp. 447-48.
140. Ibid., p. 18:
...*Raktotpalapalāśamiva kāpiśayanam*...
141. *Pāiyalacchīnāmamālā*:
Ma-iraam mahuvāro sīhū sarao mahum avakkaraso/
kāyambarī pasannā hālā taha varuṇī ma-irā//
142. Vāgbhaṭṭa, *Aṣṭāṅgahṛdaya* with a commentary by Arundatta (Lahore, 1933), V. 67-75.
Vinṭasurā piṭṭhakhauri-ā ma-irā (śloka 211, p. 28).
143. *Social Life in Northern India*, p. 301.
144. Rajaśekhara, *Karpūramañjarī* (Cambridge, 1901), p. 256.
145. *Tilaka-mañjarī*, p. 18.
146. Ibid., p. 51.
147. Ibid. :
...*gṛhopavaneṣu vanitāsakhaiḥ vilāsibhiranubhūyamāṇa madhupānotsvāḥ*+(p. 9).
Purāṇavaruṇi pānotsvā...(p. 61).
148. Ibid., pp. 18, 61.
149. Ibid,, pp. 9, 41, 169, 211, 245, 324.

150. Someśvara, *Mānasollāsa*, V : 450-65.
151. *Tilaka-mañjarī*, pp. 65, 69, 165, 173.
152. Ibid., p. 260:
 ...Nāgāvallī lālasāḥ dhaninaḥ...
153. Ibid., p. 65:
 ...Tāmbūla karaṅka vāhinā...
154. Ibid., p. 424.
155. Ibid., p. 61.
156. Srī Harṣa, *Naiṣadhacarita* ed., Siva Datta (Bombay, 1919), tr. K.K. Handiqui (Poona, 1956), XVI : 113.
157. *Tilaka-mañjarī*, p, 65.
158. Ibid,, p. 64.
159. *Tilaka-mañjarī*, pp. 68-69.
 It is noteworthy that the common strata of society during Dhanapāla's time was not neglected even in the royal dinners. It innicates the benevolent policy and affectionate attitude of Paramara rulers towards their subjects in the Medieval Hindu period.
160. Ibid., p. 69.
161. Ibid.
162. Ibid.,
163. Ibid., p. 34:
 Eṇa nābhikarpūrakaṇasantarpitā modena ca sparśendriya hariṇā candanadraveṇa-viracitāṅgarāgāṃ...
164. Ibid., p. 353:
 ...karpūrakaṇareṇunā gātrāmaccurayat......
165. Ibid., p. 17:
 ...Pratyagramṛgamadāṅgarāgamalinavapuṣo bahula-pradoṣābhisārikāḥ sudūramācakarṣa...
166. Ibid., p. 133.
167. Ibid., p. 17:
 ...kāliṇdijalaveṇikāḥ...
168. *Paīyalacchīnāmamālā*, p. 7, śloka 57:
 kābarī kuṅtalahāro dhammillo keśahatthao ma-uḍo/
 cūlā sihā sihaṁḍo siṁhaliyā chiḍāo caḍao//
169. *Tilaka-mañjarī*, p. 155;
 Pāiyalacchīnāmamālā, p. 22, ślok 190.
170. Ibid., p. 8, śloka 68:
 kuppāso kañcuayo giṁdhullovārabāṇo ya/
171. *Pāiyalacchīnāmamālā*, p. 8, śloka 69:
 Jāṇa sicayaṁ kaḍillaṁ ni-asaṇaṁ sāhulī ya parihaṇayaṁ/
172. Ibid., p. 22, śloka 175:
 U-aṭṭī uccao nīvī...
 Tilaka-mañjarī, p. 265:
 Nibiḍita paridhāna nīviravacchādya...
173. Ibid., p. 17.

174. *Tilaka-mañjarī*, p. 164:

...śaratkāla divasa iva bālatapena dūramahitacchāyāvṛddhir-vṛttanetra kūrpāsakena...

In *Pāiyalacchīnāmāmālā*, Dhanapāla uses Kūrpāsaka as synonymous with Kāñcuka and Vārabāṇa *Kuppāso kañcuayo giddhullo vārabāṇo...* (p. 8). Becaradas Jivaraj Doshi is of the opinion that Kūrpāsaka was a cola (coat of mail), p. 28. (glossary). In *Amarakośa*, 'Kūrpāsaka' is used as synonymous with colaka (*Amarakośa*, ed. Guru Prasad Shstri, Banaras, 1950, p. 119). In *Abhidhānaratnamālā* as well, it is used as synonymous with colaka. (*Abhidhāraratanamālā*. ed. Jaya Shanker Joshi, Lucknow II, 552) *kūpāsasastvardhcolakaḥ*. According to Kṣīrasvāmin the word Kūrpāsaka means a garment, the arms of which come upto the Kūrpāsa (elbow) *Amarakośa-Tīkā*, ed. Haradatta Shastri (Poana, 1941), II : 18—*kūrparo'syateanenti kūrpāsaḥ*. According to Monier Williams, it was a bodice, Jacket with short sleeves worn next the body especially by women. (*Sanskrit-English Dictionary*, Oxford, 1956, p. 300) Dr. B.N. Sharma quoting *Harṣacartia* says that feudatories of Harṣa who accompanied him on his expedition of digvijaya wore multi-coloured Kūrpāsaka (*Social Life in Northern India*, p. 278). Thus, it should have been a half-sleeved tunic. It was worn both by males and females.

175. Sachau, op. cit., I, pp. 180-181.
176. *Pāiyalacchīnāmamālā*, p. 14, śloka 116.
177. *Social Life in Northern India*, p. 281.
178. *Pāiyalacchīnāmamālā*, p. 8, śloka 69.

In *Tilaka-mañjarī* Samaraketū is described to have put on two garments [paridhāya vāsoyugalaṃ) i.e., uttariya and 'adhovastra' (p. 105).

179. *Tilaka mañjarī*, p. 108.
180. Ibid., pp. 108, 131, 155, 173.
181. Rājaśekhara, *Karpūramañjarī* (Prākṛta), ed. Sten Konow (Cambridge, 1901), IV : 20.
182. *Tilaka-mañjarī*, p. 165.
183. Ibid., p. 232:

Athoṣṇīṣapaṭṭa kṛtaśirovestanā dṛḍhākṛstakañcuka kasādhika-kṛśodaraśriyaḥ...

184. *Pāiyalacchīnāmamālā*, p. 8, śloka 68.
185. B.N. Sharma, op. cit., p. 278.
186. *Pāiyalacchīnāmamālā*, p. 8:

kuppāso kañcuayo gidhullā vārabāṇoya.

187. *Social Life in Northern India*, p. 278.
188. *Tilaka-mañjarī*, p. 115.
189. Ibid., p. 145; *Pāiyalacchīnāmamālā*, p. 8, śloka 69.
190. *Tilaka-mañjarī*, pp. 164-165.
191. Ibid., pp. 106-7. The upper garment and lower garment made of white Chinese Silk having borders are referred to in *Tilaka-mañjarī* (p. 229):

...Navadaśālakṛtena śvetacīna vastradvayena...

192. Ibid., p. 164.
193. Ibid., p. 79.
194. Ibid., p. 34.
195. Ibid.
196. Moti Chandra, *Prācīna, Bhāratīya Veśa-Bhūṣā* (Hindi), p. 147.
197. V.S. Agrawal, *Harṣa Carita Ek Sāṁskṛtika Adhyayana* (Hindi), (Patna, 1953), p. 77.
198. *Pāiyalacchīnamamālā*, p. 8.
199. Amara Siṁha, *Amara Kośa*, ed. Guru Prasada Sastri (Banaras, 1950), II : 115.
200. V.S. Agrawal, op. cit., p. 78.
201. *Social Life in Northern India*, p. 273.
202. *Harṣa Carita Ek Sāṁskṛtika Adhayayana*, p. 68.
203. Kṣiraswamī, *Amarakośa Tīkā*, ed., Haradatta Sastri (Poona, 1941), p. 157.
204. *Tilaka-mañjarī*, p. 180.
205. Ibid., p. 368.
206. Ibid., p. 180.
207. *Pāiyalacchīnāmamālā*, p. 37, śloka 272.
208. *Tilaka-mañjarī*, p. 105.
209. *Pāiyalacchīnāmamālā*, p. 27, śloka 205.
210. Ibid., p. 14. śloka 115.
211. *Tilaka-mañjarī*, p. 158.
212. Ibid., p. 160.
213. Ibid., p. 115.
214. Ibid., p. 120.
215. *Pāiyalacchīnāmamālā*, p. 14, śloka 118.
216. Ibid , p 17, śloka 140.
217. Ibid., p. 30, śloka 228.
218. Ibid., p. 14, śloka 115.
219. Ibid., p. 39, śloka 272.
220. *Tilaka-mañjarī*, p. 160.
221. *Pāiyalacchīnāmamālā*, p. 36, śloka 265.
222. Ibid.
223. Ibid., p. 14, śloka 116.
224. Ibid.
225. Ibid., p. 6, śloka 52:

    uttaṁso avayaṁso kannolī kaunauro ya
226. *Tilaka-mañjarī*, p. 161.
227. Ibid. p. 210:

    Pratikṣaṇaṁ ca sphuratā dakṣiṇena cakṣuṣā bhujaśikhareṇa ca dviguṇīkriyamāṇagamanatsāhaḥ...
228. Ibid., p. 198.
229. *Tilaka-mañjarī*, p, 77:

    ...Gugguludhūpa dhūmāndhakāra dhūrīkṛtaduṣṭacakra vakrakṣi sañcāram...
230. Ibid., p. 65.

231. Ibid., p. 63.
232. Ibid., p. 74.
233. Jagdish Chandra Jain : *Life in Ancient India as Depicted in Jain Canons* (Bombay, 1947), p. 148.
234. Op. cit. (f.n.)
235. *Tilaka-mañjarī*, p. 64:
   ...*Divāniṣamupāsyamānanaimittikam*...
236. Ibid., p. 95.
237. Ibid., p. 132.
238. Ibid., pp. 64, 95, 131-132.
239. Ibid., p. 403.
240. Ibid., p. 10:
   ...*Akalitāḍhyā nāḍhyavivekaiḥ*...
241. Ibid. :
   ...*Agṛhīta paṇḍitā paṇditavibhaktiḥ*...
242. Ibid. :
   ...*Anavabuddhasādhvasādhu viśeṣaiḥ*...
243. Ibid., p. 10:
   ...*Anavadhāritadhārmikādhārmikaparicchittibhiḥ*...
244. Ibid. :
   ...*saṁtuṣṭaiḥ*...
245. Ibid. :
   ...*Rājasabhāvāptakhyātibhirojasvibhirapi prasannaiḥ*...
246. Ibid. :
   ...*Propakāra pravaṇaiḥ*...
247. Ibid :
   ...*san mārgavartibhiḥ*...
248. Ibid. :
   ...*Adhitanītibhirapyakuṭilaiḥ*...
249. Ibid. :
   ...*jñataniḥśeṣapurāṇetihāsasaraiḥ*...
250. Ibid. :
   ...*Dṛṣṭasakalakāvyanāṭaka prabandhaiḥ*...
251. Ibid. :
   ...*Paricitanikhilākhyāyikākhyānavyākhyanaiḥ*...
252. Ibid. :
   ...*Abhyasta nāṭyaśāstraiḥ*...
253. Ibid. :
   ...*Adarśitabhrū netravikāraiḥ*...
254. Ibid. :
   ...*sarvabhāṣā vicakṣaṇaiḥ*...
255. Ibid. :
   ...*sarvairapicchekokti kovidaiḥ*...
256. Ibid. :
   ...*kāmasūtra pāragairapi*...

257. Ibid. :

...Aviditavaiśikaiḥ...

258. Ibid. :

...sarvasya guṇa grāhibhiḥ...

259. Ibid. :

...Sātvikairapi...

260. Ibid., p. 10:

...Parānupahāsabhirnarmaśīlaiḥ...

261. Ibid. :

...Ojasvirapi prasannaiḥ...

262. Ibid. :

Udāra viśeṣaiḥ...

263. Ibid. :

...Aśikṣitalaṭoktibhiḥ...

264. Ibid. :

...sakṛtayugeva satpuruṣa vyavahāraiḥ...

265. Ibid. :

...Anandita dvijā...

266. Ibid., pp. 10, 75, 107. 163, 172, 237, 322.
267. Ibid., p 237.
268. Ibid., pp. 107, 169.
269. Ibid.. p. 104.
270. Ibid., p. 108.
271. Ibid., p. 108.
272. Ibid., p. 172.
273. Ibid., p. 18:

...Svaracita subhāṣitāni...

274. Ibid., p. 18:

Kadācidvadana maṇḍanādibhirviḍambanāprakārai rūpahasanvidūṣakāntaḥpurikā janamahāsayat |

275. Ibid., p. 323:

Avasite ca vāsare viralibhavatṣukṛtrimaturaṅga vāraṇakrīḍā pradhāneṣu prekṣaṇakeṣu...

276. Ibid., p. 353:

...Aparaḥ sarastīravighaṭitaśuktimuktaira muktā phalairdyūta kriyāṁ prāvartayat |

277. Ibid.
278. Ibid., p 183:

...Mṛgayāvyasaunibhiḥ kṣitipatikumāraiḥ...

279. Ibid., p. 17.
280. Ibid., pp. 18, 168, 170, 292.
281. Ibid., p. 27.
282. Ibid., pp. 11, 17, 33, 35, 78. 180.
283. Ibid., pp. 8, 180, 370.
284. Ibid., pp. 17, 18, 168:

Kadācidbhavanadīrghikāmbhasi pravṛttanirbharkrīḍārasārāmantaḥ puravilāsinīnāṁ patitāṅgulīyakamudrānveṣaṇādinā tena tena vyājena nimajjya gṛhītajaghanāṁśuko...(p. 18).

285. *Tilaka-mañjarī*, pp. 17, 106, 173, 178, 180, 418.
286. Ibid., pp 353, 363.
287. Ibid:, p. 168.
288. Ibid,, p. 365.
289. Ibid., pp. 12, 213.
290. Ibid., p. 19.
291. Sachau, op. cit., II, pp. 178-79.
292. *Tilaka-mañjarī*, p. 338.
293. B P. Majumdar, *Socio-Economic History of Northern India* (Calcutta, 1960), p. 275.
294. *Tilaka-mañjarī*, p. 154.
295. Bhoja, *Yuktikalpataru*, ed,, I.C. Sastri (Calcutta, 1917) III : 462-64.
296. *Tilaka-mañjarī*, pp. 115, 271.
297. B.P. Majumdar, op. cit., p. 376.
298. Ibid., p. 428.
299. Ibid., p. 344.
300. Ibid., pp. 77-78, 263.
301. Ibid., p. 108.
302. Ibid., pp. 10, 104, 163, 184, 186, 193.
303. Ibid.
304. Ibid., pp. 263, 323, 391.
305. Ibid. pp. 10, 41, 57, 270, 292, 372, 399.
306. Ibid., pp. 7-9.
Here Ayodhya is an imaginary name. It denotes Dhara, the capital of the Paramāras of Malwa.
307. Ibid., p. 9:
...*Satatagṛhavyāpāra niṣāṇṇamāsābhirnisargato*...
308. Ibid.:
...*Guruvacanānurāgiṇībhiḥ*...
309. Ibid., p. 331:
...*kulapatisamādeśādatithivargamupacarantī*...
310. Ibid.:
...*khede'pyakhaṇḍitocitapratipattibhiḥ*...
311. Ibid.:
...*śālīnatayā*...
312. Ibid.:
...*Sukumāratayā*...
313. Ibid., p. 7, 9:
...*khidyamanābhiḥ*...
314. Ibid.:
...*Rateśvapitāmayantībhiḥ*...
315. Ibid:, p. 331:
...*Svakulācāra kauśalaśālinībhiḥ*...

316. Ibid., p. 9:

...vyalīke'pyanujjhitavinayābhiḥ...

317. Ibid.:

...kope'pyadṛṣṭamukhavikārābhiḥ...

318. Ibid.:

...kalahe'pyaniṣṭhurabhāṣiṇībhiḥ...

319. Ibid.:

...kulaprasūtābhiralaṁkṛta vadhūbhiḥ...

320. Damodaragupta: *Kuṭṭanīmata*, ed. Tansukhram, M. Tripathi (Banaras, 1924), śloka 436.

321. *Tilaka-mañjarī*, p. 9:

...Sakalapuruṣārthasiddhibhiriva śarīrabaddhābhiḥ...

322. Ibid.:

...Uddhataībhistāruṇye kṛtakusaṅgābhiścaraṇayarna svabhāve...

323. Ibid.:

Svapne'palaṅghayantībhirdvāratoraṇam...

324. Ibid.:

...Aṅgīkṛta satīvṛtābhirapyasatīvṛtabhiḥ...

325. Ibid.:

...Atṛptābhiraṅgaśobhīyām...

326. Daṇḍin, *Daśakumāracarita*, ed. M.R. Kale (Bombay, 1917), pp. 164-165:

Amba kiṁ bravīmi / daurbhāgyaṁ nāma jīvanmaraṇamivaṅganānāṁ, viśeṣataśca kulavadhūnāṁ// (p. 164).

Bhagavati, patireva daivataṁ vanitānām, viśeṣataḥ kalajānām/ (p. 165).

327. *Tilaka-mañjarī*, p. 67:

...Niskuṭalatāmaṇḍapāvalambiṣu prapikākarpareṣu karārpitonmṛṣṭatāratāmrabhājāṇāsu divasalakṣamīṣviva sabhāsvanmaṇḍalāsu hiṇḍantīṣu devatāyatanamaṇḍaleṣu vimalāmbaradharāsu vṛddhāsu...

328. Ibid., p. 331:

...Devatārcanakusumānyaāharanti...

329. Ibid., p. 67:

Bhartṛsaṁdhyopāsanotsukāsu gṛhṇantīṣvabhu(?)...
dvijātigṛhiṇīṣu...

330. Vātsyāyana, *Kāma-sūtra*, ed. D.L. Goswami (Banaras, 1939), 1:3:16.

331. *Tilaka-mañjarī*:

Seyaṁ kramaprāptayauvanā prakarṣamāgatena gītanṛtyādikalākauśalena deśantareṣu... (p. 343).

ucitasamaye ca yathāśuktyādhītarājakanykocita vidyā sopaniṣadi nāṭyavede gīta vadyādiṣu ca kalāsu kṛtaparicayā... (p. 264).

332. Ibid., p. 363:

...Kṛtsne'pi vidyādharaloka iha labdhapatākā kalāsu sakalāsvapi kauśalena vatsā Tilaka-mañjarī / yadi ca kautukaṁ tataścitrakarmāṇi vīṇādivādye lāsyatāṇḍava gateṣu nāṭyaprayoaeṣu-

ṣaḍjādisvaravibhāganirṇayeṣu pustaka karmaṇi draviḍādiṣu patracchedabhedeṣvanyeṣu ca vidagdhajana vinoda yogyeṣu vastuvijñādeṣu...

333. Ibid., p. 342:
Sā daśavarṣadesīyā suvela parvate piturgṛhama dhivasantī vaitāḍhyagirinivāsenā mātāmahena rājakanyocitābhiḥ sahakalābhirakāla eva pariṇataṁ lāsyavidyā rahasyaṁ...

334. Ibid., p. 170:
Sakhi citralekhe ! tvaṁ hi citra karmaṇ paraṁ pravīṇā...

335. Ibid., p. 169:
...Sarvakalāśāstrakuśalena sarvadeśabhāṣāvidā sarvapaurāṇikakhyānaka-pravīṇena strījanena...

336. Ibid., p. 331:
...Anekalalitapatralekhānsvastikānabhilikhantī...

337. Rājaśekhara, *Viddhaśalabhañjikā,* ed. Jitendra Bimala Chaudhari, (Calcutta, 1934), pp. 68, 166.

338. Rājaśekhara, *Karpūra-mañjarī,* II:34, II:9.

339. *Tilaka-mañjarī,* p. 156:
...Dhanurvedaṃ sikṣayantīḥ...

340. Ibid., p. 341:
...Anekaśatusaṁkhyābhiraṅgarakṣādhikāraniyuktābhiraṅganābhiḥ...

341. N.K. Shastri, *The Age of Nandas and Mauryas* (Banaras, 1952), p. 170.

342. *Karpūra-mañjarī,* pp. 97-99.

343. *Tilaka-mañjari,* p. 419, 421.

344. Ibid., p. 110.

345. Ibid., p. 341:
sakalakośāgārasaṁrakṣaṇādhikāraniyuktāmuktāvalīnāmapālikā...

346. Ibid., p. 110.

347. Ibid.. p. 375.

348. Ibid., p. 341.

349. A.S. Altekar, *The Position of Women in Hindu Civilization* (Delhi, 1962), p. 112.

350. pp.*Tilaka-mañjarī,* p. 78.

351. E.C. Sachau, op. cit., II, p. 155.

352. *Tilaka-mañjarī,* p. 343. Kusumaśekhara married Gandharva Datta in *Tilaka-mañjarī,* in a Gandharva-style marriage :
Samyagvihitena vivāha vidhinā gandharveṇa...
In Gandharva marriage, the bride and bridegroom made their own choice without the knowledge of their guardians and were married without rites or ceremonies.

353. Ibid., pp. 127, 142.

354. Ibid., p. 127:
...Priyadarśanānāṃ tasya Jalaketoḥ sutā sutāravṛttamauktika prakalapitaṁ hāramādāya piturājñayā gatā tadgṛham...

355. Ibid., p. 423:

Āsīdati samuditairgrhagaṇitavidbhirāveditaṁ karagrahaṇa lagnaṁ...

356. Ibid., p. 424.
357. Ibid., p. 64.
358. Sachau, II, p. 155.
359. Op. cit., II, p. 154.
360. Somadeva, *Nītivākyāmṛta*, ed., Panna Lal Soni (Bombay, 1922), p. 196:

Dvādaśavarṣā st ī ṣoḍaśavarṣaiḥ pumānprāptāvyavahāro bhavataḥ...

361. Ibid., p. 127.
362. Ibid., p. 343:

Seyaṁ kramaprāpta yauvanā...

363. Ibid., p. 363.
364. Ibid., p. 129:

...jāmātṛpratipattyā dattvā jīvaṅamati prabhūtakṛtaḥ prabhurakhilaśyāpi nāvikatantraśca/

365. See Pratipal Bhatia, *Paramāras* (Delhi, 1970), p. 286. Dr. Bhatia has quoted from *Tilaka-mañjarī*, 1903 edition, This particular reference is not traceable in the edition of 1938, which the author has used for his thesis.
366. Sachau, Part II, p. 155.
367. *History and Culture of Indian People*, Vol. IV, p. 395.
368. Amara Canda, '*Kāvyakalpalatāvṛtti*. ed , Jagannatha Sastri (Banaras, 1951), p. 25, śloka 64.
369. *Tilaka-mañjarī*, pp. 9-10.
370. *Social Life in Northern India*, p. 29.
371. Sachau, II, p. 157.
372. *Tilaka-mañjarī*, p. 9:

...Kuberapurapaṇḍyāṅganābhirivā...

373. Ibid.:

...Pādaśobhayāpinyakkṛtapadmābhiruruśriyāpi...

374. Ibid.:

...Laghūkṛtarambhāstambhābhirgauryāpichāyayā...

375. Ibid., p. 9:

...Saubhāgyahetorupāsitābhirindunāpi pratidinam...

376. Ibid.:

...Prārthyamāna mukhakamalakāntibhirmakaradhvajenāpi...

377. Ibid.:

...Narendrāṇāmapi sarvasvamākarṣayantībhiḥ...

378. Ibid., p. 10:

...surataśilpapragalbhatāvaṣṭambhena rūpamapinirupayogamavagacchantībhiḥ...

379. Ibid.:

Prasādhanāḍambaramapiviḍambanāpakṣe...

380. Ibid.:
Tāruṇyamapi tṛaṇalaghugaṇayantībhiḥ...
381. Ibid.:
Vilāṣānapihāsyakoṭau...
382. Ibid.:
Ābharaṇa saṁbhāramapi bhāramavadhārayabtinhiḥ...
383. Ibid.:
Navasurateṣu baddharāgābhirapi nīcarateṣvaśaktābhiḥ...
384. Ibid.:
Na punarekāntatorthānurāgiṇībhiḥ...
385. Ibid.:
Lakṣmī manovṛttibhiriva puruṣottamaguṇahāryābhiḥ...
386. Ibid., p. 9:
...kṛtapuñyajanocitābhiḥ...
387. Ibid.,p. 65:
...sakalalokācārakuśalābhiḥ...vāravanitābhiḥ...
388. Ibid., p. 10:
...saṁsare'pi sāratābuddhinibandhanabhūtābhiḥ...
389. Ibid., p. 9:
...Aprayuktayogābhiḥ...
390. Kṣemendra, *Kalāvilāsa* (Bombay, 1886), IV, 2-11. (See Appendix I),
391. *Tilaka-mañjarī*, p. 10.
392. Ibid.:
...Kulakramāgata vaiśikakalāklāpavaikṣaṇyābhiḥ...
393. *Life in Ancient India As Depicted in Jain Canons*, p. 164.
394. *Tilaka-mañjarī*, p. 170.
395. *Bṛhatkalpa Bhāṣya* (Bhavanagar), p. 262.
396. *Tilaka-mañjarī*, p. 17.
397. Ibid., p. 75:
...sāṁdhyamārabdhamapsarobhiḥ prekṣāntṛyam...
398. Ibid., p. 260.
399. Ibid., p. 174:
...Vāravanitābhiḥ saṁvāhyamāna caraṇapallava...
400. Ibid., p. 323.
401. Ibid., p. 70.
402. Ibid., p. 119.
403. Ibid., p. 128.
404. Chakladar, *Studies in Vātsyāyana Kāmasūtra* (Calcutta, 1929), pp. 199ff.
405. Bhartṛhari, *Nītiśataka* (Bombay, 1948):
Vidyānāmanarasya rūpamadhikaṁ pracchanna guptaṁ dhanaṁ/
Vidyā bhogakarī yaśaḥ sukhakare vidyāgurūnāṁ gurū//
Vidyā vandhujano videśa gamane vidyā paraṁ daivātaṁ/
Vidyā rajasu pūjitā nahi dhanaṁ vidyā vihīnah paśuḥ//
(*Śloka* 16)
406. *Tilaka-mañjarī*, p. 79.
407. Ibid , p. 78. Harivāhana was admitted to school at the age of six.

408. Bāṇa, *Kādambarī*, ed. K.P. Parab, (Bombay, 1834), p. 8.
409. Jineśvara Sūri *Kathākośa Prakaraṇa* (Bombay, 1949), p.8. Uddyaotana Sūri, *Kuvalayamālā kahā*, ed. A.N. Upadhye. (Bombay, 1959), p. 21.
410. *Tilaka-mañjarī*, p. 79:

Upaninye ca tebhyaḥ śobhana dina muhūrte nivartita samastetika-rttavyaḥ snāvamanupahata sūkṣmakṣauma kalpitottarāsaṁgama-nuliptaṅgamā modinyamalayajarasena pratyerasamāmuktāmuktā kalāpamuparacitarocanātilakarucina lalāṭamuttamāṅga ghaṭita-mālatī mukulaṇḍamālamavadāta veṣatayā saviśeṣadarśitādarama-bhyutthitāvāḥ puraḥ.

Sarasvatyāḥ sitāṁśudhavalayā śarīracchāyayevachuritamātmaja-mavanipatipūjā viśeṣavardhita prītayaśca...

411. Ibid.:

...Daśabhirabdaiścaturdaśāpi vidyāsthānānisaha sarvābhirūpa vidyābhirvidāncakāra kalāśāstra nirvaśaṣaṁ viveda.

412. Ibid.. p. 79.
413. Ibid , p. 13. King Meghavāhana is described to have got mastery over four Vidyās:

Catasṛṣvapi vidyāsulabdha prakarṣaḥ...

414. Ibid., p. 79. Dhanapāla gives importance to the subject of grammar and makes it a point to mention that prince Harivāhana has acquired mastery over grammar among other subjects. It appears that Grammar was regarded to be the key to the knowledge of various sciences and it was held in high estimation. That the study of 'Grammar was considered important is proved by the fact that one of the inscriptions of the time of king Udayāditya and Narvarmana discovered from the Bhoja Śālā of Dhārā containts an alphabetic chart and rules of Saṁskṛta grammar' (*E.I.* XXXI, pp. 25-30).
415. Ibid., p. 403. Astrology wielded great influence on the popular mind. The royal court, we are told by Dhanapāla, used to maintain an Astrologer known as 'Rājanaimittika'. A number of works on astrology and astronomy were composed during the period. Bhoja, the scholar king, was an astrologer and astronomer who is said to have composed many works on these subjects. It is a fair guess that this subject was quite popular in the saṁskṛta schools and colleges during Dhanapāla's time.
416. *Tilaka-mañjarī*, p. 13.
417. Ibid., p. 79. Prince Harivāhana in *Tilaka mañjarī* is descril ed to have acquired mastery over fourteen vidyās.
418. *Yājñavalkyasmṛti* (Bombay, 1926), 1 : 3.

Purāṇa nyāya mīmāṁsā dharmaśāstrāṅgamiśritāḥ Vedah sthānāni vidyānāṁ dharmasyaca caturdaśa|

419. *Tilaka-mañjarī*, p. 163. Prince Harivāhna is described to have acquired proficiency in dancing, music and painting:

Ekasūnurnṛtya gītacitrāvikala śāstrapāradṛśvā|
Harivāhanonāma kumāraḥ|

At another place we read that prince Harivāhana has attained mastery on all subjects, specially the arts of painting and flute-playing:

...viśeṣatascitrakarmaṇi vīṇavādye ca pravīṇatām prāpa...
(*Tilaka-mañjarī*, p. 79).

420. Ibid.. p. 10:
Adhītanītibhiḥ...
421. *Tilaka-mañjarī*, p. 363. Dhanapāla has mentioned 'Vṛttis' (which are four in number, namely, 'Bhāratī', Satavatī, 'Kaiśikī', and 'Ārabhaṭī'), 'Rītis' ('Vaidarbhī', 'Gauḍīyā' and 'Pāñcālī') and 'Upajāti' which are two in number, namely, 'Indravajrā' and 'Upendravajrā'.
422. Ibid., p. 10.
423. Ibid., p. 24.
424. Ibid., p. 78. There are several references to 'Vaidyas' in *Tilaka-mañjarī*. Bhoja is known to have written a book on medicine known as *Rājāmṛgāṅka*.
425. Ibid., p. 91.
426. Ibid.
427. Ibid., p. 129.
428. Ibid., p. 132.
429. Ibid., p. 133; p. 22.
430. Ibid., p. 10.
431. Ibid.
432. Ibid., p. 159. Dhanapāla's lexicon *Pāiyalacchīnāmamālā* has already been cited.
433. See Appendix II.
434. *Milindapañho*, ed. E.V. Trenckner (London, 1880), p. 3.
435. *Tilaka-mañjarī*, p. 343. Malaya Sundarī was adept in the art of music and dancing.
436. Ibid., p. 391. Malaya Sundarī portrays Harivāhana on the board. Citralekhā, the nurse in *Tilaka-mañjrī*, was proficient in this art of painting.
437. Ibid., p. 156.
438. Ibid., p. 169.
439. Ibid., p. 10.
440. Ibid.
441. Ibid., p. 220:
Aṣṭādaśalipivyaktivyatirektaḥ...
442. Bhola Nath Tiwari, *Bhāṣā Vijñāna* (Allahabad, Kitab Mahal, 1971), p. 84.
443. *Tilaka-mañjarī*, ed. Śāntyācārya, Pt II, p. 188.
444. *Tilaka-mañjarī* (Bhavadatta), pp. 18, 67, 394.
445. Bāṇa, *Harṣa Carita*, ed., K.P. Parab (Bombay, 1834 Śaka) I, p. 7, II, p. 56.
446. *Tilaka-mañjarī*, p. 79.
447. Ibid., p. 67.
448. Ibid., p. 352.

449. Ibid., p. 182. Kalhaṇa informs us that king Yaśaskara of kashmir made a gift of 55 agrahāras provided with all sorts of material resources (*Rājataraṅgiṇī*, VI ; 89).
450. Kalhaṇa, *Rājataraṅgiṇī*, ed., Durgā Praśad (Bombay, 1892) VI : 87.
451. *Tilaka-mañjarī*, p. 78:

 ...Vinayaropāṇāya rājā rājakulābhyantara eva kāritanavadya-vidyāgṛhaḥ saṁyogāve śitagurukulānām...
452. Ibid., p. 79.
453. Ibid.
454. Ibid.:

 ...Upalabdhasarvabudhajanasādhuvādaṃ...
455. Ibid., p. 78.
456. Ibid., p. 79:

 ...Labdhaparipūrṇasarvāvayavaśobham....
457, B.G. Gokhale, op. cit., p. 140.
458. *Tilaka-mañjarī*, p. 79:

 Bhujabalaṁ cāsyavismāpita surāsuraṁ kesarikiśorasyeva sahajaṁ śarīramabhavat.
459. Ibid., p. 13.
460. Ibid.
461. Ibid,, p. 79:

 Kalāśāstraṁ niravaśeṣaṁ viveda.
462. Ibid., p. 463.
463. *Prabhāvaka Carita*, p. 139, śloka 53:

 Veda-smṛti śrutistomapāragāḥ paṇḍito'grajaḥ/
 kṛtyākṛtyeṣu niṣṇātaḥ saveвektu yathā ruciṁ//
464. Dhanapāla : *Bhavisayattakahā*, (Baroda, 1923) II : 2.
465. *Tilaka-mañjarī*, p. 127.
466. Ibid.. p. 129.
467. Ibid., p. 115. *...sitādukūlavāsāḥ.*

 Dr. B.P. Majumdar, quoting Kauṭilya, says that white dukūla was produced in Lower Bengal, black dukūla in North Bengal and othsr varities of dukūla, manufactured in Kāmarūpa, had the 'colour of a rising Sun'. (*Socio-Economic History of Northern India*, Calcutta, 1960, p. 193).
468. Ibid., p. 145; *Pāiyalacchīnāmamālā*, p. 8, śloka 69.
469. Ibid., p. 197:

 ...saṁdhyārāgaraktāṁ śukadhāriṇyo vilāsanya iva...
470. Ibid., p. 164.
471. Ibid., p. 79.
472. Ibid., pp. 64-65.
473. *Pāiyalacchīnāmamālā*, p. 35, śloka 261.
474. *Tilaka-mañjarī*, p. 203.
475. *Pāiyalacchīnāmamālā*, p. 22, śloka 175.
476. Ibid., p. 8, śloka 69.

477. Ibid., p. 14, śloka 116.
478. *Tilaka-mañjarī*, p. 164.
479. *Pāiyalacchīnāmamālā*. p. 8, śloka 68.
480. *Tilaka-mañjarī*, p. 165.
481. Ibid , p. 131.
482. B.P. Majumdar, op. cit. p. 195.
483. Ibid., p. 193.
484. *Pāiyalacchīnāmamālā*, p. 32, śloka 238.
485. Ibid., śloka 236.
486. Ibid., śloka 237.
487. *Tilaka-mañjarī*, p. 67:

    Vipaṇivīthīṣu prtyāpaṇadvāraṃghataṅta kālāyasa'ālakāni...
488. *Pāiyalacchīnāmamālā*, p. 28, śloka 211.
489. Ibid., p. 31, śloka 231.
490. P.T.S. Ayyangar, *Bhojā Rājā*, pp. 94-95. *History and Culture of Indian People*, Vol. V, p. 519.
491. *Tilaka-mañjarī*, p. 69.
492. Ibid.
493. Ibid., p. 168.
494. Ibid., p. 8.
495. Ibid., p. 275.
496. Ibid., p. 368.
497. Ibid.
498. Ibid., p. 72.
499. Bhoja *Yuktikalpatru*, ed., I.C. Sastri (Calcutta, 1917), p. 80, śloka 5.
500. B.P. Majumdar, op. cit., p. 204.
501. *Pāiyalacchīnāmamālā*, p. 14.
502. *Tilaka-mañjarī*, p. 131:

    Dṛḍhakāṣṭhagumphaniṣṭhuranāvaḥ...
503. *Yuktikalpataru*, pp. 224-229.
504. *Pāiyalacchīnāmamālā*, p. 30, śloka 223.
505. Ibid., p. 37, śloka 269.
506. Ibid.
507. *Tilaka-mañjarī*, p. 70.
508. Ibid., p. 262.
509. Ibid., p. 267.
510. *Pāiyalacchīnāmamālā*, p. 12, śloka 103.
511. *Tilaka-mañjarī*, p. 34.
512. N.K. Bhattasali, *The Iconography of the Buddhist and Brahmanical Sculptures in Dacca Museum* (Dacca, 1929), p. 109.
513. Brijendra Nath Sharma, *Social and Cultural History of Northern India* (Delhi, 1972), p. 144.
514. *Pāiyalacchinānamamālā*, p. 18, śloka 143.
515. *E.I.*, XIV. p. 310.
516. *Pāiyalacchīnāmamālā*, p. 14, śloka 118.
517. See *Yuktikalpataru*, XXXVI, pp. 62-63.

518. *I.A.*, XII, pp. 201 ff.
519. *Tilaka-mañjarī*, p. 166.
520. Ibid., p. 70.
521. Bhoja, *Sṛṅgāramañjarī-kathā* (Bombay, 1968), p. 46.
522. *Mānasollāsa*, II : 126.
523. Ibid., III. 16; 1943-44.
524. Op. cit., 18 : 1970-71.
525. *Tilaka-mañjarī*, p. 34.
526. Ibid., p. 72.
527. Ibid., p. 368.
528, Ibid., p. 63.
529. *Pāiyalacchīnāmamālā*, p. 15, śloka 119.
530. *Tilaka-mañjarī*, p. 101.
531. *South Indian Inscriptions*, II : 93.
532. *Tilaka-mañjarī*, p. 43.
533. Ibid., p. 63.
534. For a detailed description of ornaments, See Chapter IV.
535. *Tilaka-mañjarī*, pp. 17, 34.
536. *Pāiyalacchīnāmamālā*, p. 37.
537. *Tilaka-mañjarī*, pp. 70, 87, 104.
538. *Pāiyalacchīnāmamālā*, p. 27.
539. Ibid., p. 15.
540. Ibid., p. 22, śloka 172; p. 12, śloka 104
541. Ibid., p. 32.
542. Ibid., p. 13.
543. Ibid., p. 37.
544. Ibid., p. 15.
545. Ibid., p. 31.
546. Ibid., p. 34.
547. Ibid., p. 16.
548. Ibid., pp. 37. 875.
549. Ibid., p. 18.
550. *Tilaka-mañjarī*, p. 117.
551. Ibid., p. 260.
552. Ibid., p. 117.
553. *Prabandhacintāmaṇi*, p. 106.
554. *Tilaka-mañjarī*, p. 66.
555. Ibid., pp. 67, 130.
556. Ibid., p, 260.
557. *Pāiyalacchīnāmamālā*, p. 14.
558. *Tilaka-mañjarī*, p. 67.
559. *Pāiyalacchīnāmamālā*, p. 30.
560. *E.I.*, XIV, pp. 300 ff.
561. *Tilaka-mañjarī*, p. 8.
562. Ibid., p. 293.
563. Ibid., p. 132.

564. Ibid., p. 95.
565. Ibid., pp. 131, 138, 140.
566. Buddha Prakash, *Studies in Indian History and Civilization* (Agra, 1962), p. 337.
567. *Tilaka-mañjarī*, p. 18:

    kadācidīṣryāruṇapratipramodākaṭākṣakarburamuparikṣipta raktotapalāśamiva kāpiśayanaṁ svayamutkṣipta māṇikya-caṣakaścandrikāprahā siṣuprāsādataleṣu premaparavaśaḥ-praṇayakupitāḥ preyasīḥ sānunayamapāyayat.
568. Kauṭilya, *Arthaśāstra*, ed., R. Shumshastri (Mysore, 1919-1929)), II: 26. p. 120:

    ...Madvikāraso madhu|
    tasya svadeśo vyākhyānam kāpiśāyanaṁ hārahūrakamiti||
569. M.E. Masson, *New Light on An Ancient Civilization* (Soviet Union, December, 1954), pp. 28-29.
570. Elliot and Dowson, *History of India as Told by Its Own Historians*, 8 Vols. (London, 1866-77), Vol. I, p. 14.
571. Sachau, I, 198.
572. Kālidāsa, *Raghuvaṁśa*, ed. Sita Ram Chaturvedi; Kālidāsa Granthāvali, (Banaras) VI, śloka 61:

    Pārasīkāṁstato jetuṁ pratasthe sthalavartmaṇā|
    indriyākhyāniva ripūṁstattvajñānena saṁyamī ||
573. Yādavaprakāśa, *Vaijayantī*, ed., G. Oopert (Madras, 1893), p. 111, 1: 189.
574. Op. cit., p. 252, 1:51.
575. *Tilaka-mañjarī*, pp. 106, 157.

    "Silk, one of the most important articles of trade in this whole period alongwith spices and cotton came from China and was unloaded at the Indian ports". (*India's Contribution to World Thought and Civilization*, p. 301).
576. Mahāvīrācārya, *Gaṇitasārsaṅgraha*, ed. M. Rangacarya (Varanasi, 1912), IV: 19-20.
577. Lallanji Gopal, *The Economic Life of Northern India* (Varanasi, 1965), p. 155.
578. *Jaurnal of Numismatic Society of India*, XX, p. 13.
579. Lallanji Gopal, op. cit., p. 111.
580. *Tilaka-mañjarī*, p. 127.
581. Ibid., pp. 133, 135, 137, 140.
582. Ibid., p. 133.
583. Haribhadra Sūri, *Samarāicchakohā*, ed., M.C. Modi (Allahabad, 1935), VI, p. 42.
584. Op. cit., VI, pp. 38-39.
585. *Tilaka-mañjarī*, p. 101.
586. Someśvara, *Mānasollāsa*, II: p. 1040,
587. *India's Coutribution to World Thought and Civilization*, p. 581.
588. Sayyid Sulaiman Nadvi, *Araba aur Bhārat ke Saṁbandna*, Hindi, tr. Ram Chandra Verma (Allahabad, 1930), p. 56.

589. Abūziad Sīrāfi, *T-avel Account* (Paris, 1811), p. 135.
590. Masūdī, *Murūjuz Dhahb*, Vol., II, (Paris), p. 488.
591. *India's Contribution to World Thought and Civilization*, p. 582. Ubla (Basrah), Suhar, Jar (Bahrein) and Adan were chief eentres of Sea trade with India, (p. 581).
592. *Pāiyalacchīnāmamālā*, p. 8.
593. Ibid., p. 15.
594. Ibid., p. 35.
595. Ibid., p. 33:

    Śālirakkhiā
596. Ibid., p. 29:

    Paripāsa utticchette jo puriso su-a-imrā-īe.
597. Ibid., p. 34.
598. B.P. Majumdar, *Socio-Economic History of Northern India* (Calcutta, 1960), p. 178.
599. *Pāiyalacchīnāmumālā*, p. 19.
600. Ibid., p. 34.
601. Ibid., p. 18.
602. *Sṛṅgāra-mañjarī-kathā*, pp. 67-68.
603. *Tilaka-mañjarī*, p. 417.
604. *E.I.*, XXXIII, p. 185.
605. *Tilaka-mañjarī*, pp. 133, 135, 137, 140, 260.
606. *History and Culture of Indian People*, Vol. IV, p. 403.
607. *Pāiyalacchīnāmamālā*, p. 16, śloka 131.
608. Ibid., p. 16, śloka 130.
609. Ibid., p. 4, śloka 28.
610. Ibid., p. 16, śloka 131.
611. Ibid., p. 16, śloka 130.
612. V. Smith, *Early History of India*, 4th ed. (Oxford, 1924), p. 41.
613. *Annual Report of Arch. Deptt. Baroda State*, 1934-35. p. 18.
614. *E.I.*, XIV, p. 182.
615. B.P. Majumdar, op. cit., p, 171.
616. Lallanji Gopal, op. cit., p. 1.
617. *Tilaka-mañjarī*, p. 182. John Garrat explains 'agrahāra' as "A village granted to the Brāhmaṇa by government free or at a favourable assessment; there are three kinds: (1) 'Sarvamānya'—rent free, (2) 'Jodi'—partially rent free, and (3) 'Trishvega'—one-third part of the produce is given as rent. (*A Classical Dictionary of India*, Reprint Delhi: Oriental Publishers, 1971, p. 17).
618. *E.I.*, XXXII. 148-56.
619. *Tilaka-mañjarī*, p. 352.
620. S. Beal, *The Life of Huen-Tsang* (London, 1888), p. 112.
621. R.S. Sharma, *Aspects of Political Ideas and Institutions in Ancient India* (Delhi, 1959), p. 722.
622. *I.A.*, VI, p. 53.
623. *Tilaka-mañjarī*, p. 103.

624. Lakṣmīdhara, *Kṛtyakalpataru*, ed. K.V.R. Aiyangar, p. 251.
625. Lallanji Gopal, op. cit., p. 16.
626. *Journal of Economic and Social History of India*, IV, pp. 99 f.
627. *Tilaka-mañjarī*, p. 103.
628. Lallanji Gopal, op. cit., p. 15.
629. Ibid., p. 13.
630. *E.I.*. XXXIII, p. 50.
631. Lallanji Gopal, op. cit., p. 13.
632. *E.I.*, XIV., pp. 156-63.
633. Ibid., V, pp. 113-114.
634. *E.I* , XXX (1953), pp 56-57.
635. *Mānassollāsa*, I: 113-47. Dr. Dasharatha Sharma mentions two types of taxes levied on the land, namely, Udraṅga or bhāga or dānī, a land tax paid in kind, generally at the rate of 1/6 or more of the procedure and Hiraṇya, a land tax paid in cash (Dasharatha Sharma, op. cit., p. 17). We are told by Alberunī, that one-sixth of the income made from the crops or from the cattle was to be paid to the ruler in recognition of the protection which he afforded to the subjects, their property and their families (Sachau, II, p. 149).
636. *E.I.*, XIX, p. 73, 1.27
637. *E.I.*, II, p. 48.
638. *I.A.*, XXI, p. 256.
639. *History and Culture of the Indian People*, Vol. II, p. 634.
640. *Tilaka-mañjarī*, p. 293.
641. Ibid:, p. 95.
642. Ibid., p. 74.
643. Ibid., p. 132. According to Dr. B D. Shukla, Dvīpāntara consisted of Burmā (Brahmā), Malāyā, Jāvā, Sumātrā, Bālī, Indonesia, Suvarṇabhūmi), Siam, Indo-China, Borneo, and the Philippines. (*Bhāratīya Saṁskriti kā Itihāsa*, Agra, 1971-72, p. 253.).
644. *Tilaka-mañjarī*, p. 427.
645. Ibid., p. 127.
646. See Muni Kanakāmara, *Karakaṇḍa Cariu*, ed Hiralal Jain (Delhi, 1964), p. 46.
647. Lallanji Gopal, op.cit , pp 131-32.
648. *History and Culture of Indian People*, Vol. IV, p. 443.
649. *Studies in Asian History and Culture*, ed. Buddha Prakash (Meerut, 1970), pp. 72-76.
650. Buddha Prakash, op. cit., pp. 76-78.
651. *History and Culture of Indian People*, Vol. IV, pp. 443-44.
652. *Tilaka-mañjarī*, p. 106.
653. Ibid., p. 127.
654. Ibid.
655. *I.H.Q.*, XIII, 590.
656. *B.K I.*, XC, pp. 73f.
657. R.C. Majumdar, *Suvarṇadvīpa*, Part II (Dacca, 1937-38), p. 351.

658. Op. cit.
659. *India's Contribution to World Thaught and Culture*, p. 20.
660. K.A. Nilakanta Shastri, *The Age of the Nandas and Mauryas* (Banaras, 1952), pp. 218-19.
661. *Tilaka-mañjarī*, pp. 134-35.
662. Ibid., p. 134:
   Tāḍaparṇakot kīrṇakarṇāṭādilipiṣu pustakeṣu virlamavalokyamānasaṁskṛtānuviddhasvadeśabhāṣānibaddha kāvya prabandhāni...
663. Ibid.:
   ...*Stokārthe lokāmi*...
664. Ibid.:
   ...*Svalpadharmādharma vivekāni*...
665. Ibid.:
   ...*Virala varṇāśramācārāni*...
666. Ibid.:
   ...*Paramita pākhaṇḍivyavahārāṇi*...
667. Ibid.:
   ...*Rucirodbhaṭastrīveṣaracanāni*...
668. Ibid.:
   ...*Duravabodhabhaṣā vacanāni*...
669. Ibid.:
   ...*Svabhāvabhīṣaṇakāraiḥ*...
670. Ibid.:
   ...*Vikṛtaveṣāḍambara dhāribhiḥ*...
671. Ibid.:
   ...*Ravaṇādivotpanna paradāra grahaṇābhilāṣaiḥ*...
672. Ibid,,
   ...*Laṁkāniśacaralokādiva saṁkrāntakāyakāla kāntibhiḥ*...
673. Ibid.:
   ...*Anyāya priyatayā*...
674. Ibid.:
   Aṅgīkṛtāti vikaṭakalahāḥ kaṭībhāgennā kalayadbhiḥ...
675. Ibid.:
   Niṣādādhipaiḥ saṁrakṣitāni...
676. Siddharṣi Sūri, *Upamitībhavaprapañca-kathā*, ed. P. Peterson (Calcutta, 1899), pp. 996-98.
677. *Karpūramañjarī*, ed. Rajkumara Acharya. p. 10.

5

Religious Condition

ŚAIVISM AND VAIṢṆAVISM

The works of Dhanapāla furnish fairly sufficient evidence with regard to the principal religious systems—Hindu and Jaina—prevailing in his days. Not only that, there are scattered in his works allusions to various other religious sects popular at that time. By collating and coordinating these references, we can form a fairly good idea of the religious climate of the age.

What lends great credibility to the material provided by Dhanapāla and renders it of positive, permanent value is the poet's non-sectarian, broad and catholic outlook in religious matters as evidenced everywhere in his works and, more significantly, at the very outset of his masterpieces, *Tilaka-mañjarī* and *Pāiyalacchīnāmamālā*. In spite of his being a staunch follower of Jainism, Dhanapāla invokes (without compunction) in the introductory verses of *Pāiyalacchīnāmamālā* and *Tilaka-mañjarī* a whole host of Jaina and Hindu deities like Ṛṣabhadeva,[1] Brahmā,[2] Viṣṇu,[3] Maheśa,[4] Rāma,[5] Kṛṣṇa,[6] Balarāma,[7] Pārvatī,[8] Bhavānī. Durgā, Kālī Caṇḍī, Kātyānī,[9] Sūrya,[10] Candra,[11] Agni,[12] Madana,[13] Indra,[14] Skanda,[15] Kubera,[16] Buddha[17] etc.

This invocation may be taken as a pointer to the preponderance of Śaivism, Vaiṣṇavism, Jainism and Buddhism during Dhanapāla's time. The kings of the time appear to have been generally tolerant towards all religions.

Śaivism

A considerable body of people during Dhanapāla's time were Śaivites who followed the customary veneration of the

'Śiva-liṅga' (phallus worship) in their temples. We learn from *Tilaka-mañjarī* that Śiva-liṅgas were worshipped in the pagodas (phallus-shaped temples) situated in the capitals of the enemies of king Bhoja. The Śiva-liṅgas were bathed and anointed with flowers.[18] Śiva was known by several names like 'Śambhu', 'Śūlina', 'Giriśa', 'Bhava', 'Pinākin', 'Sthāṇu',[19] 'Mahābhairava',[20] 'Mahākāla'[21] and 'Trayambaka'.[22] Śiva seems to have been the guardian deity of the Paramāra kings whose inscriptions invariably begin with the salutation 'Om namaḥ Śivāya'.

In the Paramāra inscriptions, Śiva, is called as 'Śrīkaṇṭha', 'Śambhu', 'Bhavānīpati', 'Amareśvara', 'Omkāra', 'Mahākāla', 'Kālakāleśvara', 'Siddhanātha', 'Nīlakaṇṭheśvara', 'Maneśvara', 'Udaleśvara', 'Vaidyanātha' and 'Gohaḍeśvara'.[23]

Śaivism was practised in medieval India in various forms. Pratipal Bhatia names the four principal schools of Śaivism as 'Śaiva', 'Kāpālika', 'Paśupata' and 'Kāruṇika-Siddhānta' or 'Karkasiddhāntā' and holds that the first three were prevalent in Paramāra's period, as references to these are found in Paramāra Inscriptions.[24] Dhanapāla's imagination appears to have been particularly stirred by the blood-curdling practices of the Kāpālikas. In *Tilaka-mañjarī*, we get a hair-raising, real-life picturization of a Vetāla (Kāpālika) whose black body[25] is terrifying to look at.[26] He is deformed[27] and his emaciated, stony-hard, rugged and rough body[28] is reduced to a skeleton.[29] He wears anklets of bones[30] and has a thick crop of yellow and glittering hair on his head.[31]

The Vetāla has fat feet[32] and long legs[33] on which raised and thickly lined veins are clearly visible.[34] He has big and pointed nails[35] on the fingers of his feet. His lean, skinny knees are capped with knobs of bones.[36] His ribs are visible from a distance.[37] The infant-snakes are sleeping in the cavities and the pits of the ribs.[38] He has small, hardened fingers with sharp nails jutting therefrom.[39] Around his waist he wears a pelt of lion-skin drenched with turbid blood dripping out of the wound over his thigh.[40] The wound has been caused by repeated strikes of stings inflicted on his thigh by the poisonous snakes coiled round the Kāpālika's waist.[41] He wears the garland of a human-skull cleared of the jaw by the Kāpālika himself to bring about the fruition (siddhi) of his supernatural spell or incantation (mantra).[42] He has a long and thin chin wherefrom hangs a long beard[43] which has the effect of accentuating the weirdness of his jet-black visage. His loud laughs are terrifying.[44]

His big, bloodshot, circular eyes blazing out of their uncanny sockets strike terror on others.[45] He holds a human-skull, in his left hand, filled with blood-wine[46] and carries a sharp dagger in his right hand.[47] Two snakes with raised hoods are curled round his ears.[48] A deadly snake is hanging on his forehead[49] which is laced with finger-prints drenched in blood.[50] He peels dead bodies and eats the flesh and bones of corpses.[51] The bits and pieces of bones and flesh entrapped in his teeth, while eating, are visible.[52] He wears round his neck a string of human skulls hanging up to the knees.[53] The avowed object of the Vetālika who worships Śiva in the shape of Mahābhairava[54] is the attainment of supernatural yogic powers known as the 'siddhis'.[55]

The Kāpālika system was highly tantric in its texture. The Tilakawādā inscription of Bhoja refers to an ascetic who had taken a Māhavrata.[56] In this copper plate, the Mahāvratin is described as Śankara in Kapālī form.[57] In *Tilaka-mañjarī*, king Meghavāhana is described as having a Mahābhairava dagger.[58]

Śiva worship, by and large, took the form of veneration of the Śivaliṅgaṁ in Dhanapāla's time.[59] Descriptions regarding Śiva temples frequently occur in *Tilaka-mañjarī*.[60] The kings of Paramāra dynasty followed this religion. Śīyaka II has been described as one who heard the whole of Śaiva Siddhānta and was like a Śiva on Kailāśa.[61] Vākpati Muñja is said to have worshipped Bhavānipati (Śiva) at the time of making his land grant.[62] The same inscription also refers to a Śiva-lake which was dug by Vākpati II as a mark of his veneration towards Śiva.[63] Muñja is said to have built many Śiva temples at places like Ujjain, Maheśvara and Māndhātā.[64] King Sindhurāja like his fore-fathers was a great devotee of Śiva. He is described to have established a Śiva-Liṅgaṁ which was presented to him by Śaṅkhapāla in his Kularajadhānī Dhārā.[65] Śaivism registered tremendous progress under king Bhoja who was a devout Śaivite (till his alleged conversion to Jainism).

He worte *Tattvaprakāśa*, a famous work, to propound the essentials of Śaiva philosophy.[66]

Archaeological survey of the period also corroborates the statements cited from *Tilaka-mañjarī* and testifies that Śaivism was a popular religion during Dhanapāla's time.

The *Udaipur Praśasti* informs us that Bhoja beautified the world by covering it with temples dedicated to Kadāreśvara, Rāmeśvara, Somanātha, Suṁdīra, Kāla, Anala and Rudra.[67]

A large temple, known as Bhojeśvara temple, stands at Bhojapura, 20 miles to the south of the city of Bhopal. It appears to have been built by king Bhoja Paramāra and named after him. Inside the temple stands a colossel 'Śiva-Liṅgaṁ', seven and a half feet high and more than seventeen feet in girth on a platform made of three superimposed blocks of standstone.[68] The Samidheśvara or Tribhuvana Narāyaṇa temple of Chittor, dedicated to Śiva, is also believed to have been built by Bhoja Paramāra.[69]

The most beautiful temple in India named Nīlakaṅṭheśvara Mahādeva temple was built by king Udayāditya Paramāra (A.D 1070-86) at Udaipura, a village twenty miles to the north of Bhilsā.[70] There is a big stone 'Liṅgaṁ' inside the interior part of the temple known as 'garbhagṛha' (sanctum. sanctorum).[71]

An important group of Śiva temples built during Paramāra kings exists at Ūna in the Nīmar district of Madhya Pradesh.[72]

Bundelkhanḍ was also an important stronghold of Śaivism during the rule of Candellas in the X, XI &XII centuries. The Copper-plates of the Candella dynasty refer to Śiva as one who holds the moon (from whom Candellas claimed their descent) on his head. The biggest temple of Khajurāho is dedicated to Śiva and is known today as Kanḍariya Mahādeva temple. Besides, Śiva-Liṅga in large numbers have been found in Khajurāho.[73] An image of Nandī, one of the two chief attendants of Śiva, and an image of a bull, the conveyance (Vāhana) of Śiva, have also been found at Khajurāho.[74] Kīrtivarman of the Candella dynasty, the patron of poet Kṛṣṇa Miśra, who wrote *Prabodha-candrodaya*, built a temple dedicated to Śiva at Mahobā.[75]

During Dhanapāla's time splendid Śiva temples were built also by Cāhamāna rulers at Puśkara, Maṇḍalgarh and Jahāzpur. Other important Śiva temples of the time had been found at Bijolia, Bādolī, Nāgdā and Kalayāṇapur.[76]

Vaiṣṇavism

Like Śaivism, the cult of Viṣṇu too commanded a sizable following during Dhanapāla's time as adduced from references in *Tilaka-mañjarī* and *Pāiyalacchīnāmamālā*. Dhanapāla says that Vaiṣṇavties practised their religion strictly in accordance with the established norms and hoary traditions of Vaiṣṇavism.[77]

The Vaiṣṇavties swore by Avatāravāda or the belief that the God (Viṣṇu) incarnated himself again and again on Earth to reward the virtuous and to punish the wicked of the world. In *Tilaka-mañjarī*, king Meghavāhana is equated with God Acyuta (Viṣṇu) who holds the conch-shell (Śaṅkha) in one hand and the wheel (cakra) in the other.[78] The 'Śaṅkha' was the emblem of the supremacy of the good, while the 'Cakra' stood for the destruction of Evil in the Vaiṣṇavite lore. Viṣṇu was variously known as 'Trivikrama'[79] 'Vāmana-avatāra' 'Sauri', 'Daśarhanātha', 'Vaikuṇṭha', 'Madhumaṭha', 'Urvida',[80] (Upendra), 'Acyuta'[81] etc.

The 'Nara Siṁha-avatāra' (the Man-Lion incarnation), the 'Varāha-avatāra' (the Boar incarnation) and the 'Vāmana-avatāra' (the Dwarf incarnation) were among the more popular names under which Viṣṇu was venerated in the country[82] during Dhanapāla's time.

The epigraphic evidence also confirms that the Viṣṇu cult was in a position of ascendancy during Dhanapāla's time. The Paramāra rulers were worshippers of Viṣṇu. They adopted 'Garuḍa' (a Species of the heron eagle) the vehicle of Viṣṇu, as their State Emblem. Garuḍa is usually delineated at a corner of the Viṣṇu image doing obeisance with folded hands (namaskāramudrā). Sometimes he is shown carrying his master at his back.[83] Sīyaka II of Paramāra dynasty was a devotee of Viṣṇu. He invokes the blessings of 'Nara Siṁha' (the Man Lion incarnation of Viṣṇu) in his Harsola Copper Grant.[84]

Vaiṣṇava cult maintained its sway even after Dhanapāla's times Various incarnations of Viṣṇu have been invoked in the *Nāgapur praśasti* of Naravarman's time.[85]

Temples dedicated to Viṣṇu are also referred to in *Tilaka-mañjarī*.[86] From epigraphic sources we learn of a Viṣṇu temple of Paramāra period viz., the temple of Daityasūdana built near Māndhātā.[87] There is an incomplete temple of Viṣṇu at Nīmar which belongs to the period of Paramāra dynasty.[88] Another temple dedicated to the Varāhāvatāra of Viṣṇu (Boar-incarnation) of the times of Dhanapāla is situated at Candrāvatī.[89] The famous temple of Paṭanārāyaṇa stood at Girwar, a village four miles to the east of Madhusūdana.[90] The temples of Kayadrān, Candrāvatī, Girwar and Karoḍī-Dhaj contain the images of Viṣṇu, Garuḍa, and Kalkī-Avatāra[91] (the last incarnation of Viṣṇu which is yet to come).

Rāmaite and Kṛṣṇite were the two major cults of Vaiṣṇavism and references to both the cults are found in Dhanapāla's works. In *Tilaka-mañjarī*, we hear of Kinnaras who sing songs in praise of Rāma's miraculous actions.[92] Other *Rāmāyaṇa* characters such as Saumitra, Sītā, Aṅgada, Jatāyu, Urmilā, Sugrīva, Rāvaṇa, Kumbhakarṇa, Akṣa, Mārīca etc. are also mentioned in *Tilaka-mañjarī*,[93] in the context of the roles played by them in the epic. It may be presumed that the study of *Rāmāyaṇa* of Vālmīki was wide-spread in those days and the position of Rāma as an 'Avatāra' of Viṣṇu had received popular acceptance. Rājaśekhara describes Rāma in terms of "Viṣṇu with the name of Rāma and the seventh avatāra of Vaikuṇṭha".[94] Dhanapāla expresses his admiration of the character of Saumitra in *Tilaka-mañjarī*.[95]

The Kṛṣṇite cult was equally strong and popular in the days of Dhanapāla. Keśava was worshipped as another avatāra of Viṣṇu. We read in *Tilaka-mañjarī*[96] that a sizable segment of the population consisted of strong devotees of Bhagavāna Kṛṣṇa. Dhanapāla invokes God Kṛṣṇa in the opening verse of *Pāiyalacchīnāmamālā*.[97] The worship of Kṛṣṇa as Kālīdamana was in vogue.[98]

The epigraphic evidence also testifies to the popularity of Kṛṣṇite cult. A sleeping female and a child sprawling on a cushion beside the mother represented on a black stone sculpture has been found at Arthuna belonging to the XI or the first quarter of the XII century.[99] Shri Agarwal and U.C. Bhattacarya hold that this sculpture represents Yaśodā resposing with the infant Kṛṣṇa.[100] Several episodes associated with Kṛṣṇa's life such as three cows standing before Kṛṣṇa, Kṛṣṇa's fight with the horse demon, Śakatabhanga and Kṛṣṇa's fight with the bull demon, have been depicted to the left of the entrance of Someśvara temple belonging to Dhanapāla's time.[101]

The worship of Balarāma alongwith Kṛṣṇa was also prevalent. Dhanapāla has invoked Balarāma in *Pāiyalacchīnāmamālā.*[102] In his treatise *Samarāṅgaṇa Sūtradhāra* Bhoja has laid down that the temples of Brahmā, Indra, Balarāma and Kṛṣṇa should be built in the centre of the city.[103] This description proves that temples dedicated both to Kṛṣṇa and Balarāma existed in Dhanapāla's time. Balarāma was also known by the name of Saṁkarṣaṇa.[104]

JAINISM AND BUDDHISM

Jainism

Dhanapāla's works provide conclusive evidence to show that Jainism had become firmly established in the northern and central parts of India in his days. Moreover, being a 'śrāvaka' (i.e., a devout, initiated Jina faithful), Dhanapāla freely displays a first hand knowledge of the fundamental postulates, tenets and doctrines of Jina Dharama and Metaphysics. In the hymns composed in honour of Ṛṣabhadeva and Mahāvīra Dhanapāla reveals his rare understanding of the character, personality and spiritual attainments of the First and the Last Jaina Tīrthaṅkaras ("ford makers") respectively, the two most famous of the twenty-four[105] teachers of Jainism. In other words, Dhanapāla's works not only furnish reliable data to help determine the state of Jainism in his times but also render positive help to the interested reader to come to grips with the essential spirit of Jaina faith.

Dhanapāla has written *Ṛṣabhapañcāśikā* in praise of Āditīrthaṅkara 'Śrī Ṛṣabhadeva and *Satyapurīya Śrī Mahāvīra Utsāha*' in praise of Lord Mahāvīra. In the opening verses of

Tilaka-mañjarī[106] Dhanapāla prays for the blessings of the Tirthaṅkaras. He invokes Ādi Tīrthaṅkara Ṛṣabha at the conclusion of *Ṛṣabhapuñcāśikā.*[107]

The Jaina temples are frequently referred to in *Tilaka-mañjarī.*[108] King Meghavāhana, a devotee of Ṛṣabhadeva,[109] goes along with his servants to the temple of Ṛṣabhadeva which had high spires and arched gateways. The Jaina temple of Ṛṣabhadeva was so beautiful and magnificent that even deities from 'Devaloka' supposedly came to see its beauty out of curiosity.[110] The popularity of Jaina temples is proved by the fact that during the reign of Bhīma I Calukya of Anhilwāḍa, his minister, Vimala of the Prāgvāta family, built at Ābū the most magnificent temple of Ādinātha, Ṛṣabhadeva. Even now the temple is considered to be unique in the world.[111]

Dhanapāla got a Jaina temple built at Sācore and installed there the image of Ṛṣabhadeva.[112]

The practice of idolatory had come into force among the Jainas in Dhanapāla's time. The poet speaks of the idols of Tīrthaṅkaras installed in the temples and adored by the laity.[113] Magnificent images (idols) of Tīrthaṅkara Mahāvīra were installed in the temples.[114] We read in *Tilaka-mañjarī* of a high idol of Lord Mahāvīra seated on a throne, wrought in gold, installed in the interior part of the temple (garbhagṛha).[115] The installation of golden dols testifies to the piety and the economic prosperity of the Jaina community which continues to the present day. An image of Ṛṣabhadeva belonging to the X century A.D. established in Surohar district in Bengal is a specimen of remarkable iconography on account of its rare features.[116]

From the pages of *Tilaka-mañjarī* we learn that Lord Mahāvīra's birth anniversary[117] ('Janma mahotsava') and death anniversary[118] ('nirvāṇa divasa') were observed with unbounded devotion and due decorum and ceremony. The death anniversary fell on the full-moon's day in the month of Kārttika.[119]

Pilgrimages to the holy shrines (Tīrthayātrā of Siddha Kṣetras) are also mentioned in *Tilaka-mañjarī.*[120] The Siddhakṣetras were closely associated with the life of the Tīrthaṅkaras. These were the places where they had attained miraculous powers of Control. Going on a pilgrimage has been a very old practice among the Jainas. The pilgrims worshipped at the Jaina temples situated at various Tīrthas.[121] The poet Dhanapāla, visited various holy places during his life time.[132]

Besides the Tīrthaṅkaras, the Gaṇadharas and other devatās (gods) were also worshipped among Jainas during Dhanapāla's time. Dhanapāla, in an introductory verse of *Tilaka-mañjarī,* invokes the aid of the first Gaṇadhara, Indrabhūti or Gautama.[123] According to Jagdish Chandra Jain, there existed eleven orders of Gaṇadharas in ancient India. He states, "Mahāvīra had eleven Gaṇadharas or heads of the schools. The eldest Gaṇadhara was Indrabhūti. He was followed by Aggibhūi, Vāubhūi, Viyatta, Suhamma Maṇḍiya, Moriyaputta, Akampiya, Ayalabhāyā, Meijja and Pabhāsa....... These Gaṇadharas were all Brāhmaṇa teachers and all except Indrabhūi and Suhamma, died during the life time of Mahāvīra....... Goyama Indabhūi cut as-under the tie of friendship which he had for his Master and attained Kevalinship the same night when Mahāvīra died. He survived Mahāvīra for twelve years and finally achieved salvation at Rāyagiha at the age of ninety two....... After Mahāvīra's death Suhamma, the fifth Gaṇadhara, became the head of Jaina Community".[124]......

As referred to in *Tilaka-mañjarī,*[125] there were four orders of devatās. The *Tattvārthasūtra*[126] defines the four orders as: (i) 'Bhavanavāsī', (ii) 'Vyaṅtara', (iii) 'Jyotiṣka', (iv) 'Vaimānika'. Bhavanavāsī devas are sub-divided into ten categories,[127] namely, 'Asura Kumāra', 'Nāga Kumara', 'Vidyuta Kumāra', 'Suparṇa Kumāra', 'Udadhi Kumāra', 'Dvīpa Kumāra' and 'Dikka Kumāra'. Of these, the AsuraKumāra devas generally dwell inside the houses, hence they are known as Bhuvanavāsī. The remaining nine kinds of Bhavanavāsī devas dwell somewhere in the atmosphere between the poles of earth and heaven at a distance of about 1000 Yojanas from the centre of the earth.[123]

Eight types of Vyantaras are 'Kinnara', 'Kimpuruṣa', 'Mahoraga', 'Gandharva', 'Yakṣa', 'Rākṣasa', 'Bhuta' and 'Piśāca'.[129] These Vyantaras have their further sub-divisions. For instance, Kinnaras are of ten types, namely, 'Kimpuruṣa',

'Hṛdyagama', Kinnara, 'Rūpamālī', 'Kīnnara-kīnnara', 'Anindita', 'Manorama', 'Kinnarottama', 'Ratipriya' and 'Ratiṣreṣṭha'. Kimpuruṣa are of ten types viz., 'Puruṣa', 'Puruṣottama' 'Satpuruṣa', 'Mahāpuruṣa', 'Puruṣaprabha', 'Stipuruṣa', 'Maruta', 'Marudeva', 'Marutprabha' and 'Yaśasvata'.

Mahoraga are divided into ten classes in their angelic hierarchy, namely, 'Bhujaga', 'Bhujaṅgaśālī', 'Mahākāya', 'Atikāya', 'Skndhaśālī', 'Manohara', 'Aśanijava', 'Maheśvarya', 'Gambhīra' and 'Priyadarśanā'.

Ten types of Gaṇdharvas are, 'Hāhā', 'Hūhū', 'Nārada', 'Tumburuka', 'Kadamba', 'Vāsava', 'Mahāsvara', 'Gītarati', 'Gīta-Yaśa' and 'Daivata'.

The angels, known as 'Yakṣas', have twelve divisions in their order, viz., 'Maṇibhadra', 'Pūrṇabhadra', 'Śailabhadra', 'Manobhadra', 'Bhadraka', 'Subhadra', 'Sarvabhadra'. 'Mānuṣa', 'Dharmapāla' 'Surūpayakṣa', 'Yakṣottama' and 'Manohara'.

The Rākṣasas are of seven categories i.e., 'Bhīma', 'Mahābhīma', 'Vighnavināyaka', 'Udaka', 'Rākṣasa', 'Rakṣasa-Rakṣasa' and 'Brahma-Rākāṣasa', while Bhūtas are seven in number i.e., 'Surūpa', 'Pratirūpa', 'Bhūtottama', 'Pratibhūta', 'Mahābhūta', 'Praticchana', and 'Ākāśabhūta'. The Piśacas are of fourteen denominations viz., 'Kūṣmaṇḍa', 'Rākṣasa', 'Yakṣa', 'Sammoha', 'Tāraka', 'Acaukṣa', 'Kāla', 'Mahākāla', 'Caukṣa', 'Satālaka', 'Deha', 'Mahādeha', 'Tūṣṇīka' and 'Pravacana'.[130]

On Gṛddhapiccha's authority we come to know that the Vyantara devas move on earth and by air from one country to another. They are dressed in fine clothes and ornaments. As a rule Caity trees are found growing before the dwellings of these devas.[131]

We learn from the same authority that 'Jyotiṣka' devas are of five types, namely, 'Sūrya-Candra', 'Gṛha', 'Nakṣtra', 'Prākīrṇaka' and 'Tāraka'.[132] Jyotiṣka devas who are resplendent dwell at the height of nine hundred Yojanas from this earth and are generally itinerant.[133]

Vaimānikas are of two categories—'Kalpopapannā' and 'Kalpātīta'.[134] These devas dwell in the sky. The devas who dwell in 'Kalpa' are called 'Kalpopapannā' and those living above the Kalpa are 'Kalpātīta'.[135] The Vaimānikas dwell in 'Saudharma aiśana',[136] 'Sānat-Kumāra-Māhendra', 'Brahma-

Brahmottara', 'Lāntava-Kāpiṣṭha', 'Sukra-Mahāṣukara', 'Śatā-ra-Sahastrāra', 'Ānata-Prāṇata', 'Āraṇa-Acyuta', 'Naugraive-yaka', 'Vijaya', 'Vaijayanta', 'Jayanta', 'Aparajita' and 'Sar-vārtha siddha'.[137]

Among the four categories of the gods discussed above, Dhanapāla makes specific mention of 'Vaimānikas'.[138] In *Ttlaka-mañjarī*, we read Vidyādharamuni[139] and Sumālī deva[140] getting down to earth to see its beauty. Vaimānikas are suppos-ed to practise an art (mantra) by which they attain the power of moving in the sky.[141]

In the spirit of a devout Jaina, Dhanapāla commends the Jaina doctrine of 'Trīratna' (three jewels) viz. 'Samyag darśana', 'Samyag jñana' and 'Samyak carita' (right faith, right knowledge and right conduct) which constitute the path-way to emancipa-tion. The life of Lord Mahāvīra represents the enshrinement of 'Trīratna'[142] in its pristine glory.

In *Ṛṣbhapañcāśika*, Dhanapāla has touched upon the concept of mithyātva. The Āgamic epistemology regards the rightness or wrongness of knowledge as ultimately dependant upon the rightness or the wrongness of the attitude. If the soul is possessed of perverted attitude (mithyātva) its knowledge is necessarily wrong. If it is possessed of right attitude (Samya-ktva), its knowledge is right. Knowledge is the 'intrensic' character of the soul. But it is vitiated by 'mithyātva' which is the Jaina equivalent of the principle known as 'avidyā' in other systems. The mithyātva vitiates the very texture of the soul and all the imperfections of the worldly existence are ultimately due to it. Dhanapāla is very much assured that mithyātva can be annihilated by hearing vacanāmṛtam.[143]

> *Ṇamo arhaṁtāṇāṁ, ṇamo siddhāṇaṁ, ṇamo āiriyāṇaṁ,*
> *ṇamo Uajjhāyāṇaṁ, ṇamo, loye sabba sāhūnaṁ//*

In *Vīrastuti* Dhanapāla has described Lord Mahāvīra to be the abode of 'Guṇas'.[144] It is a basic postulate of Jaina faith that the soul passes through an infinite number of states while reaching from the lowest to the highest stage of spirtual development. The Jaina philosophers have analysed the various stages of spiritual development. They refer to fourteen successive stages leading to the purity of soul, purity of tence and purity of consciousness. These stages, called 'Guṇasthāna',[145] are: (1) 'mithyādṛṣṭi-guṇasthāna', (2) 'Sāsādana-Samyag-dṛṣṭi', (3) 'Samyag mithyā dṛṣti', (4) 'Avitrata Samyag dṛṣti', (5) 'Deśavirata' (6) 'Pramattasaṁyata', (7) 'Apramatta Saṁyata', (8) 'Apūrva Karana', (9) 'Anivṛtti Samparāya', (10) 'Sūkṣma-Samparāya', (11) 'Upśaṅtamoha', (12) 'Ksīṇa-moha', (13) 'Sayoga Kevalī', (14) 'Ayoga Kevalī'.

Ṛṣabhapañcāśikā[146] has reflected upon the doctrine of Nayavāda. Eulogising the Nayavāda theory Dhanapāla asserts that even opponents are reconciled in no time by putting before them the seven forms of naya. Mallisena says in his *Syādvāda-mañjarī* (śloka 30) that "just as disputants cease from their quarrels after restoring to an impartial judge, similarly, the other nayas, though mutually hostile, are reconciled in the system of 'Arhat', their differences being smoothed over by the use of expression Syāt, "may be".[147] The doctrine of 'Syādvāda' is claimed to be a great synthesis comprising all the Nayas without any distinction.

In *Vīrastuti*, Dhanapāla refers to Syādvāda—another important doctrine of Jainism.[148] As a matter of fact the cardinal feature of Jaina metaphysics is found reflected in the doctrine of 'may be' which asserts that no single proposition can express the whole of Reality fully. The term Syādvāda is derived from the term 'Syāt', meaning 'may be'. Dasgupta explains the significance of the term 'may be' as follows: 'The truth of each affirmation is . . . only conditional and inconceivable from the absolute point of view. To guarantee correctness, therefore, each Affirmation should be preceded by the phrase 'Syāt' (may be). This will indicate that the affirmation is only relative, made somehow from some point of view and under some reservations and not in any sense of absolute. There is no judgment which is absolutely true and no judgment which is absolutely false. All judgments are true in some sense and false in another".[149]

The seven modes of predication (Syādvāda) are:[150]

1. May be, Reality is (Syāt asti dravyam).
2. May be, Reality is not (Syāt nāsti dravyam).
3. May be, Reality is and is not (Syād asti ca nāsti ca dravyam).

4. May be, Reality is indescribable (Syādavakt-avyam dravyam).
5. May be, Reality is and is indescribable (Syād asti ca avaktavyam dravyam).
6. May be, Reality is not and is indescribable (Syāt nāsti ca avaktavyam dravyam).
7. May be, Reality is, is not and is indescribable (Syād asti ca nāsti ca avaktavyam dravyam).

In *Ṛṣabhapañcāśikā* Dhanapāla has discussed the bondage which is caused by false views, lack of self-restraint and other factors such as passions and yoga or the vibrations produced in the soul by the activities of mind, body and speech.[151] In one of the verses of *Srī Vīrastuti*, Dhanapāla has referred to four passions (kasāyas) viz. anger (krodha), pride (māna) deceit (māyā) and greed (lobha) and quasi-passions which are nine in number, namely, laughter (hāsya), abdication (rati), bewailing (arati) disappointment (śoka), fear (bhaya), disgust (jugupsā), hankering after women (strīveda), hankering after men (puruṣa-veda), hankering after men and women (napuṅsaka veda).[152] The quasi-passions coexist with the passions and are also inspired by them. According to Dhanapāla, 'Vedatrayī' (three-fold hankering) is the enemy of the man who desires to advance on the path to emancipation.[153] According to K.K. Handiqui, vedatrayī is held to be the cause of transmigration.[154]

During Dhanapāla's time Jaina 'mantravāda' had come into existence as is evident from allusions in his work *Tilaka-mañjarī* to the 'Vidyādharas',[155] 'Ākāśagamanadāynīvidyā',[156] 'Aparājitavidyā',[157] 'Siddhamantra vidyā',[159] the veneration and cultivation of the Mantrika deities like 'Aṣṭavidyās'[159] etc.

We are told by Dhanapāla that the Sādhaka (devotee) had to meditate for a period of six months for getting 'siddhi' (fulfilment) to become Vidyādhara narendra. The procedure was a difficult one entailing numerous hardships and hurdles. The sādhaka, after taking bath thrice in the water-fall, having worshipped the images of Vidyādevāḥ, which were installed there, sat in a mountain cave with a very narrow entrance. It was a dark closet known as 'rasātalagṛha' where light could not enter. On all the sides of the cave there were big trees. Flowers and incense were brought for worshipping the vidyādevāḥ. The sādhaka sat in a 'padmāsana' posture, holding 'rudrākṣamālā' in his right hand. He brought his mind to the pinpoint of complete concentration (nigṛhītacetāḥ). Then began certain natural disturbances but the sādhaka was required to remain undeterred. Frightful apparitions and nightmares ensued—in short, almost every thing which would make the sādhaka give up the sādhana. As soon as the sādhaka began the chanting of mantra, gatherings of demons would come there, to terrify the sādhaka and divert him from his path.[160]

Further distraction would come in the shape of Vidyādharas who would stage plays, sing and play on musical instruments. They would visit the sādhaka daily to divert him with music and dance. When the efforts of the demons and merry-makers (Vidyādharas) could not divert him from his devotions, the immovable and unchangeable (*adarśa vikāra*) sādhaka was subjected to physical violence. He was assaulted with thunderbolts, and fires were set raging on all sides. Some disturbing elements made ear-piercing loud laughs. But the sādhaka was not unnerved or frightened and continued his 'japa' (recitation) with the fullest concentration (*ekagreṇa manasā*). After the expiry of six months (*Saṭasumāṣesu parisamāptāyāṁ*), all of a sudden a celestial damsel (surabadhū) glittering like lightning appeared before the sādhaka and asked him to open his eyes. She informed the 'sādhaka' that 'aṣṭapradhānavidya' devatas being very much impressed by his meditations had come down to the earth from heaven and wanted to know, what they could do for him.[161]

The king Meghavāhana in *Tilaka-mañjarī* is said to recite the mantra of 'Aprājitavidyā' thrice daily with the intention of having a son. The mantra was to be recited before Rāja-Lakṣmī.[162] The king is actually said to have pleased Lakṣmī with his sādhanā. His son also becomes a Vidyādhara by virtue of his single-minded recitations of the mantra of 'Asṭavidyās'.[163]

As stated earlier, Bhoja Paramāra was tolerant towards all religions and through the softening influence of Dhanapāla, he had become favourably inclined towards Jina Dharma.[164] During his reign in the early part of the XI century A.D., the great Jaina Śvetāmbara teacher, Amma Deva, flourished in

Khandesh in the southern division of the Paramāra kingdom. He was a forceful preacher and was able to convert many people to his faith. Numerous Jaina temples were erected in that province, in one of which was installed the image of Munisuvrati.[165] A number of Jaina temples, which were built in the middle of the XI century have been discovered at Ūn in Nīmar district.[166] A group of three images of Jaina Tīrthaṅkaras have been discovered in a small temple outside the fort at Shergarh, which was a great religious establishment of the Jainas in the early medieval period. The three Tīrthaṅkaras represented are 'Śāntinātha', 'Kuṅthanātha' and 'Aranātha'.[167] A number of fanes dedicated to Jaina Tīrthaṅkaras were constructed in Ābū during the reign of Paramāras.[168]

It thus becomes evident that during Dhanapāla's time, Jainism was not limited to Khandesh but had extended further east into the Central Provinces, within the boundaries of the Paramāra dominion, as a result of the liberal religious outlook of Bhoja.

The Paramāra kings patronised Jaina ācāryas, poets and scholars. Amitagati, Mahāsena, Dhanapāla and Dhaneśvara received the royal patronage of Muñja Vākpati II. Dhanapāla, Prabhācandra, Devabhadra, Jineśvarasūri, Abhayadeva, Buddhisāgara, Nemicandra, Nayanandi and others were patronized by Rājā Bhoja.

Jainism found a new life in Gujarat under the patronage of Cālukya Kumarapāla (A.D. 1145-1172). Jainas received encouragement from him and therefore they carried on the propagation of their religion with vigour and without any let or hindrance.

Buddhism

Dhanapāla is, for the most part, silent about Buddhism, in spite of the fact that Buddhism was the State religion of the Pālas of Bengal during his time. Dhanapāla's silence bears eloquent testimony to the fact that Buddhism did not command any sizable following within the territorial limits of the Paramāra kingdom. As Dhanapāla was the court-poet of Muñja and Bhoja Paramāra, he has, for obvious reasons, written about those religions and cults—directly or by implication—which were professed by the subjects of the Imperial Paramāras of Malwa.

Of the better-known Buddhist theories and doctrines, Dhanapāla has alluded to vo-id ('Śūnyavāda'[169] or 'Śūnyatā') and 'Middle path'[170] in *Tilaka-mañjarī.*

It will not be out of place here to mention that with the passage of time Tāntrika phase, mantra, mudrā and maṇḍala developed in Buddhism as it had done in the case of Hinduism and Jainism.

The development of Tāntrism, during Dhanapāla's time effected a radical change in the outlook and character of Buddhism. About Tāntrika Buddhism N.N. Das Gupta comments: "So far as the theological speculations and philosophical doctrines are concerned, the Śaiva and Śākta Tantras accept the Brahmaṇical philosophical systems as authority, and utilise their fundamental tenets, while the Buddhist Tantras likewise adopt and put to use the Buddhist, or more precisely Mahāyāna principles .... In point of fact, Buddhism in their later phases of Mahāyāna had adopted, or had been engrafted into, these esoteric principles and practices which had an entirely independent growth and an independent history of their own".[171]

The 'Vajra-yàna', 'Kālacakra-yāna' and 'Sahaja-yāna' evolved the course of Buddhism in this period. "The system of Tāntrism, compounded with the principles of Sexo--yogic practice is conventionally known by the general name of Yajra-yāna".[172] The outstanding feature of 'Vajra-yāna' is the identification of the ultimate reality with the conception of a Lord Supreme (Bhagavāna). Coition is considered compulsory in this mode of Sādhanā to secure 'Mokṣa' (salvation). The consort or Śakti is considered to be a sādhaka.

The supreme deity in 'Kālacakrayāna' is called Lord Sri-Kālacakra. "Kāla means the ultimate immutable knowledge (prajñā) or the state of Śūnyatā, while Cakra means the cycle of the world process, or the body of the Lord containing the potency of the existence of the Universe, which is just the principle of 'upāya'. Kālacakra, therefore, implies the absolutely unified principle of prajñā and upāya and he is thus the Bodhicitta".[173] The Kālacakrayāna gained foothold in Bengal, Magadha and Kashmir.

The sphere of influence of the Sahaja-yāna cult was for the most part confined to Bengal and probably to some extent, its western and south-western environs. Sahajiya Buddhists called their path 'the easiest'. They also followed Sexo-yogic practices. They laid stress on making the body sufficiently strong and sound before starting with Yogic practices.[174] This cult flourished under Pāla kings.

The state and fortunes of Buddhism in the times of Dhanapāla may be briefly recapitualated here. After the age of Harṣavardhana to the XII century, Bengal and Bihar continued to be the principal centres of Buddhism in India, though it had quite a good following in other parts of India also in the period—A.D 1000 to A.D. 1200.

The Pāla rulers of Bengal were the staunch followers of Buddhism. Mahīpāla I (A.D. 988—1038) did a lot for the spread and revival of Buddhism in India. He repaired a large number of Buddhist buildings at Banaras and Nalanda. He constructed two temples at Bodh Gayā and several monuments at Nalanda.[175] He tried to rouse Buddhism from the stupor into which it had fallen in the X century A.D. After him, his son tried to maintain the tempo of progress of Buddhist revival.[176] During the reign of Rāmapāla (*c.* A.D. 1077—1120) Buddhism was again active and stirring. He established a new Mahāvihāra in North Bengal called Jagaddala.[177]

Pāla rulers of Bengal got erected Vihāras or Samghāramas at Nalanda and Vikramaśīla. These vihāras played a very important role for the propagation of Buddhism and maintaining its influence.

To the vihāras and mahāvihāras learned scholars flocked from all quarters of India. The monks from Tibet also came to these mahāvihāras from the time of Mahīpāla I. This resulted in bringing Tibet closer to India than ever before. On the invitation of Tibetan kings, the vihāras used to send forth pre-eminent scholars who went there to spread Buddhism. They also translated Buddhist works from Saṁskṛta into Tibetan.[178]

Dr. V. C. Pandey clinches the issue with his considered

opinion that the Rājpūts collectively refused to follow Buddhism. They made Hinduism their State religion. Thus Buddhism could not take roots or gain a popular base in the areas under Rājput sway and in the course of time declined in the land of its birth.[179]

OTHER RELIGIOUS CULTS

There were many other esoteric religious cults and groups in Dhanapāla's time, references to whose existence and religious practices are found in *Tilaka-mañjarī* and *Pāiyalacchīnāmamālā*. Of these, the more popular and well-entrenched was the cult of Śakti or the worship of the Mother Goddess as Power Incarnated. As a matter of fact, Mother Goddesses had been venerated under different names at different periods in ancient India. The concept of Śakti may be broadly understood as the veneration of the Active Principle in the Divine Female in whose resplendent person the transcendent and inactive attributes of God become active and immanent. As Dr. A.L. Basham has observed : "It was thought that God was inactive and transcendent, while his female counterpart was active and immanent and by Gupta period the wives of the Gods whose existence had always been recognised but who had been shadowy figures in earlier theology began to be worshipped in special temples".[180]

The most prominent Śakti Cult was the Cult of 'Śiva Śakti' which had as the object of its veneration the spouse of Śiva who was variously known as 'Dākṣāyaṇī', 'Bhavānī', 'Śailasutā', 'Pārvatī', 'Umā', 'Gaurī', 'Ārya, 'Durgā', 'Kālī', 'Śivā', 'Kātyayānī', and 'Caṇḍī'.[181]

There are references to the temples of Pārvatī at many places in *Tilaka-mañjarī*.[182] Her importance and popularity is proved by the fact that she is invariably mentioned alongwith Śiva in various Paramāra inscriptions.[183] The Cauhān ruler Vigraharāja II built the temple of Āśāpurā at Broach towards the end of the X century. Indrarāja Cauhān (A.D. 942) was a worshipper of Vāṭayakṣinī. His prayer to the Goddess describes her variously as 'Mahisāsuramardinī', 'Durgā', 'Kātyayānī' and 'Varadā'.[184]

According to Dr. D.C. Sircar, Ujjain and Ābū were the famous 'Śaktipīṭhas'[185] (the centres of the worship of Śakti).

Daśaharā or Durgā-pūjā was a famous festival in Malwa. In Navarātra (the nine-day period sacred to the Goddess Durgā) which fell in the month of Āśvina, Durgā was worshipped from the 7th to the 10th day of the bright-half or Śukla Pakṣa.[186]

The worship of Pārvatī was prevalent in Candella kingdom. Pārvatī was known among the Candellas as 'Kālī', 'Ambikā', 'Tārā', 'Tripurā', 'Kāmākṣyā', 'Harasiddhi', 'Camuṇḍā' and 'Kālikā'.[187]

The Goddess Caṇḍī was regarded to be in possession of infinite power of curbing evil. Dhanapāla refers to the prevailing belief that the recitation of 'caṇḍikā-stotra' brought emancipation from all evil effects.[188] *Mārkaṇḍeya Purāṇa* states that 'a man gheraoed by decoits or enemies, by lions or elephants of the forest, may be saved by reciting 'Caṇḍikā-stotra'.[189] We also read in *Tilaka-mañjarī* that human-beings were sacrificed to propitiate Goddess Caṇḍī.[190]

Another 'Śakti Cult was associated with the 'Śakti' or spouse of 'Viṣṇu' who was called 'Kamalā,' 'Śrī' and 'Lakṣmī'.[191] The worship of 'Śrī' or 'Lakṣmī' was quite prevalent during Dhanapāla's time. King Meghavāhana in *Tilaka-mañjarī* is advised by Vidyādhara to worship Rāja-Lakṣmī.[192] On the advice of Vidyādhara king Meghavāhana got built a Lakṣmī temple. In it he installed an ornamented idol of Lakṣmī. The king worshipped Lakṣmī everyday in order to be blessed with an offspring.[193]

Sarasvatī, the spouse of Brahmā, was the centre of another Śakti Cult. She was variously known as 'Vāṇī', 'Vācā', 'Bhaṇitī', 'Sarasvatī', 'Bhāratī', 'Girā' and 'Bhāṣā'.[194] In an introductory verse of *Tilaka-mañjarī*, Dhanapāla invokes Sarasvatī.[195] The devotion of the Paramāra kings to Goddess Sarasvatī becomes obvious from the title of 'Sarasvatī' which Vākpati Muñja conferred on Dhanapāla to honour the poet.[196] Moreover, an archaeological survey records that king Bhoja got built a temple dedicated to Sarasvatī at Dhārā, wherein the great University was founded by the king. A beautiful idol of Sarasvatī was installed in that temple. An inscription on the pedestal dated A.D. 1035, as translated tentatively by Dr. K.N. Diksit, runs as follows:

"Om, the Vidyādharī of the town Bhoja, the moon among

kings, having first made the mother goddess of speech . . . . great in fruit, created the auspicious image. This was made by Manabhala, the son of the craftsman Sahira, written by Śivadeva in Samvat year 1091".[197]

"She (Sarasvatī) is conceived with four hands, having a rosary, a book, a vīṇā or a kamaṇḍalu or a goad, and the expounding gesture (vyākhyānamudrā). She wears . . . the holy thread and the breast-bands (kuca-bandha)".[198]

It is interesting to note that Sarasvatī worship transcended the bounds of caste and creed. In Jainism and Mahāyāna form of Buddhism, Sarasvatī (and to some extent, Lakṣmī) enjoyed an extra-ecclesiastical status. We find Jaina poet, Somadeva (10th century), invoking Goddess Sarasvatī in *Yaśastilaka*.[199] The following verse marks the conclusion of his invocation to Sarasvatī:

kaladhauta kamala mauktikadukūlamaṇijālacāmara-
prāyaiḥ |
ārādhayāmi devīṁ Sarasvatīṁ sakala maṅgalairbhāvaiḥ ||
syādvāda bhūdhara bhavā munimānanīyā devairanaya
śaraṇaiḥ samupāsanīyā |
svāntāśritā khila kalaṁka harapravāhā vāgāpagāstu-
mamabhodhagajāvagāhā ||

"I worship Goddess Sarasvatī with all-auspicious objects comprising golden lotuses, silken scarves studded with pearls, bejewelled curtains and fly-whisks. Like an elephant entering the waters of river, may my intellect plunge into the River of Speech, whose current cleanses the mind of all its impurities (the River) that rises from the mount of Syādvāda doctrine, is worthy of the veneration of the sages and fit to be adored by the gods having no other refuge."[200]

River Cults had become deeply rooted among the masses by Dhanapāla's time. The rivers originating in inaccessible mountains were held to be sacred and worshipped in the form of Goddesses upto our own times. The river Gaṅgā was held to be the most sacred of all the rivers of India and worshipped as a mother Goddess during Dhanapāla's time. From *Tilakamañjarī*, we learn that 'Gaṅgā-stotra' was recited in the morning in praise of Mother Gaṅgā.[201] To take a dip in the river Gaṅgā was considered to be an act of purifying oneself of all sins. According to the *Matsya* and *Kūrma Purāṇas*, the mere rememberance of Gaṅgā even from the distance of thousand Yojanas was sufficient to wash away all the sins of an evil doer and ultimately to lead him to emancipation.[202]

Other rivers held specially sacred mentioned by Dhanapāla were the 'Yamunā',[203] 'Sarayū'[204] and Godāvarī[205] and 'Narmadā'.[206] Purificational bathing in rivers and oceans is, as a matter of fact, repugnant to Jainism as recorded by Somadeva Sūri in *Yaśastilaka*.[207] But Dhanapāla, in spite of being a Śrāvaka (a devout Jaina) has drawn a factual picture of the society of the day and has not cast any aspersion on the faith of the common masses in the purifying powers of the holy rivers.

The sacred rivers were worshipped in the form of representational images. "The images of Gaṅgā and Yamunā have been found in the ruins of the Bherāghāta temple in the centre of which probably stood an Umā-Maheśvara group according to Coomaraswamy".[208]

The worship of some of the prominent gods of Hindu Pantheon has been alluded to by Dhanapāla. The worship of God Brahmā, one of the gods constituting the Hindu Trimūrti, had gained currency during Dhanapāla's time. Dhanapāla invokes Brahmā in the introductory verses of *Pāiyalacchīnāmamālā*[209] and *Tilaka-mañjarī*.[210] The worship of Brahmā is also confirmed by the images and temples of the period. A figure of God Brahmā having two arms and three faces has been discovered from Vasantagarh.[211] Dr. Dasharatha Sharma mentions a number of images of God Brahmā which have been discovered from Sevādi (Jodhpur), Bijolia (Mewar) and Osia (Jodhpur).[212] Three Brahmā temples have been discovered from the territory of Paramāras—one at Vasantagarh, the other at clinch in Bansawara and the third at Chandravatī.[213] The most famous and sacred temple dedicated to Brahmā stands at Pushkar near Ajmer.

Sun (Sūrya) worship also seems to have been fairly popular during Dhanapāla's time. Dhanapāla invokes the blessings of the God-Sun (Dinamaṇi) in the opening verses of *Pāiyalacchīnāmamālā*.[214] In *Tilaka-mañjarī*, we read that oblation of water was made to the Sun-God by the devout after bathing.[215] The worship of Sūrya had become so popular that temples were erected to the god during Dhanaāpla's time all over India. Bhinmāla seems to have been a major centre of Sun-worship in Rājasthan. The famous sun-temple known as 'Jagat-Svāmin' ('Lord of the Universe') has been discovered there. A Brāhmaṇa is described to have offered a kalaśa (spire) of gold at this temple at his own expenses in A.D. 1066.[216] During the days of Sirohī regime in Rājasthan the Sun-worship had become so popular that, according to G.H. Ojhā, no well-populated village of the period (A.D. 600—1400) was without a sun-temple.[217] A Sūrya image was found at Kotālipāda (Faridpur) which belongs to the XI century A.D. The image has been acquired by the Vangiya-Sāhitya Parishat Musuem, Calcutta.[218]

Another inscribed Sun image (XI century) has been acquired from Dinājpur village. The pedestal inscription refers to the God as 'Samasta-rogānām hartā' (Curer of All Ailments).[219]

We read in *Sṛṅgāra-mañjarī-kathā* that Sun was worshipped on the Vijayasaptamī day by those desiring male offspring.[220]

Next to the God of Life (Sūrya), the God of Love (Kāmadeva) was worshipped far and wide in the days of Dhanapāla.[221] He was variously known as 'Makaradhvaja', 'Anaṅga', 'Ratinātha', 'Manmatha', 'Kusumabāṇa', 'Kandarpa', 'Pañcasara', 'Madana' and 'Sankalpayoni'.[222] 'Anaṅga-Utsava dina (the festival of the God of Love) was celebrated as the day of great rejoicing and merriment.[223] In Dr. Dashratha Sharma's opinion, "Such a god received fervent devotion from lovers but he was worshipped also by married women for saubhāgya".[224] The temples dedicated to Kāmadeva are frequently referred to in *Tilaka-mañjarī.*

In *Tilaka-mañjarī*, there are references alluding to the worship of kula-devatā[225] numbering five: 'Siva', Viṣṇu', 'Śakti', 'Gaṇeśa' and 'Sūrya', 'Gṛahadevatā',[226] 'Udyāna-devatā',[227] 'Nagara-devatā',[228] 'Jala-devatā',[229] 'Vana-devatā',[230] and 'Dikdevatās' or 'Loka-pālas',[231] (Indra, Varuṇa, Kubera, Yama, Agni, Nairṛtya, Vāyu and Īśāna).

Dhanapāla alludes to numerous religious practises and

rituals prevailing in his days. The recitation of Gāyatrī mantra was one such practice highly prized by the pious and the virtuous. In *Tilaka-mañjarī* we read that Malaya Sundarī recites Gāyatrī mantra as an act conducive to piety.[232] All sins are said to be expiated by a pious repetition of this mantra.[233] Bhagvatī Śaṣṭhī (the mother of Skanda) was worshipped on the sixth night after the birth of a child.[234]

The worship of the planets or the Solar System (Nava-grahas) is also identified from the account furnished by Dhanapāla in *Pāiyalacchīnāmamālā*.[235] This practice has been continuing from antiquity, but with the advances made in the field of astrology and the growth of people's belief in things supernatural, it received further impetus. The Nava-graha slab in the collection of the Āśutosh Museum, Calcutta University, is a very fine piece of sculpture. It shows the nine planets, Ravi, Soma, Maṅgala, Budha, Bṛhaspati, Śukra, Śani, Rāhu and Ketu standing side by side on lotus pedestals.[236] We find the group representation of the Nava-grahas from the Verman temples.[237]

The worship of other demi-gods like Yakṣa[238] (associated with God Kubera, the God of Wealth), Kārtikeya[239] (the War God, Skanda, also called Kūmara, the eldest son of Śiva and Pārvatī) and Gaṇeśa[240] seems also to be prevalent in Dhanapāla's time. An XI century six-armed stone image of the God Gaṇeśa has been discovered from North Bengal. It shows Gaṇeśa dancing on the back of his mount, attended by two other dancing figures,[241] one on each side, playing on musical instruments. Images of dancing 'Gaṇeśa have also been found at Harṣa and Ābānerī.[242]

In ancient India the performance of auspicious rites had become an essential part of everyday life. From *Tilaka-mañjarī* we learn that on the eve of a voyage God Ratnākara (Lord of the Seas) was worshipped. Oblations of curds, kuśa-grass, rice, flowers, animals and jewellery were made to the God.[243]

The Brāhmaṇas were specially honoured at the religious festivals and functions. On special ceremonial occasions, like the royal birth-day festivities, they were given gifts of precious ornaments, scores of milch-cows and loads of gold.[244]

King Meghavāhana in *Tilaka-mañjarī* gives the gifts of cows to the Śrotriyas (the reciters of the Vedas who were generally Brāhmaṇas) on the occasion of yajña.[245] Yajñavalkya has prescribed that apart from the daily duty of bestowing gifts on the Brāhmaṇas etc., these must be given on special occasions too, and if so made, are more meritorious than the gifts made daily.[246]

The gifting of lands to the Brāhmaṇas was regarded to be an act of great religious merit in ancient India. Ancient law codifiers have laid down that whatever sin a man may commit when in straightened circumstances, he was purified therefrom by making a gift of only as much land as would be covered by the hide of a cow.[247] Queen Madirāvatī in *Tilaka-mañjarī* is found making donations of lands known as 'agrahāra' to the Brāhmaṇas on the occasion of Sun eclipse.[248] It was a widely held belief 'that gifts of gold, cows and land save even the wicked'.[249]

Worshipping and revering of saints ('Munīs'), preceptors (Ācāryas) and mentors (Gurus) was a common practice in ancient India. Vidyādhara, the saint, in *Tilaka-mañjarī*, is worshipped by king Meghavāhana with the offerings of flowers, fruits and ornaments made of gems.[250] The offering of flowers and ornaments appears to have been the common practice among the people for the appeasement of Gods. We read in *Tilaka-mañjarī* that king Meghavāhana offers a garland of jewels at the feet of the idol of Goddess Lakṣmī.[251]

Many other religious practices in the form of sacrifices (yajña), fasts (vrata) and pilgrimage (tīrtha-yātra) were observed during the Rājpūt period. The yajña in *Tilaka-mañjarī* is performed with the help of the Purohita who offers oblations to the fire. The Purohita, with green kuśa grass in his hand, pours water from the jar made of gold. The yajña maṇḍapa has been decorated with due propriety demanded by the solemn occasion. The purpose of this yajña was to bless the king with an heir.[252] The offerings at the yajña consisted mainly of incense, flowers, sweets and scent etc.[253] We gather from *Tilaka-mañjarī* that a number of fasts (vratas) were observed during Dhanapāla's time.[254] Of the various religious practices prescribed for the attainment of svarga and other objectives, the vratas were by far the most popular. In *Tilaka-mañjarī*, we read that the 'Cāndrāyaṇa vrata[255] ("A fast which is observed for one month, quantity of food taken by the observer increases and diminishes according to the waxing and waning of the Moon in each fortnight of the month")[256] is observed by Malaya Sundarī who wears Valkala like an ascetic.

We are also told by Dhanapāla that those who had set their minds on attaining a 'siddhi' renounced the world and took to living in the forests[257] and the caves of the mountains,[258] ate fruits and herbs[259] and did not take cooked food.[260]

Pañcatapa, a very difficult mode of meditation and mortification, prevalent in ancient India,[261] has also been referred to in *Tilaka-mañjarī*[262] by Dhanapāla. In this type of meditation an ascetic meditated amidst five fires. In addition to the fire of the Sun, fires were lit on all the four sides (east, west, north and south) of the ascetic. In *Tilaka-mañjarī* we read that ascetics meditated by way of standing in water immersed upto their neck.[263]

Tirthayātrā of holy places situated on the banks of holy Gaṅgā[264] and the places where ascetics[265] attained 'siddhi' are alluded to by Dhanapāla in *Tilaka-mañjarī*.

From the above account it becomes evident that apart from religious practices of later extraction, Vedic rites of yore were still continuing in the Rājput period.

REFERENCES

1. *Pāiyalacchīnāmamālā*, p. 1, śloka 1.
2. Ibid., śloka 2.
3. *Tilaka-mañjarī*. p. 1, śloka 5, *Pāiyalacchīnāmamālā*, p. 3, sloka 21.
4. *Pāiyalacchīnāmamālā*, p. 3, śloka 21.
5. Ibid., p. 3, śloka 23.
6. Ibid., p. 1, śloka 1.
7. Ibid., p. 3, śloka 23.
8. Ibid., p. 1, śloka 2.
9. Ibid., p. 1, śloka 3.

10. *Paiyalacchīnāmamālā*, p. 1, śloka 4.
11. Ibid., śloka 5.
12. Ibid., śloka 6.
13. Ibid., śloka 7.
14. Ibid., p. 3, śloka 25.
15. Ibid., śloka 23.
16. Ibid., śloka 28.
17. Ibid., śloka 20.
18. *Tilaka-mañjarī*, p. 6:

    Prāsādeṣu truṭitaśikharaśvabhralabdhapraueśaiḥ
    prātaḥ prātastuhinasalilaiḥ śārvaraiḥ snāpitāni/
    dhanyāḥ śunye yadarinagare sthaṇuliṅgāniśākhā-
    hastastrastaiḥ kusumanikaraiḥ pādapāḥ pūjyanti//
    (*Śloka 47*)
19. *Paiyalcchīṇāmamālā*, p. 3, śloka 21.
20. *Tilaka-mañjarī*, p. 14.
21. Ibid., p. 192.
22. Ibid., p. 203.
23. *I.A.*, Vol. VI, p. 42, *E.I.*, Vol. XI, p. 182, *E.I.*. Vol. IV, p. 49, *I.A.O.S.*, Vol. III, p. 30, *I.A.*, Vol. XI, p. 22, *I.A.*, Vol. VI, p. 56, *E.I.*. Vol. XIX, p. 71, *J.A.S.B.*, Vol. XVII, p. 347.
24. Pratipal Bhatia, op. cit., p. 251.
25. *Tilaka-mañjarī*, p. 46:

    ...Alikulakomalena prasaratā samantataḥ kāntikālimnā kajjala-mayīmiva saśailadvīpakānanāmurvīṁ kurvāṇam/
26. Loc. cit.:

    ...Nidarśanamivāśeṣatribhuvanabhīṣaṇānām...
27. Ibid., p. 49:

    ...Ativikṛtarūpa...
28. Ibid., p. 46:

    ...Attkṛṣaprāṁśuvikarālakarkaśakāyam...
29. Ibid., p. 48:

    ...Avayavānapyasthiśarān...
30. Loc. cit.:

    ...Asthīnūpurairapi...
31. Ibid.:

    ...kapiśabhāsureṇa keśabhāreṇa...
32. *Tilaka-mañjarī*, p. 46:

    ...Sthavīyasā carṇayugalena...
33. Loc. cit.:

    ...Ganganaśimollaṅghinā jaṅghādvitayena...

    In Saṁskṛta the word 'Jaṅghā' denotes leg, while in Hindi it is used for thigh.
34. Loc. cit.;

    ...Akṣudrasaralaśirādaṇḍanicitena...

35. Loc. cit.:

...Sthūlapṛthulayā nakhaparamparayā prakāśita nijaprabhātt-nijaprabhātīmirtīrohatacaraṇa yugalāṅgulivibhāgam...

36. Ibid., p. 47:

...Ulbaṇāsthigranthinā jānuyugalena kṣīṇamāṁsena...

37. Ibid :

...Duradarśitonnatīnāṁparśukānāṁ...

38. Ibid.:

...Antarāladroṇīṣu nidrāyamāṇaśiṣusarīsṛpa...

39. Ibid.:

...Ati kaṭhinakharvaparvābhiraṅguliveṇudaṇḍikābhiḥ parigṛhītaiḥ kuṭilatīkṣṇāyatāgrakoṭibhiḥ...

40. Ibid.:

...Gāḍhīkṛtakṣatajakvāthāraktādrarśārdulacarma sicayam...

41. Ibid.:

...Utsarpatā parikarāśī viṣavadana...

42. Ibid.:

...Acirakhaṇḍitāṁ maṅtrasādhakamuṇḍamindu khaṇḍa śraddhya dhavalakuṭilāndaṣṭrāṁnir gamānapaharantāṃ āsāditam vidhuṁtu-damiva galāvalambitaṁ bibhrāṇam...

43. Ibid.:

...Kūrcakaca klāpena kavalitamakhilaromarandhra nirgatadrudhi-ragaṇduṣamiva pralamba pṛthulaṁ cibukamudvahaṅtam...

44. Ibid., p. 46:

...Nitānta bhīṣaṇo...ḥāsadhvanirudalasat...

45. Ibid., p. 48:

...karālaparimaṇḍalākṛtinā nayanayugalena...

46. Loc. cit., p. 47:

...Raktāsava kapālamauu bhāvadarśitātyadbhutbhujāyāmena pāṇinā vāmena...

47. Ibid.:

...Dakṣiṇena ca pratikṣana vyāpāritaniśitakartiken...

48. Ibid.:

...Śravaṇayugama mūrdhavalitapucchanālanibiḍāliṅgitāṅgamut-phullaphaṇa karparaṁ kāla sarpadvayamivod vahantam...

49. Ibid.:

...Atibhīṣaṇāmābhogīnā lalāṭasthalena...

50. Ibid.:

...Sadyaḥ sthāpitamasṛkpanka pañcāṅgulaṁ...

51. Ibid., p. 47:

...Gātrapiśitamutkṛtyatkṛtya kīkaśopadaṁ śamaśnantaṁ. kavali-tapiśitacarvaṇāyā-saṁcalena...

52. Ibid., p. 48:

...Daśanamālayāpyantarālapraviṣṭakuṇapāsthiśakalayā...

53. Ibid., p. 49:

Ājānulambamānaśava śiromālamekaṁ-vetālamadrākṣhi|

54. Ibid., p. 14.
55. Ibid., p. 49:
   ...Miṭrīkṛte hi mayi sādhakānāmabhīṣṭa siddhiḥ...
56. *P.A.I.O.C.*, 1919 (Poona Session), p. 319.
57. Op. cit.
58. *Tilaka-mañjarī*, p. 14.
59. Ibid., p. 46.
60. Ibid., p. 8.
61. *Noties of Sanskrit Manuscripts and Select Palm Leaves in the Durbar Library, Nepal*, ed., H.P. Shastri (1905), p. 215.
62. *I.A.* VI, pp. 51-52.
63. Op. cit.
64. D.C. Ganguly, op. cit., p. 63.
65. *Nava Sāhasāṅkacarita*, XVIII, ślokas 53, 64.
66. S.N. Das Gupta, *History of Indian Philosophy*, Vol. V (Cambridge 1955), p. 159.
67. *E.I.*, pp. 235-36.
68. D.C. Ganguly, op. cit., p. 270.
69. Dasharatha Sharma, op. cit., p. 99.
70. *J.A.S.B.*, Vol. IX, p. 548.
71. D.C. Ganguly, op. cit., pp. 258-61. "It is one of the few temples in Malwa which were spared complete demolition by the Mohammedan iconoclasts".
72. *Progress Report of the Archaeological Survey of India, Western Circle for the year ending 31st March, 1919*, pp. 61-64, Plates XVIII-XXI.
73. N.S. Bose, *History of the Candellas* (Calcutta, 1956), p. 99.
74. *A.S.R.*, Vol. II, p. 423.
76. *History and Culture of Indian People*, Vol. V, p. 443.
76. Dasharatha Sharma, op. cit,, p. 99.
77. *Tilaka-mañjarī*, p. 12:
   ...yasyāṁ ca...vaiṣṇavānāṁ kṛṣṇavartmani praveśaḥ...
78. Ibid., p. 13:
   Acyuta iva śaṁkha cakrābhyām...
79. Ibid., p. 240.
80. *Pāiyalacchīnāmamālā*, p. 3:
   Sa urī dasāranāho vaikuṇṭho mahumaho uvidoya.
   (*Śloka* 21)
81. *Tilaka-mañjarī*, p. 13.
82. N.S. Bose, op. cit., pp. 156-57.
83. *History and Culture of Indian People*, Vol. IV, p. 318.
14. *E.I.*, XIX, p. 241.
85. Op. cit., II, p. 182, śloka 2.
86. *Tilaka-mañjarī*, p. 43:
   ...Asurārimandiramāśrayantyāḥ...
87. *E.I.*, IX, p. 109.

88. *PRAS, WC.* 1920-21, pp. 98-106.
89. *ASR* (Cunn), II, pp. 269-70.
90. *ASI*, 1906-7, p. 209.
91. Pratipal Bhatia, op. cit., p. 246.
92. *Tilaka-mañjarī*, p. 135:
    ...kinnaramithunagīyamānarāmalandra caritādbhuteṣu...
93. Ibid., pp. 135-137, 104.
94. Quoted by Dasharatha Sharma, op. cit., p. 98.
95. *Tilaka-mañjarī*, p. 204.
96. Ibid., p. 11:
    ...Gāḍhadhṛta bhūbhṛtpādaṁ Vāsudevamapi...
97. *Pāiyalacchīnāmamālā*, p. 1, śloka 1.
98. *Tilaka-mañjarī*, p. 52.
99. *I.H.Q.*, XXX, pp. 343-44.
100. Ibid.
101. Ibid., p. 350.
102. *Pāiyalacchīnāmamālā*, p. 3. V. 23.
103. *Samarāṅgaṇasūtradhāra*, ed. T. Ganapati Shastri (Baroda, 1924-25), pp. 46-50.
104. *Tilaka-mañjarī*, p. 52.
105. The twenty-four Tīrthaṅkaras according to *Samavāva Kalpasūtra*, and *Āvaśyaka Niryukti* are : (1) Usabha (Ṛṣabhanātha), (2) Ajiya (Ajitanātha), (3) Sambhava, (4) Abhinandan, (5) Sumai (Sumatinātha), (6) Paumappabha (Padmaprabha), (7) Supāsa (Supārśvanātha), (8) Candappaha (Candraprabha), (9) Suvihi (Suvidhinātha, (10) Siyala (Śītalanātha), (11) Śejjaṁ sa (Śreyāṁsanātha), (12) Vasupujja (Vāsupūjya), (13) Vimala (Vimalanātha), (14) Ananta (Anantanātha), (15) Dhamma (Dharmanātha), (16) Santi (Śantinātha), (17) Kunthu (Kunthunātha), (18) Ara (Arhanātha), (19) Malli (Mallinātha), (20) Muṇisuvvaya (Muni Suvrata), (21) Nami (Naminātha), (22) Ariṭṭhanami (Ariṣṭnemi), (23) Pāsa (Pārśvanātha), (24) Vaddhamāna (Vardhamāna Mahāvīra). Quoted by Jagdish Chandra Jain, *Life and Ancient India As Depicted in Jain Canons*, p. 371.
106. *Tilaka-mañjarī*, p. 1:
    Sa vaḥ pātu jinaḥkṛtṣanaṁ samīkṣate yaḥ pratikṣaṇam/
    rupairanantairekaika jaṅtorvyāptaṁ jagatrayam//1//
    (*Śloka* 1)
    Prājyaprabhāvaḥ prabhāvo dharmasyāstarajastamāḥ/
    dadatāṁ nivṛtātmāna ādyo'nye'pi mudaṁ jināḥ//2//
    (*Śloka* 2)
107. *Ṛṣabhapañcāśīkā Virastutidvaya rūpa kṛti kalāpaḥ*, p. 162, śloka 50.
108. *Tilaka-mañjarī*, p. 40.
109. Ibid., p. 35:
    ...Bhagavatoyugādijanasyakṛtvāpraṇāmam...
110. Ibid.
111. *History and Culture of Indian People*, Vol. V, p. 428.

112. *Pāiyalacchīnāmālā* (Introd.), p. 30.
113. *Tilaka-mañjarī*, p. 256:

    ...*Prāsādakeṣupratiṣṭhitā jināpratimāḥ krameṇāpūjat/*
114. Ibid., 319:

    ...*Mahāvīrajinavarapratimayāprasādhitasya*...
115. Ibid., p. 275.
116. *History and Culture of Indian People*, Vol. IV, p. 296.
117. *Tilaka-mañajrī*, p. 428:

    ...*Jinajanma mahotsva*...
118. Ibid., p. 344:

    ...*Mahāvīrājinavarasyanirvāṇa divasa*...
119. Ibid.
120. Ibid., p. 428:

    ...*Darśayannanekasura siddha sāddhya saṁboddhāni tīrthasthānāni*...
121. Ibid., p. 427.
122. See *Chapter 1, Dhanapāla's Life.*
123. *Tilaka-mañjarī*, p. 3:

    Namo jagannamasyāya munīndrāyendrabhūtaye/
    yaḥ prāpya tripadīṁ vācā viśvaṁ visṇurivānaśe////

    (*Śloka* 19)
124. *Life in Ancient India As Depicted in Jain Canons*, p. 25.
125. *Tilaka-mañjarī*, p. 39:

    ...*Ārādhyaścaturvidhasyāpisuranikāyasya*...
126. Gṛddhapiccha, *Tattvārtha Sūtra*, ed., Phula Chandra Siddhanta Sastri (Banaras, V.N.S. 2476), p. 167.
127. Op. cit., p. 24:

    Bhavanavāsino' suranāgavidyutsuparṇāgnivātastani todadhidvīpa-dikkumārāḥ/
128. Op. cit.
129. Op. cit., pp. 175-175:

    Vyantarāḥ kinnara kimpuruṣamahoragagandharva yakṣa rākṣasa bhūtapīśācāḥ/
130. *Tattvārtha Sūtra*, ed., Phula Chandra Siddhanta Sastri, pp. 174-75.
131. *Tattvārtha Sūtra*, p. 174.
132. Op. cit., IV, 24:

    Jyotiśkāḥ sūryyācandramasau grahanakṣatra prakīrṇa-katārakāśca//
133. Op. cit., p. 175.
134. Op, cit. IV, 17:

    kalpopannāḥ kalpātītaśca//
135. Op. cit., p. 180.
136. Op. cit.
137. Op. cit., pp. 179-180.
138. *Tilaka-mañjarī*, p. 38.
139. Ibid., p. 25.
140. Ibid., p. 40.

141. *Tilaka-mañjarī*, p. 33:
Ākāśagamanadainīvīdyā...
142. *Ṛṣabhapañcaśikā Vīrastuti dvayarūpā Kṛti Kalāpaḥ*, p. 208, śloka 4.
143. Op. cit,, p. 112:
Micchattavisapasuttā, saceyaṇā jiṇa/ na huṁti kiṁ jīvāḥ?/
kaṇṇammi kama-ī ja-i-ki-ttiaṁ pi tuha vayaṇa mantassa//
(*Śloka* 38)
'a' (अ) denotes Viṣṇu, 'Ra' (र) denotcs Brahmā and 'ha' (ह) denotes Hara.
Akāreṇocyte Viṣṇu refe Brahmā vyavasthitaḥ /
hakāreṇa haraḥ prokta-stadante paramaṁ padaṁ//
(*Jaina Sāhitya Saṁśodhaka*, II : I, pp. 10-12).
144. *Ṛṣabhapañcāśikā Vīrastuti dvayarūpa Kṛti Kalāpaḥ*, p. 214:
Gayagāravaṁ pi guruaṁ nayaṇāṇa mahūsavaṁpi sisirmahaṁ/
taṁ biṁtti khīṇa mohaṁ pi kaha ṇu paḍhomaṁ guṇaṭṭhānaṁ?//
(*Śloka* 7)
145. *Tattvārtha Sūtra*, ed. Phula Chandra Shastri, p. 409.
146. *Ṛṣabhapancāśikā Vīrastuti dvayarūpa Kṛti Kalāpaḥ*, p. 117. śloka 40. Jainism does not merely maintain that there are many reals but also accepts that each of the reals in its turn is so complex that it is difficult to understand it fully. The infinite number of the qualities possessed by the complex reals and the equal number of relations into which they enter point to the fact that Reality may be comprehended from different angles. "The attempt at comprehending anything from a particular stand point is known as naya" *Ekadeśa viśisto'rtho nayasya viṣayo mataḥ* (*Nyāyavatāra*, śloka 29) Dasgupta's translation of the term nayavāda into doctrine of relativc pluralism is extremely significant since it points to the perspective from which nayavāda itself is to be understood. He writes: The Jainas regarded all things as anekānta (na-ekanta) or in other words, they hold that nothing could be affirmed absolutely as all affirmations were true only under certain conditions (Dasgupta; *History of Indian Philosophy*, Cambridge University Press, 1963), Vol. I, p. 175.
147. Quoted by K.K. Handiqui, op. cit., p. 289.
148. *Ṛṣabhapañcāśikā Vīrastuti dvayarūpa Kṛti kalāpaḥ*, p. 289, śloka 9.
149. Dasgupta, op. cit., Vol. I, p. 179.
150. Gopalan, *Outline of Jainism* (Delhi, 1973), p. 162.
151. *Ṛṣabhapañcāśikā*, p. 9:
Diṭṭho kahāvi vihaḍiyc ganṭhimmi kavāḍa-saṁpudaghaṇuṁmi/
mohaṁdhayāracāraya-gayeṇa jiṇa / diṇayaruvva tumaṁ//
(*Śloka* 3)
152. *Vīrastuti*, p. 204:
Khaviakasāyacaukko vi nokasāyakkhayaṁ kaha karesi ?/
kaha naṭṭha nāmagutto jaya guru / jaya pāyaḍo hosi//
(*Śloka* 2)

153. *Vīrastuti*,., p. 235:

Sāma pauttipasatto kahaṁ si veattaīkkasattū vi/
kahaṇu visaṁko vi payāvai tti payaḍaṁ vahasi saddaṁ//
(*Śioka* 19)

154. K.K. Handiqui, op. cit., p, 288.
155. *Tilaka-mañjarī*, p. 25.
156. Ibid., p. 33.
157. Ibid., p. 30.
158. Ibid., p. 311.
159. Ibid., p. 400.
160. Ibid., pp. 398-99.
161. Ibid., pp. 399-400.

1Aṣṭapradhāna vidyā devatāḥ are:

(1) Prajñpti, (2) Rohiṇi, (3) Vajrasṛ-ṅkhalā, (4) Ajitabalā, (5) Śrī, (6) 'Sarasvatī', (7) Hṛī, and (8) Aparājitā (For the names of the Aṣṭapradhānavidyā devatāḥ, the aurhor is deeply indebted to Śrī 108 His Holiness Muniśrī Vidyā Nandajī, who enlightened on the subject during his stay at Jaina dharmaśālā, Baraut, on 11.3.74).

162. *Tilaka-mañjarī*, p. 30:

Amūṁ ca bhaktipravaṇena cetasā gṛhāṇa nirvikalpa malpa-puṇḍyajanadurlabhāṁ tribhuvanākhyātayaśa samaparājitā bhidhā-nāmaśeṣa vidyādharendra pūjitāṁ vidyāṁ/
Kuru divasasya ratreśca bhāgatrayamaśūnyaṁ devatārcanenāvasāne japaṁ ca tasya japyacaritasamāhitena cetasā/

In *Yaśastilaka*, we read that the blessings of Aparājita are invoked on the occasion of the mahānavamī festival by a bard for the victory of the king on the battle field.

(K.K. Handiquui op. cit.. p. 157).

163. Ibid,. p. 401:

...Rājño meghavāhanasya tanayoṁ nayena kenāpyadyaiva kuru vidyārādhana paraṁ Harivāhanākhyaṁ kumāram/

164. *Prabandhacintāmaṇi*, p. 52.
165. D.C. Ganguly, op. cit., p. 249.
166. *P.R.A.S.*, *W.C.* (1919), pp. 61-66.
167. *E.I.*, XXXI, pp. 81-86.
168. *E.I.*, IX., pp. 146-155.
169. *Tilaka-mañjarī*, p. 28. The Mādhyamika theory of void ('Śūnyatā) formed an important subject of discussion during Rājpūt period. The theme of the doctrine is that Śūnyatā is nothing but the law of causation known as 'pratītya-samutpāda', that is, whatever is subject to cause and condition is really unborn, has no real origination, and is hence called Śūnya or void. (*Mādhyamikārikā*, 24.18).
170. Ibid., p. 43:

kevalamavalambya madhyampanthānamupacayāmi te'ñjalim/

171. *History and Culture of Indian People*, Vol. V, p. 405.
172. Ibid., p. 410.

173. Op. cit., p. 412.
174. Op. cit., p. 414.
175. *History and Culture of Indian People*, Vol. V, p. 26.
176. Ibid., p. 415.
177. Ibid., p. 416.
178. Ibid.
179. V.C. Pandey, *Prācīna Bhārat kā Itihāsa* (Hindi) (Meerut: Kedar Nath Ram Nath, 1969), p. 57.
180. A.L. Basham, *The Wonder That Was India* (London, 1954), p. 311.
181. Dhanapāla, *Pāiyalacchīnāmamālā*, ed. Becardasa Jivaraja Doshi (Ahemdabad, 1960), p. 1:

    Dakkhāyaṇī Bhavāṇī salasuā pavvaī umā gorī|
    ajjā duggā kālī śivā ca kaccāyaṇī caṇḍī|| (*Śloka* 3)
182. *Tilaka-mañjarī*, p. 9.
183. *E.I.*, XXXII, p. 137 (Nagpur Stone Inscription). *E.I.*, II, p. 182, śloka 1.
184. Dasharatha Sharma, *Lectures on Rajput History and Culture* (New Delhi, 1970), p. 100.
185. D.C. Sircar, *The Śakti Piṭhās*, *J.R.A.S.B.*, XIV, No. 1 (1948), pp. 20, 22.
186. *A.B.O.R.I.*, XXXVI, pp. 323-27.
187. N.S. Bose, op. cit., p. 157.
188. *Tilaka-mañjarī*, p. 200.
189. Ibid.:

    Dasyubhirvāvṛttaḥ sūnye gṛhītovāpi śatrubhiḥ|
    siṁhavyāghrānuyāto vā vane vā vana hastibhiḥ||
    smaranmamaitaccaritaṁ naro mucyate saṁkaṭāt||

    Quoted by Sāntyācārya (ed.), *Tilaka-mañjarī*, Vol. III, p. 64, f.n.
190. Ibid., p. 200:

    ...*Pratidivasaṁanviṣyamāṇacaṇḍikopahāra puruṣābhiḥ*...
191. *Pāiyalacchīnāmamālā*, p. 11.
192. *Tilaka-mañjarī*, p. 30.
193. Ibid., pp. 33-34.
194. *Pāiyalacchīnāmamālā*, p. 6.
195. *Tilaka-mañjarī*, p. 1, śloka 2.
196. Ibid., p. 7.
197. P.T. S. Aiyanagar, op. cit., p. 93.
198. Op. cit., p. 94.
199. Somadeva, *Yaśastilaka*, Part I (Bombay, 1901), p. 401.
200. K.K. Handiqui, op. cit. 282.
201. *Tilaka-mañjarī*, p. 358. (See Appendix II for Gaṅgā-strota).
202. *Matsya Purāṇa* (Calcutta, 1954), pp. 267-68 C III, 13. *Kurma Purāṇa* (Calcutta, 1890), I : 36:29-30.
203. *Pāiyalacchīnāmamālā*, p. 31.
204. *Tilaka-mañjarī*, p. 67.
205. *Pāiyalacchīnāmamālā*, p. 16.

206. *Pāiyalacchīnāmamālā*.
207. Quoted by K,K. Handiqui, op. cit., p. 253.
208. *History and Culture of Indian People*, Vol. IV (Bombay, 1954), p. 342.
209. *Tilaka-mañjarī*, p. 1, śloka 3.
210. *Pāiyalacchīnāmamālā*, p. 1, śloka 2.
211. *P.R.A.S.*, *W.C.*, 1905-06, p. 50.
A.S.I., 1906-07, p. 175.
212. Dasharatha Sharma, op. cit., p. 101.
213. *P.R.A.S* ,*W.C.*, 1905-06, p. 50.
214. *Pāiyalacchīnāmamālā*, p. 1:

Akko taraṇī mitto mattaṇḍo diṇamaṇī payaṁgoya|
ahimayaro paccūho diasayaro aṁsumālī ya||

(*Śloka* 4)

215. *Tilaka-mañjarī*, p. 257.
216. *Bombay Gazetteer*, I, Pt. II, pp. 473-74.
217. G.H. Ojha, *Sirohī Rājya kā Itihāsa* (Hindi), 2nd ed. (Ajmer, 1937), p. 24.
218. *History and Culture of Indian People*, Vol. IV, p. 349.
219. Op. cit., p. 349.
220. Bhoja, *Śṛṅgāramañjarī-kathā*, ed. Dr. (Miss) K. Munshi (Bombay), 1958, p. 19.
221. *Tilaka-mañjarī*, p. 260:

...Anaṅga pūjā devārcanam...

222. *Pāiyalacchīnāmamālā*, p. 1:

Mayaraddhao aṇaṁgo ra iṇāho vammaho kusumābāṇo|
Kaṁdappo pañcasaro mayaṇo saṁkappagoṇi ya||

(*Śloka* 7)

223. *Tilaka-mañjarī*, p. 338:

...Parmānanda hetoranaṅgotsavadinapradosasya...

224. Dasharatha Sharma, op. cit., p. 103.
225. *Tilaka-mañjarī*, p. 30.
226. Ibid.. p. 17.
227. Ibid., p. 107.
228. Ibid., p. 66.
229. Ibid., p. 206.
230. Ibid., p. 41.
231. Ibid., p. 63.
232. Ibid., p. 257:

Japanti pavitrāṇi gāyatrī padāni...

The practice of reciting 'Gāyatrī mantra' originated in antiquity. It is a Ṛgveda mantra of 21 syllables and runs thus:

"Oṁ bhūrbhuvaḥ svaḥ tatsaviturvareṇyam bhargo
devasya dhīmahī dhiyo yo naḥ pracodayāt"||

(3:62:10)

233. Apte, *Sanskrit-English Dictionary* (Bombay, 1912), p 404.
234. *Tilaka-mañjarī*, p. 77.
235. *Pāiyalacchīnāmamālā*, p. 12.

236. *History and Culture of Indian People*, Vol. IV, p. 351.
237. *P.A.R.S., W.C.*, 1916-17, pp. 71-72.
238. *Tilaka-mañjarī*, p. 216:
...Pratiṣṭhitā yakṣa devatā prati yātanāsanātha dvārabhāgasya...
239. *Pāiyalacchīnāmamālā*, p. 3:
Kuṅcārī khaṁdo chhaṁmuho visāho guho kumāro ya/
240. Ibid., p. 11:
...Herambo gayamuho gaṇāhivai...
241. *History and Culture of Indian People*, Vol. IV, p. 348.
242. Dasharatha Sharma, op. cit., p. 102.
243. *Tilaka-mañjarī*, p. 127.
244. Ibid , p. 78:
Dattvā samāropitābharanāḥ savatsāḥ sahastrśo gaḥ svarṇaṁ ca pracuramārambha niḥspṛhebhyo viprebhyaḥ.
245. Ibid., p. 64:
...Aharahaḥ śrotriya viśrāṇaaārthamāhir yamāṇānāṁ kuṇḍa parimaṇḍalāgṛīnām gavāmūtkarṇa tarṇa kānusṛtābhiḥ paramparābhirāpūryamāṇa bāhyakākṣāntaram...
246. *Yājñavalkyasmṛti*, 'Anand Swami Sanskrit Service' No. 46 (Poona, 1903-04), I : 203.
247. P V. Kane, *History of Dharma Śāstras*, Vol. II, Pt. II (Poona, 1930), pp. 858-59.
248. *Tilaka-mañjarī*, pp. 181-82:
Eṣa daśasīrasasahastrasaṁmitasīmasūryagrahaṇa parvaṇi pūrvamapavarijito Madirāvatī devya sarvamaṇḍalagrāmāṇāmagrimo devāgrahāraḥ/
249. P.V. Kane, op. cit., p. 859.
250. *Tilaka-mañjarī*, p. 31:
Saṁjñādiṣvaparijana sampāditaitisca sāmānyamanujeśvaragṛha-durlabhaiḥ puṣpaiḥ phalaiḥ patrairaṁśukai ratnābharaṇaiśca bhūribhiḥ paramayā bhaktyā romāñcitatanurmunimarcyāṁ-cakāra/
251. Ibid., p. 46:
Divyā hi mūrtayo bhājanaṁ devyābharaṇānāṃ/
...punstridaśalokasthita samucitaṁ śobhātiśayaṁ ityabhedhāya taṁ hāra-ratnaṁ devatāyaścaranayoḥ pura stādmuñcat/
252. Ibid., p. 63.
253. Ibid., p. 151:
...Devatārcanārambhapiśunamapūrva saurabhaṁ divyakusumdhūpāmodam...
254. Ibid., p. 236:
...Nānāvidha vratairārādhayadbhiśca...
A 'vrata' means a vow taken for the atta inment ot specinc aim,
255. Ibid., p. 345:
...Vṛkṣa valkalanivasana samārabdhopavāsakṛcchracāndrāyaṇādi-vividha vratavidhiradhvaśrameṇa...

256. Bhargava's *Standard Illustrated Dictionary*, ed. R.C. Pathak (Banaras, 1946).
257. *Tilaka-mañjarī*, p. 235:
    ...*Siddhinimitta maṅgīkṛtarṇyavāsaiḥ*...
258. Ibid., p. 236:
    ...*Giriguhādhyāsibhiśca*...
259. Ibid.:
    ...*Phalamūlaprāyahāraiśca*...
260. Ibid.:
    ...*Parityaktābhyavahāraiśca*...
261. Kālidāsa, *Raghuvaṁsa*, ed. Sita Ram Caturvedi, Kālidāsa Grantha mālā (Banaras):
    Havirbhujāmedhavatāṁ caturṇāmadhye lalāṭaṁ tapa sapta-saptiḥ (13:41).
    Māgha, *Śiśupāla-vadha*, ed. Durga Prasad and Siva Datta (Bombay, 1917):
    Tejasvi madhye tejasvī davīyānamapi gaṇyate
    pañcamaḥ pañca tapasastapano jāta vedaśām/ (2:52)
262. *Tilaka-mañjarī*, p. 236:
    ...*Pañcatapaḥ sādhana vidhāna saṁlagnaiḥ*...
263. Ibid.:
    ...*Ākhanṭamudakam*...
264. Ibid., p. 371.
265. Ibid., p. 428.

6

Arts and Learning

ARCHITECTURE

Dhanapāla's *Tilaka-mañjarī*, which presents a panoramic view of the social and cultural conditions of the age, also throws interesting light on the state of contemporary architecture. It contains references to various architectural aspects such as construction of palaces, forts, temples, tanks, roads, shops and other important buildings. The *Yuktikalpataru* and *Samarāṅgaṇasūtradhāra*, the treatises attributed to Bhoja, are the other available sources for understanding the architectural achievements of the time. *Yuktikalpataru* deals, inter alia, with such diverse topics as furniture-making, ship-building, palace-architecture, construction of public and private buildings and city-planning. *Samarāṅgaṇasūtradhāra* discourses upon the building of houses, halls and palaces and the planning of cities and villages.

One of the striking features of the cities in ancient India was their artistic lay-out which duly incorporated and harmonized with the prevalent architectural styles. Dhanapāla, while describing the city of Ayodhyā in *Tilaka-mañjarī*, incidently reflects on the beauties of its planning and architecture. The technical term for the architect was 'sthapati',[1] who says *Samarāṅgaṇasūtradhāra*, was fully conversant with all the intricate aspects of the science of architecture and held the important charge of designing and planning the city.[2]

The forts were also built under his supervision in accordance with the instructions mentioned in ancient treatises.[3]

From *Tilaka-mañjarī* we learn that the city had an outer wall ('prākāra') which was circular in form[4] and was white-washed.[5]

The wall was built around the city which stood on a mound.[6] *Samarāṅgaṇasūtradhāra* mentions that 'prākāra' was of impressive height and built of bricks.[7] According to Kauṭilya also, the city-wall was built upon a mound ('vapra') and was known as 'aistakaprākārā'.[8] According to *Tilaka-mañjarī*, on the top of the city-wall there were to be accumulated deadly weapons,[9] while stones to be used as hand-missiles were to be accumulated near the city-wall.[10] Bhoja also recommends that on the top of the city-wall were to be accumulated destructive weapons in great plenty.[11]

In *Tilaka-mañjarī* we find references to the circular,[12] triangular and the square shapes of the cities.[13] The *Yuktikalpataru* of Bhoja recommends two shapes for the cities namely, 'dīrgha' (rectangular) and 'caturaśra' (square-shape).[14] Kauṭilya recommends cities of circular ('vṛta'), rectangular ('dīrgha') and square ('caturaśra') shapes.[15] According to *Samarāṅgaṇasūtradhāra*, the people living in circular town were prone to die at an early age.[16] In the *Yuktikaplataru* we read that the citizens of the circular city are always in the grip of disease,[17] while the triangular shape of the city caused a three-fold loss—that of the wealth, the religious merits and the completion of the wishes of the citizens.[18] On the other hand, the square-shaped city brings four-fold blessings to the king who builds it, namely, wealth, spiritual gains, the fulfilment of desires and release from the corporeal existence.[19]

A moat encircled the entire city-wall.[20] The moat, says Dhanapāla, was filled with water and it was impossible to cross it.[21] *Samarāṅgaṇasūtradhāra* recommends three types of moats to be thrown around the forts, namely, the water—the mire—and the parched ditch-moat.[22] We find mention of water-moats in *Samarāṅgaṇasūtradhāra*.[23] In the *Navasāhsāñkacarita*, we read that the city of Ujjainī was protected by a water-moat.[24] The moat filled with water is also mentioned in the *Arthaśāstra* of Kauṭilya.[25]

According to Dhanapāla's narration in *Tilaka-mañjarī*, the city-wall had four high gate-ways ('gopura') to the east, west, north and south.[26] Kauṭilya also mentions that the city-wall was to be pierced by main gates known as 'gopura'.[27] Like Dhanapāla, he has also recommended the formation of four gates, namely, 'Brāhmadvāra' to the north, 'Aindradvāra' to the east, 'Yāmyadvāra' to the south and 'Senāpatyadvāra' to the west.[28]

The subsidiary gates in the city-wall have been referred to as 'pratolī' in *Tilaka-mañjarī*.[29] The tradition of providing 'pratolī' gates in the city-walls in India is very old. Kauṭilya in *Arthaśāstra* has recommended the provision of 'pratolī' gates in the city-walls.[30] Megasthenes mentions that the wall of Pātaliputra contained sixty-four gates of which four were the main gates ('gopura') and the remaining sixty were the subsidiary gates.[31] The 'pratolī' gates, according to *Tilaka-mañjarī*, had strong planks.[32] In the event of the country being attacked by an enemy, all the 'pratolī' gates were protected by the king's trusted men, e.g., 'gulmaka'[33] (crack-troops).

As for the interior of the city, sufficient information can be gleaned from *Tilaka-mañjarī*. Inside the city was the king's main palace[34] which was studded with ruby stones.[35] On the grounds of the palace were built pavilions ('vedikās') which were decorated with precious stones.[36] The king's retiring room was made of ivory and was situated on the top floor of the palace. Inside the room there was a pavilion ('vedika') made of precious stones ('maṇiśilā'). The king's bed, set with 'vidruma dāru', was laid on that 'vedika'. The king rested there.[37] In *Pāiyalacchīnāmamālā*, this room on the roof is called 'candraśālā'.[38]

Tilaka-mañjarī mentions a whole variety of royal palaces whose number was legion.[39] There were separate palaces for princes. The king Meghavāhana got built a separate palace for Prince Harivāhana, when the prince completed his education.[40] The palace for the prince was built outside the city.[41] It was encircled by a moat. The palace had a high 'toraṇa' gate. Both the sides of the gate were decorated with golden jars. The palace contained enclosures for elephants and horses.[42] Kauṭilya has recommended separate palaces for princes and princesses.

Some of the more prominent royal buildings referred to in *Tilaka mañjarī* include the harem[43] ('antaḥpuraprāsāda'), assembly hall[44] ('sabhā-maṇḍapa'), art-gallery[45] ('citraśālā), bed room decorated with paintings or drawings room[46] ('śayanacitraśālā'), kitchen[47] ('bhojanaśālā'), dinner-hall[48] ('bhojanabhavana-maṇḍapa'), bath room[49] (snāna-maṇḍapikā'), water cooled house[50] ('dhārāgṛha'), wedding hall[51] ('vivāha-maṇḍapa'), pleasure palace[52] ('ratigṛha'), stadium for staging dancing concerts[53] ('līlālatā-maṇḍapa'), mechanized water-cooled house[54] ('yantradhārāgṛha'), and woodside palace[55] ('madana-vanaprāsāda').

Dhanapāla refers to the nursing home—('prasūti-gṛha')—which was situated near the harem.[56] Kauṭilya too has recommended separate homes for pregnant and sick women.[57]

Tilaka-mañjarī throws a lot of light upon the plan and lay-out of the palaces. In the construction of the palaces thousands of masons were engaged.[58] These palaces either belonged to the royal house-hold or to the aristocrats and the nobility. The palaces are described to be high like mouutains[59] as they were many-storeyed.[60] The princesses' palaces having seven storeys are referred to in *Tilaka-mañjarī*.[61] The palaces were built on high mounds plateform and had turrets.[62] They were fitted with high 'pratolī' gates.[63] Kauṭilya mentions that the 'gopura' i.e., the main city-gate was to be six times the width of the 'pratolī'.[64] Many animals were depicted over the arches ('toraṇa') which were decorated with garlands of 'harican-dana'.[65] The palaces were furnished with courtyards and pavilions ('vedikas').[66]

The courtyards had swings.[67] Every palace had a dramatic hall where plays were staged.[68] The palaces were white-washed with stone from outside.[69]

After the king, nobles and aristocrats, come the men of common stock. Dhanapāla mentions that there were well-decorated and well-furnished houses in the city for the citizens to live in.[70] The houses are described to be built of stones.[71] There were separate houses for the prostitutes.[72] There was a water-reservoir near every house for water-sports.[73] There were also a number of artificial tanks ('vāpīs') containing stairs to go down into the water.[74] The women in *Tilaka-mañjarī* are described to take bath in the 'vāpīs' near their houses after finishing the house-hold chores.[75]

There were markets in the city.[76] The city had broad streets leading to markets.[77] The shops were built in rows.[78] The city was skirted with parks and pleasure gardens.[79]

In *Tilaka-mañjarī*, Dhanapāla makes a mention of many other magnificent buildings which added to the splendour of the city. The city had a number of high pinnacled temples. The 'śikharas' (spires) were shaped into the jars of gold on the top.[80] The temple consisted of a 'garbhagṛha' or a womb-house, where the presiding diety was enshrined. In *Tilaka-mañjarī* we read that the statue of Lord Mahāvīra made of hard pearl stone was installed in thc 'garbhagṛha' of the temple.[81] Temples were built for thousands of gods[82] or whom the more conspicuous were the temples dedicated to 'kāmadeva', 'Pārvatī',[83] 'Śiva',[84] 'Lakṣmī',[85] 'Ṛṣabhadeva',[86] and 'Viṣṇu'.[87] King Meghavāhāna in *Tilaka-mañjarī* is described to have built a temple for goddess Lakṣmī. It had a spacious courtyard and was adorned with ruby stones.[88] Another temple dedicated to Ṛṣabhadeva had a high pinnacle and a carved toraṇa gateway.[89] King Bhoja Paramāra is said to have built as many as one hundred and four temples. According to *Udaipur Praśasti*: "He made the world worthy of its name by covering it all-round with temples dedicated to Kedāreśvara, Rāmeśvara, Somanātha, Sundira, Kāla-nada, Anala and Rudra".[90] The above facts are corroborated by D.C. Ganguly who writes: "During the happy reign of Paramāras a large number of superb and magnificent temples were built in Malwa".[91]

Dhanapāla has given a very beautiful account of a 'Jala-maṇḍapa' (lake-house). It was a cool house, which provided welcome relief from the scorching heat of the summer. It was built amidst beautiful natural surroundings ('nitānta-subhage-bhūvibhāge'), flanked by mango-trees ('sahakāra khaṇḍa') and newly planted plantain trees, where the presence of Cuckoos (kala-kanṭhakulasya), pea-cocks and swans lent the atmosphere a rare charm. The front portion of the house had 'sirīśa' trees which were newly budded ('aciravikacānām'). Thc walls of the 'jala-maṇḍapa' were decorated with 'visasūtracāmaras'. The gates had buntings ('vandana-malam') of 'haricandana'. The pillars were decorated with the figures of 'sālabhañjikās' made of 'himaśilā'. The fragrant incense named 'kālāgurudhūpa' was burnt in the windows. The pots made of pearls were filled with 'aṅgarāga' (fragrant powder). The ceilings had canopies made of Chinese silk ('Cīnāṁśuka'). There were pots filled with water to make the palace cool ('atiśiśiratyāca jalakalaśairapi'). There were mini-water falls on all the sides of 'jala-maṇḍapa'. The water falling down from the water-falls in a straight sweep on all the sides of 'jala-maṇḍapa' created the illusion of a crystal wall encircling the 'jala-maṇḍapa' ('sthavīyasāpāthasāṁ pravāheṇa prākāra valayeneva phātikena prānteṣu kṛtaparikṣepam'). There were drains made of 'candrakāntamaṇi', It had a number of extraordinary 'citraśālās'. The beautiful young prostitutes sat at the windows ('abhinava yauvanābhirvāraramaṇībhiradhyāsitavitata vātāyanam').[92]

Jala-maṇḍapa also served as a hospital for those attacked by heat-stroke.[93] It was an ideal resort for the summer season but only kings could afford it.

Dhanapāla mentions tanks of all sizes which added to the grandeur of the city. The water in the tanks was transparent like glass.[94] Muñja is mentioned to have beautified his capital Dhārā with many tanks, one of which is still called 'Muñjasāgara'.[95] Bhojapura lake, constructed during the reign of Rājā Bhoja was a great feat of engineering.

The caves having rooms made of pearls are also mentioned in *Tilaka-mañjarī*.[96]

From the evidence provided by *Tilaka-mañjarī*, it becomes abundantly clear that Indian architecture had reached a very high level of conceptual designing and workmanship in Dhanapāla's time.

PAINTING

'Ālekyam' (painting) is one of the sixty four 'kalās' (arts) mentioned in the *Kāmasūtra* of Vātsyāyana. It occupies the fourth place in the list.[97] The princes and painters converse about it in *Tilaka-mañjarī* and various technical terms used therein such as 'citrapaṭṭa'[98] (paintings on the canvas), 'bhitticitra'[99] (wall-paintings or frescos), 'citraphalaka'[100] (paintings on the panel or board), 'citraśālā',[101] 'nipuṇa citrakāra'[102] (master-painter), 'citravidyopādhyāya'[103] (painting-teacher), 'pratibimba'[104] (imaginative reproduction), 'viddharūpa'[105] (engravings on hard surface), and 'tūlikā'[106] (brush) reveal the importance which was attached to this art during Dhanapāla's time. The princes and princesses were not only connoisseurs of art but also took pains to learn painting. Prince Harivāhana, besides being proficient ('pāradṛśvan) in dance (nṛtya) and music (gīta) knows the art of painting (citra-kalā) quite well.[107]

Tilaka-mañjarī is quite adept in the art of painting.[108] Besides, she is avidly interested in looking at works of art.[109] Even Citralekhā, Tilaka-mañjarī's nurse is not the less proficient in this art.[110] On one occasion, Patralekhā, Tilaka-mañjarī's mother, bids Citralekhā to show Tilaka-mañjarī (who had vowed not to marry)[111] portraits of eligible princes painted by master-painters so that art should so effect her as to romove her deep-seated scorn of men and bring her round to give her consent for marriage.[112]

Various kinds of paintings[113] were done on walls,[114] canvas[115] and board.[116] The methodology or process of drawing remained nearly the same in all genres. The imagination of the artist, vis-a-vis, the picture in mind was of real importance. The colours employed most often in paintings were white,[117] blue, red and yellow.[118]

The prominence enjoyed by the art of painting during Dhanapāla's time is brought out eloquently by the lovers in *Tilaka-mañjarī* who engage themselves in drawing portraits of each other. Malaya Sundarī who is in love with Harivāhana makes his portrait on the board.[119] Similarly, Harivāhana also portraits Malaya Sundarī.[120] Dhanapāla gives a graphic account of how Malaya Sundarī paints the portrait of her lover. A casket full of brushes is placed near her and a big board for delineating the portrait is placed before her by her maid servants; she starts the work and imagining again and again the model fixed in her mind, she portrays. Now and then she pauses to think of him again, adds a touch on the canvas here and there and stops to see the correctness of her delineations.[121]

The frescos were also in vogue during Dhanapāla's time. In *Tilaka-mañjarī*, the courtesans of the royal harem paint the picture of 'Vidyādhara-couples' and the pairs of birds and deers on the walls in such a way as is indicative of their love and affection towards each other.[122]

The members of the royal family generally passed their day time in visiting picture galleries and feasting their eyes on the portraits of beautiful princesses painted by the master-painters. So great was the passion for painting in those days.[123]

The master-painters of yore were confident of their powers and capabilities. In *Tilaka-mañjarī*, Gandharvaka, a celebrated painter, agrees at the request of Citralekhā to delineate a male portrait which when presented to Tilaka-mañjarī would capativate her and rid her of her apathy for men. The portrait, asserts Gandharvaka, would approve as miraculous as 'siddhi-garuḍa mantra'.[124] Gandharvaka's is not lone example of master-painter. There are numerous references of such painters scattered in the annals of ancient India. Jagdish Chandra Jain writes: "We are told that a Parivvāiyā painted the portrait of the princess Sujeṭṭhā on a board and showed it to king Seniya who fell in love with her. Similarly, prince Sāgaracanda became enamoured of Kamalāmelā when her portrait was shown to him".[125] Dhanapāla describes in *Tilaka-mañjarī* that prince Samaraketū spends a forenoon in beholding the portrait of a charming maiden delineated on the canvas by master-artist, in the company of painting-teachers (Citravidyopādhyāya), curious-town-folk, and those who were proficient in the art of painting and other people who came to see the painting. The prince tries to evaluate the 'cārutvatattva' (aesthetic appeal) of the portrait.[126]

Picture-galleries (citra-śālā) were acquisitions of great pride for the kings in ancient India. Art-galleries were generally magnificent places artistically decorated. Dhanapāla has mentioned three types of citra-śālās namely : (1) 'citra-śālā'[127] (art-gallery), (2) 'citra-śālīkā'[128] (a small art-gallery, which existed probably in every palace), and (3) 'śayana-citra-śālā'[129] (drawing-room, or a bed-room decorated with paintings). Describing a śayana-citra-śālikā', Dhanapāla states that a 'ratna-maṇḍapa' is situated in the courtyard of the gallery . . .The maṇḍapa stands on pillars of gold. A beautiful large carpet is spread on it, laid upon with a bed of gold.[130] There is a window made of śaśikānta (candra-kānta) pearls on the left wall.[131] At another place we are told by Dhanapāla that the floor of the hall of 'citraśālā' has been decorated by beasmearing it all over with rich sandal paste.[132]

The paṭṭas on which pictures had been drawn[133] were carefully rolled up and preserved in silken covers.[134] They were unrolled and displayed as and when required.[135]

The painters of Dhanapāla's time were patronized by the members of the Royalty. The artists respected and set great store by the sense of artistic discrimination possessed by their royal patrons. Thus they brought their creations to their patrons for approval and appreciation which determined the worth of the paintings and made or unmade the career and fame of the painter. The female gate keeper in *Tilaka-mañjarī* presents a painting to prince Harivāhana for comments. The prince attentively looks at the picture which is the portrait of a comely maiden who seems to surpass the three worlds: (the Earth, the Heaven and the Nether World—mrityūloka, svargaloka and pātāla loka) in beauty. The portrait is so captivating that the prince repeatedly looks at the curly locks, the moon-like face, the parted lips, the intoxicated eyes, the slender neck, the rounded breasts, the thin waist, the alluring omphalos, the shapely thighs and the lotus-like feet of the girl. Thoroughly enchanted, the Prince shows it to his friends, Samaraketū and Kamalagupta. He enquires of the gate-keeper from where she had procured the painting of such surpassing beauty which was rare on this earth.[136]

Gandharvaka also presents for Prince Harivāhana's expert comments the picture done by him on canvas of a young girl standing in the midst of natural surroundings. Though a celebrated painter, Gandharvaka urges his princely patron in all humility to give him the benefit of his sound judgment. At it, Prince Harivāhana commends him by saying, "Who can teach you ? You are the originator of this art in the world".[137] The natural landscape painted by Gandharvaka in this picture shows an extensive tank on the top of a mount. All around the tank 'Campaka', 'Aśoka', 'Tilaka', 'Tālī' and 'Tamāla' trees are growing in abundance. The lotus flowers are blossoming on the fringes of the tank. The beautiful avenues of 'Lavalī', betel-nut trees, betel leaves have also been painted. The ground is made visible. The girl in her multi-coloured dress of red, yellow, blue and white and surrounded by her maids-in-waiting is shown moving on the sand amidst these objects of nature.[138] The various limbs of her body are set in their due proportions and symmetry and their contours and curves are masterfully delineated by the artist. The pairs of birds are shown flying away as if they are afraid of the movement of the women. The couples of deers also move hither and thither. The courtesans in white dress are shown attending upon the girl. The swans, obviously attracted by the sound of the nupura of the girl, have swarmed to her and obstructed her movements. The girl is trying to remove the swans by waving her hands.[139] Although in the opinion of Prince Harivāhana, the picture is perfect in all respects, yet he traces the want of a male figure in it.[140] There upon Gandharvaka replies that he has not portrayed it intentionally as Tilaka-mañjarī is not favourably disposed towards men.[141] But if the Prince commands him to insert a male figure, he would gladly do it.[142]

Such a vivid and in-depth description of works of art and art-galleries available in Dhanapāla's *Tilaka-mañjarī* establishes beyond doubt the keen interest and deep understanding Dhanapāla possessed in the art of painting. It may be reasonably surmised that he was something of a painter himself, else it would have been difficult for him to describe the portrait with such accuracy of detail. The description incidently brings to light other facts too. For instance, the kings used to give liberal patronage to 'Citrakāras' (painters and artists). Similarly, the word 'citravidyopādhyāya' is indicative of the existence of art teachers in those days. Evidently, painting was a subject of study both for men and women. Even women of lower status (courtesans) were adept in this art. Most significantly, patricians and plebeians alike exhibited artistic taste by frequenting the art-galleries. The climate of the age was indeed rich in art and culture.

MUSIC

vīṇāvādana tattvajnaḥ śrutijāti viśāradaḥ |
tālajñaścā prayāsena mokṣa mārgaṃ prayacchati ||

Yājñavalkyasmṛti

The technical word used for music in ancient India is Saṅgīta, which originally included, as in ancient Greece,[143] vocal and instrumental music, dancing and drama (*Gītaṁ vādyaṁ ca nṛtyaṁ ca trayaṁ saṁgītamucyate*).[144] The God Śiva is supposed to have been the creator of this art and his mystic dance (Tāṇḍava) symbolizes the rhythmic motion of the universe.[145] The origin of music is traditionally traced from Sāmadeva (*Sāmaveḍādidaṁ gītaṁ sajjagrāha pitāmahaḥ*).[146]

The earliest extant work on the theory of Indian music, dancing and drama is Bharata's *Naṭyaśāstra* written in early sixth century A.D. The twenty-fifth chapter of the *Naṭyaśāśtra* deals with the 'svaras' 'śrutis', 'grāmas', 'mūrchanā' and 'jātis'.[147]

The kings and aristocrats in ancient India took delight in music and were its chief patrons. We are told by Dhanapāla that every palace during his time had a dramatic-hall where plays were staged.[148] Dhanapāla, himself a musician of some stature, has touched upon the different aspects of music in his works.

There were several categories of singers and dancers testifying to the highest standards of proficiency which India had attained in the sphere of music. The 'Gandharvas'[149] (celestical musicians), the Apsarasas[150] (heavenly musicians), Kinnaras[151] (centaur like performers on musical instruments), Abhisārikās[152] (dancers), Kuśilavas[153] (actors or singers), Cāraṇas[154] (panegyrists), Gaṇikas[155] (dancers) who were most conspicuous in their respective attainments are referred to in *Tilaka-mañjarī*.

Music was an important subject in the curriculum of both male and female education. Prince Harivāhana in *Tilaka-mañjarī* is described to have mastered the art of playing on the flute.[156] He was also quite adept in the art of dancing, singing and painting.[157] King Meghavāhana too is described playing on the flute, reclining restfully on the bed in the after-noons attended by the music teachers.[158]

Singing, dancing and playing on musical instruments were accomplishments befitting a noble damsel.[159] In *Tilaka-mañjarī*, Malaya Sundarī,[160] Tilaka-mañjarī[161] and Gandharvadatta[162] are described to be quite adept in music. We read in Bāṇa's works that Kādambarī and Mahāśvetā had received systematic training in music.[163]

Members of the royal families were keenly interested in both vocal and instrumental music.[164] Music conferences were organised in which queens, princes and courtiers, besides professional singers and musicians, participated.[165] Someśvara in *Mānasollāsa* describes that seats were allotted to the participants according to their status. Of the artists the vocalists sat in front, stringers and harpers at their back, flute players on their sides, next to them sat the lady singers and the last of all the drummers. It was a popular belief that singing in praise of a king brought prosperity as the kings often rewarded the musicians.[166]

According to the evidence provided by *Tilaka-mañjarī* and *Mānasollāsa,* instrumental music could be classified under four categories, that which was played in accompaniment with song and dance as in: (1) 'nāṭya,"[167] (2) with dance alone as in 'prekṣā'[168] or 'tāṇḍava', (3) with song alone as in 'Gangāstotra Gītakāni',[169] (4) without song and dance as in soloplaying on any instrument.[170]

The most commonly used instruments according to *Tilaka-mañjarī,* were of four varieties :

(1) 'Tata' (stringed), such as 'Vīṇā' (lute),

(2) 'Avanaddha', such as 'mṛdaṅga' and 'muraja',

(3) 'Suṣira' such as 'Veṇu' (flute), 'Śaṅkha' (conch-shell) and 'Kāhalā',

(4) 'Ghana', such as jhallarī.

Besides, 'Vīṇā', 'mṛdaṅga', 'muraja', 'veṇu', 'śaṅkha', 'kāhalā' and 'jhallarī', other musical instruments then common were 'paṭaha', 'paṇava', 'tūrya' 'kāṅsyatāla' and 'dundubhī'.[171]

Accomplished ladies acquired skill in playing on musical instruments like vīñā. Malaya Sundarī in *Tilaka-mañjarī* harps on the lute.[172]

Dhanapāla's period was one of great literary activity as the rulers were the patrons of poets and men of letters. The office of the poet and the scholar was one of honour. Literary compositions received appreciations from the king. Sometimes the king recited or sang poems composed by himself. The poems recited by the king were generally of amorous type, that is, of śṛaṅgāra rasa.[173] Devotional songs, e.g., hymns and mantras, were also sung or recited. 'Gaṅgāstotra' was recited in the morning in praise of Goddess 'Gaṅgā'.[174] Malaya Sundarī, recites Gāyatrī mantra.[175] The king Meghavāhana in *Tilaka-mañjarī* is advised by Vidyādhara to listen to the songs sung in praise of devas.[176]

Alongwith music, dancing had become a highly accomplished and much-acclaimed art in Dhanapāla's time. Royalty provided it with due patronage and recognition. On festive occasions, such as the birth or the marriage of a prince, victory in war or at the celebration of the spring festival, dance performances were arranged by kings in the vast courtyards of the royal palace or on the spacious lawns of the royal garden. The ladies of the royal harem and of the nobility graced these dance shows with their presence.[177] In these performances courtesans entertained the royalty and the nobility with exquisitely rendered dances and songs.[178] Sometimes, even king participated in dancing.[179] Apsaras are also described to arrange dancing concerts in the evenings.[180]

Dancing was not, however, confined to courtesans. The princesses and the daughters of the nobles were equally interested in the art of dancing and learnt it with great care. The sage Vātsyāyana lists dancing as one of the sixty four principal arts and observes: "a king's daughter or the daughter of the noble man, well-skilled in these arts (singing, dancing etc.), will have her husband under her sway, even if he has one thousand wives".[181]

In *Tilaka-mañjarī*, Malaya Sundarī has been represented as a superb dancer.[182] Tilaka-mañjari, the heroine is also proficient in dancing.[183] Gandharvadattā, a girl of ten, is described to be quite adept in the art of dancing.[184] The royal damsels in *Tilaka-mañjarī* are described to have presented dance performances on the occasion of a coronation.[185] In *Karpūramañjarī*, there are references to maidens who off and on used to give a dance performance in the court before a select audience without incurring thereby any special approbrium.[186]

Various types of dances, namely, 'tāṇḍava',[187] 'nāṭya',[188] 'lāsya',[189] 'prekṣā'[190] and 'lāghava'[191] are mentioned in *Tilaka-*

mañjarī. Someśvara in his *Mānasollāsa* has referred to six types of dances: viz., 'nāṭya', 'lāsya', 'tāṇḍava', 'lāghava', 'viṣama' and 'vikaṭa'.[192] We hear of 'veśyārāsa-maṇḍalīs' (a party of courtesans who performed circular dance, imitating the dance of Kṛṣṇa) in *Tilaka-mañjarī*.[193]

Dancing in India is assumed to have had a divine origin and was usually practised with a deeply religious attitude. Unfortunately, human feelings being what they are, the precepts of the holy sages were often forgotten. Merutuṅga in his *Prabandhacintāmaṇi* describes that one day in the presence of king Paramardin a low dancing girl was made to dance topless with nothing but a short petticoat on.[194]

Dramatic performances, besides musical and dancing concerts, had apparently become an integral part of the way of life of the royalty and the nobility. References to dramatic halls frequently occur in *Tilaka-mañjarī*, where plays were staged on all festive occasions.[195] Ladies could also take part in dramatic performances[196] Dancers (nartakīs) gave shows of 'lāsya' dance in the raṅgaśālās (dramatic halls).[197]

In Dhanapāla's *Tilaka-mañjarī*, we get references to several musical airs and notes such as 'maṅgalagīta;[198] 'Karuṇa gīta',[199] 'kākalīgīta'[200] and 'kekāgīta'[201] expressive of different moods and states of the human heart.

The importance attached to song and dance during Dhanapāla's time is eloquently brought out by the numerous references to music teachers[202] and dance teachers[203] in *Tilaka-mañarī*. A case in point is that of king Meghavāhana who despite his advanced years, is described to be learning music from music teachers to gain proficiency in this art.[204]

Dhanapāla has incidently mentioned 'śruti',[205] 'svara',[206] 'grāma',[207] 'mūrchanā',[208] 'jāti'[209] and 'rāga'[210] in *Tilaka-mañjarī* which shows his intimate knowledge of the whole intricate gamut of the musical art as practised in his times.

'Śruti' produces 'svara', 'svara' produces 'grāma', from 'grāma', 'mūrchanā' is produced and 'mūrchanā' produces 'rāga'.

1. '*Srutis*' (*Quarter tones*)

Sruti is a fundamental fact of scale. Each note (śvara') can be elaborated with half and quarter tones ('śrutis'). There are twenty two quarter tones in each octave, namely, 'tīvrā', 'kumudvatī', 'mandā', 'chandovatī', 'dayāvatī', 'rañjanī, ratikā', 'raudrī', 'krodhā', 'vajrikā', 'prasāriṇī', 'prītiḥ', 'mārjanī', 'ksiti', 'raktā', 'sandīpanī', 'ālāpinī', 'madantī', 'rohiṇī', ramyā', 'ugrā' and 'kṣobhiṇī'.[211]

'Śruti' is a part of 'svara'. Every 'svara' is constructed upon the two or more 'srutis'. For example, 'ṣaḍja' 'svara' is produced from first to four 'srutis', likewise 'ṛṣabha' from fifth to seventh, 'gāndhārā' from eighth and ninth, 'madhyama' from tenth to thirteenth, 'pañcama' from fourteenth to seventeenth, 'dhaivata' from eighteenth to twentieth. The last two 'srutis', produce 'niṣāda'.[212]

The tuning of 'vīṇā' is called 'śruti'. The vīṇā is said to stand in 'pañcama śruti' or 'madhyama śruti'. The 'śrutis' are all equal in size.[213]

Michael Edwards says about quarter-tones: "The use of 'quarter tones' produces a characteristic sound which to unaccustomed ears gives the impression that the musician is out of tune".[214]

2. '*Svaras*' (*Notes*)

The Indian scale has seven notes, namely, 'ṣaḍja', 'ṛṣabha', 'gāndhāra', 'madhyama', 'pañcama', 'dhaivata' and 'niṣāda'.[215] Now-a-days these are generally abbreviated to 'sa', 'ri', 'ga', 'ma', 'pa', 'dha' and 'ni'.[216] Svaras are of four kinds namely, 'vādī', 'saṁvādī', 'anuvādī' and "vivādī'.[217]

3. '*Grāmas*'

A.L. Basham calls it a scale in music.[218] Seven grāmas namely, 'ṣāḍava', 'pañcama', 'Ṣaḍjagrāma', 'sādhāritā', 'kaiśikā', 'madhyama', and 'madhyama grāma' are referred to in *Nāradīya Śikṣā*.[219] 'Ṣaḍja', 'madhyama' and 'gāndhāra' were the popular grāmas in ancient Indian music.[220] Dhanapala in *Tilaka-mañjarī* has specifically mentioned 'gāndhāra grāma'.[221] Umesh Joshi is of the opinion that for the last five centuries Indian music remained absolutely based on 'ṣaḍja grāma'.[222]

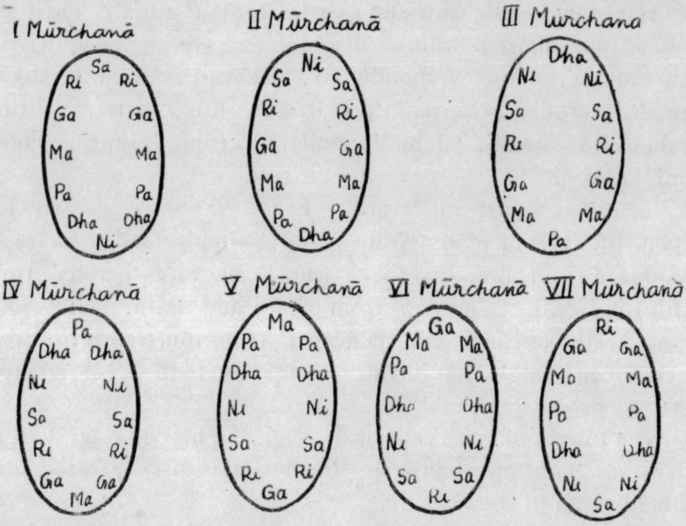

4. *Murchanās*

These are modulations in music. The seven mūrchanās, according to 'devatā', 'pitṛ' and 'gandharva' variations are, 'nandī', 'viśālā', 'citrā', 'sumukhī'. 'citravatī', 'sukhā' and 'balā'. According to 'pitṛgaṇa', they are called, āpyāyanī,'viśvabhṛtā', 'candrā', 'hemā', 'kapardinī', 'maitrī' and 'varhatī'.[223]

The seven mūrchanās are shown above in circles. Every circle has twelve places.[224]

5. *Jātis*

Jātis are eighteen in number, namely, 'ṣāḍji', 'ārṣabhī', gāndhārī, 'madhyamā', 'pañcamī', 'dhaivatī', 'naiṣādi', 'Ṣaḍjakaiśīkī', 'ṣaḍjodīcyavā', 'ṣaḍja madhyamā', 'gāndhārodicyavā', 'raktagāndhārī', 'kaiśikī', 'madhyamodīcyavā', 'kārmāravī', 'gāndhāra pañcamī', 'āndhrī' and nandayantī'.[225]

6. *Rāgas*

A rāga is a series of five or more notes upon which melody is based. "According to orthodox theory, there are six basic rāgas, the others being rāginīs, personified as the wives of masculine rāgas. The six original rāgas are 'Bhairava', 'Kauśika', 'Hiṇḍola', 'Dīpaka', 'Śrīrāga' and 'Megha.''[226]

Thirty-four rāgas are mentioned by K. Vasudeva Shastri, namely, 'Śudhasādhārita', 'ṣaḍjagrāmarāga, 'suddhakaiśika-rāga', 'suddhaṣāḍavarāga, 'bhinna kaiśika madhyama', 'bhinna tānarāga', 'bhinnakaiśika', 'gauḍakaiśkamadhyama', 'gauḍa-pañcama', 'gauḍakaiśika', 'vesaraṣāḍava', 'boṭṭarāga', 'mālava-pañacama', 'rūpasādhāra', 'śakarāga', 'bhammānapañacama', 'nartarāga, 'ṣadjakaiśika'; 'madhyamagrāmarāga', 'mālavakai-śika', 'śāḍavarāga', 'bhinnaṣaḍja'. 'bhinnapañcama', 'pañca-masāḍava', 'ṭakkarāga', 'hiṇḍola', 'suddhakaiśika-madhyama', 'gāndhāra pañcama'. 'travaṇā', 'kakubha rāga', 'vegarañjī', 'Sauvīra', 'piñjarī', 'karnāṭabhangāla'.[227] Each of the rāgas is associated with the particular time of the day or night—dawn, morning, afternoon and evening. There are also other associations with such emotions as joy, fear and love.

Besides 'śruti', 'svara', 'grāma', 'mūrchanā', 'jāti' and 'rāga', Dhanapāla has also touched upon 'tālas' which occupy an important place in the art of music. 'Tālabaddha' and 'anibaddha' are the two main parts of a 'gīta' (song). 'Tāla' is an equally integral part of the art of dancing. Dhanapāla specifically mentions 'karṇatāla'[228] and 'karatalatāla'[229] in *Tilaka-mañjarī.* One hundred and twelve 'tālas' are listed by K. Vasudeva Shastri.[230]

Dhanapāla has cited various techniques ('vyāpāra'), employ-ed by musicians playing on musical instruments, viz., 'vīṇā', 'Veṇu' and the like. For instance, kings and princes practising on the 'vīṇā' are represented beating simultaneously on 'tantrī' (chords) of the 'vīṇā' with the finger of their right hand.[231] This is called 'śkhalita vyāpāra'.[232]

The use of musical terminology by Dhanapāla (detailed above) together with other evidence provided by his works may lead one to believe that he, himself was not only a good musician but also a musicologist. Besides Dhanapāla, other contemporaries who display intimate acquaintance with music in their writings are Dhanañjaya, Dhanika, Kṛṣṇa Miśra, Nārada, Someśvara and Jayadeva. Dhanañjaya, who was the court-poet of Vākpati Muñja, composed *Daśarūpaka,* a treatise on dramaturgy. Dhanika, the younger brother of Dhanañjaya, wrote a commentary upon *Daśarūpaka*, known as *Avaloka*. Kṛṣṇa Miśra (XI century) wrote a drama named *Prabodha-Candrodaya*. It discusses musical notes, melodies, dancing etc. *Saṅgīta Makaranda*, attributed to Nārada, probably belongs to the eleventh century. It deals with music and dance in two separate parts. *Mānasollāsa* of Someśvara (XII century) devotes 2500 ślokas to music and musical instruments. Jayadeva's *Gīta Govinda* (XII century) is one of the most celebrated poems in Saṁskṛta, rich in lyrical beauty.

Michael Edwardes says about ancient Indian music and musicians: "Indian music has no harmony, and cross-rhythms and counter point take its place. Tune is usually unlike that in European music, and very often the rhythmic figure is exteremely complex. Within this framework, the Indian musician was—and remains—an improviser, probably because no true system of musical notation was developed in India. The musician, having chosen the rāga and the time, would, after perhaps playing a well-known melody based upon it, proceed to simple and then elaborate variations".[233]

In spite of this, obviously, great popularity of music among all sections of society in Dhanapāla's days, it is a matter of some sad reflection that, unlike their counterparts in the West, there existed no tradition among the Indian maestro to write out their individual musical compositions for posterity a la Beethovan and Mazart. The Indian maestro was an improviser so that every single performance (involving, as it did, the artist's impromptu variations on a well-known melody) became virtually a new composition. Owing to this built-in characterstic, the music of India's ancient masters has vanished for ever. That this should happen in a land which valued music as an instrument of culture and held that (so runs an ancient Indian proverb) "The man who knows nothing of literature, music or art is nothing but a beast without the beast's tail and horns" is a sobering thought indeed.

SCIENCE AND TECHNOLOGY

It is now universally acknowledged that science and technology had developed to great hieghts of attainment in ancient

India. Several branches of science and technology, viz., astronomy, astrology, medicine, surgery, metallurgy and engineering had registered tremendous progress by the Xth and XIth centuries A.D. Similarly, in the field of mathematics and chemistry, Indian knowledge was far superior to that of other countries of the day.

Dr. B.V. Subharayappa in his article, 'India's Contribution to the History of Science', dwells upon the impressive progress of science and technology in ancient India and its impact upon the world. He observes: "India, as the home of one of the earliest civilzations, has played a significant role in the history of scientific ideas and techniques. It is generally recognised that a number of scientific ideas which originated in India not only attracted the attention of thinkers in Greece, Arabia and Central Asia, but also influenced in no small measures the growth of different sciences in those regions. There was considerable exchange of ideas too between India and those regions from time to time resulting in the reformulation or evolution of some of the sciences in India itself. India's pre-eminent geographical position proved to be of pivotal importance in the movement of scientific ideas and technological practices".[234]

Said-ul Andalusi, an eminent historian and astronomer of the XIth century A.D., in his book '*Kitab Tabakatal-Umam* (The Categories of Nations), assigns the first place to India among the contemporary nations which had developed sciences by then.[235]

In the allied fields of astronomy and astrology Indian science had taken big strides of progress. In *Tilaka-mañjarī*, we come across references which unmistakably give us a peep into the extent of astronomical knowledge of the Indian people in the XIth century. The sailors in *Tilaka-mañjarī* make practical use of astronomy. At the time of the ship being threatened by a storm Tāraka, addresses his crew thus: "Rājā Tilaka, the ship, is sailing towards the south, even when I had ordered otherwise. It seems that you have lost all sense of direction. Even on being told, you are unable to locate the north. Look at the 'sapta-ṛṣi' (group of seven stars) and turn the ship back".[236]

As regards the knowledge and practice of astrology, it seems to be at its peak in those days.[237] Not only the man-in-the-street, but also the royalty and nobility placed deep faith in this science and often consulted the State astrologer whom they called 'Naimittika'.[238] Good or bad omens were interpreted by him and only on obtaining clearance from him were the journeys embarked upon.[239] Various, astrological terms as 'horā',[240] 'aṅguṣṭhakādipraśna',[241] 'karṇapiśācikāvidyā'[242] are mentioned in *Tilaka-mañjarī.*

Books on astronomy and astrology written by renowned authorities on the subjects were quite popular in Dhanapāla's time. *Rājamārtthaṇḍa*, *Rājamṛgāṅka*, *Vidvajjanavallabha*, *Ādityapratāpasiddhānta* by Bhoja[243] and *Bhāsavatī* by Sutānanda all belong to XI century. Two chapters of the work, *Siddhāntaśiromaṇi*, captioned 'Grahagaṇita' and 'Golā' contain very valuable material on astronomy[244] and Dhanapāla mentions in *Tilaka-mañjarī* that people consulted *Sāmudrikaśāstra*[245] and *grahagaṇita*[246] for gaining astronomical knowledge.

In the all-important field of medical sciences India was decidedly on the top of the world. The Indian system of medicine 'Āyurveda', is characterized by an all-embracing and cosmic outlook and seeks the preservation of all life—human, animal or plant. It has been rightly observed : "In the field of medical science, the methodological concepts of Āyurveda and systematic therapeutic practices have a distinct place. They not only developed into a full-fledged 'Science of Life' in India but also appear to have exercised profound influence on the growth of medical knowledge in other cultured areas".[247]

Different types of drugs and medicines used by women for preserving pregnancy[248] and medicinal preparations prescribed by 'Dhanavantari',[249] the famed physician, are referred to in *Tilaka-mañjarī*. Dhanapāla has ascribed four principal functions to medicine in *Tilaka-mañjarī*, namely, 'stambha' (astringency), 'stobha' (excitement), 'udvāsanā' (torment) and 'vidveṣaṇa' (reaction).[250]

Surgery was equally well-advanced in the time of Dhanapāla. In *Tilaka-mañjarī*, Dhanapāla refers to the high degree of skill and proficiency possessed by contemporary physicians in dressing and bandaging injuries and wounds.[251]

Physicians, proficient in all the branches of Āyurveda (medicine and surgery), are referred to in *Tilaka-mañjarī*.[252]

There was no dearth of authentic treatises and reference works on medical sciences in Dhanapāla's days. Cakrapaṇḍita, an XI century scholar of Bengal, wrote commentaries under the titles *Āyurvedadipikā* and *Bhānumatī* on the works of Caraka and Suśruta respectively. Cakrapaṇḍita also wrote a treatise on Āyurveda which stands as an important milestone in the history of Indian medicine. Its merit lies in the remarkable advance, it registers in the direction of metallic preparations introduced since the time of Vāgbhaṭṭa and Vṛṇda. Cakrapaṇḍita also wrote *Śabdacandrikā*—an encyclopaedia on vegetables and mineral substances—and *Dravyaguṇa Saṁgraha*—a work on dietetics. Another scholar Sureśvara wrote *Śabdapradīpa* and *Vrikṣāyurveda* which are highly-informed botanical treatises. *Āyurveda Sarvasvam Viśrāntavidyāvinoda*, *Śālihotra* (a Veterinary Manual)—all ascribed to Bhoja—are other important medical works of the period. *Śālihotra* constitutes a landmark in the field of veterinary science and is full of exhaustive information about horses, their common diseases and the most effective remedies thereof.[253]

In the field of medical chemistry (alchemy), the progress made by Indians was of a remarkably high order. "The chemical knowledge, which the Indians possessed in respect of the use of alkalis, acids and salts, preparation of cosmetics and perfumes, pyrotechnics and the like, was undoubtedly at a high level".[254] Dhanapāla in *Tilaka-mañjarī* alludes to various chemical preparations (rasāyana) whose effect was miraculous. The deadly vegetable poison, Kālakūṭa, (aconitum ferox) could be made ineffective, so also the fatal bite of the deadly snake 'Takṣaka' could be prevented from causing death, by administering specific compound medicines (rasāyana). Similarly, the things of far away could be seen by applying collyrium to the eyes. Onc could fly by applying unguent upon the legs or disappear by applying 'tilaka' on the forehead. Likewise, one could keep the dreaded old age and diseases at bay, one could banish the feeling of fear and even control death—all these and other miracles could be brought about by taking appropriate rasāyana.[255]

Alberunī, the famous traveller, who visited India in the XI century, and was well-versed in Arabic and Greek Astronomy and Chemistry, testifies to the achievements of Indian Rasāyana thus: "They have a science similar to alchemy which is quite peculiar to them. They call it 'Rasāyana', a word composed with 'rasa' i.e., gold. It means an art which is restricted to certain operations, drugs and compound medicines, most of which are taken from plants. Its principles restore the health of those who are ill beyond hope and give back youth to fading old age, so that people become again, what they were in the age near puberty, white hair become black again, the keenness of the senses is restored as well as the capacity of juvenile agility and even for cohabitation and the life of the people in this period is even extended to a long period".[256]

The Sanskrit equivalent of the term alchemy is 'rasavidyā' or 'rasasiddhiveda' and that of the alchemist, 'rasasiddha' or 'dhātuvādika'.[257] The word rasa, as used in the alchemical literature, means generally mercury while together with sulphur and mica is central to the whole of Indian chemical thought.[258] The use of 'Rasāyana', according to Alberunī, "could make men immortal, victorious, invincible and capable of doing every thing they desired".[259]

Rasāyana, according to Dhanapāla was capable of "transforming the three worlds into golden ones".[260] Alberunī's testimony is worth-quoting in full :

"In the city of Dhārā, the capital of Malwa, which is in our days is ruled by Bhoja Deva, there lies in the door of the Government house an oblong piece of pure silver, in which the outlines of the limbs of a man are visible. Its origin is accounted for by the following story—once in olden times a man went to a king of theirs, bringing him a Rasāyana, the use of which would make him immortal, victorious, invincible and capable of doing everything, he desired. He asked the king to come alone to the place of their meeting and the king gave orders to keep in readines all the man required. The man began to boil the oil for several days. Until at last it acquired consistency. Then he spoke to the king, 'Spring into it and I shall finish the process'. But the king terrified at what he saw, had not the courage to dive into it. The man on perceiving his cowardice, spoke to him, 'If you do not have the required courage and will not do it for yourself, will you allow me to do it myself' ? Whereupon the king answered, 'Do as you like'. Now he produced several packets of drugs and instructed him that when such and such symptoms should appear, he should throw upon him this or that packet. Then the man stepped forward to the cauldron and threw himself into it and atonce he was dissolved and reduced into pulp. Now the king proceeded according to his instructions, but when he had nearly finished the process and there remained only one packet, that was not yet thrown into the mass, he began to be anxious and to think what might happen to his realm, in case the man should return to life as an immortal, victorious, invincible person. And so he thought it preferable not to throw the last packet into the mass. The consequence was that the caldron became cold and the dissolved man became consolidated in the shape of the said piece of silver."[261]

In the field of engineering the masterly skill of Indian engineers is eloquently testified by the whole plethora of ancient tanks, lakes, bridges, bunds, dams, highways and the like. Bhojapur lake constructed in the reign of Bhoja is a veritable feat of hydraulic engineering. Dr. D.C. Ganguly says that Bhojapur lake is an example of the engineering skill and workmanship achieved by the people of Malwa under the rule of Paramāras.[262] P.T.S. Ayyangar observes that "The skill of the engineers of this period can be judged from the fact that the blocks were laid, one on the other without mortar, but yet their edges fitted so truly that the bund was absolutely water tight. . . . Its position so far from the dam affords another proof of the practical ability of the Hindu engineers of the time, for any error in the levels would have quickly destroyed the dam, which though stone-faced on both sides, was filled in by earth and could not long have withstood an overflow".[263]

A considerable progress had been made in the field of metallurgy in Northern India during Dhanapāla's time. Iron came to be used for a variety of purposes during X and XI centuries, specially in building temples. Utbi in his *Tārikh-i-Yāminī* mentions that on both sides of the city of Mathurā, "There were a thousand houses to which ideal temples were attached, all strengthened from top to bottom by rivets of iron".[264] A colossal iron pillar discovered at Dhārā, belonging to the time of Rājā Bhoja, bears eloquent testimony to the metallurgical advancement of the time.

The process of purification of iron as known to Hindus has been discussed by P.C. Ray in his book, *History of Hindu Chemistry*.[265] Vṛnda (*c.* 900 A.D.) prescribes that iron is to be lighted first and then "macerated in the juice of the emblic myrobalan and trewia nudiflora and exposed to the sun and again to be macerated in the juice of certain other plants and then to be rubbed in a mortar".[266] Cakrapāni of the XI century A.D. prescribes a better method of purification of iron: "After the bar of iron is rubbed with impalpable powder, the iron is to be heated to fusion point and plunged into the decoction of the myrobalans and roasted repeatedly in a crucible".[267]

The pages of *Tilaka-mañjarī* provide valuable information about the extent to which Mathematical knowledge had advanced in Dhanapāla's time. Dhanapāla speaks of Geometry (Kṣetra gaṇita) and mentions various geometrical terms like 'Lamba' (perpendicular), 'Bhuja'[268] (the side of a triangle), 'karṇa' (diagonal) etc. In the X and XI centuries India was most fortunate in having outstanding mathematicians like Āryabhaṭṭa, Śripati, Śrīdhara and Bhāskara, but for whose contributions Science could not have made much headway in India.[269] Āryabhaṭṭa deals with a number of intricate mathematical problems including that of zero in the chapter 'Kuṭṭakādhyāya —of his monumental work, *Mahāsiddhānta*. Śrīdhara is credited with the discovery of a method of solving quadratic equations in his work *Gaṇitatilaka*.[270] India's renowned mathematician, Bhāskara has applied himself with prodigious skill to solving problems of Arithmetic, Algebra and Geometry in his magnum opus, *Siddhānta Śiromaṇi*, which is divided into two parts— 'Līlāvati' and 'Bījagaṇita'. He gives a correct assessment of the division of a finite number by zero.[271]

We get an interesting insight into the state of Indian Ship Building Industry from the pages of *Tilaka-mañjarī*. We learn that ships were made of wood. In the account of the naval expedition undertaken by Samarketu, Tāraka, the chief sailor, speaks of ships made of strong and durable timber.[272] Al-

Masūdī also confirms that the ships operating in the Indian ocean were made of teak-wood.[273]

The *Yuktikalpataru* of Bhoja acquaints us with all the necessary materials and the characteristic qualities of different types of boats. Boats are classified by him on the basis of the wood used in them. Boats like men fell into classes: (a) light, soft and pierceable wood, which can be easily joined to any other kind of wood belonged to the Brāhmaṇa class, (b) light and yet strong and not easily pierceable wood belonged to Kṣatriya class, (c) soft and heavy wood belonged to the Śūdra class.[274] Bhoja recommends that the Kṣatriya wood was the most suitable for the construction of boats. According to *Yuktikalpataru*, the ship built of Kṣatriya class of wood brings wealth and happiness. It was most suitable and serviceable where the communication link was long and arduous over stretches of vast water. Ships made of other kinds of timber were not likely to last long and were liable to rot in salt water and split at the slightest shock and sink.[275]

The use of iron nails in ship-building was not favoured during Dhanapāla's time. *Tilaka-mañjarī* informs us that nails of wood were used in ships.[276] The same information is gathered from *Yuktikalpataru* which states that nailed timbers should not be used in sea going vessels as iron was bound to be attracted by load stone and consequently the ship would sink. For this reason Bhoja favours rope joints.[277] Al-Maśūdī traces the tendency among Indian ship-builders to avoid iron nails to the high degree of salinity in the Indian ocean remarking, "Now this kind of structure (stitching) is not used except in the Indian ocean, for the ships of the Mediterranean and those of the Arabs (there) all have nails, whereas in ships on the Indian Ocean iron nails do not last because the sea-water corrodes the iron and the nails grow soft and weak in the sea; and, therefore, the people on its shores, have taken to threading cords of fibre instead, and these are coated with grease and tar".[278]

As the ships were made of wooden planks switched together, there was an ever-present danger of their sinking as a result of water entering through leaks.[279] Therefore, it was incumbent upon the sailors to throw out water entering through the leaks and to plug the holes. *Tilaka-mañjarī* refers to the important practice of caulking.[280] Before the ships set sail, the seams and crevices were thoroughly caulked. The chief sailor (the captain of the vessel) examined all the joinings and got even the smallest holes caulked with wood and wax.[281]

Tilaka-mañjarī makes it abundantly clear that the ships of the day were fitted with cabins. Samaraketū proceeding to punish the turbulent feudatories of Dvīpāntara is described to enter the cabin erected in the forefront of the vessel.[282] Bhoja's *Yuktikalpataru* divides the ship into two kinds viz., with or without cabins.[283]

Tilaka-mañjarī furnishes information with regard to the method by which sails and masts were handled and regulated by the sailors. The first thing that Tāraka, the chief sailor, does after hearing of the proposed naval expedition of prince Samaraketū, is to get ropes tied to the sails.[284] When the wind is favourable, the sails are raised and the ship sets on its course.[285] The ship proceeds on, while the mast is erect and the ropes are attached to the sails.[286] The commander says that the crew should take rest because among other reasons most of them are too tired to keep the mast erect. They decide to sew the sails instead which had become tattered by the on-slaughts of violent wind and to tie ropes to them.[287] In order to halt the ship the sails are loosened and collected.[288] Tāraka proves his efficiency by replacing broken ropes with new ones and testing even strong sails.[289]

In *Tilaka-mañjarī*, we read that when a ship halted, the heavy anchors made of rocks were lowered down.[290] The sanskrit word for anchor is 'nāngara'.

Dhanapāla mentions that before setting sail the sailors paid special attention to replenish the stocks of ointment used for going into sea-water, kerosene oil and other necessary provisions. They also blocked the holes in the flanks of the reservoir of sweet water.[291]

Tilakā-mañjarī informs us that sailors got a sound practical training in seamanship. Tāraka was made the chief of the sailors by Candraketu. Soon he graduated in the Art and Craft of seamanship (naupracāravidyā), learnt all the duties of the helms man, journeyed back and forth in deep waters several times, visited the countries of dvīpāntara even though they were far removed, saw with his own eyes even small waterways and carefully observed rough and smooth areas.[292]

LITERATURE

The X and XI centuries turned out to be a period of great literary activity in Saṁskṛta, Prākṛta and Apabhraṁśa. The literature of this period is marked by richness, depth and variety in content and form. The period was distinguished by an all-round progress in the field of Kāvya, drama, romance and campū. A large body of scientific literature in such diverse fields as lexicography, grammar, poetics, metrics, medicine, mathematics, astronomy and astrology was penned down in this period. Religious, philosophical and devotional literature was also written in great plenty. This period saw the rise of a special form of prose composition—the Campū. The most important contribution of this age to Saṁskṛta literature is in the field of poetics which reached it high water-mark of development during this period.

The rulers of Rājpūt period were liberal patrons of art and literature. The Paramāra kings under whose benevolent and magnanimous patronage Dhanapāla produced his master-pieces were great votaries of the Goddess of Learning and were in reality at the very heart of the great literary movement of the period.[293] In fact, no other part of Northern India can boast of having gathered together such a bright galaxy of literary men as adorned the royal court of Malwa in the days of Paramāras. Beside extending patronage to men of letters, many Paramāra rulers were gifted poets themselves. Muñja Paramāra was an accomplished poet who cultivated eloquence, poetics and logic.[294] His verses have been extensively quoted in works of poetry. For instance, the Kashmiri poet Kṣemendra, in his books *Suvrittatilaka*, *Kavikaṅṭhābharaṇa* and *Aucityavicāracarcā*, quotes three different stanzas composed by Utpalarāja (Vākpati Muñja).[295]

The tradition of the poet-king bursts into its fullest flowering and attains the point of culmination in the person of Bhoja Paramāra. The *Udaipura Praśasti* glorifies Bhoja as the king of poets. Being a versatile genius, he is said to have fathered a large number of books in diverse disciplines. Authorship of the following works is generally ascribed to him by scholars and historians :

I. *Astronomy and Astrology* :
(1) *Rājamṛgāṅka*,
(2) *Rājamārttaṇḍa*,
(3) *Vidvajjanavallabha*,
(4) *Ādityapratāpasiddhānta*.
II. *Medicine* :
(5) *Āyurveda Sarvasvam*,
(6) *Visrāntavidyāvinoda*,
(7) *Śālihotra* (a veterinary Manual).
III. *Śilpaśāstra* :
(8) *Samarāṅgaṇasūtradhāra*.
IV. *Grammar* :
(9) *Śabdānuśasanam*.
V. *Philosophy* :
(10) *Rājamārttaṇḍa* (Vedânta),
(11) *Tatvaprakāśa* (Śaivism),
(12) *Siddhāntasaṅgraha*,
(13) *Śivatatvaratnakalikā*,
(14) *Yuktikalpataru*.
VI. *Dharmaśāstra* :
(15) *Vyavahārasamuccaya*,
(16) *Cārucaryā*.
VII. *Arthaśāstra* :
(17) *Cāṇakyanīti* (Daṇḍanīti).
VIII. *Alaṅkāra* :
(18) *Sarasvatī Kaṇṭhābharaṇā*,
(19) *Sṛṅgāra Prakāśa*.
IX. *Poetry and Prose* :
(20) *Rāmāyaṇa Campū*,
(21) *Vidyāvinodakāvyam*,
(22-23) Two Prākṛta poems (lately discovered at 'Dhārā),
(24) *Mahākālivijayam*,
(25) *Śṛṅgāramañjarī*,
(26) *Subhāsitapradandha*.

X. *Lexicography* :
(27) *Nāmamālikā*.[296]

Commenting upon the authorship of the books ascribed to Bhoja, Dr. Ganguly says: "It is doubtful whether Bhoja himself wrote so many books on different subjects. Some of them might have been his own productions, but the rest seem to have been written by a group of literary men under his guidance. Of all the books in the above list, *Rājamṛgāṅka* alone contains the date of composition which is expressed in the Śaka Era as A.D. 964—1042—1043".[297]

Among the scholars and litterateurs who flourished under Paramāra kings the most illustrious and talented were Dhanapāla, Śobhana, Dhanika, Padmagupta, Bhaṭṭa Halāyudha, Dhanañjaya, Amitagati, Uvaṭa, Sītā, Devasena, Mahāsena, Hariṣena, Prabhācandra, Śrīcandra, Nemicandra and Nayanandī. A bird's eye-view of the life and works of the writers listed below will suffice to furnish a fair idea of the literary wealth of the age:

Dhanapāla

Endowed with versatile and prolific genius, Dhanapāla composed numerous works in Saṁskṛta, Prākṛta and Apabhraṁśa under the patronage of Vākpati Muñja and Bhoja.[298]

Śobhana

Śobhana (second half of the X century), the younger brother of Dhanapāla, composed *Śobhanastuti*, a 'stotra' in Saṁskṛta in which all the twenty-four Jinas are extolled.[299] In this work, Śobhana "has displayed his skill in employing the most difficult metres and alaṁkāras".[300]

Dhanañjaya

Dhanañjaya was the court-poet of Vākpati Muñja. His father's name was Viṣṇu. He composed a work on dramaturgy named *Daśarūpa*. The book is divided into four chapters: the first chapter deals with different elements of drama, the second with various kinds of heroes and heroines, the third addresses itself to the practical problems connected with staging plays and the fourth dilates upon rasa theory.[301] *Daśarūpa* was composed between A.D. 9749—96.[302]

Dhanika

Dhanika was the brother of Dhanañjaya.[303] He was a native of Ahicchatra but later on settled in Malwa in A.D. 974.[304] He held the important portfolio of Mahāsādayapāla under Vākpati Muñja[305] and was also his court-poet. He wrote a commentary on Dhanañjaya's *Daśarūpa*, entitled *Avaloka* around A.D. 1000. "The commentary of Dhanika is a learned one and is full of quotations. Over 330 verses are quoted, including about 20 verses of Dhanika himself, some of which are in Prākṛta".[306] We learn from Dhanika's commentary that he also wrote a work on poetics called Kāvyanirṇaya.[307]

Halāyudha

Halāyudha was originally an inhabitant of Mānyakheṭa and was patronised by Rāṣṭrakūṭa king, Kṛṣṇa III (A.D. 939—967) but later on he migrated to Ujjain and was admitted into the patronage of Vākpati Muñja. Halāyudha wrote *Kavi-rahasya*, a book on poetics and *Abhidhānaratnamālā*, a lexicon. He also wrote a commentary under the title, *Mṛtasañjīvanī* on Pingala's *Chandaḥsūtra*. The work is a treatise on metrics. Halāyudha has followed in the footsteps of Amaradatta, Vararuci, Bhāguri and Vopālita in writing *Abhidhanaratnamālā*. *Mṛtasañjīvanī* was composed in honour of king Vākpati Muñja of Dhārā, while *Kavirahasya* eulogizes the deeds of Kṛṣṇa III of Rāṣṭrakūṭa dynasty.[308]

Padmagupta

Padmagupta *alias* Parimala, the son of Mṛgāṅka Gupta, lived in the court of Vākpati Muñja.[309] He also enjoyed the patronage of Sindhurāja.[310] He wrote his famous historical epithalmium named *Navasāhasāṅka-carita* as a compliment to his latter patron. The book, divided into eighteen cantos, celebrates the marriage of king Sindhurāja with Śaśiprabhā, daughter of Nāga king, Śaṅkhapāla.[311] It is an important work from the historical point of view, in that it describes the origin and genealogy of the Paramāras. Many verses of Padmagupta have been quoted by later writers.[312]

Amitagati

Amitagati, a well-known Digambara Jaina monk, the disciple of Mādhavasena, flourished in Malwa at the end of the X century and beginning of the XI century A.D.[313] He wrote *Subhāṣitaratna-saṁdoha* a didactic poem on Jaina ethics in A.D. 994 and *Dharma-parīkṣā* in A.D. 1014.[314]

Subhāṣitaratna-saṁdoha is divided into 32 Prakaraṇas, each Prakaraṇa consisting of 20 or 25 verses.[315] *Dharmaparīkṣā* contains a number of interesting and amusing stories which teach different morals. Amitagati's aim in both these works was to satirize the practices of Brāmaṇical religion.[316] *Dharmaparīkṣā* consists of 1945 verses[317] and is said to have been composed within a period of two months.[318] Other works ascribed to Amitagati are *Pañcasaṁgraha, Upāsakācara, Ārādhanā Sāmayikapāṭha, Bhāvanā-Dvātriṁśatikā* (prakaraṇa of 32 verses) and *Yogasāra Prābhṛta*.[319] All the works of Amitgati are in Saṁskṛta.[320] Nathu Ram Premi calls him a jewel of the court of Vākpati Muñja.[321]

Uvaṭa

Uvaṭa, the son of Vajraṭa, resident of Ānandapura (the modern Vednagar in Gujarat), who migrated to Avanti in the first quarter of the XI century composed *Mantrabhāṣya*, a commentary on *Vājasneyi Saṁhitā*, during the reign of Bhoja.[322] His other known works are *Prātiśākhya* and *Nigama-bhāṣya* commentaries on *Ṛgveda* and *Yajurveda*, respectively.[323]

Sīta

Sītā, an eminent poetess, flourished during the reign of Bhoja.[324] Padmagupta in his *Navasāhasāṅka-carita* has referred to her. She composed songs eulogizing the deeds of Upendra Paramāra.[325]

Devasena

Devasena was a Jaina writer. His famous work is *Darśanasāra* in Prākṛta.[326] In one of the concluding verses of this work, Devasena has referred to the place and time of its composition. From it we learn that *Darśanasāra* was written in the year V.S. 990 (A.D. 993). while he was staying in Pārśvanātha Caityālaya at Dhārā. Two other works, *Tattvasāra* and *Āradhanāsāra* are also attributed to Devasena.[327]

Mahāsena

Mahāsena, a staunch Jaina, was the court-poet of Vākpati Muñja. He was the guru of Mahattama Parpaṭa and wrote *Pradyumanacarita* at the request of Mahattama Parpaṭa.[328] *Pradyumanacarita* was composed between V.S. 1031—1066= A.D. 974—1009.[329]

Hariṣeṇa

Hariṣeṇa was the son of Gobardhana-Dhakkara and disciple of Siddhasena. He was originally an inhabitant of Cittore, but later on migrated to Acalapura. There he composed *Dharmapurīkṣā* in V.E. 1044 (A.D. 987) during the reign of Vākpati II.[330]

Prabhācandra

Prabhācandra, a Jaina, was the resident of Dhārānagarī. He was one of the main literary figures of the reign of king Bhoja and Jayasiṁha[331] of Paramāra dynasty. He wrote a commentary on *Ādipurāṇa* and *Mahāpurāṇa*.[332] His other known works are : *Prameya Kamala Mārtaṇḍa, Nyāya Kumuda Candrikā, Ratnākāṇḍasrāvakācāraṭīkā, Kriyā Kalāpaṭīkā, Samādhitantraṭīkā, Atmānuśāsanaṭīkā, Dravya-Saṁgraha-pañjikā, Pravacanasarojabhāskara, Sarvārthasiddhiṭippaṇa* and *Āradhanā-Kathā-kośa*.[333]

Śrīcandra

Śrīcandra was the court-poet of king Bhoja and resident of Dhārānagarī. He was a Jaina and is credited with the authorship of *Purāṇasāra, Mahāpurāṇatippaṇa* and a commentary on *Padmacarita* of Ravisenācārya.[334]

Nemicandra

Nemicandra was the contemporary of king Bhoja Paramāra. According to Nathu Ram Premi, Nemicandra, the disciple of Abhayanandi, wrote *Gommaṭasāra* and *Trilokasāra*.[335]

Nayanandī

Nayanandī, a Jaina poet, was the principal disciple of the great scholar, Māṇikyanandī. He wrote an epic named *Sudarśana-carita* in Apabhraṁśa. The work was completed in 1100 V.S. (A.D. 1043) during king Bhoja's regime.[336] Another work, *Ārādhanā*, is also attributed to Nayanandī.[337]

Muñja Rāsa:— K.M. Munshi in his erudite work, *Gujarata and Its Literature* has referred to *Muñja-Rāsa*, a love poem of the eleventh century which describes the adventures of Muñja, the king of Malwa.[338] The author of this love-story is still untraced.

Puṣpādanta

Puṣpādanta was born in a Brāhmaṇa family of Kaśyapa gotra. His father's name was Keśavabhaṭṭa and that of his mother was Mugdhādevī. The parents of the poet had been Śaivas and were later converted to Jainism.[339] Nathu Ram Premi is of the opinion that the poet might have belonged to Berar.[340] Puṣpādanta, who remained a life-long bachelor and averse to sensuous pleasures, had an extremely dark complexion and was ugly in appearance.[341] Puṣpadanta enjoyed the patronage of Bharata and Nanne (who were father and son), ministers of the Rāṣṭrakūṭa emperor Kṛṣṇa III (A.D. 939 968).[342] Thus he may be placed safely in the second quarter of the X century. He was Dhanapāla's contemporary. Puṣpādanta was an acknowledged poet of Apabhraṁśa and is still regarded in high esteem. Works attributed to Puṣpādanta include *Mahāpurāṇa* (*Tisaṭṭhimahā-purisaguṇālaṅkara*) which is a Kāvya and two epics, *Nāgakumāracarita* and *Yaśodharācarita*.[343] Puṣpādanta has alluded fo the rape of the city of Māṇyakheṭa by Sīyaka.[344]

Kanakāmara

Muni Kanakāmara was born in a Brāhmaṇa family of Candarṣī gotra. Later on he was converted to the Digambara sect of Jainism and studied at the feet of Mangaladeva, a great scholar of his time. These particulars are gleaned from the second introductory stanza and the last two stanzas which form the author's *praśasti*[345] in his epic named *Karkanḍacariu*, composed at about A.D. 1065.[346] Dr. Hira Lal Jain also assigns the work to the middle of the XI century.[347]

Dhanpāla (*Dhakkara*)

The name of Dhanapāla's father was Māyesara and his mother's name was Dhanaśrī. He was connected with the Dhakkara Vaiśya family.[348] He composed *Bhavisattakahā*, an epic in Apabhraṁśa. It is a poem in twenty-two sandhis and narrates the life of a merchant, Bhaviṣyadatta, who suffered immensely on account of the jealousy of his step-brother, Bandhudatta.[349] Dr. Jacobi assigns the work to the X century A.D.,[350] while Dr. Devendra Kumara Śāstrī places Dhanapāla in the XIV century.[351] According to Kastruchand Kasliwal, Dhanapāla was a X century poet and scholar.[352]

Padma Kīrtī

Padma Kīrtī composed a poem named *Pāśanātha-cariu* which is still unpublished. It deals with the life of Pārśvanātha, the twenty-third Tīrthaṅkara, in eighteen sandhis. The work was completed on the new-moon day of Kārtika in V.S. 999 (A.D. 942).[353]

Indranandin

Indranandin wrote *Jvālāmālinī-kalpa* in Saṁskṛta. It deals

with a mystic fire-cult associated with the Goddess Jvālā-mālinī. The work was composed in A.D. 939 at Māñyakheṭa when Rāṣṭrakūṭa king Kṛṣṇa Rāja was on the throne.[354]

Kṣemendra

The Kashmiri poet, Kṣemendra, wrote *Bṛhat-kathā-mañjarī* (Flower Bunches of Great Tales) and *Daśāvatāra-carita* in Saṁskṛta in A.D. 1066. *Bṛhat-kathā-mañjarī* is in eighteen books called 'Lambakas'. In *Daśāvatāra-carita* Kṣemendra gives an interesting account of the ten incarnations of Viṣṇu and touches upon a number Paurāṇic stories.[355]

Somadeva

Somadeva, another Kashmiri poet, who flourished in the second half of the XI century A.D. wrote *Kathāsaritsāgara*. The work is divided into eighteen books. Somadeva's treatment of the mythological material is more elaborate than that of Kṣemendra and as such the stories of *Kathāsaritsāgara* are much more interesting.[356]

Rājaśekhara

Rājaśekhara, the spiritual preceptor of the Pratihāra king Mahendra Pāla, is a famous personality in Indian literature. His wife, Avantisundarī, was an accomplished princess of the Cāhamāna family. Rājaśekhara was the "son of the minister Darduka and Sīlavatī, grandson of Akāla-Jalada and descendant of Surananda, Tarala and Kavirāja, all poets by name". He belonged to the Yāyāvara family of Maharashtra and was a moderate Śaiva by faith. He composed *Bālarāmāyaṇa* (a drama in ten acts), *Bālabhārata* (another drama), *Viddhasālabhañjikā* (a play in four acts). *Karpūramañjarī*, (Saṭṭaka in Prākṛta), *Bhuvana Kośa*, *Kāvyamīmāṁsā* (a treatise on poetics) and *Haravilāsa* (untraced Mahākāvya). He lived in the first-quarter of the X century.[357]

Bilhaṇa

Bilhaṇa, son of Jyeṣṭha Kalasa and Nāgadevī was a

Kashmiri by birth. He was educated in Kashmir and obtained proficiency in grammar and poetics. He went to the south and became a favourite poet and friend of Cālukya king, Vikramāditya VI Tribhuvanamalla (*c.* A.D. 1076—1197) of Kalayāṇī. The king honoured him and gave him the office of Vidyāpati. He had visited many famous places in the course of his migration. He composed a historical poem named *Vikramāṅkadeva-carita.* The main theme of the poem consists of royal wars and royal marriages. C. Kunhan Raja considers it to be the best among the historical poems.[358] Bilhaṇa also wrote shorter poems and plays. He is also credited with the composition of *Caurapañcāśikā*, a beautiful collection of fifty stanzas in the 'vasanta tilaka' metre on the subject of secret love. The work is in Saṁskṛta. Bilhaṇa must have lived in the second and third quarter of the XI century.[359]

Kṛṣṇa Miśra

Kṛṣṇa belongs to the second half of the XI century. He wrote *Prabodhacandrodaya*, a Saṁskṛta drama, at the instance of Gopāla (the vassal of Candella ruler, Kīrtivarman, *c.* 1060—1100). The drama was staged in the very presence of Kīrtivarman. It glorifies the doctrine of Advaita Vedānta with a bias for the worship of Viṣṇu, the great God. In this drama Gopāla is compared with the lion and boar incarnations of Viṣṇu and is credited with raising up the earth.[360] It throws light upon the political, social, religious and economic conditions of the time.

Soḍḍhala

Soḍḍhala wrote *Udaya Sundarī Kathā* which is regarded as Campū. He was born in a Kāyastha family of Gujarat. He flourished around A.D. 1000 and lived in the court of king Mummunirāja of Konkaṇa. The book, *Avanti Sundarī Kathā*, is supposed to have been written between A.D. 1336 and A.D. 1050.[361]

Abhinavagupta

Abhinavagupta is one of the most remarkable personalities of medieval India. He was a scholar of encyclopaediac erudition. His father's name was Narasiṁha Gupta and his mother was Vimlā. His ancestors originally resided in Antarvedi (the Doab between the Ganges and Yamuna) but later on migrated to Kashmir at the instance of Kashmiri king, Lalitāditya Muktāpīḍa. Abhinavagupta was a Śaiva and remained celibate throughout his life. He is attributed with the authorship of : *Abhinavabhāratī*, *Locana*, *Tantrāloka*, *Mālinīvijayavārtika*, *Tantrālokasāra*, *Bodhapāñcadaśikā*, *Kāmastotra* and *Īśvarapratyabhijñāvimarśinī*. It is generally said in Kashmir that Abhinavagupta accompanied by 1200 disciples entered a cave repeating a Bhaīravastotra and was seen no more. He may be placed between the last quarter of the X and first quarter of the XI century.[362]

Somadeva

Somadeva, a Jaina Ācārya and theologian, made substantial contribution to Jaina religious literature. "He is one of the most versatile talents in the history of Indian literature. He is a master of prose and verse, a profound scholar, an authority on Jaina dogma, a close student of the art of government, a political thinker and a keen observer of men and manners".[363]

Somadeva was a contemporary of Rāṣṭrakūṭa king, Kṛṣṇa III (A.D. 939—968). He belonged to an order of Jaina monks known as Devasaṁgha and was the disciple of Nemideva who in turn was the disciple of Yaśodeva. Somadeva wrote *Yaśodhārā-mahārāja-carita* (*Yaśastilaka*), *Sannavatiprakaraṇa*, *Mahendra-mātali-Saṁjalpa*, *Yukticintāmaṇisūtra* and *Nītivākyāmṛta*. Of all these works, *Yaśastilaka* and *Nītivākyāmṛta* are the most prominent.[364] *Yaśastilaka* is a Campu-Kāvya composed in A.D. 959.[365] *Nītivākyāmṛta* is a treatise on polity in which Somadeva has discussed the principles of State-craft and of the welfare state. He gives a picture of the imperial court besides throwing side lights on the problems of government affecting war and peace. Somadeva has been placed in the X century A.D.

Vrinda

Vrinda (X century A.D.) made substantial contribution in the field of medicine. His work, *Siddhiyoga*, deals with the common ailments and diseases and their treatment.[366]

Āryabhaṭṭa II

Āryasiddhānta of Āryabhaṭṭa II is an important treatise on such diverse topics as mathematics, astronomy and astrology. Āryabhaṭṭa is generally placed around A.D. 966.[367]

During Dhanapāla's times Jainas made an impressive contribution to Saṁskṛta, Prākṛta and Apabhraṁśa literature. The X century produced a number of Jaina and non-Jaina writers, scholars, thinkers and theologians. By their writings of high intrinsic value, these men of letters contributed to the cultural advancement of the age.

REFERENCES

1. *Tilaka-mañjarī*, pp. 14-15.
   The word 'sthapatya' has got double meaning. It denotes the architect as well as the attendant posted outside the harem. 'Sthāpatya-kalā' denotes the science and craft of architecture.
2. Bhoja, *Samarāṅgaṇasūtradhāra*, ed. T. Ganapati Sastri (Central Library. 1924), p. 44.
3. *Tilaka-mañjarī*, p. 82:
   ..*Śāstramārgānusāreṇa durgasaṁskāramanavaratma nvaṭiṣṭhat/*
4. Ibid , p. 7:
   ...*Parigatāprākāreṇa*...
5. Ibid., p. 7:
   ...*Tuṣāradhavalabhittinā*...
6. Ibid., p. 7:
   ...*Viśālavapreṇaparigatā prākāreṇa*...
7. *Samarāṅgaṇasūtradhāra*, p. 41.

8. Kauṭilaya, *Arthaśāstra*, ed. Vacaspati Gairola (Varanasi, 1962), p. 105.
...Vaprasyopari prākāraṁviṣkambhakadviguṇatsedha maiṣṭakaṁ...
9. *Tilaka-mañjarī*, p. 82:
...Prākāraśikharotsaṅgasūtritavicitrayaṅtranicayāṁkāmcīnagarīmakarot...
10. Ibid.:
...Pāṇikṣepaṇīyapāṣāṇa kūṭasthapuṭitaprākārā sannasthalāṁ...
11. *Samarāṅgaṇasūtradhāra*, p. 42.
12. *Tilaka-mañjarī*, p. 7:
...Vṛittojjvalavarṇaśalinī...
13. Ibid., p. 167:
...Caturaṅgadyūtamiva sunirūpitatrikacatuṣka racanaṁ rathanūpuracakravālaṁ nāma Vidyādhara nagaraṃ|
14. Bhoja, *Yuktikalpatru*, ed. Ishwar Chandra Shastri (Calcutta, 1917), p. 22.
15. *Arthaśāstra*, ed. Vacaspati Gairola, pp. 103-4:
Vṛttaṁ dirghacaturaśaram.
16. *Samarāṅgaṇasūtradhāra*, p. 32:
...'Svalpāyuścajāyantejanāvṛttapurāśryāḥ'.
17. *Yuktikalpataru*, p. 23.
18. Ibid.
19. Op. cit., p. 22:
'Caturstraṁ caturvargaphalāya pṛthvīpateḥ'.
20. *Tilaka-mañjarī*, p. 8:
...Mahatākhāta valayena veṣṭitā...
21. Ibid.:
...Manorathānām'api durbalaṅghayena...
22. *Samarāṅgaṇasūtradhāra*, p. 39:
'Vidheyaṁ parikhātrayaṁ'
23. Op. cit., p. 42:
...Vāribhirāpūrṇam...
24. Padmagupta, op. cit. I. 18.
25. *Arthaśāstra*, ed. V. Gairola, p. 104:
...Pradakṣiṇodakaṁ paṇyapuṭabhedanamasaṁvāripathābhyāmupetam|
26. *Tilaka-mañjarī*, p. 8:
...Nirgamamārgāyamāṇaiścaturbhirtyuccairgopurairupetā...
27. *Arthaśāstra*, ed. Gairola. p. 108.
28. Op. cit., p.112:
Brāhmaindrayāmyasaināptyānidvārāṇi...
29. *Tilaka-mañjarī*, p. 82.
30. *Arthaśāstra*, cd. V. Gairola, p. 107.
31. M.C. Crindle, *Megasthenes*, Fragment XXVI (London, 1877), p. 66.
32. *Tilaka-mañjarī*, p. 83.
...'Pratalī'kapāṭa'...
33. Ibid., p. 82:
...Āptapuruṣagulmakapratipannasakalapratoli rakṣāṁ...

34. *Tilaka-mañjarī*, p. 23:
'*Mahāprāsāda*'
35. Ibid., p. 255:
...*Maṇimayamahāprāsāda*...
36. Ibid., p. 72.
37. Ibid., p. 70.
38. *Pāiyalacchīnāmamālā*, p. 28:
'*Pāsāyassovari jā sālā sā candrasālatti*'...
39. *Tilaka-mañjarī*, p. 68:
...*Anekaśata saṁkhyairyeṣāṁ sitaprādaiḥ sarvataḥ samākulaṁ rājakulamāsasāda.*
40. Ibid., p. 80:
...*kumārabhavanamakārayat*...
41. Ibid., p. 79.
42. Ibid., pp. 79-80.
43. Ibid., p. 29.
44. Ibid., p. 19.
45. Ibid., p. 41.
46. Ibid , p. 237.
47. Ibid., p. 68.
48. Ibid., p. 374.
49. Ibid., p. p. 300.
50. Ibid., p. 17. In the *Sṛṅgāramañjarī-kathā* of Bhoja, we read of Dhārāgṛha which was made of dark coloured stones to deflect the heat and keep the inside cool. There one could seek refuge from the heat of the summer days.
[*Sṛṅgāramañjarī-kathā*, ed. (Miss) K. Munshi, p. 5.]
51. Ibid., p. 175.
52. Ibid., p. 237.
53. Ibid., p. 180.
54. Ibid.
55. Ibid., p: 78.
56. Ibid.. p. 77.
57. *Arthaśāstra*, ed. Gairola, p. 81:
...*Pṛṣṭhataḥ kakṣyāvibhāge strīniveśo garbhavyādhi vaidyapratyākhyata saṁsthāḥ*...
58. *Tilaka-mañjarī*, p. 11:
...*Viśvakarmasahastrairiva nirmitaprāsādāḥ*...
59. Ibid., p. 8:
...*Giriśikharatatinibhaśāta kumbhaprāsādamālā dhyāsitobhayavibhāgaiḥ*...
60. Ibid., p. 133:
...*Anekabhūmaikaprabhūtaprāsādāni*...
61. Ibid,, p. 372:
...*Arjunasālaguptibhiḥ*...*saptabhūmaiḥ kumarīpura prāsādalakṣaiḥ*...

62. *Tilaka-mañjarī*, p. 8:
..Dhṛtoḍḍhura prākāra pariveṣaiḥ...
63. Ibid.
...Abhraṁkaṣapratolebhiḥ...
64. *Arthaśāstra*, ed. Gairola, p. 107:
...Prākāramubhayato maṅḍapakamadhyardhadaṇḍaṁ kṛtvā pratoliṁsaṭṭalāntaraṁ dvāraṁ niveśayeta|
65. *Tilaka-mañjarī*, p. 8.
66. Ibid.
67. Ibid.:
Dolāvibhūṣitāṅgaṇavedibhiḥ...
68. Ibid., p. 41.
69. Ibid. p. 68. See also Someśvaradeva, *Kīrtikaumudī*, I. 53, p. 5.
70. Ibid., p. 11:
...Nāgarikaguṇālaṁkṛtagṛhaḥ...
71. Ibid., p. 251:
...Śilāyaneṣu...
72. Ibid., p. 260:
...Vilāsī vāsabhavanaiḥ...
73. Ibid., p. 8:
...Pratigṛahaṁ svacchadhavalāyatābhirdṛṣṭibhiriva... kṛīḍāsarasībhiḥ saṁvalitā...
74. Ibid.:
...Vipulasopānasugamāvatāravāpiśatasan ākulā...
75. Ibid., p. 67:
...Gṛhakarmaviratābhirgehinībhirivagāhya mānāsubhavanavāpīṣu...
76. Ibid., pp. 67, 76, 84.
77. Ibid.:
...Pṛthulāyatairvipaṇipathaiḥ prasādhitā...
78. Ibid., pp. 67, 84:
...Vipaṇivīthīścatuḥ patheṣu... (p. 84)
79. Ibid., p. 8:
...Amarakānanānukāribhirārāmaiḥ...
80. Ibid., p. 8:
...Prāṁśuśikharāgrajvalat kanakakalaśaiḥ...
...amaramaṅdira maṇḍalaiḥ...
81. Ibid., p. 275:
...Prāsādamagrato garbhagṛha garbhe-pratiṣṭhitaṃ...atimahā pramā navajra maṇi-śilāmāyaṁ...bhagavato mahāvīrasya... bimbam...
82. Ibid., p. 11:
...Devatāsahastrairivadhiṣṭhita pradeśāḥ...
83. Ibid., p. 8:
...Manobhavabhavānī bhavanaiḥ...

84. *Tilaka-mañjarī*, p. 6.
85. Ibid., p. 34.
86. Ibid , p. 35.
87. Ibid., p. 43.
88. Ibid., p. 34.
89. Ibid., p. 35.
90. *E.I.*, Vol. I, śloka 20.
91. D.C. Ganguly, op. cit. p. 255.
92. *Tilaka-mañjarī*,, pp. 106-7.
93. Ibid., p. 107:
...Dāhajvaracikitsāgṛhamiva...
94. Ibid., p. 11:
...Aviṣkṛta vilāsasahāseva danta valabhībhiḥ-āgṛhīta darpaṇeva sarobhiḥ...
95. *Glory That Was Gurjara Deśa*, p. 162.
96. *Tilaka-mañjarī*, p. 140:
'*Maṇiguhāgṛheṣu*'...
97. Vacaspati Gairola, *Bhāratīya Citrakalā*, ed. Śri Kṛṣṇadasa (Allahabad, 1963), p. 47.
98. *Tilaka-mañajrī*, p. 18. In *Uttara Rāma carita* of Bhavabhūti, Citrapaṭṭa is known as 'Vīthikā'. (Vacaspati Gairola, op. cit., p. 89).
99. *Tilaka-mañjarī*, p. 71.
100. Ibid., p. 163.
101. Ibid., p. 41.
102. Ibid., p. 179. In *Mālavikāgnimitra*, 'nipuṇa Citrakāra is known as 'Citrācārya', (V. Gairola, op. cit., p. 89).
103. Ibid., p. 177.
104. Ibid., p. 178. In Persian, it is called 'sabīha' (V. Gairola, p. 89).
105. Ibid. p. 163.
106. Ibid., pp. 278-79.
107. Ibid., p. 163:
...Nṛtyagītacitrā vikalaśāstrapāradṛśvā Harivahanonāma...
108. Ibid., p. 363.
109. Ibid., p. 170:
...Citradarśanānurāgiṇī ca vatsā Tilaka-mañjarī...
110. Ibid., p. 170.
111. Ibid., p. 169:
...Nābhilaṣati pāṇigrahaṇa maṅgalam...
112. Ibid., p. 170:
Ato'syāḥ sakalanija parivāravārāṅganācitrakau'sala darśana vyājena darśaya nisarga sundarākṛtīṇāma vanigocaranarendra pradārakāṇāṁ yathā svamaṅkitāni nāmabhiryathāvasthitāni viddharūyāṇi/
113. Ibid., p. 171:
Upadarśitabahuvlkalpacitraśilpena ca sthitva divasamekamekāgramansā...

114. *Tilaka-mañjarī*, p. 171; p. 364.
115. Ibid., p. 18.
116. Ibid., p. 163.
117. Ibid., p. 166:
Tathā hysāvupari dhṛtasitatapatrā...
118. Ibid., p. 164:
...Nīlapītapāṭalairullasadbhiraṅgulīyakarāgairnurāga vṛddhaye rājasūnoraparamiva citrakarma narma nirmāṇamambare kurvāṇaḥ...
In Kālidāsa's works too, we find the same colours mentioned for painting—
Pītāsitāraktasitaiḥ surācala śrāntasthītairdhāturajobhirambaram/
anyatra gandharva purodayabhramaṁ babhāra bhumnoitpatitairitastataḥ//
(*Kumārasambhava*, XV : 31)
119. *Tilaka-mañjarī*, p. 391.
120. Ibid.
121. Ibid.
122. Ibid., p. 364:
...Abhilikhantī-bhittibhāgeṣvabhaṅgurāgāṇi vidyādhara pakṣhimṛgamithunāni....
123. Ibid., p. 18:
Nipuṇacitrakāraiścitrapaṭeṣvāropya sādaramupāyanī kṛtāni rūpātiśayaśālinīnamavanipālakanyakānāṁ pratibimbāni parityaktānyakarmādivasamālokyat/
124. Ibid., p. 171.
125. *Life in Ancient India As Depicted in the Jain Canons*, p. 186.
126. *Tilaka-mañjarī*, p. 177:
Makaradhvajā yatnadīrghikātīraparisare-niṣaṇṇaḥ saṁnidhānavartibhiścitravidyopādhyāyairanyaiśca janaparamparājanitakutūhalaiścitramavalokayitumāgatairālekhyaśāstravidbhimagara lokaiḥ saha vicārayannavicārya cārutva tattvaṁ tasyāścitrapuṭa putrikāyā rupam apasārita para vinodaḥ pūrvānhamanayat/
127. Ibid., p. 41.
128. Ibid., p. 265.
129. Ibid., p. 237.
130. Ibid:, p. 367:
Uttuṅgakanakastambharājīvirajinaḥ prakāśavipulayatāva kāśasya śayanacitra śālikāṅgaṇaratna maṇḍapasyā dhastālsvahastasaṁcaritenāciradhautena śucinā samantāduttaracchadapatenācchādite mṛdāvapi tāpanīye mahati paṭṭaparyaaṅke nyaveśayat/
131. Ibid., p. 368:
...Dakṣiṇetarabhittibhāgaśryiaṇu suśliṣṭamaṇibhūmikānte śaśikāntavātāyane...

132. *Tilaka-mañjarī*, p. 41:

...citraśālāsvsaṁpādyamānaharicandana paṅkopalepanaṁ...

133. Ibid., p. 168:

...Yasyā rūpalava eṣa lāvṇyanidhinācitra paṭasaṁkrāntaḥ kṛtarthīkṛto dṛṣṭipātaprasādena...

134. Ibid., 161:

...Vasanapallava prāntasaṁyataṁ divyaṁ citrapatamupa ninye/

135. Ibid., p. 162:

...Tatkṣaṇameva vistārite purastāttatra nihitadṛṣṭiratyutkṛṣṭa rūpāṁ...

136. Ibid.
137. Ibid. pp. 165-66.
138. Ibid., p. 166.
139. Ibid.
140. Ibid., p. 167.
141. Ibid.
142. Ibid.
143. "'The Word 'masikē'-the craft over which the Muses preside—means neither music nor poetry, but both...poetry and even prose were normally composed for perfoamance and presentation... to be sung with music and even dancing"... (H.C. Baldry, *Greek Literature For the Modern Reader*, Cambridge, 1959, pp. 24-25).
144. K. Vasudeva Shastri, *Sangīta Śāstra* (Lucknow: Hindi Samiti, Sucana Vibhaga, Uttar Pradesh, 1968), p. 1.
145. *Indian Inheritance*, Vol. II, eds, K.M. Munshi and R.R. Diwakar. (Naini Tal : Raj Bhavan, 1955), p. 3.
146. Quoted by K. Vasudeva Shastri, op. cit., p. 3.
147. *Indian Inheritence*, p. 8.
148. *Tilaka-mañjarī*,; p. 41: p. 61.
149. Ibid., pp. 70; p. 174.
150. Ibid., p. 75:

Sāṁdhyamārabdhamapsarodohiḥ prekṣānṛtyamī kṣitumākāṅgkṣat/

"The female counterparts of Gandharvas (the servants of Indra and heavenly musicians) were apsarās. They were beautiful and libidinous and specially delighted in tempting ascetics in their meditations. Menakā Apsrā seduced the great sage Viśvāmitra and conceived Śakuntalā, the heroine of Kālidāsa's famous drama *Abhijñānśākuntala*. Another Apsarā famous in story was Urvaśī". (A.L. Basham, *The Wonder That Was India*, London, 1944, p. 317).

151. Ibid., p. 148:

...Api ca sānau sānau niśāmyate karṇāmṛtaṁ kinnaragītam...

152. Ibid., pp. 17, 121.
153. Ibid., p. 122.
154. Ibid. p. 340:

...Śravaṇahāriṇā cārṇabandhujana jayavyāhāreṇadūranirhārī samutsāraṇadhvaniḥ...

The caranas, the court poets or rather panegyrists recited appropriate verses on diverse occasions lile birth ceremony, marriage, coronation, etc. They also described the morning and evening scenery, the beauties of the season and the gaiety of the court life. Their provision had been singing and dancing.

155. Ibid.. p. 263:
'Nanṛturnṛpāṅgaṇeṣu gaṇikāḥ'...
156. Ibid., p. 79.
157. Ibid., p. 163.
158. Ibid., p. 70:
...Gāndharvikopādhyāyaiḥ saha veṇuvīṇāvādyasya vinodena dīnaśeṣamanayat|
159. Harṣa, *Priyadarśikā* (Madras. 1935), p. 16.
160. *Tilaka-mañjarī*, p. 343.
161. Ibid., p. 363.
162. Ibid. p. 342.
163. Baṇa, *Kādambarī*, tr. C.M. Ridding, (London, 1896), p. 324 *Harṣa-carita*, ed. K.P. Parab (Bombay, 1834 śaka), p. 140.
164. *Tilaka-mañjarī*, pp. 10, 104, 163, 184, 186, 193.
165. Ibid., pp. 18, 184; *Mānasollāsa*, IV, 16, 91-93.
166. *Mānasollāsa*, IV, 16, 566.
167. *Tilaka-mañjarī*, p. 264.
168. Ibid., p. 75.
169. Ibid., p. 358.
170. Ibid., pp. 64, 79.
171. Ibid., pp. 17, 57, 70, 76, 180, 183, 209, 236, 263, 264, 360, 370, 372.
172. Ibid., p. 391:
...Ratnaviṇāṁ vādayantī...
173. Ibid., p. 18.
174. Ibid., p. 358.
175. Ibid., p. 257:
Japantī pavitrāṇigāyatri padāni...
176. Ibid., p. 32:
Śrāvayitavyāḥ śravaṇahārīṇi devatāstutigītāni...
177. Ibid., pp. 18, 61, 75, 163, 263, 302, 323, 391.
178. Ibid., p. 263.
179. Ibid., pp. 263, 323, 391.
180. Ibid., p. 75.
181. Vātsyāyana, *Kāmasūtra*, ed. D.L. Goswami (Banaras, 1929), II . 22.
182. *Tilaka-mañjarī*, p. 270:
'Kutluṁ śikṣitā svalpcna kālena lalitānetāvataḥkarona prāyogān'|
183. Ibid., p. 363.
184. Ibid., p. 342.

185. *Tilaka-mañjarī*,, p. 269:
...Apranṛttāsu pryāyeṇa tāsu kṣitipāla kanyakāsu...
186. Rājaśekhara, *Karpūramañjarī*, ed. Sten Konow (Cambridge, 1901), p. 53.
187. *Tilaka-mañjarī*, p. 180.
188. Ibid., p. 41.
189 Ibid.. p. 61.
190. Ibid., p. 65.
191 Ibid., p. 42.
192. Someśvara, *Mānasollāsa*, IV, 16, 959-60.
193. *Tilaka-mañjarī*, p. 323.
194· *Prabhandhaciñtāmaṇi*, p. 114.
195. *Tilaka-mañjarī*, pp. 10, 41, 57, 270, 292, 372, 399.
196. Ibid., pp. 270, 363.
197. Ibid., p. 61:
kuru saphalāni raṅgaśālāsu lāsikājanasyanijāvalokanena lāsyalīlā...
198. Ibid., p. 193.
199. Ibid.
200. Ibid., p. 169. It is new 'svara'. It is called 'kākalī' on account of its sweetness. (K. Vasudeva Shastri, op. cit., p. 18.)
201. *Tilaka-mañjarī*, p. 180.
202. Ibid., p. 70:
'Gāndharvikopādhyāyaiḥ'...
203. Ibid., p. 18:
'Nartakopādhyāyaiḥ'...
204. Ibid., p. 70.
205. Ibid., p. 159:
...Pañcamaśrutimivagītīnāṃ...
206. Ibid., p. 363:
Ṣaḍajādisvaravibhāganirṇayeṣu...
207. Ibid., p. 57:
Tumbarutāḍyamānavīṇāraṇaḍgāndhāragrāmamāgṛhīta veṇukinnaragaṇopagīyamāna...
208. Ibid.:
...Prasiddhamūrchanamudvilāsa...
209. Ibid., p. 159:
...Jātibhivālaṁkṛtīnām...
210. Ibid., p. 18:
Kadācitsvayamevarāgaviśeṣeṣu saṁsthāpya samarthitāni...
211. K. Vasudeva Shastri, op. cit., pp. 15-16.
212. *Tilaka-mañjarī*, p 11.
213. *The Legacy of India*, ed. G.T. Garratt (London, Oxford University Press, 1937), pp. 312-313.
214. *Every day Life in Early India* (London, 1969), p. 158.
215. K. Vasudeva Shastri, op. cit., p. 17.

216. A.L. Basham, op. cit. p. 382.
217. K. Vasudeva Shastri, op. cit., p. 16.
218. *The Wonder That Was India*, p. 382.
219. Quoted by Umesha Joshi, *Bhāratīya Saṅgīta Kā Itihāsa* (Agra, 1969), p. 172.
220. *Ṣaḍaja madhyama gāndhārostrayo gramāḥ prakīrtitāḥ*... (Nāradīya Śikṣā), quoted by Umesha Joshi, op. cit., p, 173.
221. *Tilaka-mañjarī*, p. 57.
222. Umesha Joshi, op. cit., p. 418.
223. Ibid., p. 173.
224. K. Vasudeva Shastri, op. cit.. pp. 41-42.
225. Op. cit., p. 48.
226. A.L. Basham, op. cit., p. 383.
227. *Saṅgīta Śāstra*, pp. 83-122.
228. *Tilaka-mañjarī*, p. 186.
229. Ibid., p. 182.
230. See *Saṅgīta Śāstrā*, pp. 216-220, for a complete list of the tālas.
231. *Tilakamañjarī*, p. 183:

    kevalaṁ kutūhalatpādanāya pradhānanṛpatīnāma navaratatantrī-tāḍanābhyāsa laghutarāṅguli vyāpāreṇa savyetarapāṇināsphuṭa tarāsphālita taralavīṇastadhvaniśravaṇa...
232. K. Vasudeva Shastri, op. cit., p. 257.
233. *Every day Life in Early India*, p. 159.
234. B.V. Subarayappa, "India's Contribution to the Science" in *India's Contribution to World Thought anh Culture*, ed. Lokesh Chandra *et al.* (Madras: Vivekananda Rock Memorial Committee, 1970), p. 47.
235. *See India's Contribution to World Thought and Culture*, p. 47.
236. *Tilaka-mañjarī* p. 146:

    ...*Rājatilakatarjito'pi noparamasi praguṇayāyinīmapi navam-āgastīṁ gatiṁ grāhayasyasti kaścinna te diṅgamoho yadyudā-hṛtāmapyahṛdaya na jānāsyuttarāśāvartanīm pravartanīm| Pravartya dṛṣṭavā dṛṣṭavā saptarṣimaṇḍalamityādi sādhvā-sakaraṁ ca karttvyopadeśa paraṁ*...|
237. Ibid., p. 197.
238. Ibid., p. 403.
239. Ibid., p. 131.
240. Ibid. p. 64.
241. Ibid.
242. Ibid.
243. P.T.S. Ayyangar, op. cit., p. 69.
244. *The Struggle For Empire.*, Vol. V (Bombay, 1957), p. 32.
245. *Tilaka-mañjarī*, p. 64:

    ...*Sāmudravidakhyatprasavalakṣaṇām*...
246. Ibid.. p. 423:

    Āsīdatisamuditairgrhagaṇitavidbhirāveditaṁ karagrahaṇa lagnam|

247. *India's Contribution to World Thought and Culture*, p. 54.
248. *Tilaka-mañjarī*, p. 65:
...Vividhauṣadhāni prayujjānena...garbha grahaṇopacārabhiḥ...
249. Ibid., p. 55:
...Śailakaṭakauṣadhībhiriva Dhanavantariprahitābhi raparābhiḥ...
250. Ibid., p. 234;
...Stambhastobhodvāsanavidveṣaṇādiprayogayogyābhiśca...
251. *Tılaka-mañjarī*, p. 97:
...Vraṇapaṭṭabandhanādikriyāmanvatiṣṭhat/
252. Ibid., p. 78:
...Sarvāyurvedapāragairbhiṣagbhiḥ...
253. *The History and Culture of Indian People*, Vol. V, p. 328.
254. *Indian's Contribution to World Thought and Culture*, p. 64.
255. *Tilaka-mañjarī*, p. 234:
Rasa samūhamāraṇamahitamāhātmyābhiśca...kāla kūṭasyāpi rasapātavā panodinībhistakṣakasyāpi viṣatīkṣṇatātiraskāriṇībhir-bhuvana trayasyāpi subhagakaraṇībhirañjanamātra darśitā-darśitodṛśyadūrantaritabhāvābhiraṅghrilepamātrapravartitānila-vartmagamanābhistilaka kriyāmātrakṛtasakalatanutirobhāvābhira-bhyavahāramātrajita jarārogamṛtyūbhayābhirmahā prabhāvābhir-oṣadhībhiravandhyāṁ...
256. *Alberunī's, India*, tr. E.H. Sachau, Vol. I (Delhi, 1964), pp. 187-88.
257. *Tilakamañjarī*, p. 22.
258. *Indian's Contribution to World Thought and Culture*, p. 63.
259. Sachau, p. 191.
260. *Tilaka-mañjarī*, p. 234:
Bhuvantrayasyāpisubhagaṁkaraṇībhiḥ...
261. Sachau, I, pp. 191-192.
262. D.C. Ganguly, op. cit., p. 256.
263. P.T.S. Ayyangar, op. cit., pp. 106-107.
264. H.M. Elliot and J. Dowson, *History of India as Told By Its Own Historians*, Vol. II (Aligarh, 1952), p. 44.
265. P.C. Ray, *History of Hindu Chemistry* (Calcutta, 1906), pp. 59-60.
266. See B.P. Majumdar, *Socio-Economic History of Northern India* (Calcutta, 1960), pp. 200-201.
267. P.C. Ray, op. cit., pp. 62-63.
268. *Tilaka-mañjarī*, p. 24.
269. See *India's Contribution to World Thought and Culture*, p. 49.
270. Ibid., p. 51.
271. Ibid.
272. *Tilaka-mañjarī*, p. 131:
Dṛḍhakaṣṭhagumphaniṣṭhurānāvaḥ...
273. See G.P. Hourani, *Arab Sea Faring in the Indian Ocean in Ancient and Early Medieval Times* (Princeton, 1962), p. 90.

274. R.K. Mukerjee, *A History of Indian Shipping* (Allahabad, 1962), pp. 13-14.
275. Ibid.
276. *Tilaka-mañjarī*, p. 140:
Dṛḍhanipātaniṣṭhurakāṣṭhakīla niyamita naukeṣu...
277. Bhoja, *Yuktikalpataru*, ed. Ishvara Chandra Sastri (Calcutta, 1917), p. 224:
Na Sindhugādyārhati lauhabandhaṁ tallohavantaiḥ hi lauham/
vipadyate tena jaleṣu naukā, guṇenabadhaṁnijagāda Bhojaḥ//
(*Śloka* 88)
278. Quoted by Hourani, op. cit. p. 96.
279. Lallanji Gopal, *University of Allahabad Studies*, Ancient History Section (Allahabad, 1958), p. 3.
280. *Tilaka-mañjarī*, p. 132:
...Sthagitaniḥśeṣasaṁdhirandhraya...
281. Ibid., p. 145:
...Suśliṣṭabandhānapi phalakasa...nnirundhatātūrṇa mūrṇā sikthakena...
282. Ibid., p. 131:
Saparigrahe ca purobhāgavantinaṁmattavārṇaka madhya-madhyāsya badhāsane mayi...
283. *Yuktikalpataru*, ślokas 19—25.
284. *Tilakamuñjarī*, p. 130:
...Āgatya c mayā kṛtāni sarvāṇyapi susūtrāṇi yānapātrāṇi...
285. Ibid., p. 132:
Pṛṣṭhato'nukūla pavanāsphālana taraṅgitena-phenapāṇḍunāsalila saṁghātena purastācca sitapaṭenapravartyamānayā vrajantyā-pyatijavena durvibhāvalvādgateranujjhitasthānayevohyamānyā, nāvohyamānaḥ prativelamapasaratsānuvistārānnirantaro palakṣyāmāṇasāntarālataruganānṣuvelagiri darśanāya senayā saha pracalitāniva gacchantām nāvisaha sarvaṁ taṭasthaṁ saha pracaladiva praṭibhāti...
286. Ibid., p. 134:
...kūpastambhakānuttambhayadbhiḥ sitapaṭānāsūtarayadbhiḥ...
287. Ibid., p. 138:
Śramavikalabāhavo na vāhayānti...na śaknuvanti nidrāvaśīkṛtāḥ kartumavaṣṭambhaṁ kūpastambhakeṣu karṇadhārāḥ, samīro'pi saṁprati pratīpagatiḥ pravāti...
288. Ibid., p, 140:
Mukalitasitapaṭesu...
289. Ibid., p. 145:
Anilasaṁkṣobheṣu nūṭanāḥ saṁyajayatā rajjūrajarjarasyāpi vāraṁ vāramāpādayatā sitapaṭsyāpātavaṃ...
290. *Tilaka.mañjarī*, p. 140:
Sarvato'valambitā sthūla nāgaraśilānigaḍita poteṣu...

291. *Tilaka-mañjarī*, p. 134:

...Svīkṛtasalilamadhyasaṁcāraṇocitāñjanairagnitailādidrvya saṁgraha paraiḥ...

292. Ibid., pp. 129-30:

Tatra ca kurvatādhipatyamacireṇaiva śikṣitānena sakalāpi nau pracāra vidyā, viditamkhilamapi karṇadhārāṇāṁ karma, kṛtāni bahukṛtvaḥ salilarāśau gamanāgamanāni, dṛṣṭā dūra-prakṛṣṭā api dvīpāntara bhūmayaḥ, pratyakṣī kṛtāḥ kṣudrā api jalapathāḥ lakṣitāni teṣu samyaksamaviṣamasthānāni|

293. D.C. Ganguly, op. cit., p. 275.
294. Sir Wolseley Haig, *Cambridge History of India*, Vol. III (Cambridge, 1928), pp. 41-42.
295. Quoted by K.M. Munshi, op. cit., p. 162.
296. P.T.S. Ayyangar, op. cit., pp. 68-70.
297. D.C. Ganguly, op. cit., p. 276.
298. See *Chaptnr I* for details of Dhanapāla's Life and Works which are omitted here to avold repetition.
299. S.N. Das Gupta and S.K. De, op. cit. p. 379.
300. Maurice Winternitz, *The Jainas in the History of Indian Literrture*, ed. Jina Vijaya Muni (Ahmedabad, 1946), p. 19.
301. S.N. Das Gupta and S.K. De, op. cit., p. 550.
302. P.V. Kane, *History of Sanskrit Poetics* (Delhi Motilal Banarsi Das, 1961), p. 247.
303. D.C. Ganguly, op. cit., p. 285.
304. *I.A.*, VI, p. 53.
305. H.H. Wilson, *Select Specimens of the Theatre of the Hindus* (London, 1871), 1, XX, XXI.
306. P.V. Kane, *History of Sanskrit Poetics*, pp. 245-46.
307. op. cit.
308. *History and Culture of Indian People*, Vol. IV, pp. 188-89.
309. *Glory That Was Gurjara Deśa*, p. 162.
310. D.C. Ganguly, op. cit., p. 80.
311. S.N. Das Gupta and S.K. De, op. cit., p. 349.
312. *J.B.B.R.A.S*, XVI, pp. 173-76.
313. D.C. Ganguly, op. cit., 290.
314. Maurice Winternitz, op. cit., pp. 19-20.
315. Nathu Ram Premi, op. cit.. pp. 19, 279.
316, Maurice Winternitz, op. cit., pp. 19-20.
317, Nathu Ram Premi, op. cit,, p. 279.
318. Op. cit.:

Amitagatirivedaṁ svasya māsadvayena|
prathitaviśadakīrtiḥ kāvyamudbhūta deṣam|

319. Op. cit., pp. 279-81.
320. Op. eit., p. 279.
321. Op. cit., p. 275.
322. *Bhaṇdarakara's Report* (1882-83), pp. 2-3.

323. *Peterson's 4th Report* (Introd.), p. 17.
324. *Prabandhacintāmaṇi*, pp, 63-64.
355. Padmagupta, *Navasāhasāṅkacarita*, Sarga XI, śloka 17.
326. Quoted by Nathu Ram Premi, op. cit., p. 175. f.n.1:
   Puvvāyariyakayāim gāhāiṁ saṁciūṇa eyattha,
   Siri Devaseṇa gaṇiṇā Dhārāe saṁva saṁheṇa/
   raio daṁsaṇa sāro hāro bhavvāṇa ṇāvasaenavaī,
   siri pāsaṇāhagehe suvisuddhe mahāsuddha dasamīe/
   (*Ślokas* 49-50)
327. Nathu Ram Premi, op. cit., p. 175.
328. Quoted by Nathu Ram Premi, op. cit., p. 411 f.n.:
   Āsita Śrī-Mahāsena sūriranaghaḥ Sri Muñjarājārcitaḥ
   simā darśanabodhavṛtta tapasāṁ bhavyāñjinībāndhavaḥ//3//
   Sri Sindhurājasya mahattamena Śrī Parpatenṛrcitapāda padmaḥ/
   cakāra tenābhi hitaḥ prabandhaṁ sa pavanaṁ niṣṭhita-
   maṅgajasya//4//
329. Op. cit., p. 412.
330. Op. cit., p. 247.
331. Quoted by Nathu Ram Premi, 290. f.n.:
   Śrī Bhojadevarājyeśrīmad Dharānivāsināparā parameṣṭi-
   padaprāṇāmārjitāmalapuṇya nīrākṛta nikhilamalakalaṅkena-
   śrīmat Prabhācandra paṇḍitena nikhila pramāṇa prameya
   svarūpodyota-parikṣāmukhapadamidaṁ vivṛttamiti/
332. Op. cit., 287.
333. Op. cit , p. 290.
334. Op. cit., pp. 286-87:
   Dhārāyāṁ puri Bhojadeva nṛpaterājyejayātyuccakaih-
   Śrīmatsāgarasenatoyatipaterjñātvāpurāṇaṁ mahat/
   Bhuktyarthaṁ bhavabhītibhīta jagatāṁ śri Nandī Śiṣyobudhaḥ
   kurvecāru Purānasāra mamalaṁ Śri Chandra nāmā muniḥ/
335. Op. cit., pp. 270-74.
336. R. Upadhyaya, *Sanskrit and Prākrit Mahākāvyas* (Saugar, 1962), p. 49.
337. *Catalogue of Sanskrit Manuscripts in the Jaina Bhandāra at Patna*, p. 61.
338. R. Upadhyaya, op. cit., p. 54.
339. Nathu Ram Premi, op. cit., p. 225.
340. Op. cit., p. 229.
341. R. Upadhyaya, op. cit., p. 44.
342. Nathu Ram Premi, op. cit., p. 238.
343. Op. cit., pp. 235-37.
344. Op. cit., p. 249.
345. Muni Kanakāmara, *Karakaṇḍacariu*, ed. Hira Lal Jain (Varanasi, Bhāratiya Jñānapīṭha, 1964), p. 49.
346. R. Upadhyaya, op. cit., p. 44.
347. See Hira Lal Jain on *Karakaṇḍacariu*, p. 52 (English Section).
348. Quoted by Nathu Ram Premi, op. cit., p. 408 (f.n.).

349. Devendra Kumara Śāstrī, *Bhavisyatta Kahā Tathā Apabraṁśa Kathā Kāvya* (Varāṇasī, 1970) pp. 88-95.
350 Quoted by Devendra Kumāra Śāstrī, op. cit., p. 85.
351. Op. cit.
352. *Jain Grantha Bhandāras in Rajasthan* (Jaipur, 1967), p. 229.
353. *The History and Culture of Indian People*, Vol. IV, p. 218.
354. Quoted by K.K. Handiqui, op. cit. p. 6.
355. C. Kunhan Raja, *Survey of Sanskrit Literature* (Bombay : Bharatiya Vidya Bhavana, 1965), p. 238.
356. S.N. Das Gupta and S.K. De, op.cit. p. 96. Kṣemendra also wrote *Bharatamañjarī* and *Samayamātrika* (P.V. Kane, op. cit., p. 243).
357. *History and Culture and Indian People*, Vol. IV, pp. 179-80.
358. C. Kunhan Raja, op. cit., pp. 236-37.
359. S.N. Das Gupta & S.K. De, op cit., pp. 350-51.
360. N.S. Bose, *History of the Candellas*, p. 74.
361. S,N. Das Gupta and S.K. De, op. cit., p. 766.
362. P.V. Kane, op. cit., pp. 236-43.
363. K.K. Handiqui, op. cit., p. 3.
364. Op. cit.. p. 1.
365 Op. cit., p. 2.
366. *History and Cnlture of Indian People*, Vol. IV, p. 198.
367. Op. cit., p. 199.

Appendices

APPENDIX I
SIXTY-FOUR KALĀS

हारिण्यश्चटुलतरा बहुलतरंगाश्च निम्नगामिन्यः ।
नद्य इव जलधिमध्ये वेश्याहृदये कलाश्चतुःषष्टिः ॥
वेशकला नृत्यकला गीतकला वक्रवीक्षणकला च ।
कामपरिज्ञानकला ग्रहणकला मित्रबन्धनकला च ॥
पानकला केलिकला सुरतकला लिंगनान्तरकला च ।
चुम्बनकला परिकला निर्लज्जावेगसंभ्रमकला च ॥
ईर्ष्याकलिकेलिकला रुदितकला मानसंक्षयकला च ।
स्वेदभ्रमकम्पकला पुनरेकान्तप्रसाधनकला च ॥
नेत्रनिमीलन निःसहनिस्पन्दकला मृतोपमकला च ।
विरहासहरागकला कोपप्रतिषेधनिश्चयकला च ॥
निजजननाकलहकला सद्गृहगमनोत्सवेक्षणकला च ।
हरणकला जातिकला केलिकला चौर पार्थिवकला च ॥
गौखशैथिल्यकला निष्कारणदोषभाषणकला च ।
शूलकलाऽभ्यंगकला निद्राक्षिरजस्वलाम्बरकला च ॥
रुक्षकलातीक्ष्णकला गलहस्त—गृहार्गलार्पणकला च ।
सत्यवक्ताकामुकाहृति दर्शनयात्रास्तुतिकला च ॥
तीर्थोपवनसुरालयविहरणहेलाकला गृहकला च ।
वश्योषधमन्त्रकला वृक्षकला केशरञ्जन कला च ॥
भिक्षुकतापसबहुबिधपुण्यकला द्वीपदर्शनकला च ।
खिन्ना कलान्निषषृया पर्यन्ते कुट्टनीकला वेश्या ॥

(Kṣemendra's *Kala Vilāsa*, IV, vv. 2-11.)

APPENDIX II

EIGHTY-FIVE BRANCHES OF LEARNING ACCORDING TO SAMARĀDITYAKATHĀ

1. Lekha (writing), 2. Gaṇita (arithmetic), 3. Ālekhya (painting), 4. Nāṭya (dancing), 5. Gīta (singing), 6. Vādita (playing on stringed instrument), 7. Svargata (vocal music), 8. Puṣkaragata (playing on drum called Puṣkara), 9. Samatāla (a technical musical word), 10. Dyūta (gambling), 11. Janavāda (public speech), 12. Horā (astronomy), 13. Kāvya (poems and drama), 14. Aṣṭāpadam (meaning not clear). 15. Annavidhi (cookery), 16. Pānavidhi (preparation of drinks). 17. Śayanavidhi (directions about sleeping), 18. Āryā (composition of Āryā meters), 19. Prahelikā (riddles), 20. Māgadhikā (meaning not clear), 21. Gāthā, 22. Gīti, 23. Śloka, 24. Madhusiktham (use of wax), 25. Gandhayukti (use of scents), 26. Ābharaṇavidhi (putting on ornaments), 27. Taruṇipratikarma (toilet), 28. Strīlakṣaṇa (good and bad signs of women), 29. Puruṣalakṣaṇa (good and bad signs of men), 30. Hayalakṣaṇa (signs of horses), 31. Gajalakṣaṇa (signs of elephants), 32. Golakṣaṇa (signs of cows), 33. Kukkutalakṣaṇa (signs of poultry), 34. Meṣalakṣaṇa (signs of sheep), 35. Chakralakṣaṇa (signs of discus), 36. Chhatralakṣaṇa (signs of umbrella), 37. Daṇḍalakṣaṇa (signs of rod), 38. Aśilakṣaṇa (signs of sword), 39. Maṇilakṣaṇa (signs of jewels), 40. Kākiṇīlakṣaṇa (signs of Kākiṇī coins), 41. Charmalakṣaṇa (signs of leather), 42. Chandracharita (the behaviour of the movements of Moon), 43. Suracharita (the behaviour of the movements of Sun), 44. Rāhucharita (the behaviour of the movements of Rāhu), 45. Grahacharita (the behaviour of the movements of the planets), 46. Sūtrākāra (form of a sūtra ?), 47. Dūtākārā (the sign of an envoy), 48. Vidyāgatam (about vidyā), 49. Mantragatam (about mantras), 50. Rahasyagatam (about secrets), 51. Chāram (spies), 52. Pratichāram (counter spies), 53. Vyūha (formation of an army), 54. Prativyūha (counter formation of an army),

55. Skandhāvāranivesa (the area of camp), 56. Nagarayāna (layout of a town), 57. Vāstumāna (layout of area of a building), 58. Skandhāvāraniveśa (layout of a military camp), 59. Nagaraniveśa (layout of a city), 60. Vāstuniveśa (layout of a building), 61. Iśvastra (arrows and weapons), 62. Tattvapravāda (meaning not clear), 63. Aśvaśiksā (training horses), 64. Haśtiśikṣā (training of elephants), 65. Maṇiśikṣā (training about jewels), 66. Dhanurveda (military science), 67. Hiraṇyavāda (science dealing with hiraṇya—unminted gold), 68. Suvārṇavāda (science dealing with suvarṇa-coins), 69. Maṇivāda (science dealing with jewels), 70. Bāhuyuddha (wrestling), 71. Daṇḍayuddha (fighting with sticks), 72. Muṣṭiyuddha (boxing), 73. Asthiyuddha (fighting with bones), 74. Yuddha (fighting), 75. Niyuddha (duels), 76. Yuddhaniyuddha (combat), 77. Sūtrakrīḍā (playing with strings), 78. Vārtākrīḍā (telling stories), 79. Vāhyakrīḍā (out-door sports), 80. Nālikākrīḍā (playing with nālikā), 81. Patrachchhedya (cutting designs on leaves, etc.), 82. Kaṭakachchhedya (cutting designs on bracelets ?), 83. Prastarachchhedya (cutting designs on stones?), 84. Sajīva-Nirjīva (knowledge of animate and inanimate beings), 85. Śakunaruta (cries of birds).

APPENDIX III

GAṄGĀ-STOTRA OF ŚANKRĀCĀRYA

देवि सुरेश्वरि भगवति गंगे त्रिभुवनतारिणि तरलतरंगे ।
शंकरमौलिविहारिणि विमले मम मतिरास्तां तव पदकमले ॥ 1 ॥
भागीरथि सुखदायिनि मातस्तव जलमहिमा निगमे ख्यातः ।
नाहं जाने तव महिमानं त्राहि कृपामयि मामज्ञानम् ॥ 2 ॥
हरिपदपद्मतरंगिणि गंगे हिमविधुमुक्ताधवलतरंगे ।
दूरीकुरु मम दुष्कृतिभारं कुरु कृपया भवसागरपारम् ॥ 3 ॥
तव जलममलं येन निपीतं परमपदं खलु तेन गृहीतम् ।
मातर्गंगे त्वयि यो भक्तः किल तं द्रष्टुं न यमः शक्तः ॥ 4 ॥
पतितोद्धारिणि जान्हवि गंगे खण्डितगिरिवरमण्डितभंगे ।
भीष्मजननि हे मुनिवरकन्ये पतितनिवारिणि त्रिभुवनधन्ये ॥ 5 ॥
कल्पलतामिव फलदां लोके प्रणमति यस्त्वां न पतति शोके ।
पारावारविहारिणि गंगे विमुखयुवतिकृततरलापांगे ॥ 6 ॥
तव चेन्मातः स्त्रोतः स्नातः पुनरपि जठरे सोऽपि न जातः ।
नरकनिवारिणि जान्हवि गंगे कलुषविनाशिनि महिमोत्तुंगे ॥ 7 ॥
पुनरसदंगे पुण्यतरंगे जय जय जान्हवि करुणापांगे ।
इन्द्रमुकुटमणिराजितचरणे सुखदे शुभदे भृत्यशरण्ये ॥ 8 ॥
रोगं शोकं तापं पापं हर मे भगवति कुमतिकलापम् ।
त्रिभुवनसारे वसुधाहारे त्वमसि गतिर्मम खलु संसारे ॥ 9 ॥
अलकानन्दे परमानन्दे कुरु करुणामयि कातरवन्द्ये ।
तव तटनिकटे यस्य निवासः खलु वैकुण्ठे तस्य निवासः ॥ 10 ॥
वरमिह नीरे कमठो मीनः किं वा तीरे शरटः क्षीणः ।
अथवा श्वपचोमलिनो दीनस्तव न हि दूरे नृपतिकुलीनः ॥ 11 ॥
भो भुवनेश्वरि पुण्ये धन्ये देवि द्रवमयि मुनिवरकन्ये ।
गंगास्तवमिमममलं नित्यं पठति नरो यः स जयति सत्यम् ॥ 12 ॥
येषां हृदये गंगाभक्तिस्तेषां भवति सदा सुखमुक्तिः ।
मधुराकान्तापज्झटिकाभिः परमानन्दकलितललिताभिः ॥ 13 ॥
गंगास्तोत्रमिदं भवसारं वांछितफलदं विमलं सारम् ।
शंकरसेवकशंकररचितं पठति सुखी स्तव इति च समाप्तः ॥ 14 ॥

Stotra Ratnāvalī "Sri Gaṅgā-stotram"
18th ed. (Gorakhpur: Gita Press), pp. 267-270.

Bibliography

A. SAṀSKṚTA, PRĀKṚTA AND APABHRAṀŚA WORKS

WORKS BY DHANAPĀLA

Tilaka-mañjarī, eds. Pt. Bhavadatta Sastri and K.N. Pandurang Parab, Bombay, 1938.
(Reference in the Thesis are from this Ed.)

———, ed. Shantyacharya, Ahmedabad, V.S. 2008.

Pāiyalacchīnāmamālā, ed. Becharadasa Jīvaraja Doshi, Ahmadabad, 1960.
(References in the Thesis are from this Ed.)

———, ed. G. Bühler, Bhavanagar, V.S. 1973.

Śrī Ṛṣabhapañcāśikā-Vīrastuti-dvayarūpakṛtikalāpaḥ
Śrī Satyapurīya Śrī Mahāvīra Utsāha
Published in Jaina Sāhitya Saṁśodhaka, III, No. 3.

OTHER RELATED WORKS

Amaracanda, *Kāvyakalpalatāvṛtti*, ed. Jagnnatha Shastri, Banaras, 1951.

Amara Siṁha, *Amara Kośa*, ed. Guru Prasad Shastri. Banaras, 1950.

Bāṇa Bhaṭṭa, *Kādambarī*, ed. K.P. Parab, Bombay, 1834.

———, *Harṣacarita*, ed. K.P. Parab, Bombay, 1834.

———, *Harṣacarita*, ed. Jivanand Vidyasagar, Calcutta, 1892.

Bhoja, *Samarāṅgaṇasūtradhāra*, ed. T. Ganapati Shastri, Baroda, 1924.

———, *Yuktikalpataru*, ed. Īśvara Chandra Shastri, Calcutta, 1917.

———, *Śṛṅgāramañjarī-kathā*, ed. Dr. (Miss) K. Munshi, Bombay, 1958.

Sṛṅgāra Prakāśa, ed. G.R. Josyer, Mysore, 1969.

Bhartṛhari, *Nītiśataka*, S.J.G.M. Bombay, 1948.

Bṛhatkalpa Bhāṣya, Bhavanagar, 1933—38.

Daṇḍin, *Daśakumāracaritam*, ed. M.R. Kāle, Bombay, 1917.

Dāmodaragupta, *Kuṭṭanīmata*, ed. Tansukharama Mansukharama Tripathi, Banaras, 1924.
Dhanañjaya, *Dasarūpaka*, ed. Sudarśnacharya Shastri, Bombay, 1914.
Dhanapāla, *Bhavisayattakahā*, ed. C.D. Dalal and P.D. Guṇe, Baroda, 1923.
Gṛddha Piccha Ācārya, *Tattvārtha Sūtra*, ed. Phul Chand Siddhanta Shastri, Banaras, V.S. 2476.
Halāyudha, *Abhidhānaratnamālā*, ed. Jaya Shanker Joshi, Varanasi, Saka, 1879.
Hema Candra, *Dvyāśrayamahākāvya*, Bombay, 1915.
———, *Deśīnāmamālā*, ed. Pischel, with introduction, critical notes and glossary by P.V. Rāmānuja Swami, Poona, 1938.
———, *Deśīnāmamālā*, ed. Harivallabha C. Bhayani, Banaras, 1953.
———, *Abhidhānacintāmaṇi*, Bhavanagar, 1914, 1919.
Harṣa, *Priyadarśikā*, Madras, 1935.
Haribhadra Sūri, *Samarāicchakahā*, ed. A.H. Jacobi, Calcutta, 1926.
———, *Samarāicckahā*, ed. M.C. Modi, Ahmadabad, 1935.
Jina-Vijaya-Muni, *Purātanaprabandha Saṅgraha*, SJGM., Calcutta, 1936.
Jayāṇaka, *Pṛthvīrājavijaya*, eds. G.H. Ojha and G.S. Guleri, Ajmer, 1941.
Jinaprabhasūri, *Vividha-Tīrthakalpa*, ed. Muni Jina Vijaya, Bombay, 1944.
Jineśvara Sūri, *Kathākośaprakaraṇa*, Bombay, 1949.
Jayadeva, *Gītāgovinda*, Delhi, 1955.
Kālidāsa, *Raghuvaṁśa*, ed. Sita Rama Chaturvedi, Banaras, 1953.
Kalhaṇa, *Rājataraṅgīṇī*, ed. Durga Prasad, Bombay, 1892.
———, *Rājataraṅgiṇī*, ed. Pandeya Ramtej Shastri, Kashi, 1960.
———, *Rājataraṅgiṇī*, tr. M.A. Stein, Westminster, 1900.
Kṣīrasvāmī, *Amarakośa Tīkā*, ed. Haradatta Shastri, Poona, 1941.
Kṣemendra, *Aucityavicāracarcā*, Bombay, 1918.
Kūrma Purāṇa, Calcutta, 1890.
Lakṣmīdhara, *Krityakalpataru*, ed. with an introduction by K.V. Ranga Swami Aiyangar.

Vol. I. *Grhastha Kāṇḍa*, Baroda, 1944.
Vol. II. *Rājadharma Kāṇḍa*. Baroda, 1943.
Vol. III. *Vyavahārakāṇḍa*, Baroda, 1953.

Laghu Āsvalāyana Smṛti, ed. Vinaya Ganesh Apte, Poona, 1929.

Merutuṅga, *Prabandhacintāmaṇi*, ed. Muni Jina Vijaya, Shantiniketan, 1933.

———, *Prabandhacintāmaṇi*, tr. C.H. Tawney, Calcutta, 1894.

Manusmṛti, Bombay, 1923.

Medhatithi, *Manusmṛti-bhāṣya*, ed. G.N. Jha, Calcutta, 1932—39

Matsya Purāṇa, Calcutta, 1954.

Mitra Miśra, *Vīramitrodaya*, *Rajanītiprakāśa*, ed. Vishnu Prasad, Banaras, 1916.

Milindapañho, ed. E.V. Trenckner, London, 1880.

Muni Kanakāmara, *Karakaṇḍacariu*, ed. Hira Lal Jain, Delhi, 1964.

Padmagupta, *Navasāhasāṅkacarita*, ed. V.S. Islampur-Kar. Bombay, 1895.

Rājaśekhara, *Karpūramañjarī*, ed. Stein Konow, Cambridge, 1901.

———, *Kavyamīmāṁsā*, Baroda, 1934.

———, *Viddhaśālabhañjikā*, Calcutta, 1943.

Someśvara, *Mānasollāsa*, ed. Srigondekar, Baroda, 1925—1930.

———, *Kīrtikaumudī*, ed. Puṇya Vijaya Sūri, Bombay, 1961.

Somadeva, *Nītivākyāmṛta*, Bombay, 1922.

———, *Yaśastilaka*, Bombay, 1916.

Stotra Ratnāvalī, Gītā Press, Gorakhpur, 18th Edition.

Siddharṣi Sūri, *Upamitibhavaprapañcakahā*, eds. P. Peterson and A.H. Jacobi, Calcutta, 1909.

Śukrācārya, *Śukranīti*, ed. G. Oppert, Madras, 1882.

———, *Śukranītī*, ed. Jivananda Vidyasagar Bhattacarya, Calcutta, 1890.

Śrī Harṣa, *Naiṣadhacarita*, ed. Śivadatta, Bombay, 1919.

———, *Naiṣadhacarita*, tr. K.K. Handiqui, Poona, 1956.

Uddyotana Sūri, *Kuvalayamālākahā*, ed. A.N. Upadhye, Bombay, 1959.

Vātsyāyana, *Kāma Sūtra*, ed. D.L. Goswami, Banaras, 1929.

Vādibha-Siṁha, *Kṣatra Cūḍāmaṇi*, ed. Kuppu Swami Shastri, Tanjore, n.d.

Vāgbhaṭṭa, *Aṣṭaṅgahṛdaya*, with a commentary by Arunadatta. Lahore, 1933.

Viṣṇupurāṇa, Gorakhpur, Samvat, 2018.

Vyāsasmṛti, ed. Vinaya Ganesh Apte, Poona, 1929.

Yādava Prakash, *Vaijayantī*, ed. G. Oppert, Madras, 1893.

Yājnavalkya Smṛti, Bombay, 1926.

PERSIAN AND ARABIC WORKS

Abul Fazl, *Āin-i-Akbarī*, 2 Vols. trs. H. Blouchman and Jarret, Calcutta, 1948.

Alberunī, *Tarikh-i-Hind*, tr. E.C. Sachau, two volumes in one, Delhi, 1964. (First Indian Reprint).

Masūdī, *Murujuz-Dhabb*, Paris, n.d.

MODERN WORKS

Agrawal, V.S., *Harṣa Carita eka Sāṁskṛtika Adhyayana*, Patna, 1953.

Agrawal, Moti Chandra, *Bhāratīya Veśa Bhūsā*, Prayag, n.d.

Aiyyangar, P.T.S., *Bhoja-Rājā*, Madras, 1933.

Altekar, A.S., *The Rāṣṭrakūṭas and Their Times*, Patna, 1953.

———, *State and Government in Ancient India*, Banaras, 1949 (Rep. 1972).

———, *The Position of Women in Hindu Civilization*, Delhi, 1962.

Apte, *Sanskrit-English Dictionary*, Bombay, 1912.

Awasthi, A.B.L., *Rājpūt Polity*, Lucknow, 1968.

Baldry, H.C., *Greek Literature For the Modern Reader*, Cambridge, 1959.

Basham, A.L., *The Wonder That Was India*, London, 1954.

Beal, Samuel, *Life of Yuan Chwang*, London, 1888—1911.

Beni Prasad, *State in Ancient India*, Allahabad, 1928.

Bhatta Sali, N.K., *The Iconography of the Buddhist and Brahmanical Sculptures in Dacca Museum*, Dacca, 1929.

Bhatia, Pratipal, *The Paramāras*, Delhi, 1970.

Bose, N.S., *History of the Candellas*, Calcutta, 1956.

Buddha Prakash, *Studies in Indian History and Civilization*, Agra, 1962.

Buddha Prakash, ed. *Studies in Asian History and Culture*, Meerut, 1970.

Chatterji, B.R., *History of Indonesia*, Meerut, 1967.

Choudhary, Gulab Chandra, *Political History of Northern India from Jaina Sources, c.* A.D. 650—A.D. 1300, Amritsar, 1963.

Dasgupta, S.N., *History of Indian Philosophy*, Vol. V, Cambridge, 1963.

Dasgupta, S.N. and S.K. De, *A History of Sanskrit Literature*, Vol. I., Calcutta, 1947.

De, S.K., *History of Sanskrit Poetics*, Calcutta, 1960.

Edwardes, Michael, *Every Day Life in Early India*, London, 1969.

Elliot, H.M. and Dowson, *History of India As Told By Its Own Historians*, Vols. I-III, London, 1866—77.

Farquhar, J.N., *An Outline of the Religious Literature of India*, Oxford, 1920.

Ganguly, D.C., *The History of the Paramāra Dynasty*, Dacca, 1933.

Garrett, John, *The Classical Dictionary of India*, Delhi, 1971 (Reprint).

Gokhale, B.G., *Ancient India, History and Culture*, Bombay, 1962 (Reprint).

Gopal, Lallanji, *Economic History of Northern India*, (c. A.D. 700--1200), Delhi, 1965.

Gopalan, *Outlines of Jainism*, Delhi, 1973.

Haig, Sir Wolsely, *Cambridge History of India*, Vol. III, Delhi, 1958.

Handiqui, K.K., *Yaśastilaka and Indian Culture*, Sholapur, 1949.

Hourani, G.P., *Arab Sea Faring in the Indian Ocean in Ancient and Early Medieval Times*, Princeton, 1951.

Jain, Champat Rai, *Jaina Penance*, Allahabad, 1930.

Jain, Jagdish Chandra, *Life in Ancient India As Depicted in Jaina Canons*, Bombay, 1947.

Jayaswal, K.P., *Hindu Polity*, Banglore, 1943.

Joshi, Umesha, *Bhāratīya Saṅgīta Kā Itihāsa*, Agra, 1969.

Kaṇe, P.V., *History of Dharmaśaśtras*, Vols. I—IV, Poona, 1930—53.

———, *A History of Sanskrit Poetics*, Delhi, 1961.

Kasliwal, Kastoor Chand, *Jain Granth Bhandāras in Rajasthan*, Jaipur, 1967.

Keith, A.B., *A History of Sanskrit Literature*, Oxford, 1928.

Lokesh Chandra, ed. *India's Contribution to World Thought and Culture*, Delhi, 1970.

Majumdar, B.P., *Socio-Economic History of Northern India*, Calcutta, 1960.

Majumdar, R.C., *Ancient India*, Delhi, 1960.

———, *Suvarṇa Dvīpa*, Dacca, 1937.

———, & A.D., Pusalkar, eds. *History and Culture of the Indian People*, Vols. I-V.
Vol. IV: *The Age of Imperial Kanauj*, Bombay, 1957.
Vol. V: *The Struggle for Empire*, Bombay, 1957.

Masson, M.E., *New Light on the Ancient Civilization*, Soviet Union, 1954.

Mishra, V.B., *The Gurjara Pratihāras and Their Times*, Delhi, 1966.

Mookerji, R.K., *Chandragupta Maurya and His Times*, Madras, 1943.

———, *Indian Shipping*, Second ed. Calcutta, 1957.

Munshi, K.M., *Glory That Was Gūrjara Deśa*, Bombay, 1954.

———, and R.R. Diwakar, eds. *Indian Inheritance*, Nainital, 1955.

Nadvi, Sayyid Sulaiman, *Arab Aur Bhārat Ke Saṁbandh*, Allahabad, 1930.

Ojha, G.H., *Rājapūtāne-kā-Itihāsa*, Second Edition.

———, *Sirohī Rājya Kā Itihāsa*, Ajmer, 1911.

Om Prakash, *Food and Drinks in Ancient India*, Delhi, 1961.

Premi, Nathu Rama, *Jaina Sāhitya Aur Itihāsa*, Bombay, 1956.

Puri, B.N., *The History of the Gurjara Pratihāras*, Bombay, 1957.

Raja, C., Kunhan, *Survey of Sanskrit Literature*, Bombay, 1962.

Ray, H.C., *Dynastic History of Northern India*, Calcutta, 1931, 1939.

Ray, P.C., *History of Hindu Chemistry from the Earliest Times to the Middle of the XVI Century*, Calcutta, 1905.

Sharma, Brijanandan, *Social Life in Northern India* (A.D. 600—1200), Delhi, 1966.

Sharma, Brijendra Nath, *Social and Cultural History of Northern India* (c. A.D. 1000—1200), Delhi, 1972.

Sharma, R.S., *Aspects of Political Ideas and Institutions in Ancient India*, Delhi, 1959.

Sharma, Dasharatha, *Lectures on Rājpūt History and Culture*, Delhi, 1970.

Shastri, Devendra Kumar, *Bhavisayattakahā Tathā Apabhraṁśa Kathā Kāvya*, Delhi, 1970.

Shastri, K. Vasudeva, *Saṅgīta Śāstra*, Lucknow, 1968.

Shastri, N.K., *The Age of the Nandas and Mauryas*, Banaras, 1952.

Shukla, B.D., and K.S. Bhatnagar, *Bhāratīya Saṁskṛti kā Itihāsa*, Agra, 1971.

Sirāfi, Abuziad, *Travel Account*, Paris, 1811.

Sircar, D.C., *The Śākta Pīṭhās, J.R.A.S.B. Letters*, XIV. No. 1 (1948).

Śivarāmamūrti, C., *Indian Sculpture*, New Delhi, 1961.

———, Arts Asiatiques, Paris, 1955.

Smith, V.A., *Early History of India*, Oxford, 1924 (Reprint 1962).

Tatia, Nathmal, *Studies in Jaina Philosophy*, Banaras, 1951.

Tiwari, Bhola Nath, *Bhāṣā Vijñāna*, Allahabad, 1971.

Tripathi, R.S., *History of Ancient India*, Delhi, 1960.

———, *History of Kanauj*, Delhi, 1964.

Upadhyaya, R., *Sanskrit and Prakrit Mahākāvyas*, Varāṇasi, V.S. 1992.

Watters, T., *On Yuan Chwang* (Si-Yu-Ki), two Vols. London, 1904-5.

Winternitz, Maurice, *The Jainas in the History of Indian Literature*, Ahmedabad, 1946.

CORPS OF INSCRIPTIONS

Bombay Karnataka Inscriptions (SII, XI, Pts. I and II) Madras, 1940—1943.

Inscriptions of C.P. and Berar, ed. R.B. Hiralal, Nagpur, 1932.

Jaina Lekha Saṁgraha, ed. P.C. Nahar, Calcutta, 1918—1929.

South Indian Inscriptions, ed. and tr. E. Hultzch, Madras, 1890—1903.

JOURNALS, PERIODICALS AND MAGZINES

Anekānta (Hindi), Delhi.

Arts Asiatiques.

Annals of Bhandarkar Oriental Research Institute.

Epigraphia Indica, Ootacamund.
Indian Antiquary, Bombay.
Indian Historical Quarterly, Calcutta.
Jaina Sāhitya Saṁśodhaka (Hindi), Ahmadabad.
Journal of American Oriental Society.
Journal of Asiatic Society of Bengal, Calcutta.
Journal of Bihar Research Society, Patna.
Journal of Indian History (University of Kerala).
Journal of the Royal Asiatic Society of Bengal, Calcutta.
Journal of the Royal Asiatic Society (Bombay Branch).

ARCHAEOLOGICAL REPORTS

Annual Report, Archaeological Survey of India.
Annual Report of Archaeological Deptt., Baroda State 1934-1935.
Annual Report of Indian Epigraphy.
Proceedings of the All India Oriental Conference.
Progress Report of Archaeological Survey of India, Western Circle.

INDEX

ERRATA

Page	*Line*	*Incorrect*	*Correct*
viii	8	Parmāra rulers,	Paramāra rulers,
xvii	9	Religious condition?	Religious conditions
11	35	and Rāmeśvara	at Rāmeśvara
42	1	years (93-948)	years (939-948)
48	20	Gāya Karṇa	Gayā Karṇa
54	13	'*Sṛngāramañjarī kathā*	'*Śṛṅgāramañjarī kathā*',
55	25	Durabharāja	Durlabharāja
60	24	his subjects.[95] providing succur	his subjects[95] providing succour
64	17	Mantrin	Mantrin (Home Minister),
67	28	*Nārma-Saciva*	*Narma-Saciva*
69	2	superintendence.	superintendent.
70	14	know as	known as
70	18	'Dharmādhikaramika'	'Dharmādhikaraṇika'
72	8	Daṇḍāpāśika:	Daṇḍapāśika:
72	22	Samaraketū	Samaraketu
73	11	nārācā	nārāca
74	28	and quite	and quiet
85	Ref. no. 155	C.N. Puri	B.N. Puri
105	23	had of the	head of the
107	18	part of the bady	part of the body
108	11	silk cloths.	silk cloth.
108	34	'Mekhatā'	'Mekhalā'
110	30	'Kalāyuga'	'Kṛtayuga'
114	24	goods families	good families
122	1	The teachers. born	The teachers born
123	3	Dhanapāla, Dhakkara	Dhanapāla Dhakkara
123	29	white-dukula	white-dukūla
167	9	Vaiṣṇavties	Vaiṣṇavites
"	12	"	"

167	21	'Daśarhanāṭha'	'Daśārhanāṭha'
173-74	last	purity of tence	purity of existence
203	11	or whom the	of whom the
209	8	Sāmadeva	Sāmaveda
210	23	'Vīḥā'	'Vīṇā'
219	16	*Ā) urveda Sarvasvam*	*Āyurveda Sarvasvam,*
226	last	*Subhāsitapradandha.*	*Subhāṣitaprabandha.*
234	33	A.D. 1336 and	A.D. 1026 and
251	11	निजजनाकलहकला	निजजननीकलहकला